RADIOLOGY DEPARTMENT COMPLIANCE MANUAL

2003 Edition

Highlights

New and updated legal and regulatory information affecting compliance in your Radiology Department, including

- Medicare requirements for X-ray interpretations and payment for telecommunication, OSHA requirements for illness and injury reporting, indoor air quality, disaster response, exposure control plans, workplace violence

New interview section containing first-person accounts of Joint Commission process from perspective of Radiology Department, including

- Focus of recent Joint Commission surveys (equipment maintenance, teleradiology, documentation of competencies, crash carts, patient confidentiality, and more)
- Surprising information on questions surveyors did **not** ask
- Comments in anticipation of the 2004 Joint Commission survey process

New forms, policies and other reference materials to implement compliance in your Radiology Department, including

- Advance directives
- Sharps-Safety and Needlestick-Prevention Device Assessment Form
- Emergency Management Plan
- How to Develop Competency in Your Department
- Risk Management Process Flow Chart
- Radiologist On-Call Policy
- Brachytherapy Policy
- Diagnostic Radiology Policy
- Policy for Pregnant or Potentially Pregnant Patients
- Radiation User Training & Personal Data
- Recommendations Regarding Pregnant Employees in the Radiology Department
- Request for Radiation Exposure History and/or Training Verification
- Disaster Procedure
- Preconstruction Checklist
- Infection Prevention and Control Policies and Procedures for MRI Department
- Safer Needle Device Compliance Form
- Exposure Control Plan Compliance Form
- Workplace Violence Checklist

Aspen Publishers
Health Law and Compliance Series

Radiology Department Compliance Manual

2003 Edition

Aspen Publishers
Health Law and Compliance Series

Aspen Publishers
Health Law and Compliance Series

Radiology Department Compliance Manual

2003 Edition

Consulting Editor

Glenda Redd, MS, RT(R)

Contributors

Christopher Holt, JD
Ruth Elzer, RN, MS
Ken Weinberg, PhD
Kathleen McGuire Gilbert

ΛSPEN

PUBLISHERS

1185 Avenue of the Americas
New York, NY 10036
www.aspenpublishers.com

This publication is designed to provide accurate and authoritative information in regard to the Subject Matter covered. It is sold with the understanding that the publisher is not engaged in rendering legal, accounting, or other professional service. If legal advice or other expert assistance is required, the service of a competent professional person should be sought. (From a Declaration of Principles jointly adopted by a Committee of the American Bar Association and a Committee of Publishers and Associations.)

Library of Congress Cataloging-in-Publication Data

Radiology department compliance manual / Aspen Health Law and Compliance Center; consulting editor, Lisa Hayden; contributors, Kara Kinney Cartwright . . .[et al.]—5th ed.
p.; cm.—(AHLCC compliance series)
Includes index.
ISBN 0-7355-4161-2
1. Hospitals—Radiological services—Standards—Handbooks, manuals, etc.
2. Hospitals—Radiological services—Administration—Handbooks, manuals, etc.
I. Hayden, Lisa. II. Cartwright, Kara Kinney. III. Aspen Health Law and Compliance Center.
IV. Aspen Health Law and Compliance Center compliance series.
[DNLM: 1. Radiology Department, Hospital—standards—United States.
2. Accreditation—standards—United States.
3. Licensure, Hospital—standards—United States.
4. Radiology Department, Hospital—legislation & jurisprudence—United States.
5. Radiology Department, Hospital—organization & administration—United States.
WN 27 AA1 R12 2001]
RA975.5.R3 R326 2001
362.1'77—dc21
2001022194

Orders: (800) 638-8437
Customer Care: (800) 234-1660

Editorial Services: Amy Frevert
Library of Congress Catalog Card Number: 2001022194
ISBN: 0-7355-4161-2

ISSN available upon request.

Printed in the United States of America

1 2 3 4 5

About Aspen Publishers

Aspen Publishers, headquartered in New York City, is a leading information provider for attorneys, business professionals, and law students. Written by preeminent authorities, our products consist of analytical and practical information covering both U.S. and international topics. We publish in the full range of formats, including updated manuals, books, periodicals, CDs, and online products.

Our proprietary content is complemented by 2,500 legal databases, containing over 11 million documents, available through our Loislaw division. Aspen Publishers also offers a wide range of topical legal and business databases linked to Loislaw's primary material. Our mission is to provide accurate, timely, and authoritative content in easily accessible formats, supported by unmatched customer care.

To order any Aspen Publishers title, go to *www.aspenpublishers.com* or call 1-800-638-8437.

To reinstate your manual update service, call 1-800-638-8437.

For more information on Loislaw products, go to *www.loislaw.com* or call 1-800-364-2512.

For Customer Care issues, e-mail CustomerCare@aspenpublishers.com; call 1-800-234-1660; or fax 1-800-901-9075.

Aspen Publishers
A Wolters Kluwer Company

Table of Contents

Editorial Board

Introduction

Radiology department (RD) compliance issues can be overwhelming. Federal laws, state laws, liability concerns, and Joint Commission on Accreditation of Healthcare Organizations requirements affect nearly all aspects of patient care and departmental management. Managers must balance their compliance obligations against both patient care concerns and limited resources. This manual is an effort to assist RD managers in finding that balance by providing urgently needed information in a current, comprehensive, and easy-to-use compliance tool.

FEATURES OF THIS MANUAL

Legal Compliance Questions and Answers

This section of the manual is aimed at providing an easy reference to legal issues commonly encountered in hospital RDs. A list of questions at the front of this section will enable you to quickly locate helpful and current information on a variety of difficult legal areas such as fraud, reimbursement, the Health Insurance Portability and Accountability Act, telemedicine, regulation of radioactive materials, radiation safety, equipment regulations, recordkeeping and reporting, inspection, bloodborne pathogens, hazardous substances, staffing requirements, medical records and confidentiality, and consent. Citations to laws, regulations, and cases are provided for guiding additional research.

Joint Commission Survey Questions and Answers

This section contains valuable advice from staff members at hospitals that have successfully navigated a Joint Commission survey. Interviewees provide frank and detailed information on what surveyors looked for and how to demonstrate participation in performance improvement activities. This section is organized by topic to allow you to readily compare the experiences of different hospitals across the country.

Hospital Accreditation Standards Analysis

This section analyzes the Joint Commission standards that apply to the RD. The Joint Commission emphasizes a hospitalwide, function-based approach to evaluating compliance, making it difficult for department managers to know precisely what is expected of them. This section boils down the standards, in an accessible grid format, and designates the responsibilities of RD managers with regard to demonstrating compliance with the standards *in the RD*.

Managers should also make efforts to participate in hospitalwide compliance activities (such as performance improvement initiatives) because evaluation of interdepartmental activities is an important part of the survey process. These activities are not emphasized in this section of the manual, however, as they are usually coordinated by someone outside of the RD with facilitywide responsibilities.

The applicable standards are presented one at a time, along with the following categories of guidance:

- *Comment:* This column describes the relationship between RD and hospital responsibility for demonstrating compliance with the standard and indicates what the standard assesses.
- *Evidence:* This column lists the types of evidence that might be used to show compliance with the standard. Special emphasis is paid to documents that are developed or maintained in the RD.
- *Staff Questions:* This column lists questions that the Joint Commission surveyor might ask the RD director, RD staff members, and others to assess compliance with the standard.
- *Reference:* This column provides cross-references to the forms included in this manual that correlate with the standard.

Reference Materials for Radiology Department Compliance

This section of the manual provides documentation that hospitals across the country have used to show compliance with Joint Commission standards, as well as documentation used to meet legal requirements discussed in Legal Compliance Questions and Answers. Sample documentation includes forms and policies relating to patients' rights and responsibilities, assessment of patients, consent to radiation therapy and special procedures, job descriptions for RD staff, infection control guidelines, and radiation safety guidelines.

CMS and Joint Commission Standards Checklist

This feature was introduced in the Fourth Edition of the *Radiology Department Compliance Manual*. This tool allows you to cross-reference the Medicare Conditions of Participation to the Joint Commission Standards, and also provides a place for you to note any deviations in your own state law requirements. This checklist will simplify compliance efforts by highlighting duplications and inconsistencies in the many standards the RD must follow.

PART 1

Legal Compliance Questions and Answers

INTRODUCTION TO COMPLIANCE

The emphasis on establishing corporate compliance programs for hospitals and other health care facilities is the direct result of the government's aggressive efforts over the last five years to enforce legislative provisions governing health care fraud and abuse. Corporate compliance programs have been imposed on numerous providers by the government as part of settlements following fraud and abuse investigations, and many health care organizations have voluntarily implemented such programs to protect themselves from sanctions under fraud and abuse laws. As a result, compliance efforts have been closely linked with the subject of fraud and abuse legislation, even though an effective compliance program is much broader in scope and covers many other types of legislative requirements and prohibitions. In fact, compliance efforts should be directed at establishing a culture within a hospital that promotes prevention, detection, and resolution of all instances of conduct that do not conform to all federal and state law, private payer health care program requirements, as well as the hospital's ethical and business policies. [Department of Health and Human Services, Office of Inspector General, Compliance Program Guidance for Hospitals (Feb. 23, 1998)]

What types of legal issues are implicated in a comprehensive hospital compliance program?

The Office of Inspector General's (OIG's) *Compliance Program Guidance for Hospitals* sets forth the basic elements of an effective hospital compliance program and lists a number of risk areas that are of particular concern to hospitals. Although many of the risk areas focus on practices that could implicate fraud and abuse laws, other legal issues that should be addressed in an effective compliance program include

- medical records documentation practices
- patient confidentiality
- employment, licensure, and staffing issues
- environmental compliance issues
- informed consent issues
- quality of care issues
- antitrust issues
- tax-exempt status issues [Department of Health and Human Services, Office of Inspector General, Compliance Program Guidance for Hospitals (Feb. 23, 1998)]

What types of activities are governed by health care fraud and abuse legislation?

Both at the state and federal levels, statutory fraud and abuse prohibitions apply to the following categories of health care provider activities:

- false claims or other fraudulent billing activities
- bribes or kickbacks, including a complex array of discounts, rebates, profit-sharing agreements, or other business relationships
- illegal referrals, prohibiting physicians and other types of health care providers from referring patients for health care services to entities in which such a physician has a financial interest

The Centers for Medicare and Medicaid Services (CMS) offer this explanation of the difference between fraud and abuse:

- Fraud is an intentional decision or misrepresentation that someone makes, knowing it is false, that could result in an unauthorized payment. Keep in mind that the attempt itself is fraud, regardless of whether it is successful.
- Abuse involves actions that are inconsistent with accepted, sound medical, business, or fiscal practices. Abuse directly or indirectly results in an unnecessary cost to the program through improper payments. The real difference between fraud and abuse is the person's intent. [CMS Frequently Asked Questions, updated Sept. 14, 2001]

What are the fraud and abuse issues that are of particular concern to a radiology department?

As the above list indicates, the broad language of many of the fraud and abuse provisions in federal law and numerous state statutes makes these provisions applicable to a very wide range of potentially illegal activity. The American College of Radiology (ACR) has identified several areas of activity that should be of concern to radiology and radiation oncology practices in this regard, some of which are relevant to hospital-based radiology departments, including

- *radiology dictation*—This report is one of the primary sources of information used by billing staff when filing insurance claims, and it is important that it faithfully records what was done.
- *procedural coding*—In a rapidly evolving specialty such as radiology, it is particularly important for the business staff to stay current with procedural coding. Physicians are ultimately responsible for the coding and billing that is done on their behalf and should periodically review the way their services are coded and billed.
- *teaching physician billing*—A Department of Health and Human Services (HHS)/OIG probe launched in 1996 focused on Medicare Part B reimbursement to hospitals or faculty physicians for the services of attending physicians in cases where patients actually were treated by residents acting under the supervision of an attending physician. Radiologists and radiation oncologists that practice at teaching hospitals must make sure that they comply with current teaching physician billing rules.
- *reassignment*—In general, carriers may pay only the physician or supplier who provides the services, but under certain circumstances, a physician may reassign his or her right to payment to a third party. For example, payment

may be made to a hospital where radiology services are provided if there is a contractual arrangement between the facility and the physician under which the hospital bills for the physician's services.

- *financial arrangements with hospitals*—A violation of the antikickback statute may occur if a hospital demands payment from a hospital-based physician ostensibly for services for which the hospital has already received reimbursement under the prospective payment system (PPS). The ACR Compliance Program Guidelines contain a useful and highly detailed list of the types of hospital/physician arrangements that might generate questionable remuneration under the antikickback statute. [American College of Radiology, Compliance Program Guidelines for Radiologists and Radiation Oncologists. ACR is found on the Internet at www.acr.org.]

What specific types of contract provisions should be reviewed carefully to ensure compliance with fraud and abuse laws and other federal health care program requirements?

Radiology departments are likely to have many contracts, with suppliers, equipment providers, and temporary staff. Department heads should carefully consider with whom they contract to ensure that they are not involved or implicated in a fraud and abuse investigation. In addition, department heads should consult with legal counsel and the business office before entering into a contract. Department heads, hospitals, and legal counsel should carefully consider whether the following contract provisions are contained in their contracts in compliance with applicable federal laws and regulations:

- *identification of the parties*—Ensure that each contract properly identifies the entity or person with whom the hospital is contracting. The Balanced Budget Act of 1997 imposes civil monetary penalties against any provider who contracts with an individual or entity that the facility knows or should know is excluded from federal health care programs. The hospital also should identify the principals in the contracting organization and be sure that they are not excluded persons. [42 USC 1320a-7a(a)]
- *representation of nonexclusion*—The other party should represent that it is not excluded from federal health plan participation at the time of the contract, that it will not do anything that will cause it to be excluded during the term of the agreement, and that if it is excluded, it will promptly notify the hospital. The party also should represent that it will not arrange or contract with any employee, contractor, or agent that it knows or should know is excluded to provide items or services under the contract. [42 USC 1320a-7a(a)]
- *access to books and records*—Where appropriate, the contract should provide for access to books and records, as required by federal regulations. The hospital should require immediate notification of the nature and scope of any request for access and also should seek copies of any books, records, or documents proposed to be provided to the government to give the hospital an opportunity to lawfully oppose the production of such documents. [42 USC 1395x(v)(1)(I)]

- *compliance plan participation*—The contract should recognize the hospital's compliance program and require the other provider to cooperate, including such things as making employees available for training, providing access to necessary billing documentation, and participating in audits upon request. The contract also should require the other party to notify the hospital immediately (if the hospital is involved or merely a witness) of any violation of any applicable law, regulation, third-party reimbursement, or breach of ethics program. The hospital also should consider whether to require the other party to maintain a compliance plan.

- *compliance with applicable law*—The contract should require the other party to comply with all federal, state, and local laws, regulations, and governmental orders in providing items or services under the contract. The other party also should be required to comply, where applicable, with Joint Commission on Accreditation of Healthcare Organizations' requirements or national professional ethical guidelines. Finally, the party should be obliged to comply with the hospital's internal rules, regulations, and policies, which the hospital must then make available to the other party.

- *investigations and reviews*—The other party should be obliged, during the term of the contract and perhaps also for a period of time afterward, to notify the hospital of any complaint, investigation, inquiry, or review by any governmental agency or third-party payer regarding any of the items or services provided under the contract. The hospital also should consider whether to reserve the right to terminate the contract if an investigation or inquiry proceeds beyond a designated level.

- *termination due to changes in the environment or breach of law*—The hospital should retain the right to terminate or modify the contract in the event that a significant change occurs in any applicable health law or its interpretation; a significant payer's payment methodology that affects the continuing viability or legality of the method of doing business under the contract; the ability of either party to be reimbursed for services or items provided; or the ability to make referrals. The contract also should give the hospital the right to terminate the contract whether the other party has breached any compliance plan, or if a breach has a potential to threaten the licensure or Medicare/Medicaid certification of the hospital, or may subject the hospital to a fine, civil, administrative, or criminal penalty, or other sanction. [Adapted from Wolin & McAdams, Focus on Fraud and Abuse, Vol. 3, No. 3 (May 1999)]

REIMBURSEMENT

Billing Medicare for Radiology Services

Can a hospital bill Medicare for radiology services provided by physicians?

Medicare will pay a hospital for radiology services provided by a physician if the hospital and the physician have entered into an agreement that meets certain conditions. The agreement must specify that only the hospital may bill and receive the amounts for the services. The agreement may apply to all services furnished by the physician, or to only a particular category of services that can be distinguished from other categories. Payment will be made for only services furnished in a hospital. However, physician services furnished outside the hospital will be considered furnished inside the hospital in certain situations, including when the services are provided to an inpatient or if the services are interpretations of tests done while the patient is in the hospital. The hospital must certify that it will bill for a physician's services only as provided in its written contract with the physician. [Medicare Carrier's Manual 3060.2]

Will Medicare pay for services if an indirect contractual arrangement exists between the hospital and physician?

A hospital that has an indirect contractual arrangement with a physician—where there is a contract between the physician and an entity and a contract between that entity and the hospital—cannot bill and receive payment for the physician's services. The hospital can bill and receive payment for the physician's services, however, if the hospital enters into a direct contractual relationship with the physician and certifies that it will bill and receive payment for the physician's services. [Medicare Carrier's Manual 3060.2]

Interpreting X-rays

Does Medicare require that only radiologists provide X-ray interpretations?

CMS will reimburse non-radiologists such as emergency department physicians for X-ray interpretations furnished as part of a service covered by Medicare. The Health Care Financing Administration (HCFA), CMS's predecessor, stated that nothing in the Medicare Act indicates that only board-certified radiologists may furnish X-ray interpretations. HCFA noted that where Congress has determined that there should be special qualifications in order to furnish a Medicare service, as in the case of mammography, Congress included the provision in the Medicare statute. [60 Fed. Reg. 63,124 (1995) (comments)]

Will Medicare pay more than one physician to interpret an X-ray furnished to an emergency department patient?

Generally, Medicare will pay for only one interpretation of an X-ray furnished to an emergency department patient. Under unusual circumstances, Medicare will pay for a second interpretation. For example, Medicare will pay for a second interpretation if the first interpretation results in a questionable finding for which the physician performing the initial interpretation believes another physician's expertise is needed. In addition, a second interpretation may be justified when a second interpretation of the results of the procedure results in a changed diagnosis. Medicare will not pay for a second interpretation made for quality control purposes. Medicare requires documentation of the unusual circumstances before it will pay for a second interpretation. [Medicare Carrier's Manual 15023]

CMS has stated that if a radiologist furnishes a contemporaneous interpretation (a written interpretation or an oral interpretation that will be written later), the emergency department physician should not bill for the service. The Medicare carrier should pay only the radiologist. A "contemporaneous" interpretation is an interpretation that occurs at the same time as the diagnosis and treatment of the patient in the emergency department, not hours or days after the patient is sent home. Medicare also has stated that it will pay for an interpretation furnished by teleradiology as long as the interpretation is used in the diagnosis and treatment of the patient. [60 Fed. Reg. 63,124 (1995) (comments)]

Who will Medicare reimburse if more than one physician submits a claim for the interpretation of an X-ray?

The Medicare Carrier's Manual instructs carriers to pay the first bill they receive when the carrier receives multiple claims for the same interpretation. Carriers will no longer use physician specialty as the primary factor in deciding which claim to pay. In some cases, Medicare carriers will be required to institute recovery action. For example, if the first claim is from a radiologist, the carrier will pay the radiologist's claim because the carrier does not know that a second claim is forthcoming. However, if a second claim comes from an emergency department physician and the carrier can determine that this was the interpretation that contributed to the diagnosis and treatment of the patient, the carrier will pay that claim. If the radiologist's claim was for quality control purposes and not because the emergency department physician required a second interpretation, the Medicare carrier will institute recovery action against the radiologist. [Medicare Carrier's Manual 15023]

Services Provided by Teaching Physicians and Residents

When will Medicare reimburse physician services under the physician fee schedule for services furnished in teaching settings?

Regulations that became effective on July 1, 1996, revised Medicare reimbursement for services provided by teaching physicians working with residents. Teaching physicians are physicians, other than other residents, who involve residents in the care of their patients. The regulations require that teaching physicians must provide more than general direction to interns and residents to obtain Medicare reimbursement. Teaching physicians must be "present during the key portion of any service or procedure for which payment is sought." [42 CFR 415.172(a)]

Are there special requirements concerning a physician's presence during high-risk or other complex medical procedures?

For high-risk or other complex medical procedures, the teaching physician must be present during all critical portions of the procedure and must be immediately available to provide services during the entire service or procedure. High-risk and complex procedures include interventional radiologic supervision and interpretation. The regulation does not define the terms "all critical portions" or "immediately available." For endoscopic procedures, the teaching physician must be present during the entire procedure. However, teaching physicians do not need to be present during other diagnostic tests and may bill for test interpretations if they document that they personally performed the tests or reviewed a resident's interpretation with the resident. [42 CFR 415.172; Medicare Carrier's Manual 15016]

What are the special rules applicable to diagnostic radiology and other diagnostic tests provided by teaching physicians?

Teaching physicians receive full payment for the interpretation of diagnostic radiology and other diagnostic tests if the teaching physician performs the interpretation or reviews the resident's interpretation. CMS has indicated that it will not pay for an interpretation if the documentation is only a countersignature of the resident's interpretation. The teaching physician must document that he or she performed the interpretation or reviewed the resident's interpretation. [42 CFR 415.180; Medicare Carrier's Manual 15016]

Nurse Practitioners and Clinical Nurse Specialists

Are radiological tests performed by nurse practitioners and clinical nurse specialists eligible for Medicare reimbursement?

Under Medicare, nurse practitioners and clinical nurse specialists may perform diagnostic imaging tests without physician supervision if they are authorized to do so under state law. [42 CFR 410.32] Thus, state law must be consulted closely to determine the level of physician supervision, if any, that is necessary to support a claim for Medicare reimbursement for diagnostic tests performed by a nurse practitioner or clinical nurse specialist. The nurse practitioner's services must be services that Medicare would consider physician services if a physician furnished them.

How should the services of nurse practitioners be billed under federal health care programs?

Both Medicare and Medicaid cover the services of nurse practitioners. Effective in 1998, Congress authorized direct reimbursement to nurse practitioners, regardless of geographic area. Direct reimbursement is limited to services that would be physicians' services if furnished by a physician, that are performed by the nurse practitioner working in collaboration with a physician, and that the nurse practitioner is legally authorized to perform by the state in which the services are performed. Nurse practitioners can bill Medicare under their own billing numbers and obtain reimbursement at 80 percent of the lesser of either the actual charge or 85 percent of the physician fee schedule amount. [42 USC 1395x(s)(2)(K)] Unlike in the outpatient setting, nurse practitioner services provided in a hospital setting cannot be billed as "incident to" a physician's services.

Physician's Orders

What happens if a physician orders the wrong test, or if the radiologist realizes that additional tests are necessary?

According to Medicare guidelines, the radiologist may perform only those diagnostic tests that are ordered by the physician who is treating the beneficiary. Other tests are not considered reasonable and necessary and are therefore ineligible for payment. [42 CFR 410.32] Thus, for example, if a physician orders a computed tomography (CT) scan without contrast, and the radiologist believes that contrast is necessary, or if a physician orders a scan of part of the body unrelated to the patient's complaint, the radiologist may not revise the order. The radiologist must contact the referring physician for a new order or a clarification.

If the radiologist plans to perform the test as ordered, but believes that the service falls outside the applicable medical necessity guidelines, careful consideration should be given to whether a claim will be submitted to Medicare. If the claim will be submitted, it might be appropriate to issue an Advance Beneficiary Notice to the patient before performing the test, so that payment from the patient may be obtained if Medicare denies the claim. Hospital policy should be consulted.

Where the treating physician issues a referral to radiology for evaluation, rather than simply ordering a specific test or tests, the radiologist may have more discretion to order additional tests if, for example, an initial scan shows a mass extending into another area of the body.

There is one exception to the rule that tests ordered by only the treating physician can be reimbursed. The exception applies to mammography. A radiologist may perform a diagnostic mammogram on the basis of screening mammography results without obtaining an additional order from the referring physician. [42 CFR 410.32(a)(2)]

Outpatient Prospective Payment System (PPS)

What is the PPS for hospital outpatient services?

The Outpatient Prospective Payment System, which first went into effect in August 2000, is the Medicare payment system for hospital outpatient services, including clinical visits, emergency services and urgent care, X-rays, and surgical procedures not performed as part of an inpatient stay. Prior to the PPS, Medicare paid for services using several different payment methods that were based on reasonable costs. The PPS groups outpatient services into Ambulatory Payment Classifications (APCs). As of January 2003, there were 569 APCs. Each APC includes services that are clinically similar and that require similar resources. CMS has assigned each APC a weight based on the median costs for the services within the APC group. The payment rate, which is reviewed and adjusted annually by the Secretary of HHS, is the product of a conversion factor and the APC rate. The PPS applies to nearly all hospitals. [67 Fed. Reg. 66,718 (2002), to be codified at 42 CFR Parts 405 and 419. For detailed information on billing procedures and rates, consult the CMS Web site, www.cms.gov.]

What services are excluded from the outpatient PPS?

The following services are not paid for under the outpatient PPS:

- services provided by certain providers, including physicians, nurse practitioners, physician assistants (PAs), certified nurse midwives, psychologists, anesthetists, and clinical social workers, which will continue to be paid for under the Medicare fee schedule
- rehabilitation services
- ambulance services
- prosthetics; prosthetic supplies, devices, and implants (except for intraocular lenses); and orthotic devices
- durable medical equipment, except implantable durable medical equipment
- clinical diagnostic laboratory services
- services provided to patients with end-stage renal disease (ESRD) that are paid under the ESRD composite rate, and drugs and supplies furnished during dialysis
- services and procedures that cannot be furnished safely in an outpatient setting or that require inpatient care
- services provided to persons who are inpatients of a skilled nursing facility (SNF) and that are covered under the SNF PPS
- services not covered by Medicare, including services that are not medically necessary

ENVIRONMENTAL ISSUES AND OCCUPATIONAL SAFETY

There are special environmental concerns in the radiology department because of the use of radioactive materials. This area is heavily regulated by the Nuclear Regulatory Commission (NRC), which has specific requirements regarding licensure, radiation safety, training, equipment, recordkeeping and reporting, notices to workers, and waste disposal. HHS also regulates various aspects of radiologic services through the Medicare Conditions of Participation. In addition, the states have enacted their own regulations regarding radiologic services. There are also occupational safety concerns that apply to all areas of the hospital, including the radiology department. The bloodborne pathogen standard is of concern in the radiology department because there are invasive procedures performed in radiology that entail exposure to body fluids and because employees in the radiology department may be exposed to body fluids due to a patient's medical condition (e.g., a patient severely injured in a car accident who is in need of X-rays). Other occupational safety concerns include airborne hazards, hazardous substances (including silver from X-rays), smoking, and clearance in aisles and passageways. Each of these areas will be discussed in the following sections.

Federal Regulation of Radioactive Materials

What is the NRC's role in the regulation of radiology services?

The NRC regulates the intentional internal or external administration of byproduct material, or the radiation from the byproduct material to human beings. A specific license is required for this medical use. [10 CFR Part 35]

The NRC issues a single byproduct material license that covers an entire radioisotope program, with the exception of teletherapy, nuclear-powered pacemakers, and irradiators. Separate licenses are not usually required for departments or employees of a single hospital.

On April 24, 2002, the NRC published a new final rule on medical use of byproduct material, effective October 24, 2002, six months after publication. Among other things, the rule revises regulations on patient notification/reportable events, radiation safety committees, physician's written directions, and training and experience requirements. The rule also adds requirements for reporting unintended medical radiation exposure of an embryo, fetus, or nursing child. [Medical Use of Byproduct Material, 67 Fed. Reg. 20,250 (2002)]

Licensure

What kinds of licenses does the NRC issue?

All facilities using radioactive materials must be licensed to use them. The NRC issues three kinds of licenses for the use of byproduct material in the practice of medicine.

General License. This type of license authorizes physicians, veterinarians, clinical laboratories, and hospitals to receive, acquire, possess, or use certain small quantities of byproduct material for in vitro clinical or laboratory tests not involving administration to humans.

Specific License. Specific licenses issued to physicians in private practice are usually limited to physicians who are located in private offices, not on hospital premises. Methods of use that require hospitalization of the patient are not permitted.

Specific licenses are also issued to medical institutions. These licenses authorize byproduct material for medical uses by physicians named on the institution's license. Institutional licensees must have a radiation safety committee to oversee the use of licensed material throughout the institution and to review the institution's radiation safety program. The physicians named on the institution's license conduct their programs with the approval of the radiation safety committee.

A specific license may also be issued for a mobile nuclear medicine service. Both private practitioners and institutions may apply for authorization to use byproduct material in a mobile service.

Specific License of Broad Scope. This type of license is not appropriate for most institutions performing routine medical procedures with byproduct material. It is for medical institutions that provide patient care and conduct research programs that use radioisotopes for in vitro, animal, and medical procedures. The NRC provides guidance for preparing an application for medical use programs that specifies exactly what information the applicant must provide to the NRC. [Regulatory Guide 10.8, Guide for the Preparation of Applications for Medical Use Programs, Revision 2 (August 1987)]

Radiation Safety

Are there radiation safety standards that must be met in order to participate in the Medicare and Medicaid programs?

There are general safety standards under the Medicare Conditions of Participation. These regulations state that radiologic services, particularly ionizing radiology procedures, must be free from hazards for patients and personnel. The regulations state that proper safety precautions must be maintained against radiation hazards, including adequate shielding for patients, personnel, and facilities, as well as appropriate storage, use, and disposal of radioactive materials. In addition, periodic inspection of equipment must be made, and identified hazards must be promptly corrected. Radiation workers must be checked periodically by use of exposure meters or badge tests for amount of radiation exposure. [42 CFR 482.26]

In nuclear medicine services, radioactive materials must be prepared, labeled, used, transported, stored, and disposed of in accordance with accepted standards of practice. In-house preparation of radiopharmaceuticals must be under the supervision of an appropriately trained registered pharmacist or doctor of medicine or osteopathy. There must be proper storage and disposal of radioactive material. If laboratory tests are performed in nuclear medicine, the service must meet the requirements for laboratory tests. All equipment and supplies must be appropriate for the types of nuclear medicine services offered and must be maintained for safe and efficient performance. Equipment must be maintained in safe operating condition and must be inspected, tested, and calibrated at least annually by qualified personnel. [42 CFR 482.53]

Is a radiation protection program required under federal law?

Each licensee must develop, document, and implement a radiation protection program. Licensees must use, to the extent practicable, procedures and engineering controls based on sound radiation protection principles to achieve occupational doses and doses to the public that are as low as reasonably achievable (ALARA). There must be a review of the radiation protection program content and implementation at least annually. [10 CFR 20.1101]

What kind of information does the NRC require regarding the radiation safety program prior to granting a license?

In addition to a description of the radiation safety committee charter when applicable and radiation safety officer delegation of authority, the NRC requires copies of:

- the ALARA program
- the procedure for leak-testing sealed sources
- the rules for the safe use of radiopharmaceuticals
- spill procedures
- the procedure for ordering and receiving radioactive material
- the procedure for opening packages that contain radioactive material
- the procedure for keeping records of unit dosage use
- the procedure for keeping records of multidose vial use
- the procedure for measuring and recording molybdenum concentration
- the procedure for keeping an inventory of implant sources
- area survey procedures
- air concentration control procedures
- the procedure for radiation safety during radiopharmaceutical therapy
- the procedure for radiation safety implant therapy
- other safety procedures for specific radioactive materials described in the regulations

[Regulatory Guide 10.8, Guide for the Preparation of Applications for Medical Use Programs, Revision 2, August 1987, item 10, page 12]

What is a radiation safety officer?

Federal rules require NRC licensees to appoint a radiation safety officer (RSO) who is responsible for implementing the radiation protection program. The RSO ensures that radiation safety activities are performed in accordance with licensee-approved procedures and regulatory requirements. A licensee may have a temporary RSO for up to 60 days a year. [10 CFR 34.24]

Specific duties of RSOs that were prescribed in former NRC regulations were omitted in the revised NCR final rule published April 24, 2002. The new regulations require that the licensee give the RSO authority and resources to: (1) identify radiation safety problems; (2) initiate, recommend, or provide corrective actions; (3) stop unsafe operations; and (4) verify implementation of corrective actions. [10 CFR 34.24; Medical Use of Byproduct Material, 67 Fed. Reg. 20,250 (2002)]

An RSO must be certified by a specialty board recognized by the NRC or an Agreement State, or must have completed training and experience requirements set forth in the regulations. [10 CFR 35.57, 35.59, and 35.900]

What is the radiation safety committee?

Under the NRC's final rule for medical use of byproduct material, published April 24, 2002, the licensee's radiation safety committee is responsible for broad oversight of the uses of certain radioactive materials. Previously, specific responsibilities for the committee appeared in two regulations (former 10 CFR 35.22 and 35.23), both of which were deleted in the final rule in order to provide licensees with more flexibility in how they use the committee to oversee the radiation safety aspects of the medical use of byproduct material. Former specific responsibilities of the radiation safety committee have been transferred from the committee to licensee management. A committee is still required for certain medical licensees performing two or more higher risk activities such as those used in the treatment of cancer. The regulations continue to specify radiation safety goals or objectives for the committee, but allow licensee management flexibility in implementing those goals. [10 CFR 35.24; Medical Use of Byproduct Material, 67 Fed. Reg. 20,250 (2002)]

What is an ALARA program?

ALARA means "as low as reasonably achievable." Current NRC rules require licensees to use, to the extent practical, procedures and engineering controls based upon sound radiation protection principles to achieve occupational doses and doses to members of the public that are "ALARA." The licensee is required to review the radiation protection program content and implementation at least annually. [10 CFR 20.1101]

In its final rule on medical use of byproduct material, published April 24, 2002, the NRC deleted a regulation (former 10 CFR 35.20) that included prescriptive requirements related to the ALARA program. Medical use licensees must continue to comply with the licensing regulation (10 CFR 20.1101), which includes a more general requirement to implement an ALARA program designed to keep doses ALARA. The NRC reasons that deletion of the specific prescriptive ALARA requirements will provide licensees flexibility in developing and implementing their ALARA programs. [Medical Use of Byproduct Material, 67 Fed. Reg. 20,250 (2002)]

Does federal law require a quality management program?

The NRC formerly required licensees to have a quality management program but deleted the requirement (former 10 CFR 35.32) in its final rule for medical use of byproduct material, published April 24, 2002. Under the final rule, only certain essential requirements are necessary to provide high confidence that byproduct material will be administered as directed by the authorized user. For any administration that requires a written directive to be prepared, licensees must develop, implement, and maintain written procedures to ensure that the patient's or human research subject's identity is verified before each administration and that each administration is in accordance with the written directive. These procedures must address certain items applicable to the licensee's use of byproduct material. Beyond these requirements, the final rule allows licensees the flexibility to develop procedures to meet their needs. In addition, there is no requirement for submission of these procedures to NRC for its approval, as was previously required by the quality management rule. [10 CFR 35.40; Medical Use of Byproduct Material, 67 Fed. Reg. 20,250 (2002)]

What kind of posting is required in radiation areas?

Each radiation area must be posted with a conspicuous sign or signs bearing the radiation symbol and the words "CAUTION, RADIATION AREA."

In high radiation areas, there must be a conspicuous sign or signs bearing the radiation symbol and the words "CAUTION, HIGH RADIATION AREA" or "DANGER, HIGH RADIATION AREA."

In very high radiation areas, there must be a conspicuous sign or signs bearing the radiation symbol and the words "GRAVE DANGER, VERY HIGH RADIATION AREA."

In airborne radioactivity areas, there must be a conspicuous sign or signs bearing the radiation symbol and the words "CAUTION, AIRBORNE RADIOACTIVITY AREA" or "DANGER, RADIOACTIVE MATERIAL(S)." [10 CFR 20.1902]

What are the labeling requirements?

Each container of licensed material must bear a durable, clearly visible label bearing the radiation symbol and the words "CAUTION, RADIOACTIVE MATERIAL" or "DANGER, RADIOACTIVE MATERIAL." The label must also provide sufficient information (such as the radionuclides present, quantity of radioactivity, date for which the activity is estimated, radiation levels, kinds of materials, and mass enrichment) to permit persons handling or using the containers or working in the vicinity to take precautions to avoid or minimize exposures. [10 CFR 20.1904]

Training and Supervision

What kind of radiation safety training program is required under federal regulations?

Everyone who in the course of employment is likely to receive in a year an occupational dose in excess of 100 mrem must be

- kept informed of the storage, transfer, or use of radiation and/or radioactive material
- instructed in health protection problems associated with exposure to radiation and/or radioactive material, in precautions or procedures to minimize exposure, and in the purposes and functions of protective devices
- instructed in, and required to observe, to the extent within the worker's control, the applicable provisions of NRC regulations and licenses for the protection of personnel from exposure to radiation and/or radioactive material
- instructed of his or her responsibility to report promptly to the licensee any condition that may lead to or cause a violation of NRC regulations and licenses or unnecessary exposure to radiation and/or radioactive material
- instructed in the appropriate response to warnings made in the event of an unusual occurrence or malfunction that may involve exposure to radiation and/or radioactive material
- advised of the radiation exposure reports that workers may request [10 CFR 19.12]

In addition to the requirements listed above, the licensee must instruct the supervised individual in the licensee's written radiation protection procedures, written directive procedures, regulations of this chapter, and license conditions with respect to the use of byproduct material. [10 CFR 35.27]

The NRC has created a model training program that meets the requirements of the federal regulations. The introduction to the model program indicates that site-specific training should be given to all workers. Ancillary personnel, such as clerical and housekeeping staff, whose duties may require them to work in the vicinity of radioactive materials must be informed about radiation hazards and appropriate precautions. Training should be tailored to meet the needs of the audience. Under the model training program, personnel must be instructed

- before assuming duties with, or in the vicinity of, radioactive materials
- during annual refresher training
- when there is a significant change in duties, regulations, or the terms of the license

Alternatively, applicants may develop their own training program and submit it to the NRC for review.

Do the regulations address supervision of technologists?

The regulations permit technologists to receive, possess, use, or transfer byproduct material under the supervision of an authorized user. [10 CFR 35.11] The licensed facility is required to do the following:

- Instruct the supervised individual in the principles of radiation safety and the facility's quality management program.
- Require the supervised individual to follow the instructions of the supervising authorized user, follow the facility's written radiation safety and quality management procedures, and comply with federal regulations and license conditions.
- Periodically review the supervised individual's use of byproduct material and the records kept to reflect this use.

There are similar requirements when the facility permits the preparation of byproduct material for medical use by an individual under the supervision of an authorized user.

The regulations, as revised by the NRC's final rule for medical use of byproduct material, published April 24, 2002, delete former training requirements (former 10 CFR 35.25) and impose similar requirements in a new regulation. [10 CFR 35.27; Medical Use of Byproduct Material, 67 Fed. Reg. 20,250 (2002)]

Are there training requirements for authorized users?

Applicants for licensure for radioactive materials must be qualified by training and experience to use the requested radioactive materials for the purposes requested. [10 CFR 30.33(a)(3)] The regulations provide specific criteria for acceptable training and experience.

Authorized users involved in medical use have the following special responsibilities:

- examination of patients and medical records to determine if a radiation procedure is appropriate
- prescription of the radiation dosage or dose and how it is to be administered
- actual use of, or direction of technologists or other paramedical personnel in the use of, byproduct material
- interpretation of results of diagnostic procedures and evaluation of results of therapy procedures

These responsibilities may be delegated to a physician who is under the supervision of an authorized user. Technologists or other personnel may use byproduct material under an authorized user's supervision when permitted under applicable federal, state, or local laws. [Regulatory Guide 10.8, Guide for the Preparation of Applications for Medical Use Programs, Revision 2, August 1987, item 7, page 8]

Equipment and Procedures

Are there any "broad scope" federal regulations regarding equipment in the radiology department?

The Conditions of Participation set out some general equipment requirements for nuclear medicine services. All equipment and supplies must be appropriate for the types of nuclear medicine services offered and must be maintained for safe and efficient performance. Equipment must be maintained in safe operating condition and must be inspected, tested, and calibrated at least annually by qualified personnel. [42 CFR 482.53]

Do federal regulations impose requirements for calibration of instruments used to measure activity of unsealed byproduct material?

NRC licensees must possess and use instruments to measure the activity of unsealed byproduct material before it is administered to each patient or human research subject.

A licensee is responsible for calibrating the instruments in accordance with nationally recognized standards or the manufacturer's instructions. The licensee must also retain a record of each required calibration. [10 CFR 35.60 (formerly 35.50); Medical Use of Byproduct Material, 67 Fed. Reg. 20,250 (2002)]

Are there federal requirements regarding calibration and checking of survey instruments?

Licensees must calibrate the survey instruments used to show compliance with federal regulations before first use, annually, and following repair. There are specific requirements regarding calibration, including calibrating two separated readings on each scale or decade that will be used to show compliance. A licensee must retain a record of each survey instrument calibration for three years. [10 CFR 35.61 (formerly 35.51); Medical Use of Byproduct Material, 67 Fed. Reg. 20,250 (2002)]

Does federal law address measurement of dosages of unsealed byproduct material for medical use?

The regulations, as amended by the NRC's final rule on medical use of byproduct material published April 4, 2002, require a licensee to determine and record the activity of each dosage before medical use. For a unit dosage, the determination may be made by direct measurement of radioactivity, or a decay correction based on activity determined by the manufacturer or a licensee. For other than unit dosages, the determination is made by direct measurement, a combination of measurement of radioactivity and mathematical calculations, or a combination of volumetric measurements and mathematical calculations. The licensee must retain a record of the dosage for at least three years. [10 CFR 35.63 (former 35.53); Medical Use of Byproduct Material, 67 Fed. Reg. 20,250 (2002)]

What do federal regulations require with regard to syringe shields and vial shields?

Licensees must keep syringes that contain byproduct material to be administered in a radiation shield and must conspicuously label each syringe or syringe radiation shield that contains a syringe with a radiopharmaceutical. The label must show the radiopharmaceutical name or abbreviation, the clinical procedure, or the patient's name.

Each person who prepares a radiopharmaceutical kit must use a syringe radiation shield when preparing the kit and must use a syringe radiation shield when administering a radiopharmaceutical by injection unless the use of the shield is contraindicated for the patient. [10 CFR 35.69]

Each person preparing or handling a vial that contains a radiopharmaceutical must keep the vial in a vial radiation shield. Vial radiation shields that contain a vial of a radiopharmaceutical must be labeled. [10 CFR 35.69]

What are the requirements regarding surveys for ambient radiation exposure rate?

A survey with a radiation detection survey instrument must be done at the end of each day where radiopharmaceuticals are routinely prepared for use or administered, and once a week where radiopharmaceuticals or radiopharmaceutical waste is stored. The regulations indicate acceptable detection rates. There must be a survey for removable contamination once a week where radiopharmaceuticals are routinely prepared for use, administered, or stored. Trigger levels must be established for these surveys. A record of each survey must be kept for three years. [10 CFR 35.70]

What are the requirements for storage of volatiles and gases?

The NRC's final rule on medical use of byproduct material, published April 4, 2002, deleted specific requirements for storage of volatiles and gases (former 10 CFR 35.90). Licensees are instead required to comply with general public and occupational dose limits and to maintain exposures that are ALARA. In deleting the detailed storage requirements, the NRC reasoned that licensees should have flexibility in complying with general provisions, and, therefore, a prescriptive requirement was not needed. [10 CFR 20.1101; Medical Use of Byproduct Material, 67 Fed. Reg. 20,250 (2002)]

Are there federal regulations governing control of aerosols and gases?

The NRC's final rule on medical use of byproduct material, published April 4, 2002, deleted specific requirements on control of aerosols and gases (former 10 CFR 35.205). Licensees must instead comply with the occupational and public dose limits in 10 CFR 20.1101. In deleting the specific regulation, the NRC indicated prescriptive requirements for limiting airborne concentrations of radioactive material are not needed. [10 CFR 20.1101; Medical Use of Byproduct Material, 67 Fed. Reg. 20,250 (2002)]

Are there federal regulations regarding radiopharmaceutical use for therapy?

The NRC's final rule on medical use of byproduct material, published April 4, 2002, provides that a licensee may authorize the release from its control of any individual who has been administered unsealed byproduct material or implants containing byproduct material if the total effective dose is not likely to exceed 5 mSv (0.5 rem). The licensee must provide the released individual, or the parent or guardian, with instructions concerning effective doses and concerning the consequences of failing to follow instructions. The licensee must also follow recordkeeping requirements. [10 CFR 35.75, 35.2075]

For a patient or research subject who cannot be released, a licensee must provide a private room or sanitary facility, or a shared room with another individual who has also received radiopharmaceutical therapy. The licensee must take the following precautions:

- The room must be posted with a "RADIOACTIVE MATERIALS" sign.

- A notice must indicate where and how long visitors may stay in the room.

- The licensee must either monitor material and items removed from the room to determine radioactivity, or handle the material as radioactive waste.

A licensee must notify the RSO or designee and the authorized user as soon as possible if the patient or human research subject has a medical emergency or dies. [10 CFR 35.315]

For what reasons do courts typically hold hospitals or staff liable for radiology equipment malfunctions?

Generally, a hospital is responsible for the condition and safety of equipment used in the diagnosis and treatment of hospital patients. This responsibility derives from the hospital's overall duty of care toward patients. Thus, failure to periodically assess, adequately maintain, or provide for the proper use of radiology equipment in accordance with the standard of care may result in liability if a patient is injured. The standard of care will be established by examining the practices of similar hospital radiology departments, equipment manufacturer guidelines, recommendations of professional associations (such as the Joint Commission Environment of Care standards), and expert testimony.

In addition to the "direct" or "corporate" liability discussed in the previous paragraph, hospitals are liable for the negligence of hospital employees. This form of liability is known as "imputed," "vicarious," or *"respondeat superior"* liability. Thus, a hospital may be held liable if a hospital employee negligently carries out equipment-related duties, resulting in harm to a radiology patient, even if appropriate procedures and safeguards were in place.

How can hospitals reduce equipment-related liability?

Hospital leaders should consider

- equipment inspection procedures
- quality control measures
- risk manager review of departmental practices
- staff orientation and continuing education
- detailed policies and procedures
- other techniques for improving the safety of equipment and quality of patient care

In addition, a hospital may attempt to limit liability for radiology equipment malfunction by contracting with a provider group that furnishes all radiology services and assumes responsibility for the safety and condition of radiology equipment. However, courts may not look favorably on such contracts and may continue to reason that the hospital remains liable for injuries caused by radiology equipment under the hospital's direct duty of care toward its patients.

Recordkeeping and Reporting

In what form must records be maintained?

Records required under federal law must be legible throughout the retention period specified in each regulation. The record may be the original, a copy, or a microform, as long as the copy or microform is authenticated by authorized personnel and the microform can produce a clear copy throughout the required retention period. The record can also be stored on electronic media. Records such as letters, drawings, and specifications must include all pertinent information such as stamps, initials, and signatures. The licensee must maintain adequate safeguards against tampering with and loss of records. [10 CFR 35.5]

Must records be kept concerning the radiation protection program?

Federal regulations require the maintenance of records of the radiation protection program, including the following:

- The provisions of the program must be maintained until the license is terminated.
- Audits and other reviews of program content and implementation must be retained for three years. [10 CFR 20.2102]

Must records of surveys be maintained?

Records showing the results of surveys and calibrations required by 10 CFR 20.1501 and 20.1906(b) must be retained for three years.

The following records must be kept until the license is terminated:

- results of surveys used to determine the dose from external sources and used in the assessment of individual dose equivalents
- results of measurements and calculations used to determine individual intakes of radioactive material and used in the assessment of internal dose
- results of air sampling, surveys, and bioassays required pursuant to 10 CFR 20.1703(a)(3)(i), (ii)
- results of measurements and calculations used to evaluate the release of radioactive effluents to the environment [10 CFR 20.2103]

What records must be kept regarding the receipt, transfer, and disposal of byproduct material?

Records of the receipt of byproduct material must be retained as long as the material is possessed and for three years following transfer or disposal of the material. The licensee who transferred the material must retain each record of transfer for three years after transfer. The licensee who disposed of the material must retain each record of disposal of byproduct material until the NRC terminates each license that authorizes disposal of the material. [10 CFR 30.51]

What other records must be retained?

The following records must be retained (some regulations were renumbered in changes made by NRC final rule on medical use of byproduct material [67 Fed. Reg. 20,250 (2002)]:

- dose calibrator checks and tests [10 CFR 35.60 (former 35.50)]
- survey instrument calibrations [10 CFR 35.61 (former 35.51)]
- measurement of dosages of unsealed byproduct material [10 CFR 35.63 (former 35.53)]
- surveys for contamination and ambient radiation exposure rate [10 CFR 35.70]
- records of safety instructions to personnel involved in patient care when radiopharmaceuticals are used for therapy [10 CFR 35.310]

- records of doses received by all individuals for whom monitoring was required and records of doses received during planned special exposures, accidents, and emergency conditions [10 CFR 20.2106]

What are the requirements for the reporting of a medical event (misadministration)?

The NRC final rule on medical use of byproduct material deleted the former regulation on notifications, reports, and records of misadministrations. (former 10 CFR 35.33) The final rule uses the term "medical event" because of concerns that "misadministration" had a negative connotation that implied negligence on the part of the physician or other hospital workers. The term "medical event" simply means that the byproduct material or radiation from byproduct material was not administered as directed by the authorized user. [10 CFR 35.3045]

Medical events include delivery of a dose different from the prescribed dose by specified margins and administration of a dose to the wrong individual. A licensee must report the medical event by telephone to the NRC Operations Center by the next calendar day. The licensee must submit a written report to the appropriate NRC Regional Office within 15 days after discovery of the medical event. The written report must include the licensee's name, the name of the prescribing physician, a description of the event, why the event occurred, the effect on the recipient, preventative action, and certification that the licensee notified the individual or representative, and if not, why not. The licensee must also notify the referring physician and the recipient within 24 hours. [10 CFR 35.3045]

The final rule also provides for report and notification of a larger than approved dose to an embryo/fetus or a nursing child. [10 CFR 35.3046]

What are the requirements for reporting failure to comply with NRC regulations or the existence of a defect?

A defect or failure to comply that could create a substantial safety hazard, were it to remain uncorrected, must be reported to the NRC within 60 days of discovery. If the evaluation of an identified deviation or failure to comply cannot be completed within 60 days, an interim report must be submitted to the NRC. The regulations contain details regarding the content of the notification to the NRC and method of communication of transmission. [10 CFR 21.21]

What other reports must be made to the NRC?

The following reports are required:

- reports on theft or loss of licensed material [10 CFR 20.2201]
- notification of incidents—immediate report of any event involving byproduct, source, or special nuclear material that may have caused or threatens to cause an individual to receive a specific dose listed in the regulations, or the release of radioactive material so that if an individual had been present for 24 hours, the individual could have received an intake five times the annual limit [10 CFR 20.2202]
- notification of incidents—24-hour notification of discovery of an event involving loss of control of licensed material that may have caused or threatens to cause an individual to receive certain dosages within 24 hours, or the release of radioactive material so that had an individual been present for 24 hours, the individual could have received an intake in excess of one occupational annual limit on intake [10 CFR 20.2202]
- reports of exposures, radiation levels, and concentrations of radioactive material exceeding the constraints or limits [10 CFR 20.2203]
- reports of planned special exposures [10 CFR 20.2204]
- reports to individuals of exceeding dose limits [10 CFR 20.2205]
- immediate report (not later than four hours) of an event that prevents immediate protective actions necessary to avoid exposures to radiation or radioactive materials that could exceed regulatory limits or releases of licensed material that could exceed regulatory limits (fires, explosions, toxic gas releases, etc.) [10 CFR 30.50]
- report within 24 hours of an unplanned contamination event that meets certain parameters; an event in which equipment is disabled or fails to function as designed when the equipment is required to prevent releases exceeding regulatory limits, to prevent exposures to radiation and radioactive materials exceeding regulatory limits, or to mitigate the consequences of an accident; equipment required to be available and operable that is disabled or fails to function; and lack of available and operable redundant equipment to perform the required safety function [10 CFR 30.50]
- report within 24 hours of an event that requires unplanned medical treatment at a medical facility of an individual with spreadable radioactive contamination on the individual's body or clothing [10 CFR 30.50]
- report within 24 hours of an unplanned fire or explosion damaging any licensed material or any device, container, or equipment containing licensed material when the quantity is of a certain amount and the damage affects the integrity of the licensed material or its container [10 CFR 30.50]

Notices and Reports to Workers

What kinds of notices to workers must be posted?

Current copies of the following documents must be posted:

- federal regulations governing Notices, Instructions, and Reports to Workers; Inspections [10 CFR Part 19]; and Standards for Protection against Radiation [10 CFR Part 20]
- the license, license conditions, or documents incorporated into the license by reference and amendment
- the operating procedures applicable to licensed activities
- notices of violations involving radiological working conditions, proposed imposition of civil penalty, or order pursuant to applicable federal regulations, along with any response
- NRC Form 3, Notice to Employees

If the posting of documents in the first three items is impractical, the facility may post a notice that describes the document and where it may be examined.

Documents, notices, or forms required to be posted must (1) appear in a sufficient number of places so that those engaged in licensed activities can observe them on the way to or from a licensed activity location to which the document applies, (2) be conspicuous, and (3) be replaced if defaced or altered.

Postings must be made within two working days of receipt of documents from the NRC. [10 CFR 19.11]

What kinds of reports must be made to individuals regarding radiation exposure?

Radiation exposure data for an individual, and the results of any measurements, analyses, and calculations of radioactive material deposited or retained in the body of that individual, must be reported to that individual. There are specific requirements regarding what is to be in the written notification.

Each worker must be advised annually of the worker's dose as shown in the records required by federal law.

At the request of a worker formerly engaged in licensed activities controlled by the licensee, the worker must be given a report of the worker's exposure to radiation and/or to radioactive material as shown in the records for each year the worker was required to be monitored. This report must be furnished within 30 days of the time of the request or within 30 days after exposure of the individual has been determined by the licensee, whichever is later.

At the request of a worker who is terminating employment that involved exposure to radiation or radioactive materials during the current calendar quarter or current year, the licensee who employs that worker must provide at termination a written report regarding the radiation dose the worker received from operations. If the most recent individual monitoring results are not available, a written estimate of the dose must be provided with a clear indication that it is an estimate. [10 CFR 19.13]

Inspection

Is the NRC authorized to conduct inspections?

Federal law mandates that all licensees must afford the NRC at all reasonable times the opportunity to inspect materials, activities, facilities, premises, and records. During an inspection, inspectors may consult privately with workers. Hospital representatives may accompany inspectors during other phases of an inspection. If there is an authorized workers' representative, that person may have the opportunity to accompany the inspectors during the inspection of physical working conditions. [10 CFR 19.14]

Are inspectors authorized to consult with workers during inspections?

Inspectors may consult privately with workers concerning matters of occupational radiation protection and other matters related to NRC regulations and licenses to the extent the inspector deems necessary for an effective and thorough inspection. During an inspection, any worker may bring privately to the attention of the inspectors, either orally or in writing, any past or present condition the worker has reason to believe may have contributed to or caused any unnecessary exposure of a person to radiation. [10 CFR 19.15]

Can a worker request an inspection?

Any worker or worker representative who believes that there has been a violation of law or license conditions may request an inspection. If the regional officer administrator determines that the complaint states reasonable grounds to believe a violation exists or has occurred, he or she will cause an inspection to be made as soon as practicable. [10 CFR 19.16] If the inspector determines that an inspection is not warranted, he or she must notify the complainant in writing of this determination. The complainant can obtain a review of that determination by submitting a written statement to the NRC Executive Director for Operations, either by mail, or, effective December 5, 2002, by electronic submissions. Information on electronic submission is available from www.nrc.gov/site-help/eie.html. [10 CFR 19.17; 67 Fed. Reg. 57091 (2002)]

Radioactive Waste

What are the requirements regarding disposal of radioactive waste?

Radioactive wastes are classified for management and treatment purposes as high, intermediate, and low level. Health care facilities primarily deal with low-level radioisotopes in diagnosis and therapy. Federal law specifies that licensed material can be disposed of only

- by transfer to an authorized recipient who must dispose of the material in accordance with several approved handling methods [10 CFR 20.2001]
- by decay in storage [10 CFR 20.2001]
- by release in effluents (within regulation limits) [10 CFR 20.2001]
- under a plan not in the regulations but approved by the NRC [10 CFR 20.2002]
- by release into sanitary sewage if several conditions are met [10 CFR 20.2003]
- by incineration if certain conditions are met [10 CFR 20.2004]

State Regulation of Radioactive Materials

Does state law regulate radioactive materials?

In addition to NRC and other regulations discussed above, state law addresses many aspects of working with radioactive material and varies widely. Therefore, state legislation and regulation must be consulted to ascertain the requirements in each jurisdiction. This section does not provide a state-by-state breakdown of laws but rather relies largely on California and Texas law to provide illustrations of how the states regulate various aspects of law that impact the radiology department.

Licensure

Does state law require licensure for radioactive materials?

The NRC is authorized to make agreements with states to turn over regulatory authority for radioactive materials. In 2002, 32 states had agreements with the NRC that gave them the authority to license radioactive materials used or possessed within their borders. A facility that wants to possess or use licensed materials in one of the agreement states must file an application with the state's radiation control program, not the NRC. A listing of agreement states and contact information is available on the NRC Web site, www.nrc.gov.

Texas is an example of an agreement state that has legislated licensing requirements. Texas statutory provisions mandate the general or specific licensing of radioactive material and devices or equipment using radioactive material. [TEX. HEALTH & SAFETY CODE 401.104] The state regulatory code expands on the distinction between general and specific licenses and addresses other administrative matters. [25 TEX. ADMIN. CODE 289.252]

California's Radiation Control Law gives the state Department of Health Services the authority to develop programs for licensing and regulation of radioactive materials, and to adopt regulations relating to control sources of ionizing radiation. [CAL. HEALTH & SAFETY CODE 114960]

Training

Does state law address training of radiologists?

State laws generally spell out in detail the necessary qualifications of physicians who are considered "authorized users" under the facility's license, and they frequently specify the required credentials for particular uses of radioactive material. Texas law, for example, states that the licensee must require the authorized user of a radiopharmaceutical to be a physician who is certified by one of several listed radiology or nuclear medicine boards or who has successfully completed classroom and laboratory training in radioisotope handling techniques applicable to the use of prepared radiopharmaceuticals and supervised clinical experience as specified in a detailed list in the regulations. [25 TEX. ADMIN. CODE 289.252]

Does state law address training of technologists?

Several states spell out in detail the requirements of approved training programs. In California, for example, regulations set forth requirements for diagnostic radiologic technology schools. The regulations indicate that the course of study must meet at least the following:

- 500 hours of formal classroom instruction
- 50 hours of general radiographic laboratory
- 75 hours of positioning laboratory
- 25 hours of radiation protection laboratory
- 1,850 hours of supervised clinical education

Further, the regulations spell out what the classroom instruction shall include, which experiments must be performed in the radiographic laboratory, techniques that must be learned in the positioning laboratory, experiments that must be performed in the radiation protection laboratory, and the specific radiographic procedures that must be performed in the supervised clinical education portion of the program. [CAL. CODE REGS. tit. 17, 30421]

Texas also has extensive regulation of training requirements. [25 TEX. ADMIN. CODE 143.17] In addition, Texas has continuing education requirements, mandating 24 contact hours of continuing education acceptable to the department during each biennial renewal period. The regulations are very detailed and very stringent about what is and is not acceptable as continuing education.

Equipment

Does state law regulate radiology equipment?

Generally, there are extensive state laws and regulations regarding standards for radiology equipment. The state administrative code in California, for example, contains extensive requirements for radiographic equipment. [*See, e.g.,* CAL. CODE REGS. tit. 17, 30305, 30308, & 30312.] Each state's laws should be consulted to ensure compliance.

Reporting and Recordkeeping

Do states require the reporting of misadministration?

States generally require the reporting of misadministration. In California, for example, the law states that when a misadministration involves a therapy procedure, the licensee must notify the state Department of Health Services, the referring physician, and the patient or the responsible relative or guardian, unless the referring physician agrees to inform the patient or believes, based on medical judgment, that telling the patient or the patient's responsible relative or guardian would be harmful to one or the other.

The notifications must be made within 24 hours after the licensee discovers the misadministration (or as soon as practicable). The licensee is not required to notify the patient or relative without first consulting the referring physician but should not delay medical care because of that. The law requires written notification within 15 days after the initial therapy misadministration and indicates what information must be included in the report.

When misadministration involves a diagnostic procedure, the radiation safety officer must promptly investigate its cause, make a record for agency review, and retain the record. The licensee must notify the referring physician and the department in writing within 15 days if the misadministration involved use of radioactive material not intended for medical use, administration of dosage fivefold different from the intended dosage, or administration of radioactive material such that the patient is likely to receive an organ dose greater than 2 rem or a whole-body dose of greater than 500 mrem.

Licensees are required to retain a record of each misadministration for 10 years. The record must contain the names of all individuals involved in the event, including the physician, allied health personnel, the patient, and the patient's referring physician; the patient's Social Security number or identification number; and a brief description of the event, the effect on the patient, and the action taken to prevent recurrence. [CAL. CODE REGS. tit. 17, 30322]

Does state law mandate the retention of certain records?

State law may incorporate federal recordkeeping requirements, may have requirements that mirror federal requirements, and/or may require additional or different records. Texas law, for example, requires persons who possess or use a source of radiation to maintain

- records relating to the use, receipt, storage, transfer, or disposal of that source of radiation
- records showing radiation exposure of each individual for whom personnel monitoring is required
- other records the state agency may require [Tex. Health & Safety Code 401.057]

Inspection

How often must equipment in the radiology department be inspected under state law?

State laws vary in their required frequency of inspection. For example, in California, the law specifies that the average inspection frequency for ionizing radiation machines is once a year for mammography X-ray units, once every three years for high-priority sources of ionizing radiation, and once every four and one-quarter years for medium priority sources. [Cal. Health & Safety Code 115085] In Texas, the law requires routine inspection of X-ray equipment every five years, for electronic products that present a minimal threat to human health and safety. [Tex. Health & Safety Code 401.064]

State law may contain several provisions regarding inspections. For example, in addition to the inspection provision noted above, Texas law also grants general inspection authority. It states that the department or commission may enter public or private property at reasonable times to determine whether there is compliance with state law. It further indicates that state representatives can enter an area under the jurisdiction of the federal government only with concurrence of the federal government. [Tex. Health & Safety Code 401.063]

Another provision of Texas law indicates that the department or commission, with the approval of the governor, can enter into an agreement with the federal government, another state, or an interstate agency under which the state, in cooperation with the other parties, performs inspections or other functions relating to the control of sources of radiation. [Tex. Health & Safety Code 401.065]

Radioactive Waste

What does state law require with regard to disposal of radioactive waste?

The states often cite the federal regulations governing low-level radioactive waste and adopt them by reference. [*See, e.g.,* CAL. CODE REGS. tit. 17, 30470.] The state laws may or may not add exceptions or additions to the federal law.

Texas law specifies that the relevant department and commission must ensure that the management of radioactive waste is compatible with applicable federal commission standards. [TEX. HEALTH & SAFETY CODE 401.151] It also indicates, however, that the state commission directly regulates the disposal of low-level radioactive waste and that the person making the disposal must comply with commission rules. [TEX. HEALTH & SAFETY CODE 401.201]

Occupational Safety

How are the Occupational Safety and Health Administration (OSHA) and the Joint Commission working together on health care worker safety issues?

OSHA and the Joint Commission have formed a successful partnership to promote safety and health for health care workers. The joint program, initiated in 1996, was originally developed as a three-year venture, but has recently been extended in recognition of the benefits gained from the partnership. OSHA and the Joint Commission have worked together to help hospitals and other health care facilities understand how to meet the requirements of both the federal agency and the accreditation organization. As part of that effort, OSHA and the Joint Commission have jointly developed training materials and publications for health care facilities, and provided specific examples in Joint Commission accreditation manuals to illustrate how compliance with OSHA standards also satisfies Joint Commission standards. In addition, the partnership has enabled OSHA and the Joint Commission to minimize duplicative compliance activities. [*See* OSHA and Joint Commission Extend Efforts To Promote Health and Safety for Health Care Workers, OSHA Trade News Release (June 8, 2000), available on the Internet at www.osha.gov.] Joint Commission standards relating to environmental issues are discussed under Management of the Environment of Care, Part 3 of this Manual.

OSHA Injury and Illness Recordkeeping

What is injury and illness recordkeeping?

OSHA requires that all employers who employ ten or more individuals maintain records and report all work-related injuries, illnesses, and fatalities (29 CFR 1904). An illness or injury meets the general recording requirements if it results in any of the following: Death, Days away from Work, Restricted Work or Transfer to Another Job, Medical Treatment (beyond first aid), Loss of Consciousness, Significant Injury or Illness Diagnosed by a Physician *or* Other Health Care Professional. The last point is significant because a case is recordable under those circumstances, even if it does not result in Death, Day Away from Work, Restricted Work or Job Transfer, Medical Treatment (beyond First Aid) [see Part 4 for classification of first aid or medical treatment] or Loss of consciousness.

Effective January 2002, the recordkeeping requirements were revised. Additional criteria were added to the OSHA Injury and Illness reporting regulations to ensure that Needlestick and Sharps Injury cases, Tuberculosis cases, and Medical Removal cases are also recorded. OSHA anticipates that new requirements will be enacted in the near future to deal with repeat trauma disorders. In the interim, there is a space provided on the current OSHA form for recording work-related, musculoskeletal injuries.

As mentioned, the new reporting requirements that must be included on the OSHA recordkeeping log are:

Needlestick and Sharps Injuries. All work-related needlestick injuries and cuts from sharp objects that are contaminated with another person's blood or other potentially infectious material.

Medical Removal. Cases where an employee is medically removed under the medical surveillance requirements of any OSHA standard.

Tuberculosis. Cases where employees have been occupationally exposed to anyone with a known case of active tuberculosis (TB), and that employee subsequently develops a TB infection, as evidenced by a positive skin test or diagnosis by a physician or other licensed health care professional.

An injury or illness must be considered work related if an event or exposure in the work environment caused or contributed to the resulting condition or aggravated a preexisting injury or illness. OSHA has provided guidance [29 CFR 1904.4 (b) (2), see Part 4] to help employers determine if an injury or illness is work related.

Each year, in February and March, the employer is required to post the annual summary of the previous year's injury and illness records in a location that is readily accessible to all employees on the OSHA 300 A log (see Part 4).

What is medical treatment for the purpose of injury and illness recordkeeping?

Medical Treatment means the management and care of a patient to combat disease or disorder. For the purposes of injury and illness recordkeeping, medical treatment does not include:

- Visits to a physician or other licensed health care professional solely for observation or counseling

- The conduct of diagnostic procedures, such as X-rays and blood tests, including the administration of prescription medications used solely for diagnostic purposes (e.g., eye drops to dilate pupils)

What is first aid for the purpose of injury and illness recordkeeping?

First aid is defined as:

- using a non-prescription medication at nonprescription strength (for medications available in both prescription and non-prescription form, a recommendation by a physician or other licensed health care professional to use a non-prescription medication at prescription strength is considered medical treatment for recordkeeping purposes)

- administering tetanus immunizations (other immunizations, such as Hepatitis B vaccine or rabies vaccine, are considered medical treatment)

- cleaning, flushing, or soaking wounds on the surface of the skin

- using wound coverings such as bandages, Band-Aids™, gauze pads, etc.; or using butterfly bandages or Steri-Strips™ (other wound closing devices such as sutures, staples, etc., are considered medical treatment)

- using hot or cold therapy

- using any non-rigid means of support, such as elastic bandages, wraps, non-rigid back belts, etc. (devices with rigid stays or other systems designed to immobilize parts of the body are considered medical treatment for recordkeeping purposes)

- using temporary immobilization devices while transporting an accident victim (e.g., splints, slings, neck collars, back boards, etc.)

- drilling of a fingernail or toenail to relieve pressure, or draining fluid from a blister

- using eye patches

- removing foreign bodies from the eye using only irrigation or a cotton swab

- removing splinters or foreign material from areas other than the eye by irrigation, tweezers, cotton swabs, or other simple means

- using finger guards

- using massages (physical therapy or chiropractic treatment are considered medical treatment for recordkeeping purposes)

- drinking fluids for relief of heat stress

Decision tree in order to help the employer determine if an injury or illness is work related:

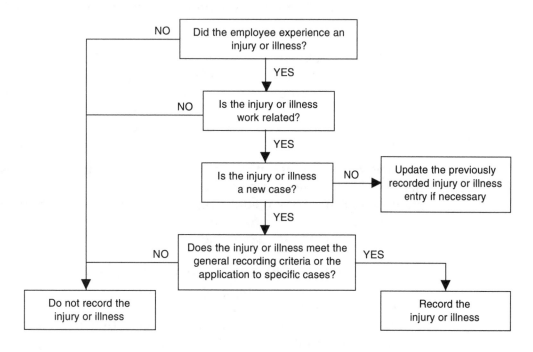

Summary of Work-Related Injuries and Illnesses (OSHA's Form 300A)

Bloodborne Pathogens

What is OSHA's bloodborne pathogen standard?

The OSHA bloodborne pathogen standard applies primarily (although not exclusively) to the health care industry. The standard was recently revised by the Needlestick Safety and Prevention Act [Pub. L. 106-430, 66 Fed. Reg. 5317], which was passed in November 2000, became effective in April 2001, and contains the following key provisions:

- Exposure Control Plan
- Engineering and Work Practice Controls
- Personal Protective Equipment
- Disposal of Waste and Cleaning of Workplace
- Employer-Provided Hepatitis B Vaccinations
- Postexposure Evaluation
- Notice of Hazards to Employees
- Recordkeeping [29 CFR 1910.1030]

How did the Needlestick Safety and Prevention Act revise the bloodborne pathogen standard?

The Needlestick Safety and Prevention Act directed OSHA to revise the bloodborne pathogen standard. The changes were directed at establishing clear requirements that employers identify and use safer and more effective medical devices in order to reduce injuries from needles and sharps. In addition, two new terms have been added to the standard, and one existing term has been modified:

Sharps with engineered sharps injury protection is defined as a "non-needle sharp or needle device used for withdrawing body fluids, accessing a vein or artery, or administering medications or other fluids with a built-in safety feature or mechanism that effectively reduces the risk of an exposure incident." This term covers a broad range of devices including:

- syringes with a sliding sheath that shields the attached needle after use
- needles that retract into the syringe after use
- shielded or retracting catheters
- intravenous medication delivery systems that use a catheter port with a needle housed in a protective covering

Needleless Systems is defined as "a device that does not use needles for : (A) the collection of body fluids or withdrawal of body fluids after initial venous or arterial access is established; (B) the administration of medications or fluids; (C) any other procedures involving the potential for occupational exposure to bloodborne pathogens due to percutaneous injuries from contaminated sharps." Examples of such devices include intravenous medication systems that administer medications or fluids through a catheter port using non-needle connections, and jet injection systems that deliver liquid medication beneath the skin or through muscle.

The original Bloodborne Pathogen Standard was not specific with respect to the applicability of various engineering controls in the health care setting. The only comments made indicated that engineering controls included devices ". . . that isolate or removed a hazard from the workplace, such as sharps disposal containers and self-sheathing needles."

The revised standard now specifies that "safer medical devices, such as sharps with engineered sharps injury protection and needleless systems" constitute an effective engineering control, and must be used where feasible.

What is an exposure control plan?

Hospitals must develop written exposure control plans that identify those employees who, by job classification or by the tasks they perform, are at risk of exposure to blood and body fluids. This identification must be done without consideration of the protective clothing or equipment in use. The exposure control plan must specify the methods that will be used to protect employees from exposure to bloodborne pathogens. In addition, the plan must include the methods that will be used to train employees about the standard and the methods used for employee protection. It must also define the methods that will be used to evaluate circumstances surrounding each exposure incident. The exposure control plan must be readily accessible to employees and must be reviewed annually or whenever job task additions or changes affect employee exposure to bloodborne pathogens (29 CFR 1910.1030 (c)).

The new additions to the exposure control plan require employers to take into account changes in technology that will lead to the elimination or reduction of exposure to bloodborne pathogens. The employer is required to solicit nonmanagerial employee input into the selection of safer medical devices for use in patient care. It is anticipated that the devices selected will not compromise employee or patient safety, and that such devices will reduce the likelihood that an exposure incident involving a contaminated sharp will occur. The employer must also document all safer medical devices that have been identified and considered for use in the facility. In addition, the employer must document the methods used to evaluate all such devices and maintain records for justification of selection of the safer devices. For sample documentation see Part 3 under Surveillance, Prevention, and Control of Infection.

What kinds of equipment or engineering controls must be used in the radiology department to help prevent the spread of bloodborne pathogens?

Hospitals must implement engineering controls such as puncture-resistant containers for used needles, self-sheathing sharps and needles, protective shields, safer medical devices such as sharps with engineered sharps injury protections and needleless systems, and biosafety cabinets. The standard requires employers to regularly inspect and repair engineering controls. [29 CFR 1910.1030(b) & (d)] In an annual review of their exposure control plan, hospitals must consider safer needle devices as part of the reevaluation of appropriate engineering controls, and must involve frontline (i.e., nonmanagerial) employees in the identification and selection of safer devices. The revised standard also mandates that in the exposure control plan employers document how they received input from the employees, either by listing the employees involved and describing the process by which input was requested, or by other documentation such as minutes of meetings or copies of requests for employees' participation.

In addition, the National Institute of Occupational Safety and Health (NIOSH) has issued an alert on preventing needlestick injuries in health care settings. The alert contains detailed recommendations for employers and employees. [NIOSH Alert, *Preventing Needlestick Injuries in Health Care Settings*, NIOSH Pub. No. 2000-108 (1999), available on the Internet at www.cdc.gov/niosh]

What are the handwashing requirements?

The Centers for Disease Control and Prevention (CDC) released new hand hygiene guidelines on October 25, 2002. In addition to traditional handwashing with soap and water, CDC recommends the use of alcohol-based handrubs by health care personnel for patient care because they address some of the obstacles that health care professionals face when taking care of patients. Handrubs should be used before and after each patient just as gloves should be changed before and after each patient. The CDC guidelines are available at www.cdc.gov/handhygiene.

Handwashing must be performed as soon as feasible after exposure to blood or other potentially infectious materials and after removal of gloves or other personal protective equipment. [29 CFR 1910.1030(d)(2)(iii) through (vi)] [For more information, *see* Centers for Disease Control and Prevention, *Draft Guideline for Infection Control in Health Care Personnel, 1997*, reprinted at 62 Fed. Reg. 47,276 (1997).]

What kinds of work practices are prohibited in the radiology department to prevent the spread of bloodborne pathogens?

Employees are prohibited from eating, drinking, and storing food in areas where there is potential for exposure to bloodborne pathogens or where blood, body fluids, or both are stored (e.g., refrigerators and cabinets, medication carts). [29 CFR 1910.1030(d)(2)(ix) & (x)] Employees also are prohibited from suctioning blood or other body fluids by mouth. [29 CFR 1910.1030(d)(2)(xii)] [For more information, *see* Centers for Disease Control and Prevention, *Draft Guideline for Infection in Health Care Personnel, 1997*, reprinted at 62 Fed. Reg. 47,276 (1997).]

What are the OSHA requirements for handling sharps in the radiology department?

Employees are prohibited from shearing, breaking, recapping, removing, or bending contaminated needles and other sharps; from picking up potentially contaminated glassware by hand; and from reaching by hand into a container that may contain contaminated reusable sharps. [29 CFR 1910.1030(d)(2)(vii) & (d)(4)(ii)(D) & (E)] [For related information, *see* U.S. Department of Health and Human Services, *Selecting, Evaluating, and Using Sharps Disposal Containers*, NIOSH Pub. No. 97–111 (1998), available on the Internet at www.cdc.gov/niosh.sharps1.html. For recommendations on preventing needlestick injuries in health care settings, *see* NIOSH Alert, *Preventing Needlestick Injuries in Health Care Settings*, NIOSH Pub. No. 2000-108 (1999), available on the Internet at www.cdc.gov/niosh.]

OSHA has clarified its policy on the prohibition of removing contaminated needles from blood tube holders. In a June 12, 2002, letter of interpretation, OSHA explains that the bloodborne pathogen standard requires blood tube holders with needles attached to be immediately discarded into a sharps container after the device's safety feature is activated. The letter of interpretation is available on OSHA's website, www.osha.gov.

It should be noted that state law also may regulate infectious waste, such as sharps. In Ohio, for example, the law specifies that all unused, discarded hypodermic needles, syringes, and scalpels must be placed in rigid, tightly closed, puncture-resistant containers on the premises before they are transported off the premises. Containers containing such wastes must be labeled "sharps" and, if the wastes have not been treated to render them noninfectious, must be conspicuously labeled with the international biohazard symbol. [OHIO REV. CODE ANN. 3734.021]

Is the hospital required to provide personal protective equipment in the radiology department?

The hospital must provide, at no cost to the employee, personal protective equipment when engineering and work practice controls cannot fully protect an employee from occupational exposure. [29 CFR 1910.1030(d)(2)(i)] Employers must also repair, replace, launder, and dispose of personal protective equipment at no cost to the employee. [29 CFR 1910.1030(d)(3)(iv) through (viii)]

What kinds of items are considered personal protective equipment?

The OSHA standard contains a comprehensive listing of such equipment, which includes gloves, gowns, laboratory coats, masks, eye protection, mouthpieces, and resuscitation devices. The standard also contains specific details regarding the adequacy of certain items of protective equipment; for example, it specifically requires the disposal of torn, cracked, or punctured gloves because their function as a barrier may be compromised. [29 CFR 1910.1030(d)(3)(i)]

Are there any exceptions to the requirement that employees wear personal protective equipment?

A limited exemption applies when the employee refuses to wear the equipment because its use "would have prevented the delivery of health care or public safety services or would have posed an increased hazard to the safety of the worker or a co-worker." An example of such an occasion would be an unanticipated emergency in which a patient suddenly begins bleeding and workers lack time to delay treatment and put on gloves, masks, or gowns. When the employee makes this judgment, the circumstances must be investigated and documented to prevent such occurrences in the future. [29 CFR 1910.1030(d)(3)(ii)]

What measures must be taken to clean the worksite and dispose of contaminated waste?

Requirements for cleaning the worksite and disposing of contaminated waste include

- implementing a written plan that describes the method and frequency of cleaning
- regular inspection and decontamination of reusable garbage bins, pails, and laundry carts that hold potentially contaminated medical waste
- ensuring that blood specimens and other potentially infectious materials are placed in properly labeled containers that will prevent leakage during handling, storage, and transport
- requiring employees who have contact with potentially contaminated laundry to wear appropriate personal protective equipment such as gloves and gowns [29 CFR 1910.1030(d)(4)]

Are hospitals required to give employees a free hepatitis B vaccine?

Employers must give all employees who have occupational exposure the option to receive a free hepatitis B vaccine and must educate them about the benefits of obtaining a vaccination. The vaccination must be made available to the employee within 10 days after initial assignment to a job task with potential exposure to bloodborne pathogens. It is the employee's choice whether to receive the hepatitis B vaccine, but an employee who chooses not to be vaccinated must sign a waiver form. [29 CFR 1910.1030(f)]

Employers are allowed to delay offering the vaccine to collateral first-aid providers, defined as employees whose primary jobs are not the rendering of first aid, until after these employees have rendered assistance in a situation presenting a risk of exposure to blood or another potentially infectious body fluid.

If the employee must travel to another location to obtain the vaccination, the employer must pay for the entire travel cost. The employer cannot require the employee to pay for the vaccine and later be reimbursed if reimbursement is contingent on the employee remaining employed by the employer for a specific length of time. Nor can the employer require that the employee's health insurer pay for the vaccine unless the employer pays the entire premium for the coverage and there is no deductible, copayment, or other expense to the employee.

Are employers required to provide an employee postexposure evaluation following an exposure incident?

Employers must conduct postexposure evaluations of employees who are exposed on the job. As part of that evaluation, to be provided at no cost to the employee, the employer must make available to the employee a confidential medical examination, including a blood test if the employee consents;

postexposure preventive treatment; and counseling. [For more information, *see* Centers for Disease Control and Prevention, *Draft Guideline for Infection Control in Health Care Personnel, 1997*, reprinted at 62 Fed. Reg. 47,276 (1997).]

The employer must also document the circumstances surrounding the employee's exposure and, if possible, identify the source individual. If an identifiable source individual exists, the employer must test that individual's blood for hepatitis B and human immunodeficiency virus (HIV), provided that the individual consents. The employer must inform the exposed employee of the source individual's test results but also must be careful not to violate state or local acquired immune deficiency syndrome (AIDS) confidentiality laws by disclosing the identity of the source individual along with those results.

The employer must provide the employee with a copy of the written medical evaluation within 15 days after completion of the evaluation. Aside from information about whether the employee should receive a hepatitis B vaccine, all other information (including blood test results) in this report must be kept confidential, even from the employer, to encourage the employee to participate in the medical examination process and to obtain follow-up care. [29 CFR 1910.1030(f)]

What must employers do to communicate the hazards of bloodborne pathogens to employees?

Employers are required to communicate the hazards of bloodborne pathogens to employees through employee training and education and proper placement of written warnings and labels. Employers must provide training when the employee is first assigned to a job in which there is occupational exposure, and then provide additional training on an annual basis or any time changes in work tasks affect the employee's risk of exposure. Employers must affix labels to containers of regulated waste. Employers must either affix a "biohazard" symbol on all transport, storage, and waste containers that hold substances contaminated with blood or other potentially infected body fluids or place such materials in red bags or containers. In addition, employers are required to appropriately label all contaminated equipment or partially contaminated equipment. [29 CFR 1910.1030(g)]

What kinds of records must employers keep regarding occupational exposure?

Employers must maintain medical records for each employee with occupational exposure for the duration of the employee's employment plus 30 years. The employer must keep the records confidential during this period, and the employer may not disclose contents of the records without the employee's express written consent. The standard also requires employers to maintain training records for a period of three years from the date of training but does not require that they be kept confidential. [29 CFR 1910.1030(h)] Employers must keep a log to track all injuries from contaminated needles or sharps, not only those cuts or sticks that lead to actual illness, while maintaining the privacy of employees who have suffered those injuries. At a minimum the log must contain a description of the incident, the type and brand of device involved, and the location of the incident (i.e., department or work area). The log may include additional information as long as an employee's privacy is protected. [66 Fed. Reg. 5317]

What will OSHA compliance investigators look for with respect to bloodborne pathogens?

In recognition of technological advances and new research, OSHA has issued guidance for compliance investigators who enforce the bloodborne pathogen standard. Since the standard itself was revised by the Needlestick Safety and Prevention Act in 2000, OSHA has updated its compliance directive to conform with the revised standard. The new compliance directive, Enforcement Procedures for the Occupational Exposure to Bloodborne Pathogens, CPL 2—2.69, 11/27/2001, can be found on the OSHA Web site at www.osha-slc.gov/pls/oshaweb/owadisp.show_document?p_table=DIRECTIVES&p_id=2570. The enforcement procedures do not carry the force of law or regulation, but health care employers are well advised to become familiar with the revised guidance, because it will direct agency officials during compliance inspections. The instruction requires investigators to assess whether

- the employer has conducted an annual review of the exposure control plan. The plan should reflect consideration and use of the safer medical devices that are now commercially available.
- engineering controls, including safer medical devices, needle devices, work practices, administrative controls, and personal protective equipment, are used to reduce occupational exposure to the lowest feasible extent. The guidance emphasizes the importance of needleless systems and sharps with engineered sharps injury protection and provides detailed guidance on what constitutes sufficient use of engineering controls.
- the employer has relied on relevant evidence (beyond FDA approval) to ensure effectiveness of devices designed to prevent employee exposure to bloodborne pathogens.
- the employer has established a log to track all needlesticks, maintaining the privacy of employees who have suffered needlestick injuries.
- employees receive effective training when safer devices are implemented. The instruction highlights the value of interactive training sessions that provide the opportunity for discussion with a qualified trainer.
- employees are solicited to give input in identifying and selecting safer devices for implementation.
- the most recent CDC guidelines on hepatitis B vaccines and postexposure evaluation and follow-up for HIV and hepatitis C are followed.

The directive also addresses the compliance responsibilities of several types of "employers." Where companies provide services on an independent contractor basis (such as radiology), both the company and the "host employer" are responsible for all provisions of the bloodborne pathogen standard. Part time, temporary, and per diem employees are covered by the standard, also. Finally, OSHA has replaced and updated its sample documentation and other appendices. The agency has provided examples of committees, sample engineering control evaluation forms, sample exposure control plan, an Internet resource list, and CDC guidelines. [*Enforcement Procedures for the Occupational Exposure to Bloodborne Pathogens,* OSHA Instr. CPL 2-2.44D (Nov. 5, 1999), available on the Internet at www.osha.gov]

Do any state laws address the control of bloodborne pathogens in the health care setting?

As of November 2001, 20 states and 2 territories have enacted some type of legislation related to health care worker bloodborne pathogen exposures. These OSHA-approved state laws typically require that state health departments or labor departments develop administrative regulations to implement the laws. State laws typically add additional safeguards for health care workers, create broader protections than the federal OSHA standard, and/or cover public employees not covered by OSHA. Although the state laws vary in their scope, they commonly include requirements for

–listing of safety devices as engineering controls
–developing a list of available safety devices by the state that employers can use
–developing a written exposure plan by employers, with periodic review
–developing protocols for identifying and selecting safety devices and involving frontline employees in the process
–using a sharps injury log to report needlestick injuries
–developing methods to increase use of vaccines and personal protective equipment
–waiving or exempting safety device use under certain circumstances (including patient and/or worker safety issues, market unavailability, etc.)
–placing sharps containers in accessible positions
–training for workers in the use of safety devices

[National Institute of Occupational Safety & Health, "Overview of State Needle Safety Legislation," available on the Internet at www.cdc.gov/niosh/ndl-law.html] Many of the state laws contain more unique requirements such as surveillance programs, strict requirements for safety device use, and the use of statewide advisory boards.

Since the revisions to the OSHA bloodborne pathogens standard, those states and territories with individual, OSHA-approved needlestick requirements have been required to comply with the new federal standards, or adopt a more stringent amendment to their existing standard, by October 18, 2001.

Airborne Hazards

What are the OSHA requirements regarding prevention of the spread of TB in the health care workplace?

The risk of TB infection, which is an airborne transmissible disease, is the major airborne pathogen transmission concern in the health care workplace. In recent years, OSHA has shown active interest in the area of TB prevention in health care settings, emphasizing in introductory comments to both its proposed TB prevention standard (discussed next) and an updated respirator standard [29 CFR 1910.139] that TB is a serious health risk, particularly because some recent outbreaks have involved drug-resistant strains of the disease.

For several years, OSHA has relied on the CDC for guidance on how to respond to the threat of TB transmission in the workplace. In 1996, for example, in response to the CDC's revision of its guidelines for preventing the transmission of TB in health care settings, OSHA issued a compliance directive incorporating CDC recommendations and providing enforcement guidance to protect workers against hazards posed by TB. [*Enforcement Procedures and Scheduling for Occupational Exposure to Tuberculosis*, OSHA Instr. CPL 2-106 (Feb. 9, 1996)]

In 1997, OSHA proposed a TB standard, based on both its compliance directive and the CDC guidelines; once the standard is finalized, it will apply to a broad range of sites where health care services are provided, including hospitals. [Occupational Exposure to Tuberculosis, 62 Fed. Reg. 54,160 (1997) (to be codified at 29 CFR 1910.1035)] The requirements in the standard vary depending on the type of facility and the associated degree of risk. However, the proposed standard requires all covered health care employers, regardless of degree of risk, to

- develop written exposure control and remedial action plans
- use engineering controls to protect the work environment
- offer free TB skin testing to employees
- undertake periodic medical surveillance
- provide employees with TB awareness training

Although the standard provides detailed recommendations as to appropriate procedures, or work practice and engineering controls, OSHA noted that it does not intend to dictate patient management practices.

OSHA reopened the period for comments on the TB rulemaking records until May 24, 2002, to address risk assessment and other issues. [67 Fed. Reg. 9934 (2002)] In the interim, before the standard becomes effective, health care employers can be cited for violations of the general-duty clause of the Occupational Health and Safety Act and/or a number of OSHA standards related to respiratory protection, reporting of occupational illnesses, and accident prevention notices.

What is latex sensitivity?

Sensitivity to latex products, or latex allergy, develops in some individuals exposed to natural rubber latex—a plant substance that is used extensively to manufacture latex gloves. Allergic reactions to latex range from skin disease to asthma and anaphylaxis that can result in chronic illness and other disabilities; there is no treatment for these problems other than complete avoidance of latex.

OSHA's sister agency, NIOSH, has issued guidance regarding prevention of latex-related health problems in the workplace. [National Institute for Occupational Health and Safety, *NIOSH Alert: Preventing Allergic Reactions to Natural Rubber Latex in the Workplace*, DHHS Pub. No. 97-135 (June 1997), available on the Internet at www.cdc.gov/niosh/latexalt.html] NIOSH recommends that hospitals implement policies and procedures to require, or at least encourage, appropriate engineering and work practice controls to reduce the risk of allergic reactions to latex. Such controls include the use of nonlatex gloves for activities that are not likely to involve contact with infectious materials, good housekeeping practice to remove latex-containing dust in latex-contaminated areas, and training materials/education programs about latex allergy.

What standards apply to indoor air quality during construction and renovation?

Indoor air quality concerns have increased dramatically over the past 30 years since the energy crisis of the 1970s resulted in energy conservation measures that led to reduced intake of outside air and increased buildup of indoor contaminants. In the mid-1990s OSHA tried to enact standards that would regulate indoor air quality, particularly in health care settings. Even though this effort was unsuccessful, other groups such as the CDC and the American Institute of Architects (AIA), recognized that air quality, especially during construction and renovation activities could be severely affected, putting both patients and health care workers at risk. The results of release of dust and the molds that might accompany the dust could cause severe respiratory problems among health care workers, especially those already suffering from asthma or other respiratory ailments, and among patients, particularly those whose immune systems are compromised and incapable of effectively dealing with molds, such as aspergillus fumigatus.

The Joint Commission has acted on the published recommendations of the AIA (2001 AIA Guidelines for Health Care Facility Construction) and on recommendations published by the CDC in a draft report on environmental infection control in health care facilities. The Joint Commission's Environment of Care Standards now require that a preconstruction risk assessment be performed prior to all renovation and construction projects in hospitals and other health care facilities in order to determine, at least in part, what steps need to be taken to prevent the spread of dust and infectious agents during the course of this work (see Section 3 under Surveillance, Prevention, and Control of Infection).

Hazardous Substances

What is the hazard communication standard?

OSHA regulations, known as the hazard communication standard, require employers to notify employees if there are hazardous chemicals present in the workplace and to train employees to work with the chemicals. [29 CFR 1910.1200]

In addition to the federal hazard communication standard, some states, such as Texas, have enacted similar laws. [TEX. CIVIL STAT. art. 5182b] The Texas administrative code states that, to avoid confusion among employers and the public, the state Hazard Communication Act must be compatible with the federal hazard communication standard. [25 TEX. ADMIN. CODE 295.1]

What must employers do to comply with the hazard communication standard?

The standard requires employers to undertake a hazard evaluation in which they identify and list all hazardous chemicals used, released, or stored in the workplace. [29 CFR 1910.1200(d)] Employers are required to maintain material safety data sheets (MSDSs) for each hazardous chemical that they use, process, or store. The MSDSs must be made available upon request to any employee, an employee's designated representative, or the Department of Labor.

In filling out the MSDS, the manufacturer, importer, or distributor of the hazardous material must identify

- the physical dangers of the hazardous chemical, such as its potential for fire or other explosive reactivity
- any health hazards linked to exposure to the chemical
- control measures and precautions to be taken in handling or using the chemical
- emergency and first-aid procedures in dealing with a hazardous exposure incident
- the responsible party (e.g., designated person for providing additional information on the hazardous chemicals present at the worksite, and appropriate emergency procedures, if necessary) [29 CFR 1910.1200(g)(2)]

The standard also requires all employers to develop and implement a written hazard communication program.

What must be included in the written hazard communication program?

The hazard communication program must include provisions for the labeling of containers of hazardous chemicals and indicate where the employer maintains MSDSs on the hazardous chemicals in the workplace. Employers must provide employees who may be exposed to hazardous chemicals with information and training on how to work safely with these materials. The standard provides that employers inform employees of the areas in their worksite where hazardous materials are present and the location and availability of the written hazard communication program. To meet the standard's requirement, an employer's training program must include methods for detecting hazardous chemicals in the workplace, the physical and health hazards of exposure to chemicals present in the workplace, and protective procedures that employees should follow when working in areas where such chemicals are present. [29 CFR 1910.1200(h)(3)]

Can employers provide the required employee access to MSDSs through electronic means?

OSHA has published a compliance directive stating that employers can meet the access requirements by relaying MSDSs to employees through computers, microfiche machines, the Internet, CD-ROM, and fax machines. However, if employers are using electronic means for this purpose, they must ensure that reliable devices are always readily accessible in the workplace, and that employees have adequate training in the use of such devices (i.e., software or Internet training). Moreover, employers must take steps to establish and maintain adequate backup systems so that access is not impaired under circumstances of system failures, power outages, or on-line access delays; as one additional safeguard, employers still must provide employees with access to hard copies of MSDSs upon request, or in the event of medical emergencies when hard copies must be provided immediately to medical professionals. [OSHA, *Inspection Procedures for the Hazard Communication Standard*, OSHA Instr. CPL 2-2.38D (1998)]

Why is there a silver recovery policy in the radiology department?

Silver recovery is required under the Clean Water Act and the Environmental Protection Agency Effluent Discharge Regulations. The radiology department should have a policy regarding the silver recovery hazardous waste program.

What are the risks of exposure to hazardous drugs in the health care workplace?

OSHA has identified health care worker exposure to hazardous drugs as an area of increasing health concern (OSHA Technical Manual, Section vi, chapter 2 "Controlling Occupational Exposure to Hazardous Drugs"). A number of drugs, including antineoplastic cytotoxic medications, anesthetic agents, and antiviral agents, have been identified as hazardous. These drugs are capable of causing serious effects including cancer, organ toxicity, fertility problems, genetic damage, and birth defects. While most people regard drugs as being exempt from coverage under OSHA's Hazard Communication Standard, hazardous drugs and pharmaceuticals in the nonmanufacturing environment are included under the provisions of the standard. Only those drugs provided in final solid form, such as pills or tablets, are exempt from inclusion in coverage by the Hazard Communication Standard. All employees who are potentially exposed to hazardous drugs must be provided adequate information and training to understand those hazards and the means of protecting themselves from exposure. Risks to employees working with hazardous drugs are related to the drug's specific toxicity and the type and length of exposure.

What work duties can place radiology department employees at risk for injury from hazardous drugs?

Work duties that may place employees who work in the radiology department at risk of exposure include direct contact with body fluids from patients who have received these hazardous drugs, and exposure to or contact with a spill of a hazardous drug. Other work activities that place health care workers at risk of exposure include drug preparation, drug distribution, and drug administration. The primary routes of exposure are inhalation of dusts and aerosols, dermal absorption, and ingestion.

Drugs that are categorized as hazardous have the following characteristics, according to the American Society of Hospital Pharmacists (Am. J. Hosp. Pharm. 47:1033–49, 1990):

- genotoxicity
- carcinogenicity
- teratogenicity or fertility impairment
- serious organ or other toxic manifestation at low doses in experimental animals or treated patients

What information concerning hazardous drugs should an employer include in a written communication program?

When preparing a written hazard communication program, the employer should also include the following information concerning hazardous drugs:

- a list of the covered hazardous drugs known to be present using an identity that is referenced on the appropriate MSDS
- methods the employer will use to inform employees of the hazards of nonroutine tasks in their work areas
- methods the employer will use to inform employees of other employers of hazards at the work site

Training of employees who are potentially exposed to hazardous drugs should include the following:

- methods and observations that may be used to detect the presence or release of a covered hazardous drug in the work area (such as monitoring conducted by the employer, continuous monitoring devices, visual appearance, or odor of covered hazardous drugs)

- physical and health hazards of the covered hazardous drugs in the work area
- measures employees can take to protect themselves from these hazards. This includes specific procedures that the employer has implemented to protect the employees from exposure to such drugs, such as identification of covered drugs and those to be handled as hazardous, appropriate work practices, and emergency procedures (for spills or employee exposure).
- personal protective equipment, and the details of the hazard communication program developed by the employer, including an explanation of the labeling system and the MSDS, and how employees can obtain and use the appropriate hazard information

WORKPLACE VIOLENCE PREVENTION

Why is workplace violence an area of concern in health care delivery settings?

Health care workers are a population who face a potentially high incidence of workplace violence, according to OSHA (U.S. Dept. Labor, Occ. Safety and Health Admin, OSHA, Pub. 3148, 1998 Guidelines for Preventing Workplace Violence for Healthcare and Social Service Workers). This increase in violence is due to a number of factors, including:

- an increase in the prevalence of handguns and other weapons among patients, family, and friends who come to the hospital for care
- increased use of hospitals by police for criminal holds
- increased number of disturbed patients seeking acute care in hospitals
- availability of drugs and money in hospitals and clinics, making them targets for robbery
- isolated work with patients during therapy or treatment, making health care workers potential targets for violence

What standards apply to prevent workplace violence?

In order to reduce workplace violence and increase worker and patient safety, OSHA has recommended the institution of a violence prevention program. This program requires management commitment and employee involvement. Each workplace needs to have an analysis performed to determine locations where hazards exist and where there is a potential for physical harm or violence to occur. In addition, all workplace incidents need to be reviewed to characterize jobs or duties that are at a higher risk for violence to occur. The analysis needs to account for frequency and timing of violent events and establish criteria for determining which patients are at a higher risk for committing violent acts or assaults against employees, patients, or visitors. Steps then need to be taken to prevent and control the occurrence of these types of workplace violence.

What steps can be taken to prevent and control the occurrence of workplace violence?

Some of the actions that can be implemented might be:

- Install alarm systems and panic buttons.
- Install closed circuit video cameras to monitor high risk areas.
- Provide patient waiting rooms that reduce stress and increase comfort.
- Arrange furniture to prevent entrapment of staff in the event of an incident.
- Provide employee safe rooms for use in emergencies.

How do written programs, education, and training help prevent workplace violence?

A written workplace violence program should be developed and implemented. The program requires that clear goals and objectives be established that will result in violence prevention. The program should be suitable and adaptable to the work environment. OSHA recommends that the first step in developing the program should be the dissemination of a zero tolerance policy for violence at work.

Employee education and training are essential for reducing the potential of workplace violence. Employees should understand the potential threats and where and when they may occur. Employees must also be prepared to deal with combative patients and to respond in a way that will maintain their safety and prevent harm to themselves and to the assailant. In addition, it is important for employees to be aware of the fact that all violent incidents must be reported immediately. This helps not only to protect the employee, but to ensure that a database is developed to better understand and analyze situations that may result in violence in the future. For sample Workplace Violence Checklist, see Part 4.

DISASTER RESPONSE

What compliance and implementation issues relating to disaster response are important in the radiology department?

Hospitals and health care providers hold a key place in disaster response. Whether the emergency occurs on hospital grounds or in the community that the hospital services, all departments and services within the hospital will be expected to respond effectively and efficiently. It is imperative that the radiology department be prepared to answer the call. Careful planning and training, as well as participation in practice drills and exercises, are a vital part of the preparation process. Key personnel need to be designated, in compliance with the hospital and community emergency response plans, so that if and when the call comes, employees and radiology staff technicians and physicians are prepared to participate in order to help patients and thier families effectively and efficiently.

Also, since the events of September 11, the Joint Commission has called for hospitals to become more aware and actively involved in helping patients in the event that a disaster or terrorist event hits their community. Preparation for such events is similar to those for any disaster in the community and requires a concerted effort. While it is not likely that patients who have not been decontaminated will enter the radiology department for treatment and care, it is important that staff understand the hazards and risks posed by such things as anthrax exposure and that they have the knowledge and confidence to deal with these potential threats.

Smoking

Is it legal to ban smoking in the radiology department?

There is no federal law that specifically provides the legal authority to ban smoking in the radiology department. It may be argued, however, that OSHA's general-duty clause, which requires employers to provide a safe working environment, provides support for a smoking ban. However, the Joint Commission does provide strong impetus to limit smoking in health care facilities. Contained in its guidelines are requirements that permit smoking in designated areas only for those patients who have been approved to do so by written order of their physician or primary care nurse because prohibiting certain patients from smoking may interfere with the provision of the optimal level of care. Others, including staff, employees, and visitors, according to these guidelines should be required to smoke in designated locations outside of the building. Many state laws do provide such authority. Maryland state law, for example, states that there will be no smoking in any area of the hospital. (MD. CODE ANN., HEALTH-GEN. 24–205]

Aisles and Passageways

What are the legal requirements regarding aisles and passageways?

OSHA regulations mandate that aisles and passageways must be kept clear, in good repair, and free from obstruction across or in aisles. In addition, permanent aisles and passageways must be appropriately marked. [29 CFR 1910.22] In the radiology department, these regulations prohibit the blockage of passageways by, for example, supplies or patient gurneys.

PERSONNEL

Radiology departments have specific personnel concerns relating to the qualifications, scheduling, and treatment of employees. Some of these concerns arise from the necessity of providing 24-hour services every day. State hospital licensure laws vary from state to state, but they generally include on-call staffing requirements that may affect radiology departments. State law also contains a variety of requirements relating to the certification and licensure of medication radiation technologists. In addition, federal labor standards are relevant to determining payment for on-call hours. Federal law prohibiting pregnancy-based discrimination may be particularly relevant to female radiology department employees; if pregnant or likely to be pregnant, a female employee cannot be discharged based on her condition and may request restricted work activities for the safety of the fetus. A different federal antidiscrimination law directed at protecting employees from gender-based discrimination may come into play if a department employee is dissatisfied with workplace grooming or dress code policies. The following questions and answers discuss state and federal laws, as well as judicial decisions relevant to these personnel issues.

Licensure and Certification Requirements

What kinds of technologists work in radiology?

Technologists in radiology generally specialize by instrumentation. As instruments and equipment have become more complex, the number of subspecialties for technologists has increased, as it has for radiologists. There are four allied health careers in radiologic technology: radiographers, also called X-ray technologists; ultrasound technologists, also known as diagnostic medical sonographers; nuclear medicine technologists; and radiation therapy technologists. Each type of technologist requires specific training and certification.

Does state law require certification and licensure of medical radiation technologists?

State laws in most jurisdictions require certification and licensure of medical radiation technologists. The laws vary from state to state, but requirements are often set forth in statutes and are expanded upon further in state regulations. Maryland law, for example, requires certification of medical radiation technologists and nuclear medical technologists, and it mandates the adoption of rules and regulations concerning qualifications, training, certification, monitoring, and enforcement requirements for radiation technologists and nuclear medical technologists.

Maryland law states that the qualifications required of applicants for certification as a medical radiation technologist or a nuclear medical technologist shall include requirements established and approved by

- the American College of Radiology—Maryland Chapter
- the Maryland Society of Radiologic Technologists
- the Maryland Association of Nuclear Medicine Technologists
- the Maryland Society of Nuclear Medicine
- any applicable federal standard for training and certification [Md. Code Ann., Health Occ. 14-606]

Each state's laws must be reviewed to determine what the certification requirements are in that jurisdiction.

Does federal law address personnel qualifications and staffing?

The Conditions of Participation, which are federal regulations that facilities must meet to qualify for provider agreements under Medicare and Medicaid, specify that if hospitals provide therapeutic services, both the therapeutic and the diagnostic services must meet professionally approved standards for safety and personnel qualifications. The regulations indicate that only personnel designated as qualified by the medical staff may use radiologic equipment and administer procedures. [42 CFR 482.26(c)(2)] Medicare rules generally require that the physician who is treating the beneficiary must order all diagnostic X-ray tests. Exceptions apply to chiropractic X-rays and mammography. Also, the Conditions of Participation allow nurse practitioners and clinical nurse specialists to perform diagnostic imaging tests if they are authorized to do so under state law. [42 CFR 410.32]

The federal regulations mandate that a qualified full-time, part-time, or consulting radiologist must supervise the ionizing radiology service and must interpret only those radiologic tests determined by the medical staff to require a radiologist's specialized knowledge. [42 CFR 482.26(c)(1)]

For nuclear medicine services, the Conditions of Participation specify that the organization of the nuclear medicine service must be appropriate to the scope and complexity of the services offered and that the qualifications, training, functions, and responsibilities of nuclear medicine personnel must be specified by the service director and approved by the medical staff. [42 CFR 482.53(a)(2)] The regulations indicate that, in the nuclear medicine service area, there must be a director who is a doctor of medicine or osteopathy qualified in nuclear medicine. [42 CFR 482.53(a)(1)] Nuclear medicine services may be ordered only by a practitioner whose scope of federal or state licensure and whose staff privileges allow such referrals. [42 CFR 482.53(d)(4)]

What is the requirement for certification as an X-ray technologist?

The general imaging section, in which X-ray technologists work, includes the routine films of extremities, chest, abdomen, skull, and spine. The fluoroscopic suites, also part of the general radiography section, provide gastrointestinal tract studies and other procedures, such as intravenous pyelograms.

Technologists generally require two years of formal training to become certified in radiologic technology, although some schools also offer bachelor's degree programs. After graduation from an approved educational program, the candidate must pass a qualifying examination for certification as an X-ray technologist.

Through on-the-job training, X-ray technologists may specialize in X-ray computed tomography, neuro or abdominal angiography, magnetic resonance imaging, gastrointestinal/genitourinary imaging, fluoroscopy, pediatrics, trauma, mammography, operating room, and so forth.

What is diagnostic ultrasound, and what are the certification requirements for an ultrasound technologist?

Diagnostic ultrasound uses high-frequency sound waves for diagnostic purposes. Ultrasound is transmitted to specific parts of the body and creates images on video screens that show the shape and composition of organs, tissues, and other masses. Ultrasound is noninvasive and, unlike X-rays, does not use radiation to create images.

The ultrasound technologist performs various studies, including examination of the inner structures of the brain, called neurosonography; examination of the heart, called echocardiography; examination of soft tissue structures of the abdomen; examination of female anatomy and pregnant females; and examination of the eyes, or ophthalmology.

There is a one-year training program in diagnostic ultrasound offered by universities, radiological institutes, and hospitals. Programs may also be two or four years, depending on the degree or certificate awarded. Prerequisites for the program are a high school education or equivalent and qualifications in a related allied health profession.

After completion of the educational and clinical experience requirements, the candidate must pass the registry examination and apply for registration as a registered diagnostic medical sonographer with the American Registry of Diagnostic Medical Sonographers. The registry credential of registered vascular technologist may be obtained by passing the Vascular Physical Principles and Instrumentation exam and the Vascular Technology exam.

What is nuclear medicine, and what are the certification requirements for a nuclear medicine technologist?

Nuclear medicine imaging uses radioactive materials for diagnostic and treatment purposes. The patient ingests, inhales, or is injected with small amounts of radioactive material, which is then traced as it makes its way throughout various body organs. Nuclear medicine is used to diagnose or treat diseases of the brain, heart, kidneys, liver, lungs, spleen, pancreas, thyroid, bone, and gastrointestinal system. Radioactive analysis is also used on blood or urine taken from the patient to measure hormones, drugs, blood constituents, and other materials.

Programs for certification as a nuclear medicine technologist include a one-year certificate, a two-year associate degree, and a four-year bachelor's degree. Certification is granted after graduation from a nuclear medicine technology program and successful completion of a qualifying examination. One of the two organizations that offer certification also requires clinical experience before certification is granted.

Positron emission tomography (PET) is a specialized branch of nuclear medicine. Nuclear medicine technologists who have received on-the-job training in PET technology staff PET facilities.

What is radiation therapy, and what are the certification requirements for a radiation therapy technologist?

Radiation therapy involves the use of equipment that produces radiation, generally a linear accelerator, to treat patients, mainly those with cancer. Radiation therapy can be used in combination with surgery or drug therapy or can be used separately. X-rays or other kinds of ionizing radiation are administered in prescribed concentrations to the area of the patient's body affected by the disease.

There are one- and two-year programs in radiation therapy technology, which have different prerequisites. Upon graduation from an approved program, the candidate must pass an exam to be granted certification as a radiation therapy technologist. Some states require radiation therapy technologists to be licensed.

How do reimbursement issues affect staffing in the radiology department?

The radiology department is a revenue center in the fee-for-service environment, but it is viewed as a cost center in the fixed payment environment introduced by diagnosis-related groups and continued by various managed care–based reimbursement methodologies, such as capitation. In this environment, it is even more important to provide radiologic services efficiently and effectively. One way to increase efficiency and keep costs down through staffing is to cross-train technologists, which is increasingly becoming the rule rather than the exception.

How do scope of practice and licensure issues affect the use of standing orders?

A standing order is a medical order written for use by nurses and other nonphysicians when a physician is not present. Another term often interchanged with standing order is "protocol," which can be defined as a detailed template for the treatment of a very specific medical problem. In most states, standing orders and protocols are a legal and convenient way for drugs and treatment to be given on a physician's order but within the discretion of the nurse or other nonphysician health care provider. Standing orders and protocols are problematic when they are not in compliance with state scope of practice laws; for example, when the standing order allows a nonphysician to make a medical diagnosis.

Nurses and PAs may not perform tasks under a standing order or protocol that are not permitted by their scope of practice rules. In addition, standing orders and protocols that do not require an appropriate level of physician oversight may lead to charges that a nurse or PA was practicing medicine without a license. Reimbursement considerations also must be considered, as direct physician involvement may be required for payment under some circumstances.

On-Call Staffing

How does state law affect on-call requirements for the radiology service?

State laws regarding radiology coverage must be carefully consulted to establish the minimum on-call requirements. Hospital licensure laws generally require hospitals with an emergency department to provide 24-hour services with adequate professional and ancillary staff coverage, including on-call staff, to ensure that all persons are treated within a reasonable length of time depending upon the priority of need for treatment. Many states require that one registered nurse be on duty in the emergency department at all times and that ancillary departments, including radiology, be staffed or provide on-call services at all times. [*See, e.g.,* ILL. ADMIN. CODE tit. 77, 250.710; MD. CODE ANN., HEALTH–GEN, 19-307.1.]

What federal laws affect payment for on-call hours?

The Fair Labor Standards Act (FLSA) [29 USC 201 through 219], a federal statute governing wage and hour issues, may affect the rate at which employees covered under the Act (or nonexempt employees) are paid for on-call hours. Most employees are nonexempt and protected under the FLSA. Employers must compensate any nonexempt employee required to work in excess of 40 hours per week at an overtime rate of at least one and one-half times the employee's regular rate. Hospitals, however, may enter agreements with employees to establish an alternative work period of 14 consecutive days and to pay the overtime for hours worked in excess of 80 hours during that period. Even under this option, the employee must be paid overtime rates for hours worked in excess of eight in any one day.

Federal regulations interpreting FLSA requirements address whether employers must pay nonexempt employees for time spent on call. If the health care employer requires an employee to remain on call either at the institution or so close to it that the employee cannot effectively use the time for his or her own purposes, then the time spent on call must be compensated as working time. For example, when a hospital employee returns home after a normal shift with the understanding that he or she is expected to return to the hospital in the event of an emergency, the time spent at home is normally not compensable. If, however, the conditions placed on the employee's activities are so restrictive that the employee cannot use the time effectively for personal pursuits, then such time on call is compensable. [29 CFR 553.221]

The Emergency Medical Treatment and Active Labor Act (EMTALA) includes requirements for on-call schedules in hospitals that receive Medicare or other federal funds. CMS issued policy memoranda on June 13, 2002, clarifying EMTALA on-call requirements. Under the CMS policies, a hospital is not strictly required to provide on-call physician services 24 hours a day/365 days a year, but must provide on-call coverage consistent with the capability of the institution and the well-being of the patient. If a hospital is unable to provide a certain service to a patient because of lack of on-call coverage, the hospital lacks capacity and may transfer the patient. CMS does not interpret EMTALA to require full coverage of a specialty when there are three physicians with that specialty on the staff (the "rule of three"). Rather, CMS considers all relevant factors, including the number of physicians in a specialty, to determine if on-call coverage should be provided. CMS allows hospitals to exempt senior staff from on-call coverage, provided that it does not adversely affect patient care. CMS will allow on-call physicians to provide coverage simultaneously at several hospitals. The CMS policies are available on the CMS Web site and are also reflected in proposed revisions to the EMTALA regulations issued May 9, 2002.

How have courts determined whether on-call time constitutes working time under the FLSA?

Courts have focused on whether restrictions placed on the employee during on-call hours prevented the employee from using the time for his or her own purposes. A Colorado appeals court, for example, ruled that four PAs employed by a multiple-site state correctional facility were entitled to overtime compensation for time spent on call. The PAs each worked 40 hours per week and also rotated through on-call time during which they would provide emergency medical services after regular working hours. The state paid the PAs one and one-half times their regular rate for hours when they were physically present at a facility on a call but did not compensate them for time spent waiting for calls. The PAs argued they should be paid for all on-call hours because the employer required a 20-minute response time to any of seven sites located within an eight-mile radius, and therefore they could not use the on-call time for personal pursuits. The appeals court agreed, concluding that the short response time, high volume of calls, number of facilities, and the geographical radius between facilities placed severe restrictions on the PAs' activities during on-call hours. The court found that the time was used predominantly for the employer's benefit and therefore was working time. [*Casserly v. State,* 844 P.2d 1275 (Colo. Ct. App. 1992)]

On the other hand, some courts have held on-call time noncompensable. The federal appeals court for the Seventh Circuit held that emergency medical technicians (EMTs) who served on standby crews that were on call after hours, and who were not required to remain on the employer's premises, were not "working" and were not entitled to on-call pay because they were free to effectively use their time for their personal pursuits. [*Dinges v. Sacred Heart of St. Mary's Hospitals,* 164 F.3d 1056 (7th Cir. Jan. 7, 1999)] Similarly, a federal trial court in Kansas ruled that hospital EMTs who work a 24-hour on-call shift during which they must remain within city limits were not entitled to compensation for on-call time. Under the hospital's procedures, the on-duty crew would respond to an emergency call, and the on-call crew would be notified to maintain a heightened sense of readiness. If another emergency call came in while the on-duty crew was responding to the prior emergency, the on-call crew was required to report to the hospital in five minutes. The court reasoned that this notification system provided the technicians with a warning that lessened the restrictive nature of the five-minute call-back requirement. [*Burnison v. Memorial Hosp.,* 820 F. Supp. 549 (D. Kan. 1993)]

What may a hospital radiology department do to ensure that its policy of payment for on-call employees does not violate the FLSA?

To avoid a potential violation of FLSA's wage and hour provisions, hospitals may wish to make a written request to the Wage and Hour Administrator for an interpretation of the FLSA as applied to the particular facts of the employer's policy of payment for such on-call time spent on and off premises.

Can hospitals be held liable when an on-call physician in the radiology department fails to respond to a call for assistance in providing emergency medical services?

Courts have held hospitals liable for injuries suffered by patients because of a physician's failure to respond to a request to attend to a patient in a timely manner. Maryland's highest court, for example, sustained a verdict against both a hospital and a physician in a case where a patient was brought to the hospital after he was struck by a car, and the physician failed to respond to a call for assistance in the emergency department. Upon the patient's arrival in the emergency department, he was not personally attended to by a physician although he was in shock, as indicated by dangerously low blood pressure. There was telephone contact between an emergency department nurse and the physician who was providing on-call coverage, but the physician failed to come to the hospital until the patient was near death. The court found that the physician's failure to respond was clearly not reasonable care, because the physician knew that wounds sustained as a result of a car accident could have been serious internal injuries that should be evaluated and treated by a physician. The court also held that the negligence of the nurse, who failed to contact the on-call physician after the patient's condition had worsened, did not relieve the physician of liability. Relying on the doctrine of *respondeat superior*, the court ruled that the hospital was liable for the nurse's negligence. [*Thomas v. Corso,* 288 A.2d 379 (Md. 1972)] A federal court in Missouri also has recognized the duty of physicians to respond to call, holding a general surgeon who attended an out-of-town medical conference while on call without notifying the hospital liable to a patient whose treatment was delayed as a result. [*Millard v. Corrado,* 14 S.W.3d 42 (E.D. Mo. 1999); *but see Anderson v. Houser,* 523 S.E.2d 342 (Ga. Ct. App. 1999), *cert. denied* Mar. 3, 2000 (Ga.) (no liability for on-call physician who was out of town because no physician–patient relationship existed).]

A physician's failure to respond to call also has ramifications under EMTALA. As explained in a June 13, 2002, CMS policy memorandum, if a physician on an on-call list is called by a hospital to provide emergency screening or treatment and either refuses or fails to arrive within a reasonable time, the hospital and that physician may be in violation of EMTALA. Under that statute, a physician who fails to respond to call may be cited and fined up to $50,000 per violation. If CMS finds that the violation was gross and flagrant or repeated, the physician is subject to exclusion from Medicare and Medicaid. [42 U.S.C. 1395dd(d)(1)] If the hospital's attempts to call in an alternate physician fail and the patient must be transferred, the physician's refusal to respond and the steps taken to find another provider must be documented carefully, and the federal transfer requirements under EMTALA followed closely.

Failure to respond to call also may trigger investigation or disciplinary proceedings under hospital rules or medical staff bylaws, or by the state medical board. Failure to respond to call also may constitute a breach of the physician's contract with the hospital. Internal reporting requirements and procedures should be followed closely.

What does developing an on-call schedule entail?

To safeguard patients, backup procedures should be in place in the event that an on-call physician becomes unavailable. The on-call lists should be posted and accessible to attending physicians, residents, and nurses, who should be trained on how to use the lists and backup procedures. When planning the on-call schedule, careful consideration should be given to how many backup physicians are necessary in light of the patient load, physician specialties, proportion of patients who present needing care in a particular specialty, whether the physicians take call at more than one facility, whether physician contracts or medical staff bylaws set forth requirements for on-call hours, whether state law requires 24-hour coverage for certain specialties, the physical health of the on-call staff, the availability of nearby hospitals for transfer, and other relevant factors.

Joint Commission standards regarding assessment of community and patient needs bear on the development of an on-call schedule. The Joint Commission standards require leaders to continually evaluate the relationship between patient needs and departmental resources. [For guidance on evaluating patient needs, see Part 3, under the headings Management of Human Resources and Leadership.]

How can staffing decisions affect the risk of liability?

Courts will consider not only whether a particular staff member acted properly, but also whether the radiology department was adequately staffed. For example, a Louisiana appeals court ruled that a hospital was liable to a patient who fell while being assisted onto an X-ray table, because providing only one X-ray technician to assist the patient onto the table constituted negligence. The patient had suffered an eye injury and was taken to the hospital to have his eye examined. The patient's right leg had been amputated years earlier. The patient, who arrived at the hospital carrying crutches and not wearing a prosthesis, was taken to the X-ray room in a wheelchair. In the X-ray room, a footstool with a handrail served as a step up to the X-ray table. As a technician assisted the patient onto the table, the patient fell. The court assessed whether one person could have safely helped the patient onto the table, considering that the patient's eye was swollen and bruised, that the patient was obviously an amputee, and that he appeared weak to the X-ray technician.

Reasoning that the patient could not step up on the footstool because he had only one leg and that the technician could not lift the patient onto the table alone, the court ruled that the hospital was negligent by failing to provide additional assistance. [*Deville v. Opelousas Gen. Hosp.*, 432 So. 2d 1131 (La. Ct. App. 1983)]

Fetal Protection Policies

What federal law prevents a radiology department from discharging or refusing to hire a pregnant female employee based solely on the risk of harmful fetal radiation exposure?

The Pregnancy Discrimination Act (PDA) of 1978 amended Title VII of the Civil Rights Act of 1964, the comprehensive federal antidiscrimination statute, by extending its prohibition of disparate employment treatment based on race, religion, sex, and national origin to disparate employment treatment based on pregnancy. [42 USC 2000e through 2000e-17] The Equal Employment Opportunity Commission (EEOC) and several federal courts have interpreted the PDA amendment to prohibit an employer from failing to hire and promote or firing a woman solely because she is pregnant; case law also generally holds that, under the PDA, if an employment practice has an adverse effect upon pregnant women, even if unintentional, an employer must be able to show business necessity to justify the practice.

The U.S. Supreme Court has specifically addressed the issue of whether one particular employment practice, the implementation of fetal protection policies, violates the PDA amendment to Title VII. [*United Auto Workers v. Johnson Controls, Inc.*, 499 U.S. 187 (1991)] The Court held that a company's policy to bar fertile women from battery making that involved exposure to lead violates Title VII. In so holding, the Court rejected the company's argument that the policy constituted permissible discrimination under Title VII because the safety of unconceived fetuses in jobs involving lead exposure is an instance where gender is a "bona fide occupational qualification" (BFOQ) necessary to the normal operation of its business. The Court explained that the BFOQ defense has a very narrow scope and does not transform concern for the safety of fetuses into an essential aspect of battery making. In this case, sex was not an occupational qualification, the Court held, noting that fertile women participate in the manufacture of batteries as efficiently as anyone else does.

In the aftermath of this significant U.S. Supreme Court decision, the EEOC issued a policy guide to assist its investigators in determining whether fetal protection policies violate Title VII. [EEOC, Policy Guidance on the Supreme Court Decision in *International Union, United Automobile, Aerospace & Agriculture Implement Workers of America v. Johnson Controls* (June 28, 1991)] According to the policy guide, fetal protection policies that exclude members of one sex from a workplace for the purpose of protecting fetuses cannot be justified under Title VII. The policy also states that, even if an employer can prove that a substance to which its workers are exposed will endanger the health of a fetus, such a factual showing is irrelevant because individuals who can perform the essential functions of a job must be considered eligible for employment, regardless of the presence of workplace hazards to fetuses.

Are hospitals obligated to reassign pregnant radiology department employees?

A pregnant medical technologist who was fired after exhausting her family and sick leave time may not sue the hospital where she worked for wrongful termination, the D.C. Court of Appeals has ruled. A hospital transferred a medical technologist to a position that required her to train for eight weeks using equipment that emitted radiation. The employee, who was six months pregnant, feared that radiation exposure would harm her fetus. The hospital denied the employee's request for a transfer because no other position was available, placing her on family and sick leave after she refused to report to work. When the employee exhausted her leave, the hospital fired her. The employee sued the hospital for wrongful termination.

The appeals court affirmed a trial court's decision to dismiss the employee's case. The court rejected the employee's argument that the hospital wrongfully discharged her in violation of a public policy of not exposing pregnant women to radiation. The employee identified the source of the public policy as a District of Columbia law prohibiting sex-based discrimination that contains language identical to the federal PDA. The court determined that the law does not create a special dispensation for pregnant women, but requires only that they not be discriminated against nor denied any employment opportunity due to pregnancy. The decision whether to continue in a particular job rests with the pregnant employee. Acknowledging that the employee was faced with a difficult choice, the court determined that she did not identify a public policy that imposes a duty on the hospital to transfer her to a new job or otherwise to accommodate her concerns. [*Duncan v. Children's Nat'l Med. Ctr.*, 702 A.2d 207 (D.C. App. 1997), *cert. denied*, 525 U.S. 912 (1998)]

What federal regulatory constraints are imposed on a radiology department in formulating a fetal protection policy for pregnant employees?

The NRC has promulgated regulations that set out embryo/fetus dose limits for a "declared pregnant woman," defined as a woman who has voluntarily informed her employer, in writing, of her pregnancy and the estimated date of conception. [10 CFR 20.1003] Specifically, the regulations provide that, for declared pregnant women, the dose to the embryo/fetus must be limited to 0.5 rem (5 mSv) over the entire pregnancy. [10 CFR 20.1208] The employer is also required to make an effort to avoid substantial variation above a uniform monthly exposure rate of 0.05 rem/month (0.5 mSv/month). [10 CFR 20.1208] In addition, declared pregnant women are not allowed to receive planned special exposures that involve whole-body doses or maternal intakes that could result in exceeding the embryo/fetus dose limit. The employer's radiation protection program should make provisions for instructing women workers about the special need to protect the embryo/fetus and to encourage them to promptly notify their employer if they become pregnant.

For clarification, the NRC has issued its Regulatory Guide Series, consisting of guides that collectively outline (1) methods acceptable to NRC staff for implementing specific parts of the Commission's regulations, (2) techniques used by NRC staff in evaluating specific problems or hypothetical radiation exposure accidents, and (3) data needed by NRC staff in their review of applications for permits and licenses. The guides of particular relevance to the formulation of fetal protection policies include

- Regulatory Guide 8.13, "Instruction Concerning Prenatal Radiation Exposure," which outlines instructions that must be provided concerning prenatal radiation exposure, and also provides the information needed by women who become pregnant to help them make an informed decision on whether or not to formally "declare" their pregnancy in accordance with regulations —instructions must describe the licensee's policy on pregnant women, including how those policies may affect the woman's work situation
- Regulatory Guide 8.29, "Instruction Concerning Risks from Occupational Radiation Exposure," which provides guidance on the instructions and information that should be provided to workers by licensees about health risks from occupational radiation exposure
- Regulatory Guide 8.36, "Radiation Dose to the Embryo/Fetus," which clarifies the methods and techniques for evaluating the dose to the embryo/fetus

The entire NRC Regulatory Guide Series is available free of charge on the Internet at www.nrc.gov.

Dress Codes

What legal claim might be triggered by hospital and/or radiology department grooming or dress code policies?

Grooming standards and dress codes have triggered lawsuits by employees claiming that the employer's policy violates Title VII, particularly its prohibition of disparate employment treatment based on gender. [42 USC 2000e through 2000e-17]

Facial hair may be an issue for health care workers who must be provided with respirators. OSHA standards require that an employer may not permit respirators with tight-fitting facepieces to be worn by employees who have facial hair that comes between the sealing surface of the facepiece and the face or that interferes with valve function. [29 CFR 1910.134(g)(i)(A)]

How have courts responded to suits based on alleged discriminatory grooming or dress code policies?

Numerous courts have upheld the employer's right to enforce a dress code. In one case, a federal appeals court upheld a county ambulance department's grooming policy for male EMTs prohibiting mustaches, beards, and hair of certain lengths. The policy was not arbitrary, the court ruled, finding that it was directed at promoting esprit de corps among EMTs; establishing a uniform, professional image for EMTs; and minimizing the possibility that the EMTs' hair would interfere with the performance of their jobs. [*Hottinger v. Pope County*, 971 F.2d 127 (8th Cir. 1992)]

Dress codes will be subjected to a different standard of scrutiny, however, in instances in which male and female employees who perform the same functions are expected to conform to two entirely different dress codes. Several courts have held that Title VII requires that similarly situated employees be treated in an equal manner with respect to dress code requirements. A state appeals court in Michigan, for example, ruled that a hospital's dress code requirements illegally discriminated on the basis of sex. The court rejected the hospital's argument that its policy of requiring female technologists to wear white or pastel-colored uniforms, while male technologists wore white lab coats over their street clothes, was justified because patients are used to seeing men dressed like physicians and women dressed like nurses. [*Michigan Dep't of Civil Rights v. Sparrow Hosp.*, 326 N.W.2d 519 (Mich. Ct. App. 1982)]

Staff Substance Abuse

What are some legal concerns arising from staff substance abuse?

The problem of employee substance abuse among health care professionals may give rise to a number of legal concerns for a radiology department. If an impaired health care provider harms a patient, both the hospital and the provider may be held liable for the patient's injuries because the provider's negligence may be imputed to the hospital. The hospital also may be subject to direct liability for negligent monitoring of a medical staff member and failing to protect the patient.

May a radiology department require drug tests for staff members?

Drug testing programs for health care workers must balance a hospital or other employer's need to drug test medical staff and employees against individual privacy.

The American Hospital Association advises its members to initiate a comprehensive drug-testing program for all hospital personnel, including employees, physicians, volunteers, and trustees. [American Hospital Association, *Management Advisory, Substance Abuse Policies of Health Care Institutions* (Jan. 1992)] The American Medical Association (AMA) takes the position that drug and alcohol testing of employees in any industry may be appropriate in the following circumstances: (1) preemployment for health or safety-sensitive positions; (2) reasonable suspicion that performance is impaired by drugs or alcohol; and (3) follow-up testing to monitor rehabilitation. The AMA also urges employers who choose to establish drug testing programs to use confirmed, positive test results in employees primarily to motivate those employees to seek appropriate assistance with their alcohol or drug problems, preferably through employee assistance programs. [AMA policy H-95.984, *Issues in Employee Drug Testing*]

Courts have upheld drug testing for physicians and hospital employees performing safety-sensitive work. In the public sector, in a challenge to the Veterans Administration's Drug Free Workplace Plan that included random drug testing of designated "safety-sensitive" medical positions (such as pharmacist, physician, nurse, and medical technician), a federal district court in California upheld testing for any medical position that involved direct patient care. [*American Federation of Government Employees, Local 2110 v. Derwinski*, 777 F. Supp. 1493, 1493 (N.D. Cal. 1991)] A federal district court in Mississippi upheld a county hospital's discharge of an employee based on her refusal to cooperate in a newly implemented facilitywide drug testing program, reasoning that the employee held a safety-sensitive position and, therefore, had a diminished expectation of privacy. [*Kemp v. Claiborne County Hospital*, 763 F. Supp. 1362, 1367–68 (S.D. Miss. 1991)]

What should a radiology department do when it becomes aware of a staff member with a substance abuse problem?

A first step for the radiology department would be to informally persuade the impaired practitioner to seek help and to refer him or her to the hospital's employee assistance program or in-house rehabilitation program, if one exists. In the absence of such a program, the radiology department should refer the employee to an external professional treatment program. The radiology department should report the impaired practitioner to the chief of the appropriate clinical service, chief of staff, or a supervisor, and then, if required, the hospital must report that practitioner to the appropriate state licensing body. In some states, state law may insulate impaired practitioners from disciplinary action, including peer review and medical board reporting, unless the impairment becomes habitual or poses a danger to patients.

Participating in a rehabilitation program should be required of any employee or medical staff member who voluntarily admits to having a substance abuse problem or whose substance test results are positive. Employees and medical staff members who successfully complete treatment should be provided with an opportunity to continue working in the radiology department under an agreement that provides for unannounced testing for a reasonable period after return to work. If an employee is unable or unwilling to rehabilitate, the hospital may have no other option than termination. [*See, e.g.,* American Hospital Association, *Management Advisory, Substance Abuse Policies of Health Care Institutions* (Jan. 1992).]

All communications should be kept strictly confidential to comply with the Americans with Disabilities Act and with state laws governing medical information and peer review. Because impaired physicians may have protected status under these statutes, department managers should consult with the hospital's human resources department and medical staff committee, as soon as a potentially impaired practitioner is discovered, for assistance in complying with disability discrimination, confidentiality, and other federal and state laws.

A federal district court in California ruled that a physician's prior chemical dependency problem constituted a disability under California law and that a health plan's termination of the physician based on that disability violated anti-discrimination provisions when the plan failed to show specifically how the physician's prior drug use made him unqualified. [*Ambrosino v. Metropolitan Life Insurance Company* (N.D. Cal. 1995) 899 F. Supp. 438] On the other hand, a federal district court in New York concluded that the Americans with Disabilities Act did not bar a hospital from demoting its chief of internal medicine after he relapsed into drug and alcohol abuse. The physician sought reinstatement to his supervisory position, asserting that the ADA required the hospital to provide him with a "reasonable accommodation" for his disability—a professional monitor assigned to observe him for any signs of relapse. The court reasoned that the health care field posed dangers of a special nature and magnitude, and that the suggested accommodation was not reasonable in light of those dangers. [*Altman v. New York City Health and Hospitals Corp.* (S.D.N.Y. 1995) 903 F. Supp. 563, *aff'd* 100 F.3d 1054 (2d Cir. 1996)]

RESTRAINT AND SECLUSION

In 2000, patients' rights issues came to the forefront, as legislators on the federal and state levels enacted new laws to ensure the safety and self-determination of patients following headlines concerning medical errors and managed care mistreatment in the popular press. Federal agencies responded as well, most notably by incorporating patients' rights guarantees in the Medicare Conditions of Participation. New standards protecting patients' right to be free of restraint and seclusion created much controversy in 2000, following the establishment of specific ordering, documentation, and time requirements for restraint and seclusion as part of the Medicare patients' rights provisions.

Do any federal regulations address the use of restraint and seclusion?

In 2000, the Medicare Conditions of Participation were amended to incorporate a patients' bill of rights, which set standards for the restraint and seclusion of hospital patients. These standards must be met by hospitals that receive Medicare or Medicaid reimbursement. The regulations establish patients' right to be free from both physical restraints and drugs that are used as restraints that are not medically necessary or that are used as a means of coercion, discipline, convenience, or retaliation by staff. The standards distinguish between the use of restraint for medical and surgical care from the use of restraint or seclusion for behavior management, setting forth separate criteria for each. [42 CFR 482.13]

What constitutes a restraint?

Under the regulations, a restraint is any manual method, physical device, mechanical device, material, or equipment attached or adjacent to the patient's body that he or she cannot easily remove, if it restricts freedom of movement or access to one's body. A drug constitutes a restraint if it is a medication used to control behavior or to restrict a patient's freedom of movement and is not a standard treatment for the patient's medical or psychiatric condition. [42 CFR 482.13]

According to CMS guidance, what constitutes a restraint depends on whether the object or technique is being used for the purpose of limiting patient movement and access to their bodies. According to the guidance, devices that serve multiple purposes, such as a gerichair or side rails, constitute a restraint when they have the effect of restricting a patient's movement and cannot be easily removed by the patient. A drug qualifies as a restraint if it used to restrict a patient's freedom of movement in medical postsurgical situations and is not a standard treatment for the patient's medical or psychiatric condition. Tucking in a patient's sheets so tightly that he or she cannot move is another example of a physical restraint under the standards. [CMS, Interpretive Guidelines, Hospital Conditions of Participation for Patients' Rights (May 2000)]

If the patient is being transported to another area for a diagnostic or surgical procedure and must wait briefly, a restraint order is not required for raised side rails or a seatbelt. In the case of a patient who is awaiting a treatment or a procedure, CMS expects that, even though an order is not required, as a matter of standard practice staff will ensure that the patient is not abandoned while awaiting treatment or care and that the patient's basic needs are met. [CMS Hospital Conditions of Participation for Patients' Rights, Questions and Answers, October 10, 2001]

Age or developmentally appropriate protective safety interventions, such as stroller safety belts or raised crib rails, that a care provider outside a health care setting would utilize to protect an infant, toddler, or preschool-aged child are not considered restraint or seclusion for the purposes of the regulation. [CMS Hospital Conditions of Participation for Patients' Rights, Questions and Answers, October 10, 2001]

How do the patients' rights standards limit the use of restraints for medical and surgical care?

The standards, which have generated much controversy in the hospital community,

- limit restraint use to those situations in which less restrictive interventions have been determined to be ineffective to protect the patient or others from harm
- require the order of a physician or qualified licensed independent practitioner
- prohibit the use of standing or as needed orders for restraints
- require consultation with the patient's treating physician as soon as possible (if the physician did not personally write the order)
- necessitate a written amendment of the patient's plan of care
- mandate that restraints be implemented in the least restrictive manner possible and in accordance with safe and appropriate restraining techniques
- require the withdrawal of restraints at the earliest possible time
- establish that restraint use must be continually assessed, monitored, and reevaluated

- impose ongoing staff training requirements [42 CFR 482.13]

Mental health provider representatives brought a suit challenging on procedural grounds the Patients' Rights Condition of Participation requirement that hospitals provide for an in-person evaluation of a patient by a physician or other licensed independent practitioner within one hour of initiating the use of a restraint or placing the patient in seclusion to address the patient's violent or aggressive behavior. [*National Association of Psychiatric Health Sys. v. Shalala*, 120 F. Supp. 2d 33 (D.D.C. 2000)] As a result of a federal district court ruling in the suit, CMS reopened the Condition of Participation in compliance with the Regulatory Flexibility Act, but was allowed to continue to enforce the requirements of the interim final rule. [67 Fed. Reg. 61,805 (2002)]

What documentation is necessary with regard to restraint orders and evaluations?

The guidance states that the rationale that a patient might fall is an inadequate basis for using a restraint. Each individual patient's history of falls, medical condition, and symptoms must be evaluated on a case-by-case basis—restraints are not a substitute for adequate staffing and monitoring, according to the guidelines. The guidelines emphasize the importance of documenting: the rationale for ordering a restraint, the rationale for the time frame for the order, continual reevaluation of patients in restraints, and that other less restricting alternatives were considered. Consistency with hospital policy and reliance on current standards of safety and technique are also factors in evaluating whether restraint use is appropriate. [CMS, Interpretive Guidelines, Hospital Conditions of Participation for Patients' Rights (May 2000)]

CONSENT

Consent to treatment is a basic concept that may seem second nature to health care providers, but that is a more complex concept than it first appears. The informed consent process can give rise to a variety of questions, such as what constitutes valid consent, whether consent must be in writing, and who can consent if the patient is not able. This section answers these and other questions that may arise in the radiology department. It is important to realize, however, that each state may have statutes and case law that dictate how the law of consent applies in that particular jurisdiction. For sample documentation related to this topic, see Part 3 under Care of Patients. The general legal principle is that patient consent to medical treatment is necessary. There are some situations, however, when patient consent is not required, such as

- in an emergency
- when the patient is not able to give consent due to minority status
- when the patient is not able to give consent due to mental incapacity
- when a therapeutic privilege is applicable

- when the law designates a substitute decision maker, such as in the case of abused children
- when a court permits treatment without consent, such as in the case of taking a blood sample pursuant to a search warrant

In many of these situations, "substituted consent" of a decision maker other than the patient, such as next of kin, a guardian, or a court, is required.

When is informed consent required?

Generally speaking, the necessity for consent is a function of the risk posed by a particular treatment or procedure. For example, informed consent should be obtained for any invasive surgical procedure, due to the risks to the patient. Informed consent also should be obtained for noninvasive, but high-risk, procedures. On the other end of the spectrum, consent is not likely to be required for drawing blood for a routine test, considering the low risk of harm to the patient.

In the radiology department, informed consent requirements should be examined carefully for compliance with hospital policy, association guidelines, state law, and any other applicable standards. For example, Georgia law states:

> . . . any person who undergoes an amniocentesis diagnostic procedure or a diagnostic procedure which involves the intravenous or intraductal injection of a contrast material must consent to such procedure. [GA. CODE ANN. 31-9-6.1]

The statute goes on to describe in detail the information that must be disclosed to the patient.

Leaders should review the spectrum of procedures performed and decide when informed consent should be required, balancing the invasiveness and risk of each procedure. Typically, hospitals require informed consent for arteriograms, biopsies, and stress tests, for example. Many hospitals also require informed consent for use of contrast dyes and radionuclides, in accordance with state law, community standard of care, or hospital policy. For examples of informed consent documentation, see Part 3 under Care of Patients.

Who should obtain informed consent for radiological procedures?

As discussed below, informed consent requires a discussion of the risks and benefits of the procedure. The physician who performs a procedure may be in the best position to discuss the required information with the patient. It is important that hospital policy be followed. If the hospital requires informed consent to be obtained by a physician, rather than a radiology technologist, that policy should be strictly followed.

The Pennsylvania Supreme Court held that it was the radiologist's duty to inform a patient undergoing an aortogram that the dye used might damage the kidneys. The medical facility where the aortogram was given could not be held vicariously liable for the physician's failure to obtain the patient's informed consent for the procedure. [*Valles v. Albert Einstein Medical Center*, 805 A.2d 1232 (Pa. 2002)]

What information must be disclosed to the patient to obtain informed consent?

The law of informed consent has been shaped by years of court cases, with each state forming its own response regarding what information must be disclosed to the patient. Generally, however, the list includes the following:

- diagnosis
- nature and purpose of the proposed treatment
- risks and consequences of the proposed treatment
- probability that the proposed treatment will be successful
- feasible treatment alternatives
- prognosis if the proposed treatment is not given

The applicability of each of the items on the list may shift from case to case, depending on the particular facts. Nevertheless, the list has value as a disclosure checklist for the practitioner.

Do all states use the same method of determining whether consent is informed?

States use two different standards in defining informed consent: (1) the professional community standard and (2) the reasonable patient standard. The first is a physician-based standard, the second a patient-based standard.

The *professional community standard* states that the duty of the physician to disclose is limited to disclosures that a reasonable medical practitioner would make under the same or similar circumstances. The *reasonable patient standard* states that the physician must disclose all information that is material to the patient's decision to accept the proposed treatment. This is considered the more modern standard. Some states have adopted this standard through legislation. In Pennsylvania, for example, state law requires physicians to inform a patient of the nature of the proposed treatment, its risks, and the alternatives that a reasonable patient would consider material to the decision of whether to undergo treatment. [2002 PA. LAWS 154, No. 13, Section 504]

The following quote from a landmark 1960 Kansas case, which involved a radiologist, states well the professional community standard:

> The duty of the physician to disclose, however, is limited to those disclosures which a reasonable medical practitioner would make under the same or similar circumstances. How the physician may best discharge his obligation to the patient in this difficult situation involves primarily

a question of medical judgment. So long as the disclosure is sufficient to assure an informed consent, the physician's choice of plausible courses should not be called into question if it appears, all circumstances considered, that the physician was motivated only by the patient's best therapeutic interests and he proceeded as competent medical men would have done in a similar situation. [*Natanson v. Kline*, 350 P.2d 1093 (Kan.), *clarified*, 354 P.2d 670 (Kan. 1960)]

In that case, the physician had failed to disclose to his patient the hazards inherent in proposed cobalt irradiation therapy, a form of treatment that was then relatively new and untried. Upon suffering serious side effects from the therapy, the patient sued, arguing that his formal consent to the treatment was invalidated by his lack of knowledge of the dangers. Although technically the complaint was grounded in assault and battery, the court treated the issue as one of professional negligence, requiring proof that the physician had deviated from the standard of care that would have been observed by other practitioners under the same or similar circumstances. Application of the professional community standard in the *Natanson* case precluded a finding of liability, because the patient had not introduced expert medical testimony regarding what other physicians would have disclosed in similar circumstances.

A well-known Texas case also involved the issue of informed consent in the radiology department. A patient was referred for cobalt therapy after surgery failed to stop her uterine bleeding. After her treatment, the patient developed a wound on her back that required plastic surgery. The injury resulted from the radiologist's miscalculation of the cobalt dosage to be administered to the patient. The cobalt source had been changed shortly before the injury, and the physician had inadvertently used the wrong set of figures in computing the cobalt dosage, based on the older source potency information. The patient sued, claiming, among other things, lack of informed consent.

The court determined that the definition of informed consent given by the court was in accordance with Texas law. That definition was "informed consent means such consent as would be given by a patient to whom the risks incident to treatment by radiation therapy have been disclosed to the patient by a general practitioner of ordinary prudence, under the same or similar circumstances." The court also ruled that neither the hospital nor the technologist had a duty to obtain informed consent; the radiologist was solely responsible. [*Nevauex v. Park Place Hosp.*, 656 S.W.2d 923 (Tex. Ct. App. 1985)]

Does the failure to disclose relevant information to a patient automatically result in liability?

Even when relevant information is not disclosed, there is no liability unless a court is convinced that the patient would have chosen a different course, and thereby avoided injury, if the information in question had been disclosed. This link between the nondisclosure and the patient's injury is called "proximate cause" or "causation."

Under the reasonable patient standard, the patient must prove that the particular danger that was not disclosed was "material" (important) to the patient's decision. Some courts measure this by what a "reasonable person" would find material to his or her decision, although other courts require the information to be tailored to the needs of the particular person. For example, it might not be material to a "reasonable person" that a procedure would cause slight stiffness in one finger joint. It might be very material, however, if that particular person were a concert pianist.

Is a signed consent form sufficient evidence of informed consent?

Simply requiring the patient to sign a form does not satisfy informed consent requirements, as the form serves merely as *evidence* of the informed consent process. On the other hand, it is important to document consent or the lack of consent. Although not legally conclusive, a well-written, properly executed consent form is strong evidence that informed consent was given.

A legally effective consent form must

- be signed voluntarily
- show that the procedure performed was the one to which consent was given
- show that the consenting person understood the nature of the procedure, the risks involved, and the probable consequences

A general consent form, worded to permit a physician to perform whatever procedures are in the patient's best interest, is invalid. It does not illustrate that the patient made an informed decision after receiving adequate information.

Consent in an Emergency

Is consent required in a medical emergency?

A true medical emergency may obviate the need for consent. The two factors necessary to trigger the emergency care doctrine are (1) the patient's incapacity to consent and (2) the need for immediate treatment. When immediate treatment is required to preserve life or prevent a serious impairment to health, and it is impossible to obtain the patient's consent or that of someone authorized to consent on the patient's behalf, the physician may perform the required procedure without liability. Consent is implied by law as a matter of public policy, because the physician's inaction in an emergency might result in greater harm to the patient.

Some states have enacted laws that formalize this emergency exception to the informed consent requirement. In Georgia, for example, an emergency is defined as a situation in which a delay in treatment would be expected to jeopardize the life or health of a patient, or where a delay could lead to disfigurement or impaired faculties. According to the statute, "consent to surgical or medical treatment or procedures suggested, recommended, prescribed, or directed by a duly licensed physician will be implied where an emergency exists." [GA. CODE ANN. 31-9-3]

How serious must a patient's condition be for a health care provider to render care without the patient's consent?

The patient's condition must be so serious that the initiation of treatment cannot be delayed until consent is obtained or the patient would suffer death or serious permanent impairment. This is a medical judgment. In cases where delay would not materially increase the hazards, although it is clear that the medical treatment in question will be needed in the near term, failure to obtain consent cannot be excused on the ground that an emergency existed.

As with all questions of fact, it is important that the need for haste in rendering treatment be documented fully and carefully. Whenever possible, the health care provider should seek confirmation of a determination that an immediate threat to life or health exists. Hospitals should insist that staff engage in such consultation as time and circumstances permit. Findings supporting the existence of an emergency should be noted in the patient's record, with particular emphasis on the nature of the threat, its immediacy, and its magnitude. The initialing of such notations by consultant physicians is advisable from an evidentiary standpoint; at the least, the consulting physicians' names should be recorded.

What kind of treatment is authorized in an emergency?

Authorized treatment during an emergency when there is no patient consent is limited to whatever is reasonable under the circumstances. Reasonable treatment is dictated by the patient's condition. Radiology services, such as a CT scan, would be considered reasonable in the assessment of a patient who has sustained a serious fall in a construction accident, for example. Whatever treatment is necessary to alleviate the threat of death or serious permanent injury would be considered reasonable.

Consent to Treatment of Minors

Can minors consent to medical treatment?

Generally, minors cannot consent to treatment. In most cases, the health care provider must secure the consent of the minor's parent or other person standing *in loco parentis* (in the place of the parents). There are several exceptions to this rule, however, including emergency situations, emancipated minors, and state laws that allow minors to consent to treatment for various conditions, such as sexual assault, venereal disease, drug or alcohol abuse, and pregnancy-related care.

What if there is a medical emergency and the parents cannot be located?

Parental consent is implied when there is a need for immediate action necessary to preserve a life or prevent permanent bodily harm, which is the definition of a true emergency.

Most states have statutes specifically addressing consent to emergency medical and surgical treatment of minors. A North Carolina statute, for example, authorizes medical treatment without parental consent if the minor's life or health is in jeopardy or if delaying treatment to seek consent would create a threat of serious injury to the minor. Surgical treatment under such circumstances requires consultation with another surgeon or physician, except in rural areas where consultation may not be promptly available. [N.C. GEN. STAT. 90-21.1 through 90-21.4] New Mexico law provides that consent may be given on behalf of a minor by anyone standing *in loco parentis* to the minor when an emergency exists and the parents cannot be located. [N.M. STAT. ANN. 24-10-2]

What is an emancipated minor?

Most states recognize the concept of the "emancipated minor," one who, although below the chronological age of majority, has assumed the lifestyle and responsibilities of an adult. Emancipation is generally accomplished by marriage and/or cessation of dependency on parental support. Having a separate home and an independent means of financial support are key determinants of emancipation. In many states, a minor is automatically emancipated upon becoming a parent. Whether or not emancipation has been effected is a factual question that depends on the circumstances of the particular case.

Most states have statutes that allow married and emancipated minors to give effective consent to medical and surgical treatment. Many of these statutes also provide that minor parents have the power to consent to care of their children. The following Delaware statute is representative:

> Consent to the performance upon or for any minor by any licensed medical, surgical, dental, psychological or osteopathic practitioner or any nurse practitioner/clinical nursing specialist, hospital or public clinic or their agents or employees of any lawful medical treatment, and to the furnishing of hospitalization and other reasonably necessary care in connection therewith, may be given by

> 1. a parent or guardian of any minor for such minor
> 2. a married minor for himself or herself or, if such married minor be unable to give consent by reason of disability, then by his or her spouse
> 3. a minor of the age 18 years or more for himself or herself
> 4. a minor parent for his or her child

5. a minor or by any person professing to be serving as temporary custodian of such minor at the request of a parent or guardian of such minor for the examination and treatment of (i) any laceration, fracture, or other traumatic injury suffered by such minor, or (ii) any symptom, disease or pathology which may, in the judgment of the attending personnel preparing such treatment, if untreated, reasonably be expected to threaten the health or life of such minor; provided, however, that the consent given shall be effective only after reasonable efforts shall have been made to obtain the consent of the parent or guardian of said minor

6. A relative caregiver acting pursuant to an affidavit giving that person the power to consent to medical treatment of the minor. [DEL. CODE ANN. tit. 13, 707]

Mental Incompetence

What is mental competency?

For consent purposes, competency is an ability to understand the nature and consequences of the treatment to which one is asked to consent. Mental incompetence is not limited to persons who have been legally declared incompetent. It also includes persons who, in the opinion of the treating physician, are either permanently or temporarily unable to give consent. Permanent inability to give consent may apply to patients who suffer from mental retardation or senility. Temporary inability to give consent may result from a head injury, alcohol, or drug abuse.

Who can consent to treatment if the patient is mentally incompetent?

If a person has been declared legally incompetent and a legal guardian or conservator has been appointed, that person's consent must be obtained. The guardian or conservator should be asked to provide proof of legal authority to make medical decisions for the patient.

In many cases, the person has not been declared legally incompetent, but, in the physician's medical judgment, the person is either permanently or temporarily incompetent to provide consent to treatment. Whenever possible, a hospital or other provider contemplating treatment of a person arguably incompetent should try to obtain "substituted consent" from the person's next of kin or a court order authorizing the proposed treatment. If the next of kin refuses to consent, it still may be possible to obtain a court order allowing the treatment.

In some cases, the patient, although competent, may have executed an advance directive (such as a durable power of attorney) relating to the provision of medical care if the person is incapacitated. Such a document may grant agents full power and authority to make health care decisions on behalf of the person who executed the document to the same extent as that person would make if he or she were competent.

In emergency situations, when death or serious harm is imminent, general rules regarding emergency treatment will protect the provider who acts reasonably and in good faith.

Refusal of Consent

What if a patient refuses to consent to treatment in the radiology department?

A competent adult patient who has been informed of the consequences of such a decision has the right to refuse to consent to treatment. To provide treatment in the face of refusal to consent would constitute battery. Nor can a physician, after a patient's refusal, wait until the patient's condition worsens or until the patient lapses into unconsciousness and then commence treatment, basing such action on the existence of an emergency or the patient's lack of competence.

If the patient refuses care in the face of pressing need, this may be evidence of incompetence. The attending physician must make a medical judgment of whether the patient is competent. This assessment must be fully documented and medically supportable.

If the patient is not competent, there may be a patient representative who is authorized to consent to treatment. However, if a patient is not capable of giving consent and a relative refuses to consent to treatment that the provider considers essential to the patient's life or health, the provider should seek a court order authorizing such treatment.

How should refusal of consent be documented?

The medical record should contain documentation of the patient's refusal to consent, documentation that the consequences of the patient's refusal to consent were explained to the patient, and documentation of the physician's assessment that the patient was competent at the time of the refusal.

It also is good policy to obtain a signed release form that exculpates the hospital and its employees and staff from liability for any consequences flowing from the refusal. It should contain the information stated above. If the patient refuses to sign a release form, a note reflecting that refusal should be added to the medical record.

MEDICAL RECORDS AND CONFIDENTIALITY

The patient-related information gathered by the radiology department is subject to various legal requirements that are defined in both federal and state law. These requirements govern the inclusion of information in a patient's medical record, the retention of records for defined periods of time, and confidentiality.

What legal requirements governing the content of medical records apply to information gathered in the radiology department?

State law and regulations that define the content of medical records frequently specify that diagnostic documentation, including X-rays, are part of a patient's record. In Colorado, for example, "medical record" is defined as "the written or graphic documentation, sound recording, or computer record of services pertaining to medical and health care, which are performed at the direction of a physician or other licensed health care provider on behalf of a patient by physicians. . . or other health care personnel," including "X-rays, electrocardiograms, electroencephalograms, and other test results." [COL. REV. STAT. 18-4-412] Under federal regulations, the Medicare Conditions of Participation provide that all records must contain all radiology reports as appropriate [42 CFR 482.24(c)] and that the records of radiologic services must be maintained. [42 CFR 482.26(d)] The radiologist or other practitioner who performs radiology services must sign reports of his or her interpretations. [42 CFR 482.26(d)]

Are there legal requirements that govern the retention of X-ray records?

The Medicare Conditions of Participation and some states have special statutory or regulatory provisions governing how long a hospital should maintain specific portions of a patient's record, such as X-rays, scans, and clinical laboratory reports. For example, under federal law, a hospital must retain copies of reports and printouts of radiologic services, as well as films, scans, and other image records, for five years. [42 CFR 482.26(d) and ALASKA STAT. 18.20.085] Liability can arise for failure to retain records in accordance with these requirements.

For example, in one case, a court ruled that state legislation governing the retention of X-rays creates the right to sue a hospital for failure to keep these X-rays. [*Rodgers v. St. Mary's Hosp.*, 149 Ill. 2d 302, 597 N.E.2d 616 (Ill. 1992)] The court noted that state law requires hospitals to retain X-rays as part of their regularly maintained records for a period of five years. The statute clearly seeks to protect the property right of persons involved in litigation, the court declared. According to the court, violating a statute that is designed to protect either property or human life is evidence of negligence. To succeed in recovering damages, however, the patient would have to prove a causal connection between the failure to comply with records retention legislation and actual injury.

What rules of patient confidentiality govern the data collected by a radiology department?

Patient information relating to medical history, examinations, diagnosis, or treatment that is gathered in a radiology department is confidential under the rules of confidentiality that govern the confidentiality of medical records in general. These rules are generally found in the Medicare Conditions of Participation and state statutes and regulations. Under federal law, a hospital must have a procedure for ensuring the confidentiality of patient records [42 CFR 482.24(b)], and patients have the right to the confidentiality of their clinical records. [42 CFR 482.13(d)] The privacy of individually identifiable patient health information is also protected by recently enacted final regulations implementing the Health Insurance Portability and Accountability Act of 1996 (HIPAA). [45 CFR Parts 160 and 164] (See further discussion under Telemedicine, below).

A few states simply specify that the medical record is confidential and impose a general obligation on hospitals to develop an appropriate policy for record confidentiality. [*See, e.g.,* MD. CODE ANN., HEALTH–GEN. §4.302] Enactments in other states similarly embody the principle of confidentiality and the patient's right of access. In Connecticut, for example, a statutory Patient's Bill of Rights [CONN. GEN. STAT. 19a-550(b)(9)] provides that patients are entitled to confidential treatment of personal and medical records. Patients may approve or refuse their release to any individual outside the facility, except in the case of the patient's transfer to another health care institution or as required by law or a third-party payment contract.

Numerous other statutes provide that medical records are confidential and may be disclosed only with the patient's consent or as provided in the statutes. Note that although the general rule establishes that the medical record is a confidential document, numerous exceptions allow disclosure or impose mandatory reporting of patient information under specific circumstances. Hospital policy governing the release of information from patients' medical records frequently stipulates that records stored in other departments, such as X-ray films, are subject to the policy if they meet the definition of "medical record" under state law.

What types of liability can arise for the unauthorized disclosure of medical records?

Health care providers can be liable to their patients for the improper or unauthorized disclosure of medical record information. Under the new federal HIPAA regulations, although there is no private right of action that would allow patients to sue for violations of the new privacy rule (see discussion that follows), HHS has authority to impose both civil and criminal penalties for violation, including a fine of $100 per violation, up to a total of $25,000 per year for unintentional disclosure of protected health information [42 USC § 1320d-5(a)], and up to $250,000 and imprisonment for knowingly disclosing protected information for commercial or personal gain or for malicious harm [42 USC § 1320d-6(b)].

In addition to federal and state statutory penalties, hospitals and practitioners may be liable in common law for defamation, invasion of privacy, professional secrets, and breach of contract. Liability under a newly recognized separate tort for the disclosure of nonpublic medical information may also exist in some jurisdictions. [*See e.g., Biddle v. Warren Gen. Hosp.,* 715 N.E.2d 518 (Ohio 1999).]

What specific patient confidentiality concerns arise in a radiology department?

Discussions or comments among radiology department staff members regarding test or film results can violate patient privacy. Like all hospital employees, radiology department staff should be aware that they are not to give out patient information or discuss patient-related information except as authorized under law. Accordingly, the department should provide an area where patients can be interviewed in private. [*See* 42 CFR 482.13(c), recognizing a hospital patient's right to personal privacy.] It also is important to ensure that the information on radiology requisitions is protected because they frequently contain confidential patient information relating to infection precautions that need to be taken for a particular patient. Appropriate security measures, depending on how the radiology reports are transmitted to the floors or to the emergency department (via computer, fax, or hand delivery), must be implemented and observed.

TELEMEDICINE

The number of radiology teleconsultations is increasing and, in fact, represents one of the dominant areas of activity for delivery of health care services via telemedicine, according to recent studies. [Department of Health and Human Services, Office of Rural Health Policy, Exploratory Evaluation of Rural Applications of Telemedicine, Health Resources and Services Administration (1997), which found that 70 percent of hospitals reporting telemedicine activity were solely providing telemedicine services for radiology.] Radiology leaders who are pioneering telemedicine at their facilities should be familiar with the legal issues triggered by the electronic transmission of health information.

HRSA, (http://telehealth.hrsa.gov) has established the Office for the Advancement of Telehealth to serve as a leader in telehealth services and education. HHS has identified five key issues affecting the telemedicine and telehealth industry:

- lack of reimbursement
- legal issues
- safety and standards
- privacy, security, and confidentiality
- telecommunications infrastructure

With respect to reimbursement, the Balanced Budget Act of 1997 expanded coverage options for telemedicine but also restricted telemedicine's use under conditions where it is commonly being used outside of Medicare. The Medicare, Medicaid, and SCHIP Benefits Improvement and Protection Act, passed in 2000, expanded the types of presenters, current procedural terminology codes, and geographic area limits that are eligible for reimbursement. [HHS, 2001 Report to Congress on Telemedicine, May 20, 2002]

What telemedicine compliance issues must be considered?

A variety of state and federal laws must be reviewed to ensure compliance with regard to telemedicine. The following checklist contains examples of the types of statutes and regulations that may come into play:

- *state health care practitioner licensing laws*—Where physicians and other practitioners are consulted across state lines, consideration must be given to whether they are authorized to participate in the care of an out-of-state patient. More than 20 states have some form of telemedicine licensing law. In Alabama, for example, out-of-state physicians seeking to treat Alabama patients must obtain a special purpose license in the state, showing that they hold the appropriate license in their home state, unless the telemedicine services are provided on an emergency or infrequent basis. [ALA. CODE 34-24-500 through 34-24-508]
- *reimbursement rules*—Telemedicine poses reimbursement challenges. Requirements related to signatures, direct supervision of nonphysicians, direct observation of the patient, medical necessity, and other issues must be examined.
- *patient consent*—Where patient information is transmitted electronically, or where a patient is being treated by a practitioner whom he or she has never met, consent issues should be reviewed carefully. Patients should receive specific information about telemedicine as part of the informed consent process, and understand that confidentiality may not be guaranteed. A consent form may be tailored to include this type of disclaimer for video consultations.
- *confidentiality*—The potential for breach of confidentiality in telemedicine is significant because telemedicine involves not only collecting and storing patient data electronically but also broadcasting it off-site. Because individuals may intentionally or unintentionally intercept video broadcasts, some telemedicine locations have decided to scramble their broadcasts to protect confidentiality. Technical personnel must be present at both ends of the transmission during a consultation broadcast, requiring that these individuals be included in institutional policies and training that relate to patient confidentiality.
- *accreditation standards and other guidance*—The American Health Information Management Association has addressed standards for telemedical records, suggesting specific actions to protect confidentiality and security. [Practice Brief, *Telemedical Records*, J. HEALTH INFO. MGMT. ASS'N, vol. 68, no. 4 (1997)] ACR also has drafted standards for teleradiology, addressing goals, qualifications for personnel, equipment guidelines, licensing, credentialing, liability, communication, quality control, and quality and quality improvement. The standard recommends that teleradiology systems provide network and software security protocols to protect the confidentiality of patients' identification and imaging data. There also should be measures to safeguard the data and to ensure data integrity against intentional or unintentional corruption of the data. [ACR Standard for Teleradiology, available on the Internet at www.acr.org]

- *Health Insurance Portability and Accountability Act (HIPAA)*—HIPAA is a federal law that addresses two separate issues: (1) health insurance reform and (2) federal standards for transfer of patient information in the health care industry. These standards are also known as the "administrative simplification" provisions. The standards are explained further in the question and answer that follow.

What does HIPAA compliance entail?

HIPAA compliance is an ongoing process that entails carefully following regulatory developments, analyzing what steps toward compliance are necessary, and then implementing appropriate policies and procedures to ensure compliance. This planning will likely take place outside of the radiology department, at the hospital or health care organization level.

By way of introduction, Congress vested authority for developing standards for electronic health industry transactions to CMS, if none were legislated by August 1999. No legislation was passed by that deadline and so CMS has now finalized a number of proposed rules. CMS's first final regulation addresses what are known as the transaction elements of the HIPAA administrative simplification provisions, adopting standards for content and format of eight electronic transactions in the health care industry. All health care providers will be able to use the electronic format to bill for their services, and all health plans will be required to accept these standard electronic claims, referral authorizations, and other transactions. [65 Fed. Reg. 50,312 (2000), amending 45 CFR Parts 160 & 162]. Providers and plans must comply with the new rule by October 16, 2002, but the compliance deadline may be extended by a year for plans and providers who submit a report detailing their compliance status and their strategies for reaching compliance within the year.

On August 9, 2002, CMS released modifications to the final HIPAA privacy rule establishing standards for privacy of individually identifiable health information. The modified final rule includes stricter written authorization requirements for using personal health information in marketing, a provision allowing direct treatment providers to use or disclose information without prior written consent, a provision permitting incidental use and disclosure of information, and a transition period allowing an extra year for bringing contracts with business associates into compliance. [Standards for Privacy of Individually Identifiable Health Information, 67 Fed. Reg. 53,182 (2002), amending 45 CFR Parts 160 and 164]

It is critical to note that the statute and its implementing regulations will touch on an extremely broad range of standards. HIPAA and its regulations will impact all aspects of the management of all patient health information, whether electronic, written, or oral, including the safety, security, and integrity of that information. Health information is defined in the final regulations as any oral or recorded information that is created or received by a health care provider, health plan, public health authority, employer, life insurer, school or university, or health care clearinghouse, if that information relates to an individual's past, present, or future physical mental health or condition, provision of health care to an individual, or future payment for providing health care to an individual.

The final privacy regulations protect all patient health information or records that have been maintained or disclosed by a hospital or other provider in any form, whether communicated electronically, on paper, or orally. Under the rule, patient health information generally may not be used or disclosed unless the disclosure is either authorized by the patient or is specifically authorized under HIPAA. Written consent to use or disclosure is not required for direct provider treatment, payment, and health care operations, but authorization requirements apply. Although full compliance with the final regulations is not required until April 14, 2003 (and one year later for small plans), hospitals should already have begun putting the appropriate privacy policies and procedures into place.

HHS has published a final rule on implementation of the HIPAA regulation requiring standardization of the identifying numbers assigned to employers in the health care industry:

- Standard Unique Employer Identifier (formerly National Standard Employer Identifiers). [67 Fed. Reg. 38,009 (2002)]

Two regulations implementing HIPAA requirements that would establish standards for providers to obtain a unique identifier, and that would establish rules for security standards to protect electronic information, remain in the proposal stage:

- Standard Health Care Provider Identifiers [63 Fed. Reg. 25,320 (1998)]
- Security and Electronic Signature Standards [63 Fed. Reg. 43,241 (1998)]

As enacted, HIPAA also included a requirement for a unique personal health care identifier, but HHS and Congress have put the development of such a standard on hold indefinitely. Congress has adopted budget language to ensure that no such standard is adopted without Congress' approval. [HHS Fact Sheet, Administrative Simplification Under HIPAA: National Standards for Transactions, Security and Privacy, October 15, 2002]

PART 2

Joint Commission Survey Questions and Answers

INTRODUCTION

This section presents first-person accounts of the Joint Commission Accreditation of Healthcare Organizations (the Joint Commission) process from the point of view of the radiology department. The following interviews describe the Joint Commission survey experience as a whole, as well as how recently surveyed hospitals demonstrate their performance improvement activities. The following pages detail the concerns of Joint Commission survey teams, including what the surveyors did and didn't ask during their visits, and the innovative methods used in some hospitals to share their performance improvement successes with the surveyors. In addition, several hospitals shared their views on the new Joint Commission survey process that will go into effect in 2004.

SURVEY FOCUS

Question: What did the Joint Commission survey team focus on when they visited your radiology department?

Answers:

Jonathan Brownlee
Director of Imaging
Hollywood Community Hospital
Hollywood, CA
Joint Commission Site Visit: October 2002

The surveyors took a lot of time to check all the licenses, to make sure they are on display in a conspicuous place and current. From the license they made sure all the yearly updates are done—physicals and that sort of thing. They want to know that everyone is working legally.

They looked at the rooms and checked to see that all the preventative maintenances are done correctly, that all the machinery is working properly, and that the machines are licensed as radiation-producing machines. They checked the aprons and the columnators for cracks and holes. The surveyors wanted to see that they were all clean and that we have a log to show the checks have been done.

The surveyors looked for weekly checks on fluoroscopy equipment using a phantom with the same settings. We have to note any deviations, calculate the percentage of deviation, and if it exceeds 5 percent, we must be able to show a service log.

Also, they checked to be sure nothing was under sinks, that there was no food in the area, and that contrasts and controlled substances are stored in locked cabinets. Contrasts used orally should be stored in one place and those used rectally in another place. Intravenous must be in yet another place and locked up.

They also looked at each individual technologist's appearance—the techs must be dressed appropriately for the hospital and be wearing a current dosimetry badge. They looked for us to have a report on all techs' current limits. If any techs are working someplace else, we must have a report from other places they work too.

They checked the log for department meetings, which should be held monthly. They wanted to see that our minutes showed topics covered and what was said. We also keep a communication binder for all memos, both received and sent.

Gary Fammartino, MBA
Director, Radiology
St. Vincent Hospital and Health Care Center, Inc.
Indianapolis, IN
Joint Commission Site Visit: September 2002

Mostly the surveyors focused on the environmental issues. The inspector did do a walk-through and was very concerned with checkoffs for safety devices like crash carts. He also made sure that fire extinguishers were checked and in order. He asked about our cleaning process for ultrasound probes. We explained how we clean it with OPA Cidex. We use the soak cycle, plus protective sheets for any endovaginal work. He also checked our written protocols for the cleaning process.

He was interested in patient privacy and areas where patients were held. We did go through some policies on the confidentiality of the patient and the patient's medical record. His greater concern was the physical layout, as in "Where are your patients held once they're in gowns?" We explained to him that when a patient comes out, they're gowned, they go into a separate area to wait, and right after their procedure they are immediately escorted back to the dressing area.

We're on PACS, so he was very interested in the electronic digital image and how it is secured. The workstations are not in areas where the patients are located. In addition, we have auto-logoff on the workstations so that when a radiologist or tech leaves a station, it will log off within a certain time period. He was extremely interested in the maintenance logs, crash carts, and drug logs sheets. There was a huge focus on that rather than on process improvements.

The surveyor was somewhat interested in procedural sedation and asked a couple of questions about that. We had to supply him with two patients that fit the criteria for reaching that level of procedural sedation, and he then pulled those charts in the medical records area to see how we were administering, monitoring, and recording the procedure.

He was very much interested in the vascular lab, particularly the narcotics and medications log. He checked to make sure those logs correlated with the pharmacy's checkoffs.

Other than that it was pretty benign. We were really surprised that he didn't ask the staff any questions at all. He was much more focused on the physical plant: cleaning and making sure the hallways and exits were not blocked by equipment.

Carol Fincher
Manager
Medical Park Hospital, Inc.
Winston Salem, NC
Joint Commission Site Visit: November 2002

The surveyors' main focus was on our lead aprons. They asked about our inventory of them, how I know when the physicist checks them, and how I know that I have them all. The surveyors examined our documentation as well, making sure that we have all the aprons, that they're checked on an annual basis, and if any don't pass inspection, how we get rid of them.

It was a very quick walk-through that they did here because we're a small hospital, and we don't have any other modalities here except radiology. It was late in the afternoon and they were running behind as well.

Addie Haverfield, ARRT(R)M
Manager, Radiology
Southwestern General Hospital
El Paso, TX
Joint Commission Site Visit: August 2002

Actually, I was surprised because the visit was very brief.

The surveyor wanted to know when the aprons and gloves were last checked, and if we had a record of that (although he did not ask to see the documentation). He also checked the cleanliness of the aprons.

Regarding paperwork for the X-ray chemicals, again he asked if we had documentation of what's in the developer and the fixer (which we did) but didn't ask to see it.

He did not look at any of my peer review information for the radiologists, but he did ask about it. He wanted to know if we did a blank peer review or put a report with it, and we had been putting a report with the jacket. Instead, he wanted us to just file the peer review sheet as "agreed" or "disagreed."

All of the outpatient clinics, including radiology, were written up for not doing follow-up on outpatient biopsies, so we've changed that process.

He focused quite a bit on cleanliness, and we really did well. We do a lot of our own cleaning in radiology, in addition to that done by housekeeping.

He also went into nuclear medicine and asked the technicians a few questions, although he generally spoke with me.

Anonymous
North Texas VA Health Care System
Dallas, TX
Joint Commission Site Visit: August 2002

The surveyors wanted to make sure that we had good labels on everything, from medical gas valves to fire extinguishers, etc. They also asked a lot of questions about signs—they liked that every room in our department had signs asking "Are you pregnant?"

They were also interested in patient flow: were the patients checked in, were they weighed, and who handles the patients at every step that they take through the department. The surveyors checked our transport time from other hospital units to the radiology department; for example, if an inpatient had a 3:00 appointment, do we have to call ahead of time to make sure they're on time?

They also asked to see who was credentialed to do conscious sedation, especially for the special procedures area. They looked at our guidelines and policies regarding conscious sedation and who administers sedation.

The surveyors wanted to make sure that all our oxygen tanks were in carts rather than sitting directly on the ground.

Another question was about crash carts: they asked about the number of carts and if we thought the number was sufficient. We had a total of three in our department and felt that was enough.

The surveyors also wanted to see the biomed log on each crash cart to be sure we were up to date, and they asked us to explain our role in a disaster plan.

Bruce Lauer, MBA, RT(R)
Technical Director
Department of Radiology
The Ohio State University Medical Center
Columbus, OH
Joint Commission Site Visit: October 2002

The surveyor focused heavily on issues we were cited for during the last visit, such as documentation for emergency cart checks. He checked to make sure the documentation was signed off every day and that the locks were checked and the paddles tested. He went through supply drawers and cabinets looking for expired items. He also looked at our separation of internal and external supplies (i.e., to make sure we do not keep topical items next to internal medications).

The surveyor examined the timely completion of our employee evaluations. He checked that we had orientation for employees, that we made sure they were qualified, how we determined they were competent to take X-rays in our facility, and that we had appropriate credentials such as ARRT registration and a state license for each technologist. In Ohio, technologists must be ARRT-registered and licensed from the state. The surveyor also wanted to see documentation that new employees had both a hospital orientation and a department orientation.

He really concentrated on our age-specific competencies, making sure we had competencies for each modality and in each profession (ultrasound, nuclear medicine, etc.), and that we covered all the different age groups. The concern was that we have the criteria in place to address the age groups according to specialty. We also had to demonstrate that the staff knew about the competencies and practiced the competency content. The surveyor questioned the staff to validate the management's explanations.

The doctor who surveyed us asked a number of specific questions about the radiation safety committee and how it functioned. Did we provide reports to specific state and federal agencies? He was also interested in how we alert staff if they have an excessive amount of radiation—how does the badge system work, and how do you explain it to staff? If you have a pregnant technologist, how do you monitor her? What do you do differently? He wanted to know which departments were represented on the committee as well.

He was very interested in our aprons; he would get an apron and ask, "How do I know it's okay to use this?" He wanted to know how we check aprons and document the checks. Another thing he looked at closely was IV contrast, in particular making sure that it was locked up, since it is considered a prescription item. Not only is it necessary to keep the storeroom locked up, but also the daily supply if staff did not have it within their line of sight.

Another area of focus was continuum of care issues with patients. As patients left the floor, how did we get pertinent patient care information from the floor to the rest of the hospital (e.g., reaction to contrast, patient not able to sit up or lie down)?

He focused quite heavily on the physician's involvement in patient assessment, especially just prior to an exam. Physicians normally receive a history and physical prior to invasive surgery. Now it is also required that they do a pre-test reassessment (checking lungs, heart, the basics) prior to the exam. He wanted to see documentation that it was done by a physician, not a nurse. The chart had to show that the physician did sign off in the chart prior to starting the exam.

The surveyors looked for documentation of pain evaluation throughout the hospital. We were asked to provide documentation of this in interventional radiology, as well as documentation of conscious sedation use and that patients returned to pre-test values before being discharged or returned to their room.

We had our clinical engineering staff available, and the surveyor asked how that process works and how often we have our machines checked. Our clinical engineering staff had switched to a PDA system with every piece of radiology equipment loaded in, so they were able to give the surveyor all the information right away: the service record, when service would be due next, the age of the equipment, the preventive maintenance date, and the date the physicist had calibrated that piece of equipment. The surveyor was very impressed with that.

He had a strong interest in nuclear medicine and asked about how we received radionucleotides, how they are checked in by technologists, how we did quality assurance monitors on those coming in, and he asked about the checks in the laboratory at the beginning and end of each day. He also asked about counts to make sure there was no radioactive activity. He wanted the staff to actually demonstrate the process. He wanted to go through the department as a patient would. He asked about some patient privacy/confidentiality issues, such as where dressing rooms are so patients aren't seen walking down the hall.

Judy Mink, RT(R), MPA
Radiology Director
Robinson Memorial Hospital
Ravenna, OH
Joint Commission Site Visit: November 2002

The surveyor wanted to start with a tour of the department. He asked what services we have and if I am responsible for all of them. He wanted to know where patients come into the department, and where outpatients go next. I showed him the male and female dressing rooms and explained that if the patients need to be dressed, they wait there, or sometimes the techs take them back to another waiting area.

He looked into the mammography room, but didn't ask any questions. I took him into the control room for one of our CT scanners, but since there was a patient on the table he did not go in. He asked if we had spiral scanners, which we do. We went into the angio tech work area and quickly looked inside the angio lab. He asked if the previous day's patients were inpatients or outpatients, but he had no other questions in that lab and didn't ask to see any charts. On the way out, he asked about wet darkrooms and the delivery and storage of the chemistry. He asked our manager of special imaging about the stains on the floor, which had resulted from a drain backup a few years ago.

The surveyor noticed the crash cart in the hallway and stopped to check the daily log. We only had one month on the clipboard, so he asked me to pull the previous month's data.

He said he wanted to see any X-ray room, preferably one where we do intravenous pyelograms. I took him into the tech area and there were patients on both tables. He asked if there was a drug box in the room, who checked it, and if it had a lock on it.

In the ultrasound area, he asked the tech about sterilization of transvaginal probes. She showed him the containers that they are transported in back and forth to central sterile, and how they come back so we know they are sterile. He asked if we had PMs on the machines and she said that we did. He didn't ask for documentation.

We went to Nuclear Medicine, where most of the questions were directed to and answered by the nuclear medicine supervisor. First the surveyor wanted to know how many cameras and what type of equipment we have, specifically if we have a dualhead camera. He had a number of questions about the hot lab. He asked if we had a generator, and the supervisor told him we receive unit doses from Mallinckrodt. He asked when doses are delivered and if anyone is here for the first delivery. She (the nuclear medicine supervisor) discussed police and protective services escort. He asked if the couriers know where to put the deliveries, so she showed him the sign indicating the appropriate counter and where cases are left for pickup. He asked how the doses are received. She discussed wipe testing and surveys, and he asked if they were documented. He also asked if we knew what was delivered. She discussed the packing slips and explained disposition records. He asked about assaying doses to ensure accuracy and if that was documented. He wanted to know if we keep track of which patients receive which dose. She discussed return of spent doses to the radiopharmacy. He asked if any were decayed in storage and if this was documented. He also asked about using syringes (these were in an injection tray on top of the hot storage unit), and she indicated that we do make up kits on call—we receive bulk tech. He wanted to know what we do with spent syringes that are not returned to the pharmacy, so she showed him the L-block with sharps container. She told him that when it is three-quarters full, it is sealed and stored in hot storage. He asked how long they are stored and what happens when they are decayed. He also reviewed the hot waste disposal log. He asked if we re-sheath, which we do not.

He asked if there was a spill policy differentiating major from minor spills, and if our spill procedure was posted. He also asked if we had had a minor spill and whether it was documented. He asked what was kept in the refrigerator and looked at the temperature monitoring log. He asked if the external thermometer alarms when the temperature goes out of range, and told us that that we don't have to record the temperature if the alarm is functional. He asked what kind of quality control is done and its frequency.

In my office, during the interview, the surveyor asked her some additional questions: how often the physicist group came, what they reviewed, and if the RSO reviewed the documents; whether we had state inspections and what the findings were; whether we did diagnostic and therapeutic and the hours of availability, staff on call; whether the department chair reviewed the policies and procedures, QC results, and documentation. Other than disposition records, waste storage, and refrigerator temp records, the surveyor did not review written documentation.

He asked our department chair how many radiologists we have and about peer review. He wanted to know if the information got into the radiologists' files.

The surveyor asked if we had teleradiology, which we do. He wanted to know if we had a station here and if each radiologist had one at home and whether we have a digitizer. I told him we don't send plain films, only CT, MRI, nuclear, and ultrasound. He wanted to know whether we monitor appropriate diagnoses for MRIs, and we do.

He asked whether we do conscious sedation and who administers it, whether we do IPs and OPs, and if we follow the policy. He asked what we use to document the information, and one of our nurses from Special Imaging explained the form. He asked what we monitor and the frequency, and if the frequency was that specified in the policy. He asked how we store narcotics, and the nurse told him about the double-lock system. He asked where we recover our patients.

After the interview, he went over to see the narcotics box and was satisfied with it. It was double-locked, so we had to locate the one RN who had the key. He went through the medications in the drawer and asked about two of them. He asked the nurse to explain the sign-out procedure for narcotics, where the sheets go when they are signed out, and who replaces them (pharmacy). He also asked her to open the controlled substance part of the drawer, and he counted the fentanyl and compared it to the count on the sheet. He asked if we had a paper that listed all the drugs in the box and how many should be there. We do, but he didn't ask to see it.

He wanted to know what type of contrast media we use, and I told him we use all non-ionic. He asked me where we got the contrast, if we have it secured, and who is responsible for that. He wanted to know if we pre-medicate patients with known contrast reactions. The nurse told him we have a protocol depending on the patient's report of the reaction, and I told him about the pre-injection checklist and that when the techs discover an allergy, they bring it to the attention of the radiologist, who decides what to do at that point.

The surveyor asked what type of changes we have seen in the department in the last three years, then narrowed it to the last 12 months. He wanted to know what kind of quality control we do since we have a lot of equipment. I told him we have a very detailed plan in place as a result of a state-mandated program which is reviewed yearly by the physicist. We have a QC tech who oversees the program and a variety of procedures, for example, daily processor QC, screen cleaning, film-screen contact tests, darkroom cleaning, and lead apron checks. He asked me if we check the aprons for the whole hospital and if I am responsible for all the X-ray equipment in the hospital. He also wanted to know if I am responsible for the imaging equipment off-site.

His other questions addressed the following:

- whether we monitor repeat rates
- if we had a radiation safety committee
- how we monitor radiation exposure for staff. He also asked what company we use and what happens with the reports.

- whether we subscribe to ALARA
- what we do for excessive exposures
- if we monitor contrast reactions and if they are reported to the pharmacy

Throughout the departmental tour, he checked several fire extinguishers for the dates they were last checked.

Ray Poston, BS, RT, RTT
Radiology Manager
Deaconess Hospital
Evansville, IN
Joint Commission Site Visit: August 2002

The thing they really focused on was our crash carts. They looked at the pediatric paddles on the equipment, at how many crash carts we had within the department, and at our documentation to make sure the carts were checked daily. They also inquired as to crash carts in certain areas (such as in areas not used over the weekend) to make sure those carts were also up to date in their documentation. They wanted to see documentation that if an area not normally open on the weekend was used, that the crash cart was checked prior to patients coming to that area.

The surveyors were interested in how often the radiologists were reviewed regarding their second readings/interpretations. For example, if an ED physician did a first reading on a film and the radiologist did the second reading, they wanted to know how we addressed any differences between the readings, and whether we had documentation to show that.

They were interested in what kind of program we had in MRI regarding zones; they wanted us to ensure that patients could not enter an area carrying metal objects that could interfere with MRIs.

The surveyors asked about nuclear medicine and about the receipt and disposal of radioactive isotopes. They wanted to know how the radioactive isotopes were brought into the hospital, who received the shipment, was it checked in, and how was it disposed of if we didn't use it. They wanted to see the paperwork that showed that information.

They were also interested in our film repeat rates.

Judy Sikes, PhD
Director of Accreditation and Medical Staff Services
Parkview Medical Center
Pueblo, CO
Joint Commission Site Visit: October 2002

The physician surveyor didn't really inspect everything. He got a sample of our departmental staff in a room and asked them questions for about 45 minutes. We had the radiology director, assistant radiology director, two radiologists, and a couple of techs present. Most of his questions were general enough that if anyone had practiced at all, they would have done well.

He asked about competency and other general questions, such as how we know that a doctor can order a test if he or she is not on staff.

He also asked whether we use teleradiology. We don't, but we do have a digitized system set up so that if our ED physician has a question in the middle of the night, he or she can ship the image to the radiologist's home computer and get some assistance with it. What the surveyor was getting at was whether we knew the physician was competent for teleradiology, but since we only used the system for staff physicians, that didn't affect us.

The surveyor wanted to know how often the physicists came in to check things. These were just basic systems questions.

Sherry Spragens, RT(R), ARDMS(A)
Director of Radiology
Rockcastle Hospital and Respiratory Care Center, Inc.
Mount Vernon, KY
Joint Commission Site Visit: August 2002

It was a very brief visit. The surveyor asked about our patient safety efforts and report turnaround times, but he did not ask to see any documentation.

Andrea Stevens
Manager of Diagnostic Imaging
MacNeal Hospital
Berwyn, IL
Joint Commission Site Visit: July 2002

The surveyors focused on nuclear medicine. Those questions were answered by the physicist. They wanted to know how we maintain our records. They asked a lot about interventional radiology; those questions were answered by our chairman. All patient charts were reviewed within the hospital chart committee. Human resources and the employee files were reviewed within the human resource committee.

He did want to know about our contract labor agency technologists, both how we checked on their competencies and that we kept their employee files within this department.

They reviewed contrast storage. They asked about the contrasts and how they are stored in all areas; in the interventional lab, the surveyors wanted to see the locked up drugs and how the nurse documented usage. They checked to make sure needles and syringes were locked. In CT and the diagnostic lab they made sure all our contrasts, needles, and syringes were locked.

They reviewed staff education and how staff competencies were managed; I explained the process to them. He didn't ask to see a lot, but there was a lot of discussion.

The surveyors checked the crash carts, making sure they were signed off and properly locked and that the dates were all correct. There were certain areas that he wasn't able to check during the initial walk-through because a patient was there and we had to protect patient confidentiality.

Patient confidentiality was a major focus. They checked to make sure there was nothing lying around with patients' names on it. They checked the front desk and all the areas that patients would be able to see, making sure that there were no lists, schedules, or requisitions with patient names on them. We also showed them that we had all our contract labor technologists sign our confidentiality policy.

When surveyors arrive, I have an entourage that includes the physicist, head radiologist, leads from all the departments, and staff director. The surveyors didn't talk to the staff that much.

PERFORMANCE IMPROVEMENT

Question: How did you demonstrate performance improvement to the Joint Commission?

Answers:

Jonathan Brownlee
Director of Imaging
Hollywood Community Hospital
Hollywood, CA
Joint Commission Site Visit: October 2002

You have to show indicators, data acquisition, the performance improvement plan, how you put the plan in effect, and the results of the plan, and that you tried. It's not necessary to be successful, but you have to show that you made the effort. Some people in the hospital put up storyboards or displays. I publish annual reports with graphs/charts, numbers, etc., in booklet form, so I just pulled out those reports for the surveyors.

We just give them the information they want, nothing more. The surveyors don't have time for dog and pony shows.

Gary Fammartino, MBA
Director, Radiology
St. Vincent Hospital and Health Care Center, Inc.
Indianapolis, IN
Joint Commission Site Visit: September 2002

We actually steered him toward our performance improvement efforts because we're proud of them, and he was so focused on the equipment and physical environment. He did ask a couple questions on key performance improvement processes that we were focusing in on, but not until the very end of the visit.

He really liked our process called "pass the doves." The symbol of our hospital is three doves representing body, mind, and spirit. When a patient comes to radiology from the registration side, we fill out a "dove card" at our front desk with a picture of a dove on the front and on the back the patient's name and time that they came. Everywhere they go, the dove goes with them, and is handed off from associate to associate. This way the patient is escorted throughout our system, and each time they reach a new area, the time is filled in when they arrive. They never really see the card, but the staff keep passing it along. Once they arrive for a procedure, a timer is set for 15 minutes from their scheduled appointment time. If they're not taken care of within that 15 minutes, someone actively finds out what's going on, talks to the patient, and resets the appointment with the patient's approval. If the alarm goes off again, a tech would come out if there is a further delay, and explain it to the patient. That seldom happens, however. The process has really gotten everyone in tune that we want to move the patient along. When the patient is seen, the card goes from clerical to the tech; if the patient then goes to ultrasound, for example, they're escorted along with their card and a new alarm is set. We're passing the care of that patient from one associate to another. We have had zero complaints since introducing this, so we're trying to roll the system out hospitalwide. We actually demonstrated it for the surveyor, and our staff explained the process as they went along.

We also do a quarterly patient survey, juggling the dates so they're not always on the same months. We ask questions about professionalism, courtesy, how were delays handled, etc., so we showed the surveyor those results.

Addie Haverfield, ARRT(R)M
Manager, Radiology
Southwestern General Hospital
El Paso, TX
Joint Commission Site Visit: August 2002

He did ask about our performance improvement projects and one of my first projects was not to let unread films leave the emergency department. The discussion was very conversational; he did not request any documentation.

Anonymous
North Texas VA Health Care System
Dallas, TX
Joint Commission Site Visit: August 2002

We created a storyboard showing how we distribute our images to the radiologists. We also had recently expanded our PAC system in radiology to other services, so we treated that as a performance improvement project as well.

Bruce Lauer, MBA, RT(R)
Technical Director
Department of Radiology
The Ohio State University Medical Center
Columbus, OH
Joint Commission Site Visit: October 2002

One surveyor addressed quality assurance activities in a very conversational way. He asked, "What are you most proud of in your department? What have you done to improve customer service and patient care? What types of things are you working on?"

We had a few storyboards we were going to present and some storyboards hanging in the department, but he really wanted the staff to articulate the projects.

We had report turnaround time available, and documentation of our improvements in that area. We're filmless here, so we could show him where we streamlined those processes.

Judy Mink, RT(R), MPA
Radiology Director
Robinson Memorial Hospital
Ravenna, OH
Joint Commission Site Visit: November 2002

He asked what our performance improvement initiatives were, and I just listed a few of the things that we did hospitalwide. There were a number of storyboards of group initiatives. I had my PI manual showing all the minutes from the meetings. It's broken down into each item that we monitor, so I could have shown him the data we collect and improvements that resulted from that.

Ray Poston, BS, RT, RTT
Radiology Manager
Deaconess Hospital
Evansville, IN
Joint Commission Site Visit: August 2002

Basically, the surveyors asked what kind of quality assurance projects we were doing, whether each area had its own quality assurance project, and where the documentation was located. I had each one of my areas represented when we sat down, and my staff brought our books with them so that the reviewer could look through and start asking questions.

Judy Sikes, PhD
Director of Accreditation and Medical Staff Services
Parkview Medical Center
Pueblo, CO
Joint Commission Site Visit: October 2002

The surveyor asked what PI activities the radiology staff has been involved in as a department, and how the physicians get involved in PI activities. He was looking for whether physicians were actively involved, or if they just rubber-stamped staff efforts.

The surveyor did not ask for any documentation in the radiology department, but the survey team looked at performance improvement in the document review portion of the survey. Every department director has to submit two reports each year on two projects they're doing, so we had documentation available to show the surveyors. Radiology discussed two projects; the first had to do with over-reads. The emergency department physicians will often do a first read on X-rays, because our radiologists don't work the midnight shift unless it's an emergency. Then a radiologist reads the X-ray the following morning as a quality assurance check.

The second project dealt with what we call "ER/TR"—someone stationed in the emergency department but who does the transport of patients to radiology.

As soon as the ED staff knows a radiology test is needed and the patient is ready to go, they notify radiology. The radiology tech then asks them to bring the patient down right away, or after a certain length of time if needed, because ED patients can't be left waiting in radiology. This way the radiology tech staff doesn't spend a lot of time waiting for the patients to be ready and actually bringing them down. It optimizes the time the tech spends actually doing the diagnostic testing rather than transporting patients and/or standing around waiting for them.

Sherry Spragens, RT(R), ARDMS(A)
Director of Radiology
Rockcastle Hospital and Respiratory Care Center, Inc.
Mount Vernon, KY
Joint Commission Site Visit: August 2002

The surveyor did not ask about performance improvement in the radiology department; that was discussed separately with the performance improvement committee for the hospital.

Andrea Stevens
Manager of Diagnostic Imaging
MacNeal Hospital
Berwyn, IL
Joint Commission Site Visit: July 2002

He did not ask very much about performance improvement. I did explain the process that we use in our department for PI, but the hospital has a PI committee, and they have a master book that shows the PI in all areas of the hospital, which gives the surveyors documentation if they look for it. They did not look at the policy and procedure manuals.

THE NEW SURVEY PROCESS

Question: Are you aware of the new Joint Commission survey process (going into effect in 2004)? If so, how do you anticipate adjusting your processes?

Answers:

Gary Fammartino, MBA
Director, Radiology
St. Vincent Hospital and Health Care Center, Inc.
Indianapolis, IN
Joint Commission Site Visit: September 2002

We've had a pretty thorough inservice on the administrative side for upper-level management—a general explanation, two or three programs giving an overview. We really haven't communicated it with the staff yet because we didn't want to confuse them on what was the focus for the current survey. The surveyors themselves were explaining the change and refocus to us. We're gearing up for the next survey. Our inservice was more of an "fyi," keeping up with some of the Joint Commission publications, which we circulate throughout our organization. All the Joint Commission standards, human resources responsibilities, issues, and policies and procedures are on our intranet, so staff have access to nearly everything within that environment.

Judy Sikes, PhD
Director of Accreditation and Medical Staff Services
Parkview Medical Center
Pueblo, CO
Joint Commission Site Visit: October 2002

I was reviewing some of the drafts for the 2004 standards, and I think the new process will help somewhat to limit the variation among the surveyors. I hope that the Joint Commission continues to work on surveyor variation. I have to give them credit, because I do know they're trying. I have done consultant work with a lot of hospitals, and the biggest complaint I hear is about surveyor variation.

Andrea Stevens
Manager of Diagnostic Imaging
MacNeal Hospital
Berwyn, IL
Joint Commission Site Visit: July 2002

I did receive notice of an upcoming seminar from the AHRA regarding the new regulations. We're not ready to be inspected again for a while, but I want to make sure our leads stay on top of things so that we don't scramble.

Hospital Accreditation Standards Analysis

INTRODUCTION

Part 3 of the *Radiology Department Compliance Manual* analyzes the standards in the *Comprehensive Accreditation Manual for Hospitals: The Official Handbook* (CAMH), published by the Joint Commission on Accreditation of Healthcare Organizations and updated quarterly. Part 3 was prepared based on the standards updated through the November 2002 supplement to the CAMH, which includes the standards that will be surveyed in 2002.

The information in Part 3 is presented in a chart format for easy reference. The chart format contains five columns: Standard, Comments, Evidence, Staff Questions, and Reference.

- The **Standard** column designates those particular Joint Commission standards that uniquely apply to the radiology department.
- The **Comments** column provides a brief explanation of each standard and special considerations for the radiology department.
- The **Evidence** column outlines specific types of evidence that may be used to show radiology department compliance with the standard. The types of evidence suggested include both written documentation review and physical inspection.
- The **Staff Questions** column lists detailed questions to use in preparing staff for the Joint Commission survey.
- The **Reference** column indexes sample forms, policies and procedures, and other items in Part 4 that can be used to demonstrate compliance with the standard.
- The **LINK** provides a cross-reference to related Joint Commission standards in other chapters. This serves as a key to recognize opportunities for streamlining compliance by avoiding duplication of efforts.

PATIENT RIGHTS AND ORGANIZATION ETHICS

Standard	Comments	Evidence	Staff Questions	Reference

RI.1 through RI.1.1	Patients' rights to treatment or service are protected, and patients are involved in all aspects of care, including the informed consent process, pain management, and disclosure of sentinel events. Standards applicable organization-wide. Require that hospitals address ethical issues in patient care.	• Interviews with patients, families, and staff
		• Open and closed medical records
		  – Admission database
		  – Surgical/invasive procedure consent forms
		  – Progress notes
		• Policies
		  – All patient rights policies and procedures
		  – Informed consent policy
		• Code of ethics
		• Staff orientation and continuing education materials, training records
		• Ethics committee minutes or evidence of functioning of ethics resolution process
		• Patient and family education committee
		• Minutes of ethics committee
		• Educational materials distributed or accessible to patients and families regarding patient rights, responsibilities, advance directives, accessing the ethics resolution process, etc.
		• Policies and procedures addressing ethical issues
		• Policies for transferring patients
			• Is the radiology staff familiar with the policies and procedures of the hospital dealing with ethical issues?
			• Describe how staff learn about patient rights and responsibilities.
			• Have you participated in any recent inservices?
			• What is the procedure staff follow when the organization cannot provide the care a patient requests? Can you discuss an example of such an incident and how staff responded?
			• Are medical records reviewed for compliance with patient rights policies and procedures? Who performs the review? How often?
			• What ethical issues have you targeted for improvement?
			• If you have an ethical patient concern, what procedure is followed?
				4–1 to 4–5
				4–14
				4–20
				4–25
				4–28 to 4–30
				4–36

RI.1.2 through RI.1.2.1	These standards must be implemented hospital-wide. They refer to the informed consent process for patients. Patients should be involved in all aspects of care, including pain management, formulating advanced directives, and care at the end of life.	• Executed consent forms • Staff, patient, and family interviews • Consent forms designed and written in terms/language the patient can understand • Policy on informed consent • Sample computer-generated consent form	• How do you involve patients in making care decisions? • Who is responsible for ensuring that patients make informed decisions about their treatment options? • How is patient understanding and consent documented?	4–2 4–6 4–13 4–20 4–25 4–28 to 4–30

continues

Patient Rights and Organization Ethics

Standard	Comments	Evidence	Staff Questions	Reference
RI.1.2 through RI.1.2.1 *continued*		• Waiver of information of consent • Authorization to disclose medical information • QA performed to ensure compliance with consent issues • Patient education handouts regarding procedures • Specific informed consent forms to include consent for contrast material injection • Sample hospital informed consent for injection of intravenous contrast materials, permission to use radioisotopes, consent to radiographic material	• Show me your consent forms for various procedures, tests, treatments, or patient types. • What mechanism do you have in place for obtaining informed consent from non-English speaking patients? How do you know that the patient understands? For radiation treatment areas: • How do you support patients' decision making at the end of life? • How are end-of-life issues communicated to caregivers?	
RI.1.2.1.1 through RI.1.2.1.5	Concern the implementation of organizationwide policies and procedures for addressing the rights of patients asked to participate in an investigational study/ clinical trial.	• Staff, patient, and family interviews • Policy on investigational drugs, clinical trials • Open and closed medical records • Executed consent forms signed, relevant discussions documented • Educational material distributed to patients on investigational drugs	• Who obtains consent for patients participating in research projects? Where will this be documented? • What information is given to patients participating in investigational studies or clinical trials? • What happens when a patient refuses to participate in a research project/ clinical trial? How does this affect the patient's access to services? • For patients returning for services (inpatient, outpatient), how do you verify that research consents have been signed?	
RI.1.2.2	References informing patients and, when appropriate, their families about the outcomes of care, including unanticipated	• Patient, family, staff, and physician interviews • Policies and procedures on communication of outcomes to patients	• What is the radiology department policy regarding communication with patients about adverse outcomes?	

continues

Patient Rights and Organization Ethics

Standard	Comments	Evidence	Staff Questions	Reference
RI.1.2.2 *continued*	outcomes. This would include informing the patient if he or she has experienced an event that was not expected such as medical error or complication.	• Open and closed medical records • Staff orientation and continuing education • Patient satisfaction surveys/results • Medical staff bylaws, rules, and regulations	• What information is given to patients or their families regarding outcomes of treatment or procedures when those outcomes differ significantly from the anticipated outcomes? • Who speaks to the patient regarding unanticipated outcomes? How are unanticipated outcomes reported inhouse? Out of house? Who is notified?	
RI.1.2.3	Relates to the family's role in the patient's consent and the patient's role in this care. Standard is implemented hospitalwide. Care may require that people other than the patient be involved in health care decision making (e.g., patient is an emancipated minor or patient lacks mental or physical capacity). If the patient cannot make health care decisions, a surrogate decision maker is identified.	• Interviews with staff, patients, and families • Open and closed medical records • Policies related to the following: guardianship, family/surrogate decision makers' involvement in care decisions, access to legal counsel regarding care decisions, and patient and family education • Staff orientation and continuing education • Documents recording surrogate decision makers or identification of active family members	• When applicable, does the family or surrogate engage in the patient's care decisions? • What is the policy when the patient does not have the mental or physical capacity to make care decisions? • How do you know who is the surrogate decision maker for patients with a mental or physical condition that impairs decision making?	4–2 4–6 4–21 to 4–22
RI.1.2.4	Standard concerns ethical dilemmas that may arise during the admission, treatment, or discharge of a patient.	• Patient, family, staff interviews • Open and closed medical records • Patient rights policies and procedures, specifically resolving conflicts in care decisions/ethical dilemmas • Minutes of ethics committee review of consultation records	• Please describe how conflicts in care (e.g., end-of-life decisions) are resolved. • Is there a committee and/or individual responsible for coordinating the ethics consultation process? • Who can consult the ethics committee? • How do you access the ethics committee?	4–1 to 4–6

continues

Patient Rights and Organization Ethics

Standard	Comments	Evidence	Staff Questions	Reference
RI.1.2.4 *continued*		• Patient and family education policies, materials, flowsheets (e.g., brochure on access to ethics resolution process) • Patient satisfaction surveys/results • Care at the end of life policies	• Can you recall a situation that required an ethics consultation? Where would this conflict and resolution be documented? • What is your mechanism for informing patients, families, and staff about your ethics resolution process?	
RI.1.2.5	References patients' right to formulate an advanced directive and have it carried out. This standard applies to all admitted adult patients, despite setting/location.	• Examples of advance directives • Policy on advanced directives • Advanced directive documentation forms • Admission database • Policies and procedures related to advance directives	• If inpatient: If the patient has an advanced directive, is it available for use by caregivers? • If outpatient: Can staff describe the process by which patients who request information on advanced directives receive it? • For patients with advanced directive: How is the presence of an advance directive communicated to you if the patient is an inpatient? How do you know a patient has an advanced directive?	4–2 to 4–5
RI.1.2.6 through RI.1.2.9	These standards address resuscitation, life-sustaining treatment, end-of-life care, and pain assessment and management. They should be implemented hospitalwide. In the absence of an advance directive, and in accord with applicable state law, the patient's wishes may be documented within the patient's chart.	• Patient and staff interviews • Open and closed medical records • Documentation of staff orientation • Records and content outlines of staff continuing education materials • Policies and procedures: – Advance directives – Forgoing or withdrawing life-sustaining treatment – Do not resuscitate (DNR) orders	• Describe how you inquire about patients' advance directive status. • What happens if a patient comes into the radiology department with an advance directive? • How is a patient's advance directive information communicated to the members of the care team? • What advance directive educational materials are distributed to patients? • Describe your procedure for assisting patients who do not have an advance	4–2 to 4–5

continues

Patient Rights and Organization Ethics

Standard	Comments	Evidence	Staff Questions	Reference
RI.1.2.6 through RI.1.2.9 *continued*		– Effective pain management, including reassessment – Care at the end of life • Treatment algorithms, clinical pathways • Patient and family educational material available concerning patient rights (e.g., advance directives, care at end of life, accessing spiritual support, etc.) • Policy regarding patient family education on pain management using medications and other pain management techniques • Patient education materials on pain assessment and management	directive but wish to create one. • If the advance directive is not with the patient, how is the patient assisted in having the advanced directive carried out? • Describe your policies and procedures for withholding resuscitative services. What are the legal requirements for your organization in your state? • What training is provided to staff regarding end-of-life ethical and legal issues? • Describe how end-of-life decisions are made. Are attempts to treat pain, provide comfort, and meet spiritual needs documented? • Describe how patients' pain is assessed by radiology staff. When does reassessment occur, if applicable? • How do you ensure that patients' pain is managed while in your area? What methods are available for ensuring communication of unmet needs to the primary care team? • Are there educational programs for staff regarding pain assessment and treatment? • Are DNR orders accompanied by a corresponding progress note by the physician?	
RI.1.3 through RI.1.3.6.1.1 **(LINK TX.1.2.1)**	Standards address patient needs for confidentiality and privacy, security, complaint management, pastoral care, and	• Staff, patient, family interviews • Open and closed medical records • Staff orientation and continuing education documentation	• Describe the mechanisms you use to ensure privacy for patients during history taking, examination, and treatment. • How do you keep patient information confidential?	4–78 4–82 to 4–84

continues

Patient Rights and Organization Ethics

Standard	Comments	Evidence	Staff Questions	Reference
RI.1.3 through RI.1.3.6.1.1 **(LINK TX.1.2.1)** *continued*	communication. They outline patients' right to communication and information including mechanisms used when communication is limited for clinical reasons. Organizational policies address how these rights are supported. Areas of particular importance include ensuring access to translation services for foreign language or services for the hearing or speech impaired.	• Patient satisfaction data, surveys, results (e.g., complaint tracking) • Performance improvement studies concerning privacy, confidentiality, security, complaints, pastoral care, and/or communication enhancements • Patient and family education materials distributed on patient rights, pastoral care, access to advocates, ethics committee, etc. • Documentation of patients' rights to privacy, security, and confidentiality of information • Evidence of appropriate referrals for pastoral/spiritual counseling • Evidence of informing patients and patients' families of patients' status and treatment • Evidence of informing patients and patients' families of the right to complain and how to access the resolution process established by the organization • Documentation or calendar of training provided to staff on protecting patient rights • Review of radiology operations for compliance with organizational policies • Policies for security and protection in circumstances involving violence and/or abuse	• What is your mechanism to resolve patient and family complaints? • How are patients' needs for spiritual or pastoral counseling assessed and provided, when appropriate? • How do you protect patients' safety while in your area? Are there any special protections for infants and children? • What protective procedures are followed to ensure the safety of victims of domestic abuse or assault? • What procedures do you follow to secure patient valuables and other possessions? • What is your policy for allowing family members to accompany patients in the radiology department? • When applicable, how do you explain restrictions to a patient's rights when required for therapeutic reasons? • How do you communicate with patients who are deaf or speak another language? • How do you access translation services? • What process do you follow for patients in need of pastoral care or spiritual services (especially in radiation treatment areas)? • How are patients informed of their right to have complaints heard? • How does the organization ensure that all	

continues

Patient Rights and Organization Ethics

Standard	Comments	Evidence	Staff Questions	Reference
RI.1.3 through RI.1.3.6.1.1 (LINK TX.1.2.1) *continued*		*Site inspections and observations* • Sign in boards for others' ability to determine patient's name and reason for visit • Examination areas • Use of curtains and partitions without compromising monitoring of patient condition and safety • Patient remaining covered during treatment • Patient surveys/ comment boxes for protection of confidential information • Patient logs, computer monitors, and communication boards for patient identifiers accessible to non-staff • Patient records are secure	Medicare recipients have received a copy of "An Important Message from Medicare"?	
RI.1.4	Each patient receives a written statement of his or her rights. The radiology department is responsible for implementing organizationwide policies and procedures supporting patient rights.	• Patient rights policies, procedures • Staff, patient, family & interviews • Written copy of patient rights and responsibilities appropriate to patient's language, age, and level of understanding for common patient populations • Posted copy of same in the department • Availability of written copy of rights for admitted patients • Educational resources (e.g., patient education channel reviewing patient rights)	• Describe your procedures for informing patients of their rights and responsibilities. • How do you communicate these rights if the patient speaks another language, cannot read, or is hearing or sight impaired?	4–2 to 4–5

continues

Patient Rights and Organization Ethics

Standard	Comments	Evidence	Staff Questions	Reference
RI.1.5	Addresses the rights of patients involved in research, investigational, or clinical trials. Applies organizationwide but only for those patients participating in research.	• Documents supporting informed consent process for research • Policy and procedure for patient participation in research • Minutes of IRB		

PATIENT ASSESSMENT

Standard	Comments	Evidence	Staff Questions	Reference
PE.1 through PE.1.1 (LINK PE.4.1)	Radiology department policies and procedures for assessment should be consistent with organizationwide standards. Standards concern performing a thorough initial assessment of patient care needs. Assessment includes information on nutritional and functional status.	• Open and closed records indicating patient assessments for physical, psychological, social status, and further assessments (when indicated) • Radiology department assessment policies and procedures, forms • Clinical pathways, algorithms for assessment • Orientation, continuing education materials • Translation services availability for performing assessments	• What assessments are conducted in the radiology department? • By whom? • Where would you find initial assessment data to assist you in the care of the patient? • Do data differ by discipline and if so, where is the discipline-specific information located? • Where would you find information on a patient's functional ability before assisting them onto an exam table?	4–6 to 4–14
PE.1.4 (LINK TX.1.2, TX.1.3)	Requires assessment of pain for all patients, not only patients at the end of life. The scope of assessment and treatment is based on the care setting and services provided.	• Documentation of assessment and intervention in open and closed medical records • Staff interviews • Organizational and department-specific policies regarding pain assessment • Clinical pathways or clinical practice guidelines • Documentation of staff orientation and educational materials re: pain management • Pain assessment system or tools allowing documentation of each pain site • Patient and family education materials • Patient interviews	• Please describe your pain assessment protocol (for children, adults, cognitively impaired patients, elderly patients). • How were you trained in pain management? • How do you record pain assessment findings? • How do you measure a patient's response to pain management interventions? Do you use specific pain scales, show examples? • For patients receiving interventional radiology or radiation therapy, what is the process for pain assessment and management?	4–7 4–9
PE.1.5 and PE.1.5.1 (LINK PE.8)	Relates to performing tests to determine patients' health or treatment needs. The radiology department will provide relevant test results, such as diagnostic testing.	• Organizational and department-specific policies regarding testing and reporting procedures and protocols • Access to testing, time frames for testing	• Is each study or treatment pursuant to a properly executed physician order? • Is there adequate clinical information provided to correctly complete and/or interpret the study?	4–14 4–23 4–31 4–35 4–51 4–77

continues

Patient Assessment

Standard	Comments	Evidence	Staff Questions	Reference
PE.1.5 and PE.1.5.1 (LINK PE.8) *continued*	Clinicians requesting study provide, in writing, relevant information needed to perform and interpret the study properly. Apply to any and all departments where diagnostic testing occurs.	• Testing order forms • Procedure for coordinating after-hours exams with the nursing unit and on-call technologist • Performance of diagnostic imaging services • Performance improvement studies of availability of clinical information at the time of study.	• When are essential diagnostic services available? Are *diagnostic* services provided 24/7? How does the hospital provide these services?	
PE.1.6 through PE.1.7.1.1 (LINK CC.6.1, IM.7.5, 2)	Initial assessments are completed within 24 hours of admission following guidelines established by the hospital.	• Patient and staff interviews • Organizational and department-specific discharge planning plans, policies, and procedures • Open and closed medical records • Clinical pathways, standards of care, algorithms • Initial assessment database • Policies and procedures regarding assessment • Questionnaires and safety checklists for specific image studies • Discharge instructions given to outpatients for invasive procedures in radiology	• What is the required time frame for completion of initial assessment forms? How do you obtain clinical information prior to this time frame? • Does the department complete any assessments? • Do they cover, at minimum, data related to providing high quality studies in a safe manner? • Who completes the assessments? • Does your department use information/questionnaire sheets for procedures? • Are patients screened for allergies or contraindications before giving them intravenous (IV) contrast? • What questions do you ask females of childbearing age? • What procedures require discharge instructions?	4–7 4–9 4–18 4–23 4–26 4–27
PE.1.8 through PE.1.8.4 (LINK TX.2–TX.2.4.1)	Relate to all procedures and locations that utilize anesthesia or sedation. Require presence of relevant diagnostic tests prior to procedure. Prior to	• Staff interviews • Policies and procedures related to the following, if applicable: sedation, preanesthesia assessment practices	• When is a consent form required to be signed for use of anesthesia or sedation? • What types of anesthesia/sedation may be administered here?	4–13 4–37

continues

Patient Assessment

Standard	Comments	Evidence	Staff Questions	Reference
PE.1.8 through PE.1.8.4 **(LINK TX.2– TX.2.4.1)** *continued*	administration of sedation or analgesia, a two-step assessment process is conducted, a plan formulated, and ongoing assessment continues to protect patient safety. Includes allowances for emergencies in which a physician note may replace a standard history and physical for surgery or invasive procedures.	• Open and closed medical records • Medical staff privileges in anesthesia for radiology physicians • Performance improvement monitoring regarding moderate sedation, anesthesia practices • Progress notes referencing plan for sedation/analgesia • Procedure forms denoting pre sedation/analgesia assessment *and* reassessment just prior to induction (two-step assessment process). • Procedure flowsheets including reassessment at appropriate intervals and criteria for discharge • Policy and procedures regarding criteria for discharge following sedation/analgesia	• What type of training have you had in administering conscious sedation? Moderate or deep sedation, if applicable? • How do you care for a patient who has just received conscious sedation? Moderate or deep sedation? What do you document? • What performance improvement data are collected in monitoring the use of conscious sedation, or other sedation, if applicable, in your organization? Do you receive feedback on your use of sedation in the radiology department? • How do you know which physicians have the credentials to perform procedures in your area?	
PE.1.9	Address identification of possible victims of abuse. Basis for radiologist role in identifying possible victims if obvious signs of abuse are noted on radiographs.	• Staff and patient interviews • Open and closed medical records • Staff records indicating attendance at mandatory orientation, continuing education sessions • Policy on reporting to protective services (children and family services, senior services) • Evidence of compliance with the organization's abuse policies, procedures, criteria, reporting procedures • Assessment tools designed to document domestic, child, elder abuse	• What training have you received to assist you in identifying victims of abuse? • Can you describe your screening mechanism for identifying victims of abuse (e.g., elder, child, sexual, adult violence, etc.)? Who performs further assessments, if needed? • How have you been educated on abuse issues? • What is the hospital policy regarding victims of abuse? • How do you deal with comments made by patients during an exam that raise concerns about abuse or neglect?	

continues

Patient Assessment

Standard	Comments	Evidence	Staff Questions	Reference
PE.1.9 *continued*		• List of private and public community agencies that provide assistance for victims of abuse	• How do you record the interaction?	
PE.1.11 through 1.15.2	Applicable only to areas that perform waived testing such as blood glucose monitoring, hemoglobin measures, etc.	• Policies designating whether tests are used for screening or definitive purposes • List of individuals or job classifications of those authorized to perform the waived test • Procedures for performing testing including quality control or calibration methods • Logs of quality control data for waived testing and results of patient studies	• Who can perform waived testing in this department? (Question usually focused on type of test used in department) • Is the test used for screening purposes or for purposes of diagnosis? • How did you become proficient in the use of that test? • Has your competency been validated for those tests used for definitive purposes?	
PE.2 through PE.3.1 **(LINK PE.4, PE.4.1, TX.1, TX.1.2, IM.7.2, IM.7.4)**	Address reassessment of patients to meet their continuing care needs. Require assessment at points in care designated in policy as appropriate to scope of care, treatment, and needs of individuals. Applicable to the radiology department depending on type of patient, condition, care received, and procedure performed.	• Radiology department policies, procedures that include scope and frequency of assessment/reassessment • Monitoring of compliance with medical staff bylaws, rules, and regulations • Open and closed medical records • Procedure and assessment forms for monitoring patients during or following procedures • Policies, procedures, standards of care, or care algorithms outlining care of patients with defined conditions • Open and closed medical records • Interdisciplinary progress notes, forms, flowsheets, care plans • Policies or mechanisms	• When are patients reassessed? • What data and information are collected as part of the reassessment? • Describe how various disciplines collaborate to prioritize special patient care needs.	

continues

Patient Assessment

Standard	Comments	Evidence	Staff Questions	Reference
PE.2 through PE.3.1 **(LINK PE.4, PE.4.1, TX.1, TX.1.2, IM.7.2, IM.7.4)** *continued*		for multidisciplinary process for care and planning • Scope of care identifying staff responsibilities		
PE.4 through PE.4.2 **(LINK PE.1– PE.1.1)**	Scope of assessment performed by each discipline must be defined in writing.	• Policies and procedures regarding the discipline, scope, and frequency of assessment • Clinical pathways and guidelines • Patient assessment policies, procedures, and protocols by discipline • Open and closed medical records	• Describe how you document the scope of assessment and care for patients.	4–6 to 4–17
PE.5 through PE.8 **(LINK PE.1.9)**	Address assessment process for special patient populations, namely, infants and children, patients with emotional or behavioral disorders, patients with substance abuse issues, and victims of alleged or suspected abuse and neglect.	• Staff interviews • Open and closed medical records • Policies and procedures describing the discipline, scope, frequency, age-specific criteria, and condition assessment elements utilized in the radiology department • Policy on responsibilities for collecting, safeguarding, and releasing evidentiary material(s) • Staff records linking responsibilities for special population assessments and evidence of training • Assessment algorithms, clinical pathways, documentation guidelines	• Describe the assessment process for infants, children, and adolescent patients. • For the assessment you provide, how do they differ for special populations? • How do you safeguard any evidence collected in the assessment process, especially in suspected abuse or neglect cases? • What procedures are in place for radiology's role in assessment of special patient populations?	4–51 4–55 4–73 4–74 4–76

continues

Patient Assessment

Standard	Comments	Evidence	Staff Questions	Reference
PE.5 through PE.8 **(LINK PE.1.9)** *continued*		• Forms or assessment tools for gathering data to meet the needs of special patient populations • Screening checklists for studies in children or mentally challenged		

CARE OF PATIENTS

Standard	Comments	Evidence	Staff Questions	Reference
TX.1 through TX.1.2 (LINK PE.1– PE.1.4, PI.1–PI.1.1)	Refer to individualizing patient care plans to meet the needs of patients served. Expectations for a multidisciplinary process focused on meeting patient needs and setting primary and other goals are set forth.	• Scope of services documents including admission and care criteria • Open and closed medical records • Documents reflecting process for goal setting and plan formation. May include standards of care, care algorithms, or care protocols. • Guidelines for assessment and care of patients with specific conditions, disorders, or injuries, and patient groups, such as geriatric, adult, pediatric, pregnant, cognitively or physically impaired victims of abuse or assault (sexual, domestic, child, and elder), and those with behavioral health or substance abuse disorders. • Policy for nursing care in medical imaging • All policies and procedures that address assessment, care of patients, and transfer or discharge • Policy and procedures for patient care and safety responsibilities • ED radiological exams policy and procedure • Policy and procedure for the appropriateness of exams • Policy for invasive and other medical imaging procedures • Policy and procedure for assessing patients when they arrive in medical imaging	• How do you participate in planning patient care following assessment? • How do you plan for modifying the treatment plan for patients with special needs? • In radiation therapy programs, how do you participate in the multidisciplinary team to plan the patient's course of treatment?	4–6 to 4–22 4–26 4–27 4–36 4–37 4–42 4–51 4–55 4–73 4–85 4–86

continues

3:16 RADIOLOGY DEPARTMENT COMPLIANCE MANUAL

Care of Patients

Standard	Comments	Evidence	Staff Questions	Reference
TX.1 through TX.1.2 (LINK PE.1– PE.1.4, PI.1–PI.1.1) *continued*		• Policy and procedure for medical records accompanying all inpatients for medical imaging exams		
TX.1.2.1 (LINK HIPAA 164.506)	Privacy of patients is provided for and respected when patient care procedures are being performed.	• Department observations of patient during studies • Guidelines for procedures outlining special privacy needs (e.g., caring for alleged victims of abuse) • Patient interviews • Staff interviews • Policy and procedures related to confidentiality and privacy • Dress code for employees and patients • Policies regarding appropriate disposal of patient information and X-rays • Policy for visitors in the medical imaging department *Site inspections* • Availability and use of private procedure rooms • Appropriate space for services • Adequate auditory and visual privacy for patients • Overhead paging that does not violate patient's privacy • Patient clothing or drapes that provide an appropriate level of privacy • Availability of a place for private conversations • Activities of staff that preserve patient	• How do you ensure that you meet patients' and families' need for privacy? • Do patient satisfaction surveys address privacy?	4–79 to 4–84

continues

Care of Patients

Standard	Comments	Evidence	Staff Questions	Reference
TX.1.2.1 (LINK HIPAA 164.506) *continued*		privacy (closing doors and drapes, patrol of changing areas to ensure privacy) • PI data regarding patient perception of privacy during exams • HIPAA policies and procedures for patient intake and treatment		
TX.1.3	Requires evaluation of goals set in care plans. Applicable hospitalwide.	• Nursing procedures and codes • Clinical pathways, guidelines, and protocols • Policies and procedures for reassessment, care planning • Open and closed medical records • Consistent application of reassessment and evaluation guidelines for specified patient groups. For instance, patients receive the same reassessment and evaluation following an angiogram whether it was done in radiology, the OR, or outpatient surgicenter. *See also* sections TX.1, TX.1.2, above.		
TX.2 through TX.2.1 (LINK RI.1.2.1, LD.1.6)	Relates to the appropriate use of moderate and deep sedation. Define the levels of sedation and requirements for each. Specific to the radiology department, it outlines requirements for: • organizationwide policies and procedures • competency needs of staff	• Anesthesia and sedation procedures consistent for all areas providing these services (medical imaging uses same process as other areas). • Preanesthesia/sedation assessment policy and procedure that includes criteria for assessment and reassessment • Policies governing selection of appropriate	• What types of anesthesia/ sedation do you administer in radiology? • Who decides the type of anesthesia or sedation for each patient? • Who completes or is responsible for the preanesthesia/sedation assessment? • Do you have separate policies and procedures for pediatric assessment?	4–37

continues

Care of Patients

Standard	Comments	Evidence	Staff Questions	Reference

TX.2 through TX.2.1 (**LINK** **RI.1.2.1, LD.1.6**) *continued*	• appropriate staffing levels
	• informed consent prior to the procedure monitoring
	• appropriate discharge
		type of sedation/ anesthesia by LIP
		• Medical staff or administrative policies governing requirements for practitioners to administer moderate and deep sedation
		• Requirements for qualifications of staff performing preanesthesia/sedation assessments
		• Policies, protocols, and forms addressing interdisciplinary team participation in assessment and care planning for anesthesia/sedation
		• Interviews revealing staff knowledge of procedures for preanesthesia/sedation assessment, and anesthesia/sedation care planning
		• Open and closed medical record review
		  – Procedure flowsheets
		  – Progress notes outlining informed consent
		  – Consent forms
		• Performance improvement efforts analyzing practice versus policy in anesthesia/sedation care
		• Policy and procedure for sedation and analgesia
		• Procedures performed in medical imaging that require moderate sedation
		• Policies regarding invasive and other medical imaging procedures
			• How are you competent to perform or assist with anesthesia or sedation in radiology?
			• How have you measured or improved the delivery of anesthesia services?
			• Where is the plan for sedation/anesthesia documented?	

continues

Care of Patients

Standard	Comments	Evidence	Staff Questions	Reference
TX.2.2 (LINK TX.3– TX.3.7)	Concerns informed consent for sedation/ anesthesia, specifically focusing on making the patient and family aware of anesthesia and sedation options and risks.	• Any performance improvement studies or activities on documentation of informed consent • Policies governing selection of appropriate type of sedation/ anesthesia by LIP and expectations for informed consent • Patient education handouts • Interviews with staff • Interviews with patients • Documentation in medical record of informed consent • Consent forms • Policy and procedures regarding sedation or anesthesia assessment and administration	• What procedures require a consent? • Where is this defined policy? • What preanesthesia/ sedation and postcare patient teaching do you do?	4–22
TX.2.3 through TX.2.4.1	Standards govern the assessment of patients before, during, and after sedation or anesthesia administration. Includes requirement for a discharge process guided by licensed independent practitioner intervention or criteria approved by the medical staff.	• Anesthesia and sedation procedures consistent in all areas providing these services (medical imaging should use same process as other areas) • Policy outlining assessment and reassessment of patients receiving sedation or anesthesia applicable to the department • Procedures including sedation scales, Aldrete score, or other tools for assessment • Policies approved by the medical staff for discharging patients by criteria following sedation or anesthesia • Protocols for monitoring during anesthesia, and for the documentation, communi-	• Who is responsible for monitoring the patient during anesthesia? • Where are the policies, procedures, and guidelines for anesthesia located? • What are the criteria for discharging a patient who has received anesthesia?	4–18

continues

Care of Patients

Standard	Comments	Evidence	Staff Questions	Reference
TX.2.3 through TX.2.4.1 *continued*		cation, and interpretation of monitoring data • Medical record review and documentation • Guidelines for sedation postanesthesia assessment • Criteria and procedures for postanesthesia discharge • Policies for ensuring patient safety after discharge • Patient discharge instructions • Medical staff bylaws delineating practitioners authorized to perform sedation/anesthesia		
TX.3 through TX.3.3	Medication use standards governing the organization processes supporting the prescription, ordering, and processing of medications. Standards apply organizationwide, but evaluation of compliance in radiology department weighs heaviest on implementation of established policies. Note that Joint Commission includes radiopharmaceuticals under these standards, and therefore assessment of compliance will include these agents. Includes appropriate administration of PCA or other parental medications. *Note:* Joint Commission has released new draft standards for medication use to take effect January 1, 2004. Organizations are encouraged to make	• P&T committee minutes • Documentation of approval of radiopharmaceutical agents added to formulary • Hospital formulary • Medication administration policies—general • Medication administration policies—specific to radiology department. • Sample drug logs, if applicable • Policies relating to storage of radiopharmaceuticals • Mechanisms for obtaining medications during off-hours • Discharge education sheets outlining post-study care and medication • Observation of security of radiopharmaceuticals • Policies denoting classification of individuals authorized to administer medications	• How are drugs selected for the radiology department? What criteria are used? • Describe the procedure for procuring drugs that are not on the formulary/drug list. • Describe how you ensure safe medication usage practices (e.g., prescription, ordering, preparing, and dispensing). • Where are drugs stored and who is responsible for them? • How often does pharmacy inspect medication areas? • What type of training do clinical staff receive concerning medication usage? How often? • Do you use sample drugs? If yes, please describe your policy and procedure for the use of samples.	4–49 4–50

Care of Patients

Standard	Comments	Evidence	Staff Questions	Reference
TX.3 through TX.3.3 *continued*	relevant changes in policy and practice to prepare for this change. For clarity, standard references are included in the next section.	• Policies addressing process for avoiding drug-contrast reactions • Protocols for sample drugs • Adverse drug reaction (ADR) reporting mechanism • Procedure if a physician orders a drug that is not on the formulary • Procurement, storage, and control of radiographic contrast material • Open and closed medical records (e.g., documentation on effectiveness of pain medication) • Staff personnel records indicating staff responsibilities for medication usage, education activities (job descriptions, orientation, performance evaluations, continuing education records) • Radiology department or organizationwide performance improvement activities concerning medication usage and pain management, as appropriate • Interview with physicians regarding knowledge and participation in recommending and placing drugs on the formulary • Evidence of radiology director involvement in developing ED medications list with staff • Formulary or drug list • Criteria for selection of medication (may include specific criteria for radiopharmaceuticals)		

continues

Care of Patients

Standard	Comments	Evidence	Staff Questions	Reference
TX.3.4 through TX.3.5.3	Standards related to the preparation, dispensing, use, prescribing, or ordering of medications. Include the availability of information about the patient to support appropriate medication ordering. Sets forth requirement for pharmacist review of all orders except when prescription dispensing and administration are controlled by licensed independent practitioners.	• Open and closed medical records – Physician orders – Medication administration records • Policies and procedures including inventory control of needles, syringes, and IV solutions • Policies governing unit dose medication administration • Policies governing injection of contrast material by physicians and nonphysicians • Guidelines for use of low osmolar contrast agents • IV contrast injection policy • Emergency drug boxes • Code Blue chart • Observations of security of contrast agents during and after operating hours • Compliance with policy regarding medication administration by authorized individuals • Observation and discussion of oversight of medication administration in the department • Pediatric crash cart • Performance improvement studies (e.g., checking crash carts)	• Describe how you control medication preparation and dispensing processes. • What type of patient medication dosage system do you use? • What is the involvement of the pharmacist in reviewing your orders? • What type of medication information do you rely upon when dispensing, prescribing, or ordering medications? • How often does the pharmacy department check your stock levels? • What information is available to clinicians for use in prescribing medications?	4–11 4–36 4–37
TX.3.5.4 through TX.3.6 (LINK 2003 Patient Safety Goal: Patient Identification)	Relate to the availability of pharmacy services and emergency medication issues. Require verification of patient identification prior to administration.	• Policy and procedures for after-hours access to medications within the pharmacy, if applicable; use of night cabinets, closets, and after-hours drug carts, emergency drug boxes, and crash carts	• What special procedures do staff members have to follow when using the emergency drug box or crash cart? • If areas of department of closed at night, how are medications secured (includ-ing those on crash cart)?	

continues

Care of Patients

Standard	Comments	Evidence	Staff Questions	Reference

TX.3.5.4 through TX.3.6 (LINK 2003 Patient Safety Goal: Patient Identification) *continued*		• Observations of storage areas and logs of after-hour pharmacy access
		• Observations of security of medications in all departments during regular and off hours
		• Emergency drug box policy
		• Policies and procedures for administering medications
		• Policies for monitoring stock and emergency medications
		• Patient identification policy
		
		Site inspection
		• Examination of crash cart to determine enforcement of policy and procedure on emergency medications and crash cart
		  –Check for compliance with inspection of carts including lock/seal (no missing spaces)
		  –May ask where locks/seals are kept
			• Where are contrast agents stored? Who oversees these medications?
			• Do radiology staff access the pharmacy after hours?
			• How do you verify patient identity prior to medication administration?
			• What two patient identifiers do you use?	

Revised Medication Use Standards go into effect January 2004. Introduction to Standards	Emphasizes importance of blame-free approach to medication use, error prevention, and performance improvement. Outlines goals related to uniform medication use systems, reduction of process variation, use of evidence-based practice, and focus on performance improvement for critical points in the medication system.	• Patient safety planning and documentation • Patient safety report to the board • Performance Improvement plan • FMEA or RCA documents, as appropriate	• What is the process for reporting medication errors? • How readily are staff willing to report errors? • Have you participated in any FMEA or RCA activities?	

continues

Care of Patients

Standard	Comments	Evidence	Staff Questions	Reference
TX.3 through TX.3.1 (similar to current standard TX.3.4)	Changes include the expectation that organizations adhere to accepted professional practice standards governing safe and appropriate medication use.	• Selection criteria for radiopharmaceuticals • Minutes of radiology department meetings denoting references to studies, articles, or information from professional societies supporting current or new processes • Observations of medication process in use in radiology department vs. other areas of the organization	• How were professional standards considered in the selection of current or new radiopharmaceuticals in use at this organization?	
TX.3.2 through TX.3.3 (Similar to current standard TX.3.5.3)	Address importance of availability of patient information to the practitioners at the time of prescribing and dispensing medications. Implications for the radiology department include ensuring that medical information (age, weight, diagnoses, medications) are available in the department for prescribing contrast agents. Focus on continued improvement of medication use processes.	• Presence of patient chart with patient during a study involving a radiopharmaceutical • Performance improvement activities for medication use in all departments	• What ongoing medication use performance improvement activities do you participate in? • Is the chart immediately available to the radiologist when a patient arrives from the ED for a contrast study?	

TX.3 through TX.3.5.2 (similar to TX.3.3.5.6)	Address selection, procurement, and storage of medications. Aspects applicable to the radiology department include process for obtaining ordered medications or contrast agents not stored in the organization. Reference storage of standard and emergency medications in a proper and safe	• Observation of medication storage areas to ensure protection of medications from
		  –theft
		  –excess temperatures
		  –contamination and spoilage
		  –moisture, condensation, and mold light, as appropriate storage hazards (spills, acid base
			• Where is the crash cart kept when this interventional area is closed?
			• What happens if a box of CT contrast solution is recalled because of contamination with glass shards?	

continues

Care of Patients

Standard	Comments	Evidence	Staff Questions	Reference
TX.3 through TX.3.5.2 (similar to TX.3.3.5.6) *continued*	manner. More direction is provided for recall mechanisms for discontinued or recalled medications.	concerns, look alike/ sound alike) – Discussion of process for medication recall – Observation of security and proper storage of emergency medications in all areas of department		
TX.3.6 through TX.3.12 (similar to TX.3, 3.4, 3.5.1, 3.7, 3.5.4)	Address policies and procedures that support prescribing, transcribing, preparation, and dispensing medications.	• Dosage scales or charts • Open and closed medical records • Observed practice of medication processes use in department	• Are all radiopharmaceuticals given based on a physician's order? • If pharmacy does not review the orders, are they given under the supervision of a physician?	
TX.3.13 through TX.3.19 (similar to 3.9, 3.5.1, 3.4)	Govern the administration of medications and the monitoring of effects on patients. Include designating in policy who can administer medications, presence of patient safety focused processes, and processes for distributing sample medications with high potential of serious drug events including a process for reporting overdose drug events. Expectations for use of self medication modalities and medications brought from home are outlined. Outline expectations for investigational medications and use of controlled substances. Specific to the radiology department, major themes likely include: • medication administration only by authorized individuals	• Medication administration records • Performance improvement documentation • Medication administration policies • Personnel records/job description • Adverse event/ incident reporting policy • Observations of medication administration	• How do you screen patients for possible drug-drug interactions specific to radiopharmaceuticals? • What do you do if a patient experiences a medication side effect? An adverse event? • Does the department provide sample medications? If so, describe the recall procedure. • Do you have any controlled substances in the department? Who administers them and what procedures are associated with their administration?	

continues

Care of Patients

Standard	Comments	Evidence	Staff Questions	Reference
TX.3.13 through TX.3.19 (similar to 3.9, 3.5.1, 3.4) *continued*	• processes surrounding controlled substances • high-risk medications • monitoring for medication side effects • response for adverse events • compliance consistent with policy and practice throughout organization • use or distribution of sample medications if applicable			
TX.5 through TX.5.1.5	Relate to assessment of patients prior to operative and other invasive procedures. Specific to the radiology department, it includes those invasive procedures performed that the medical staff has determined place patients at risk. The scope of assessment for types of procedures is determined by the medical staff and compliance measured based on the established scope. For instance, the medical staff may determine that patients undergoing a peripheral angiogram need a short-form history and physical, renal profile, and medication allergy list completed before the procedure. For a simple insertion of PICC line, the medical staff may determine that a complete medication/allergy list is the only required documentation.	• Medical staff bylaws, rules and regulations, or other supportive documentation outlining the scope of assessment for types of invasive procedures • Presence of relevant diagnostic data • Open and closed medical records documenting assessment prior to procedure • Staff interviews • Performance improvement activities, use of data collected	• How do you know what should be on the chart in preparation for an invasive procedure?	4–8 to 4–14 4–16 to 4–20 4–22 4–36 4–37

continues

Care of Patients

Standard	Comments	Evidence	Staff Questions	Reference
TX.5.2 through TX.5.2.2 (LINK IM.7.2– IM.7.3, TX.2– TX.2.4.1)	Focused on ensuring that patients receive all information necessary to give informed consent.	• Staff and patient interviews • Open and closed medical records • Documentation of informed consent (LIP note or co-signature on consent form) • Consent forms with risks and benefits explained • Documentation in medical record if informed consent cannot be obtained • Evidence that information given and informed consent obtained for patients receiving blood	• How is informed consent documented? • Where is it found in the chart?	4–21 4–22 4–25 4–28 to 4–30
TX.5.3 through TX.5.4	Concern formation and implementation of plan of care for operative or other invasive procedures that place patients at risk. Plan expected to include: • Initial assessment of patient needs, including need for additional diagnostic data • Assessment of level of care required during and after the procedure • A nursing plan of care.	• Documentation in patient record of specific information that would affect the procedure (examples include allergies to contrast/last normal menstrual period [LNMP]/pregnancy magnetic resonance imaging [MRI]/screening for metal) • Open and closed medical records including care plans, progress notes, pre-procedure notes with plan for procedure, postprocedure care, and setting and patient-risk level (may include ASA class) • Staff interviews • Procedure documentation forms • Policies governing delineation of staff responsibilities regarding procedures and post-procedure monitoring	• Describe care plans for patients undergoing operative and/or invasive procedures. • Where is the care plan located in the record? • Please describe your process for monitoring patients following a procedure. • Is there a consistent method you use to qualify a patient's level of pain?	4–6 to 4–10 4–13 to 4–15

continues

Care of Patients

Standard	Comments	Evidence	Staff Questions	Reference
TX.7 through TX.7.17.16 and TX.7.5 through TX.7.5.5	Standards address the safe and appropriate use of restraint and seclusion. Standards prescriptive for ensuring safe and appropriate use of restraint and seclusion. Generally, restraint/seclusion use is overseen through collaboration between nursing personnel and physicians. Specific to the radiology department, restraint interventions would likely be limited to maintaining restraints or restraint alternatives during visits to the department. Require competency appropriate to role in restraint management. Note that the use of restraints or papoose during a procedure is *not* considered a restraint under these standards as long as the device is removed during recovery from the procedure.	• Interviews with staff • Interviews with patients and/or families • Organizationwide policies, procedures, and protocols • Open and closed medical records, including assessment and monitoring records of patients in restraint • Observation of patient care for the patient in restraint • Restraint policy • Staff training materials and inservice/orientation records	• What is your role in restraint use? • What staff members participate in the application/use of restraints, and/or in assessing or monitoring patients in restraints? • How were they trained? • How do you protect the safety and dignity of patients in restraints? • How often is a patient in restraints monitored? By whom? • What steps do you take to try to avoid restraint use for a particular patient? • How do you document restraint use?	
TX.8	Governs effective resuscitative services. Applicable organization-wide. The radiology department maintains consistent compliance with organization policy regarding resuscitative procedures. This may include CPR training for relevant personnel, maintenance of emergency equipment, and performance improvement data on resuscitation outcomes.	• Staff training and orientation documentation • PI documentation and data • Policies, procedures, and protocols • Inspection of crash cart, code bags, and/or logs verifying availability of resuscitative services • Interviews with staff	• Which staff respond to situations requiring resuscitation services? • How are staff trained in resuscitation? • What equipment is available in the department for responding to resuscitative emergencies?	

EDUCATION

Standard	Comments	Evidence	Staff Questions	Reference
PF.1 through PF.1.1	References whether the education the hospital provides is planned and supports the coordination of patient education activities in all settings to assist in meeting the hospital's mission. Education must be relevant to the patient's unique set of circumstances and characteristics. Patient should receive information related specifically to his or her treatment and services.	• Patient education plan that includes radiology department services • Interdisciplinary patient and family education assessment and flowsheets • Patient education materials • Interdisciplinary discharge and medication summary/instructions • Open and closed medical records • Interviews with patients, staff, and families • Direct observation of patient education • Patient and family education plan, policy, procedure, and performance improvement (PI) activities • Evidence of education material for patients and families (e.g., brochures, handouts, videos, closed circuit television education channel, education display rack, bulletin boards, poster projects) • Committee minutes, budgets, staff development plans	• Do you have a Patient and Family Education Committee that coordinates activities across health settings? • Does your hospital promote and support a learning environment for staff and patients/families? • What type of patient and family education activities do you provide to improve outcomes, promote self-care? • How do you determine a patient's education needs? • How do you document teaching provided in the department? • Show me your assessment of the patient's education needs and corresponding flow sheet. • How do you assess and address cultural or language barriers to learning? • How do you assess a patient's ability to learn? • How are your patients educated on medication? Medical equipment? *Patient interview* • What education have you received regarding the test you are receiving? From whom? (Note: Surveyor would then try to verify that the education was documented.) • Do you feel you have enough information to care for yourself following this test? • Was your family included in the education process? • Were you referred to any community education resources?	4–5 4–13 4–21 4–22

continues

Education

Standard	Comments	Evidence	Staff Questions	Reference
P.F.1 through P.F.1.1 *continued*			• Were you informed where to seek additional treatment, if needed? • Was your pain addressed?	
P.F.2	Patient education should be collaborative if care involves multiple disciplines. This standard assesses whether the hospital uses an interdisciplinary approach to the provision of patient education.	• Policies, procedures, and plans related to patient education demonstrating collaborative efforts by caregivers, including radiology staff • Open and closed medical records demonstrating interdisciplinary participation in patient education • Clinical pathways incorporating patient and family education • Patient interview	• What role does the radiology department play in patient and family education? • How does the organization support patient and family education planning and implementation? • Can you describe a case that would illustrate collaborative, interdisciplinary education?	

P.F.3	Assessing patient and family education needs is critical to ensure a favorable outcome for the patient. Staff consider cultural, religious, emotional, and language barriers; readiness to learn (motivation level); physical and cognitive limitations; financial impact of treatment decisions; and the learning method (e.g., demonstration, verbal, video) preferred by the patient/family.
	
	Although this assessment is generally done by nursing personnel on admission, surveyors will monitor documentation based on whether the patient's identified needs were met by any and all members of the multidisciplinary team.
		• Patient interview
		• Open and closed medical records review
		  – admission database
		  – patient education records
		  – procedural notes or flowsheets
			• What information is assessed on admission concerning patient education needs?
			• Where are the patient's learning needs found?
			• How do you involve the patient and/or family in care or services before discharge?
			• How do you know that the patient and/or family understands the education they have received?
			• Where is this information documented?
			• What grade level do you use for instructional material?
			• What actions do you take if you discover there are barriers preventing understanding? How do you make accommodations for identified limitations? Can you describe a challenging case that was successfully managed?
				See also health literacy information on the AMA Web site.

continues

Education

Standard	Comments	Evidence	Staff Questions	Reference
PF.3 *continued*			• How do you incorporate education factors in the care planning process (i.e., creating individual education plans, prioritizing education needs, etc.)? • Where would you find any identified barriers to learning? • Before you provided patient education, how would you determine a patient or family's learning preferences?	
PF.3.1 through PF.3.5	Focuses attention on particular areas of educational need. Include: • PF.3.1 Medication Usage (instructions on medication prior to administration) • PF.3.2 Nutrition Interventions, Oral Health, and Drug-Food Interactions (diet teaching, food-drug interaction) • PF.3.3 Medical Equipment (walker or CT call button) • PF.3.4 Pain Management (how to use the pain scale) • PF.3.5 Habilitation or Rehabilitative Techniques (e.g., special adaptations provided to patient to ensure maximizing independence)	• Open and closed medical records review – patient education records – procedural notes or flowsheets – patient handouts or teaching aids	• What type of patient and family education activities do you provide? • Where is patient or family education documented? As applicable to the patient, can you show me an example of how you educated a patient on: – medications (such as contrast media)? – nutritional aspects (do not eat any food for 12 hours prior to the test)? – medical equipment (if you start to panic and want to stop the test, push this button)? – pain management (any time I hold the card during the procedure, indicate the number (0–5) with your hand)? – habitation techniques (let's review how the therapist suggested you transfer to this table)? *To patient* • Has anyone in this department discussed what you need to know about the testing or treatment you are receiving? • Who educated/counseled you regarding these issues?	

continues

Education

Standard	Comments	Evidence	Staff Questions	Reference
PF.3.4	Requires that patients be educated about pain and methods of pain management during their care and treatment.	• Documentation that patient was educated regarding – pain management options – methods of management of postprocedure pain – follow-up for management of pain at home – when to contact a physician or health care provider if pain symptoms worsen • Open and closed medical records – patient education flowsheet or notes – procedural flowsheets	• Describe policies on educating patients and families about management of pain. • What education do you provide patients and families on pain management? • Where is pain management education provided by radiology staff documented? Show examples of documented assessment of patients' pain management education needs, as well as evidence that you educated patients on pain management. *Patient* interview • What education, if any, have you received on pain management? • Who educated/counseled you regarding pain management?	
PF.3.6	Requires that patients and families are educated about outside resources and obtaining further care, services, and treatment. • Limited applicability to the radiology department other than referrals for further studies not offered at the organization or referral for follow-up care from a radiation treatment center.	• Evidence of referral for follow-up care (e.g., other hospital for further study, hospice) • Patient and family education materials • Interviews with clinical staff and patients/families	• What do you do if a patient required a more detailed study at another organization? What do you tell the patient and/or family? Where is that education documented?	
PF.3.7	Ensures that patients and families are educated on their responsibilities and role in the treatment process, specifically, their role in	• Handout/brochure of patient rights and responsibilities • Open and closed medical records for education about	• Do you have any booklet or handout to orient the patient/family to the radiology department? • How are patients informed of their responsibilities?	

continues

Education

Standard	Comments	Evidence	Staff Questions	Reference
P.F.3.7 *continued*	helping to facilitate the safe delivery of care. Patient responsibilities include • Detail of the standard outlines patient responsibilities for: – providing information, including reporting perceived risks in their care – asking questions – following instructions – accepting consequences – following rules and regulations – showing respect and consideration – meeting financial commitments • Requires that these responsibilities are outlined for patients either verbally, in writing, or both.	patient and family responsibilities • Posting of patient rights and responsibilities in treatment and waiting areas • Patient and staff interviews	• How are patients informed of their role and responsibilities for patient safety?	
P.F.3.8	Standard relates to the patient being able to care for self (e.g., hygiene, grooming). Specifies the need to educate patients to care for self (e.g., hygiene, grooming), as applicable. May include postprocedural instructions for caring for wound or insertion site.	• Open and closed medical records • Observation and interview of patients • Interviews with clinical staff • Policies and procedures related to education, self-care • Postprocedure care teaching sheets	• If indicated by visual inspection or interview of patient, what follow-up education is provided to ensure patient receives proper hygiene/grooming resources? • What instructions are given to patients following procedures or studies to assist in caring for themselves at home? • Where do you document that patients have received education on how to care for themselves at home?	
P.F.3.9	Requires that discharge instructions are given to the patient, family, or other caretakers.	• Discharge instructions or handouts for invasive procedures in radiology	• What instructions are provided to patients and their families on discharge?	

continues

Education

Standard	Comments	Evidence	Staff Questions	Reference
PF.3.9 *continued*		• Policy and procedures related to discharge planning • Open and closed medical records	• Who provides these instructions? • Are instructions given in a manner that respects the patient or family's cultural needs? • If instructions are written, are they provided in a language understood by the patient?	

CONTINUUM OF CARE

Standard	Comments	Evidence	Staff Questions	Reference
CC.1 (LINK LD.1.3)	Implemented hospitalwide, concerns the hospital's process for matching the patient's needs with the most appropriate level of care. Constitutes part of the planning process for serving patient needs with current and future needs. May include patient referral services not provided in the organization.	• Performance improvement data summarizing services ordered versus services provided and identification of future needs • Scope of service document for department • Referral or transfer log, as applicable • Transfer/referral policy • Documents summarizing availability of services not provided, such as open MRI • Waiting time performance data and performance improvement plans • Referral and transfer agreements • Leadership interviews • Waiting time measures • Handouts for community resources	• Describe the patient's initial experience when entering the radiology department. • What information do you obtain to determine what care and services the patient needs? • What is the range of care you provide? • Do you have sufficient staff and equipment to provide services to meet the needs of your patient population? • Where are patients referred when needed care cannot be provided? How do you access these services? • How are patients transported to another organization? • How do you access the services of other departments within your organization?	4–10 4–25 to 4–27 4–36 4–37
CC.2 through CC.3	Relate primarily to the selection of an appropriate setting of care based on patient needs. Specific to the radiology department, the type of study or setting is selected based on patient need such as an open MRI for obese or claustrophobic patient. May include transfer to another setting if indicated by patient's assessed needs.	• Application of the criteria that define the information needed for matching the patient to the appropriate care setting • Open and closed medical records • Transfer logs or performance data related to reason for transfer • Scope of service document	• How do you determine whether a patient will receive care in the radiology department? Who makes the decision? • When are patients transferred for services? • Are there any criteria that determine which procedures may be done here? • Do you have a scope of service document?	4–10 4–27 4–36 4–37
CC.4 through CC.7 (LINK EMTALA Regulation §§ 42 CFR 489.20 and 42 CFR 489.24)	Largely applicable to inpatient areas of the hospital. Involve the radiology department in its participation as a member of the multidisciplinary team to provide continuity of care for patients over	• Staff, leadership, and patient interviews • Referral and transfer agreements • Open and closed medical records • Departmental policies and procedures for assessment, care	• Describe the procedure for transferring a patient to another department or organization. • Describe the process for discharging a patient. • Describe the procedure for notifying and recalling patients who need	4–10 4–25 to 4–27 4–34 to 4–35

continues

Continuum of Care

Standard	Comments	Evidence	Staff Questions	Reference

CC.4 through CC.7 (LINK EMTALA Regulation §§ 42 CFR 489.20 and 42 CFR 489.24) *continued*	time. Address requirement for ensuring coordination and continuity of care when patients are transferred or discharged. Include a requirement for ensuring transfer of information to other clinicians when the patient is referred for care.	planning, patient and family education, transfer, referral, discharge, and follow-up
		• PI studies on turn-around times, recalls, rereads
		• Progress notes concerning referrals for follow-up care, especially in radiation therapy areas
		• Policy on transferring patients for services not offered by the hospital
		• Patient and family education on transfer, referral, discontinuation of services, discharge, and follow-up
		• Agreements/contracts for services by off-site organizations
		• Call-back policies, procedures
		• Open and closed medical records documenting the patient's continuing care needs following discharge
		• Policies and procedures
		  – Discharge planning
		  – Patient and family education and discharge instructions
		  – Diagnostic testing, follow-up procedure
		• Interdisciplinary pathways demonstrating flow of clinical information
		• Use of fax machines, networked personal computers assisting with the flow of patient information among providers and various health care settings
			additional radiologic studies.
			• How is a patient transported to radiology?
			• Who in the radiology department is responsible for responding to codes?
			• Is there a means of providing services not offered by the department? What is it?
			• What criteria are in place for discharging patients from medical imaging following certain procedures?
			• What are the criteria for referral and transfer? For discontinuation of services? When can a transfer take place? What information must be documented in a patient's record prior to transfer?
			• What is your role in the planning process for follow-up care?
			• What information do patients and/or families receive?
			• When do they receive it?
			• How do you ensure that a patient receives necessary follow-up care or diagnostic testing following discharge?
			• How do you assess compliance with appropriate transfers, as applicable?
			• Describe the flow of clinical information when patients are admitted, referred, transferred, and discharged, and when services are discontinued.
			• Describe how treatment information is made available to providers	

continues

Continuum of Care

Standard	Comments	Evidence	Staff Questions	Reference
CC.4 through CC.7 (LINK EMTALA Regulation §§ 42 CFR 489.20 and 42 CFR 489.24) *continued*			performing follow-up care. • How are patients notified of their testing results (discrepancies) and any follow-up care required?	

IMPROVING ORGANIZATION PERFORMANCE

Standard	Comments	Evidence	Staff Questions	Reference
PI.1 through PI.1.1	Hospital must have a hospitalwide performance improvement process. The radiology department follows the hospital's process for improving performance. Common performance improvement approaches include plan, do, check, act (PDCA). Expectations include an approach that emphasizes a multidisciplinary collaborative approach to issues that cross departmental or functional lines.	• Flowchart for getting a process improved • Quality improvement (QI) idea form • Summary of quality improvement efforts • Quality assurance (QA) policy and procedure • QA and performance improvement (PI) plan for medical imaging services • QI indicators	• How have you participated in hospital PI efforts? • What are you doing to improve patient care at this hospital in your department? • Do you participate in any cross-departmental or cross-functional PI activities? • Explain your process for identifying PI activities. • What methodology for PI has you organization adopted? Give an example of how you used the methodology to improve care in the past.	4–32 4–39 4–40 4–41
PI.2	Outlines expectations for designing new and modified processes. Includes redesign of existing or new processes such as new patient care services or new facility openings. In designing new processes, organizations draw upon information from: • Mission/vision/values, goals and objectives and plans • Needs of individuals or groups (patients, staff, or physicians) • Industry best practices (clinical and business) • Potential risks to patients, including sentinel events or near misses • Pilot studies of redesigned processes	• Staff interviews • PI planning documents, minutes of meetings prioritizing improvements • Prioritization grid • PI activity results • Information about potential risks to patients and sentinel events within the organization and at other facilities • Flowcharts, other descriptions of new processes	• How does your organization assign priorities for PI? How does your department determine its PI processes for study? • What is staff's role in selecting processes to be improved? • What improvements have you made in the past quarter/year? • Was the improvement maintained? • How did you apply the PI model in designing the new process? • Give an example of a PI project that you have participated in.	4–34 to 4–37 4–40 to 4–44

continues

Improving Organization Performance

Standard	Comments	Evidence	Staff Questions	Reference
PI.2 *continued*	• Results of PI studies These aspects are used as a basis for prioritizing opportunities for improvement.			
PI.3 through PI.3.1.3	Standards describe the organization's responsibility to systematically collect data to monitor performance and identify areas and methods for improvement initiatives. Radiology staff should be prepared to show compliance with organizationwide and department-specific data collection activities, as well as evidence that the data have been used to improve radiology processes. Includes those measures focusing on quality control (e.g., maintenance logs, pretest calibration procedures) and those focusing on improving processes (e.g., wait times or turn-around times). PI focus is on high-risk, high-volume, problem-prone processes and functions, as well as sentinel events or their risk factors. Data collection also must include areas targeted for further study and PI efforts. Measurement reflects those processes that have greatest impact on processes and outcomes.	• Staff interviews, PI team interviews • Plans, strategies for data collection • Data collection tools used (e.g., surveys, flowsheets) • Orientation, continuing education materials, attendance concerning data collection and measurement • Measurement and improvement reports, minutes (e.g., aggregate, comparative data collected) • Evidence of participation in a reference database • Nuclear medicine cardiac consent forms filled out completely—graph • All transcribed reports to medical imaging (MI) turned around in prescribed time limits—graph • Quality control logs and/or worksheets • Service log reports for nuclear medicine and MI radiation producing equipment • Retake film computation sheet • Radiology quality trend analysis • Patient care processes or outcome measurement strategies • Patient survey • Nuclear medicine wait times—graph	• What aspects of care are you measuring as part of improvement activities? • How do you select and prioritize data collected? • Where are the data reported and how will information be used? • Do you use external comparative data (e.g., Press Gainey, Gallup, peer review organization [PRO], comparisons with other organizations)? • How do you measure the quality of radiology department invasive and noninvasive procedures that place the patient at risk? • What sampling methodology do you use for PI studies? • If PI measures include aspects of the physician role, are any of the data used at the time of reappointment?	4–34 to 4–37 4–42 to 4–44

continues

Improving Organization Performance

Standard	Comments	Evidence	Staff Questions	Reference

PI.3 through PI.3.1.3 *continued*		• Noncompliance with nuclear medicine QA— consent forms
		• Nuclear medicine patient wait times— graph
		• Graphs interpreting radiology department data collected, other trend analysis
		• Documentation illustrating the periodic evaluation of common radiology department procedures
		• Use of data collection tools to measure performance of processes in the radiology department such as
		  – operative and invasive procedures
		  – medication usage
		  – quality control
		  – incident reports
		  – infection control indicators
		  – sentinel events
		  – waiting times
		  – appropriateness of procedures
		  – medical record documentation
		• Use of data collection tools to measure
		  – pathway variances
		  – timeliness, appropriateness of ancillary services, consultations
		  – patient satisfaction
		  – staff and patient views on perceived risks to patients and opportunities for improvements
		  – appropriateness/ effectiveness of pain management
		  – staff willingness to report medical/health care errors		

continues

Improving Organization Performance

Standard	Comments	Evidence	Staff Questions	Reference
PI.4 through PI.4.4	Standards focus on the hospital's assessment and analysis of collected data. Organization uses the data to identify changes that will not only improve performance and improve patient safety, but also reduce the risk of sentinel events. Radiology leaders should be prepared to discuss the analysis and use of data related to radiology services, especially where undesirable trends have been identified. Connection to the hospitalwide sentinel event policy should be outlined. Statistical analysis is helpful in comparing the organization's performance with historical trends, as well as against other organizations, and in assessing common or special variations.	• Reports on radiology process evaluation • Proof of interdisciplinary QI projects involving radiology representatives • Proof that data collected are assessed at periodic intervals • Minutes and other documentation of QI team meetings, activities • Reports evaluating collected data • Proof of data analysis that indicates poor performance, major discrepancies, undesirable patterns, and other problematic issues • Proof of action in response to the data described above • Adverse events reports • Documentation of analysis of staffing effectiveness issues • Documentation of X-ray variances, other variances, and follow-up • Root cause analysis • Material from external sources such as recent clinical and management literature, including relevant Joint Commission *Sentinel Event Alerts*	• How is statistical analysis applied in the radiology department? • Describe what techniques you use to analyze the data you've collected on a radiology-related PI project. • Have you seen any trends in the data related to ____? How have you analyzed this trend? • How does the radiology department compare with other radiology departments? How does it compare with itself over time? How does it compare with scientific and other literature? • How do you know that a QI initiative has been successful? • How do you assess variations in trends? What statistical quality control methods do you use? • What is an example of a discrepancy or unfavorable trend in radiology data? What have you done to correct it? • How do you review and respond to information and recommendations the Joint Commission provides about sentinel events? • What do you do if there is a sentinel event?	4–34 4–35 4–40 4–41
PI.5	Standard measures whether PI is sustained over time. Radiology leaders may be called on to discuss their department PI initiatives.	• Records of radiology PI activities or new services, including planning, data collection, evaluation, and implementation documentation • Proof of participation in interdepartmental PI initiatives	• In what PI projects has the radiology department participated this year? • What processes have you redesigned? What was the result? • What hospital PI initiatives have involved the participation of radiology staff?	

continues

Improving Organization Performance

Standard	Comments	Evidence	Staff Questions	Reference
PI.5 *continued*		• Communication to staff regarding implementation of PI projects	• How do you prioritize PI projects?	

LEADERSHIP

Standard	Comments	Evidence	Staff Questions	Reference
LD.1 through LD.1.2	Standards discuss leaders' role in hospital and systemwide planning. Include participation at the departmental, organizational, and when applicable, the systemic level.	• Leadership interview discussion about input sources used for organizational planning • Meeting minutes indicating department leaders' participation in hospitalwide planning activities • Planning documents for departmental needs (short term or long term) • Budget and planning documents • Planning documentation for new service, environmental space, or process changes • Discussion of budgeting and resource allocation planning for organization and/or radiology department • Systemic planning or goal documentation • Protocol for adding on examinations between 7 AM and 11 PM Mon.–Fri. • Protocol for night procedures • On-call policies and procedures • Transferring of patients to other institutions from medical imaging • Interpretation of X-rays during night hours • Patient priority procedures • Procedure for coordinating after-hours exams with nursing units and on-call technologists	*For leaders* • Describe your participation in strategic and operational planning. • How do you use staffing variances for budget planning the next year? • What is the process for requesting additional resources, such as staff? • How does organizational planning flow from the mission/vision/and values of the organization? Give an example. • What information sources are used in the organizational planning process? Do they differ for the radiology department? • If part of a hospital system, how do respective departments collaborate on issues in common? How is this planning documented?	
LD.1.1.3	Radiology staff must comply with hospital policies and procedures regarding patients under legal or correctional restrictions.	• Interviews wth staff regarding processes and patient flow in the radiology department • Department policies and procedures consis-	• What do you do when a patient arrives in handcuffs? • What if a police officer asks you to restrain a patient or put the patient	

continues

Leadership

Standard	Comments	Evidence	Staff Questions	Reference
LD.1.1.3 *continued*		tent with hospital policy on treating prisoners and other restricted patients • Documentation of treatment of patients in custody or under other restriction • Staff compliance with hospital requirements regarding patients in custody or under other legal restrictions	in seclusion? Who places the patient in restraint? • What policies govern the processing of patients in the department? Do they differ if the patient is a medical patient or psychiatric patient? • What training have you received regarding the care of patients under legal or correctional restrictions?	
LD.1.2	Addresses leadership's responsibility for communicating the hospital's mission, vision, and plans. Communication may be accomplished through formal education or policies and procedures.	• Educational materials distributed to staff • Minutes of meetings in which hospital mission/vision were discussed • Orientation materials and staff orientation attendance records • Mission and vision statements posted in the radiology department • Interviews with staff about knowledge of mission, vision, values, and plans	• What are the hospital's mission and vision? • What are the organization's key goals or plans for the current year? What are the performance improvement goals or objectives? • Where would you locate the organization's mission and value statements for reference? • How do the hospital's leaders communicate PI plans to your department? • How do radiology department PI plans relate to organization-wide PI goals or plans that support the organization's mission? • How does the radiology department accomplish the hospital's mission?	
LD.1.3 through LD.1.3.3.1	Standards govern the planning processes for establishing and maintaining services based on patient needs. Require consideration of patient satisfaction data. Include the determination of the needs of individual departments based on the scope and level of care required by the patients served.	• Planning documents showing that services are planned in response to patient needs • Radiology patient needs data analysis and action plan • Planning documentation that considers patient needs, human and material resources in planning for radiology services	• How have the needs of the patients you serve changed over the last year? • What information do you use to determine these changes? • How does the department accomplish the hospital's mission? • What are the priorities for radiology service improvement?	4–34 4–35

continues

Leadership

Standard	Comments	Evidence	Staff Questions	Reference
LD.1.3 through LD.1.3.3.1 *continued*		• Community analysis or study outlining needs of patient groups • Meeting minutes, other documents that show radiology representation in hospital planning activities • Quality assurance (QA) documents, other measurements assessing radiology needs • Patient and family satisfaction surveys, changes made in response to results	• What are you doing to measure patient and family satisfaction? • What is the process for responding to trends in the data you will collect? • What other sources do you use to determine the needs of your patients or physicians? • Have you added any services in the last year? If so, describe the planning process that took place to prepare for the new service. • If the new service indicated a need for a change in staffing levels, how has the staffing plan evolved?	
LD.1.3.4 **(LINK § 482.26 Condition of Participation: Radiologic Services)**	Standards address the provision of patient care in a timely manner either directly or through referral, consultation, contractual arrangements, or other agreements. Echo CMS requirement for essential diagnostic radiology services and nuclear medicine services. If services are provided outside the organization, the medical staff approves these sources of care and monitors the quality of care.	• Approval of off-site provider of nuclear medicine by the medical staff • Quality studies of timeliness of patient care in the radiology department. Physician satisfaction surveys concerning timeliness of radiology service. • Tools used to measure patient waiting time • Tools used to measure waiting times for test results • Patient and family satisfaction surveys • Patient treatment flowcharts • Department policy on patient waiting time • Chart review indicating radiology services provided within time frame established by hospital	• Describe how you ensure that patients' needs are being met in a timely fashion. • Describe how you ensure that physician needs are being met in a timely fashion. • What aspects of timeliness of care do you measure to improve care? • How long do you wait for diagnostic X-rays and the report? • How long does it take before the physician has access to the interpretation of a radiology department study? Is it written or oral? When does the written report become available on the chart? • How long does the average patient wait in your department? *Physician interview* • Are radiology services provided in a timely manner? • Do you have any outside sources of radiology	4–35

continues

Leadership

Standard	Comments	Evidence	Staff Questions	Reference
LD.1.3.4 (LINK § 482.26 Condition of Partici- pation: Radiologic Services) *continued*			services in which the patient leaves for the testing and returns? If so, did the medical staff approve its use? How do you monitor the ongoing quality of that service?	
LD.1.6 (LINK PE.2– PE.2.4)	Critical standard addressing adherence to a uniform provision of care across the organiza- tion. In short, it poses the question "do patients with similar conditions or treat- ments receive similar care?" Most applicable in radiology for those procedures that also take place in other areas of the organization. Applies to inpatients and outpatients.	• Policies for procedures that take place in radiology and outpa- tient area or surgery (should be one policy, not two). • Interview with staff regarding reassessment, patient flow, and discharge criteria. • Department participa- tion in organization- wide PI projects, committees (e.g., patient and family education, ethics) to ensure uniform care and interdisciplinary participation in planning • Application of organizationwide quality control policies and pro- cedures • Operative and other procedures PI moni- tors (the standard of care for conscious sedation uniform throughout the hospi- tal) • Use of housewide policies in a consistent manner in the radiol- ogy department (setting is modified but not procedural prin- ciples). • Quality controls for procedures consistent	• How do leaders and staff ensure one standard level of patient care across the organization? • Where do you keep your standards of care for the radiology department? • How often do you reassess a patient follow- ing an angiogram or vena caval filter? Is this the same as the procedure in the OR? Why or why not?	

continues

Leadership

Standard	Comments	Evidence	Staff Questions	Reference
LD.1.6 (LINK PE.2– PE.2.4) *continued*		with controls for the same procedures in other departments • Treatment protocols consistent with those implemented in other hospital departments • Cross-departmental measures for monitoring consistent level of care • Discharge, patient education, and follow-up procedures similar to those offered by other treatment areas • Patient care standards implemented in a manner consistent with that offered by other departments in the hospital		
LD.1.7 through LD.1.7.1	Require a defined scope of service for each department that defines the type of care delivered to the individual groups of patients it serves. Standards describe specific criteria for formatting the scope of service. Result in an important scope of service document that outlines clues for compliance with other standards.	• Radiology department scope of service document • Department policies and procedures consistent with services offered • Departmental goals • Description of radiology services offered • Minutes of radiology service meetings in which planning is discussed • QI documentation, other assessment tools	• Is the scope of radiology services in writing? Where? • How do you determine the scope of radiology service? • How do you identify patient needs? • Is staffing adequate to serve your patient population?	4–35 4–44
LD.1.8	Outlines expectations for collaboration of leaders in decision making and planning.	• Planning documents • Patient safety planning documents and minutes • Staff interview about budgeting process and leadership input into budgetary decisions • Meeting minutes reflecting consideration of patient needs in planning	• How does the radiology department participate in hospitalwide planning and programming? • How is the radiology department represented on the hospital's QI committee?	

continues

Leadership

Standard	Comments	Evidence	Staff Questions	Reference
LD.1.8 *continued*		• QA/PI documentation • Documentation reflecting radiology participation in development of hospitalwide programs		
LD.1.9 and LD.1.9.1 **(LINK HR.2–HR.5)**	Address requirements for establishing and maintaining an initial and ongoing training, education, and competency program that attracts and retains qualified individuals. (Note that inadequate training or orientation could result in deficiencies in the LD and HR chapter).	• Documents supporting the relationship between patient needs and educational planning. May include needs assessment or planning documents for budget. • Department staffing plan • Staff training education records • Staff recruitment materials • Staff retention plan • Minutes of meetings in which staffing issues are discussed	• Is the radiology department adequately staffed? • How do you know the radiology staff meet the needs of your patient population? • What continuing education have you received in the past year? • Do you have sufficient opportunities for training and education? • How would you describe staff turnover? Are you doing anything to reduce turnover? • Who is the most recent staff member hired? Can I see his or her orientation record? • Have any employees left because they were unhappy? Has anything been done to resolve similar problems?	4–60 to 4–62 4–64 4–65
LD.1.10 through LD.1.10.3	Govern the appropriate use of clinical practice guidelines. Organizations are required to consider their use, but not required to use them at this time. If used, standards outline expectations for a multidisciplinary approach to their use including the tracking and trending of patient outcomes for the purpose of improving care. Surveyors will focus on specific aspects outlined in the standards.	• Interviews with leaders and staff • Clinical practice guidelines, Caremaps, Carepaths, or other documents that outline the expectations and outcomes for specified patient groups or conditions • Aggregation and analysis of outcomes from clinical practice guidelines and actions plans resulting from negative trends • Minutes of meetings documenting radiology	• Are any clinical practice guidelines used in the radiology department? • Why did you decide to adopt a clinical practice guideline? • Did you utilize any benchmarks in the selection process? • Why was it adopted? • How was it selected? What were the criteria used? • How has it impacted patient care? • When was it last reviewed? Who participated in the review?	

continues

Leadership

Standard	Comments	Evidence	Staff Questions	Reference
LD.1.10 through LD.1.10.3 *continued*		department participation in discussions of clinical practice guidelines evaluation and use • Examples of guideline use or modification for PI, including results • Staff training materials	• How are staff trained regarding this guideline? • How are variances from the guideline tracked and measured? • How do physicians and staff individualize care? • How do you share the information on improving patient care that you discover from the use of clinical practice guidelines?	
LD.2.1 through LD.2.10	Outline the responsibilities of departmental leadership in departmental work and organizational collaboration. Include expectations for management of human, material, and budgetary resources while improving care processes within the department. Standards provide detail of specific expectations.	• Department policies and procedures • Meeting minutes from medical staff, governing body, interdisciplinary care, and QI committees • Planning documents for budget cycle (may include human, material, and budgetary requests based on identified needs) • Quality assessment tools • QI plans, documentation, and reports • Job descriptions and competencies for care providers who are not licensed independent practitioners • Staff orientation materials and attendance records (including physician orientation) • Radiology staffing plan • Policies on staff training and education • Contracts with entities that provide services to the radiology department • Department care plans • Radiology budget • Department leader(s) job description	*To any staff member* • What is the hospital's mission? • Do you feel there are adequate human resources for meeting the needs of the patients you serve? Why or why not? • Are the space, equipment, and supplies adequate for you to do your job? *To the director* • How do you motivate the radiology staff to improve the services provided? • How do you help staff meet the goals of the department and professional goals? • How do new staff receive initial orientation? • How do you educate contract personnel? • How do you measure the competency of contract personnel? • How do you coordinate services within the department? • How does the radiology department coordinate services with other departments? • How do you know your staff are qualified? • How do you know if staff are competent? • Who trains the nonprofessional staff?	4–52 to 4–55 4–66 4–68 to 4–78

continues

Leadership

Standard	Comments	Evidence	Staff Questions	Reference
LD.2.1 through LD.2.10 *continued*			• How are radiology physicians credentialed? What are the criteria for reappointment? How is the clinical competency of staff physicians documented? • Who supervises residents, if applicable? • What are the responsibilities of the radiology director according to medical staff bylaws?	
LD.2.11 through LD.2.11.3	Addresses qualifications of the radiology director.	• Radiology director job description • Job descriptions for other administrative and clinical personnel • Radiology director's personnel file, credentialing file	*To the director* • What are your qualifications? (Director must be a licensed physician who is a medical staff member.)	
LD.3 through LD.3.4.1	Relate the expectations for establishing and implementing the Plan for the Provision of Patient Care in a multidisciplinary and coordinated manner across departmental boundaries. The Plan serves as an overriding document from which individual scope of service documents flow. It describes the dependent, independent, and interdependent relationships between departments for fulfilling the needs of all patients. Outline the importance of patient safety as an major emphasis of this plan.	• Plan for the Provision of Patient Care • Meeting minutes • Internal communications between radiology and other departments • Communications with staff, such as bulletin boards, suggestion boxes, staff meetings • Patient care flowcharts and other documents illustrating coordination between departments • Multidisciplinary care plans • Communication with other community services • Policies and procedures that involve participation of other departments • Participation in interdepartmental QI programs	• How do you communicate with other departments? • How have you collaborated with other departments to improve the care of patients you serve? • What mechanisms are in place to ensure collaboration between departments? • What patient safety issues have you analyzed in the past year? Did the analysis result in any changes? If so, how?	

continues

Leadership

Standard	Comments	Evidence	Staff Questions	Reference
LD.3 through LD.3.4.1 *continued*		• Documentation of measurement/analysis of performance of high-risk processes that affect patient safety		
LD.4 through LD.4.5 **(LINK PI.2– PI.3.1.3)**	Hospital leaders are required to participate in hospitalwide performance improvement and safety improvement activities, including dealing with sentinel events and assessing adequacy and utilization of resources. The radiology director should be prepared to demonstrate the department's contribution.	• QI initiatives • Radiology data collection tools • Job description that includes quality and safety improvement activities • Documentation that facilitywide QI and safety improvement activities include radiology department representation • Radiology performance measurement tools • Documentation of PI and safety improvement education attended by radiology leaders • Priority planning for radiology PI and safety improvement • Reports on radiology participation in PI and safety improvement efforts • Evidence of radiology allocation of human and other resources to PI and patient safety improvement activities	• What are you doing to improve the quality of care in this hospital? • What are you doing to improve performance in the radiology department? To improve safety? • What is the methodology you use for performance improvement? • Who is responsible for PI? For safety improvement? • What are you doing better than last year? • What are your priorities for PI and safety improvement in the coming year? • How do you participate in hospital PI activities? In safety improvement activities? • What resources (human, educational, time, material, data systems) have been brought to bear on improving patient safety in this department?	4–34 4–35
LD.5 through LD.5.3	Require hospital leaders to implement and give a high priority to a hospitalwide patient safety program, including processes for identifying and managing sentinel events, risks to patient safety, and for reducing medical errors. The intent is to	• Interviews with leaders, staff • Orientation, continuing staff education re: patient safety improvement • Patient safety program initiatives, priority planning, lists, assessment tools	• What do you do when you discover that a medical/health care error has been made in the radiology department? • What is a sentinel event? Or, what would you do if a patient tried, or succeeded, in hanging himself in one of the rooms?	4–32 4–40 4–41 4–59

continues

Leadership

Standard	Comments	Evidence	Staff Questions	Reference
LD.5 through LD.5.3 *continued*	proactively identify potential patient safety risks and prevent adverse occurrences. Radiology directors should be prepared to demonstrate the department's contribution.	• Hospitalwide patient safety improvement activities that include radiology department representation • Documentation of patient safety program education attended by radiology leaders • Department and organizational evaluations of patient safety programs • Allocation of human and other resources to patient safety improvement activities • Leadership self-evaluations • Documented procedures for response to medical/health care errors • Documented mechanisms for responding to various occurrences, e.g., root cause analysis of a sentinel event • Reports on occurrence of medical/health care errors and actions taken to improve patient safety	• How would you report a sentinel event?	

MANAGEMENT OF THE ENVIRONMENT OF CARE

Standard	Comments	Evidence	Staff Questions	Reference
EC.1.1, EC.1.1.1, EC.1.5.1, EC.2.1, EC.2.8, and EC.2.10.1	Standards relate to the organizationwide safety management plan and its implementation for the protection of patients and workers. Surveyors walk through the department to assess the effectiveness of ongoing risk monitoring and compliance at the department level. Hazardous surveillance surveys should be performed in the radiology department at least every six months to reduce safety risks.	• Documents reviewed during the Environment of Care Document Review • Safety plan, including any department-specific aspects or component plans • Leadership and staff interviews • Part 4 Plan for Improvement for any existing deficiencies or equivalency documents • Documentation supporting implementation of safety plan • Feedback and action plans concerning radiology department safety surveillance rounds • Performance improvement (PI) projects, measurement of performance standards, action plans in response to safety trends • Safety orientation and continuing education materials, education schedules, staff attendance records • Mechanism for training, informing medical staff, and students of environment of care plans, policies, and procedures • Reporting of trends in occupational illness, personnel injuries • Building plans if renovation of radiology department is underway • Organization and medical imaging department safety policies and procedures accessible to staff	• Describe your safety orientation. • What activities have been implemented to increase worker safety in general? In your department? • How often are you updated on safety issues? • How do you ensure that the environment is safe to take care of patients? • Do you have any treatment rooms reserved for special types of patients (e.g., isolation, children, trauma)? • What do you allow in the hallways (e.g., portable X-ray equipment)? • How did you receive education on safety? (Give an example.) • Is there a committee that oversees the safety of the organization? How does the radiology department participate in the committee? • How is the organization's safety measured? • Where do you discuss safety-related issues at the departmental level? • Describe the frequency of any surveillance rounds in the radiology department. What data are collected? • Who monitors safety in your department? • Is safety a standard part of your department meetings? • How do you contribute to eliminating and minimizing safety risks? • What do you do if a child turns up missing from the department? What is done within the department? In the organiza-	4–39 4–42 4–47 4–60 to 4–63

continues

Management of the Environment of Care

Standard	Comments	Evidence	Staff Questions	Reference
EC.1.1, EC.1.1.1, EC.1.5.1, EC.2.1, EC.2.8, and EC.2.10.1 *continued*		• Policies or process for maintaining safety of equipment and physical environment, especially in limited egress areas of radiology • Hospital security department evidence of hazardous surveillance surveys monthly, notifying radiology department of violations, which are to be corrected • Sentinel event policy, specifically, procedures for decreasing the risks of elopement or infant/child abduction from the radiology department • Evidence of a radiation safety committee • A representative from the radiology department on the hospital safety committee—meeting minutes, agendas, attendance lists • Minutes from departmental safety committee meetings • Designation in the hospital safety manual of person to be notified when there is an immediate safety threat • Department safety policy that designates a radiation safety officer • Department orientation addressing radiology-specific issues and continuing education • Orientation manual • Documentation of orientation session • Sample radiology safety policies	tion? What processes are in place for preventing this occurrence? • Who do you contact if there is a safety threat? • How do you prevent patient falls? • What is the procedure for reporting an incident or threat involving a patient or visitor? • Describe the safety risks you encounter during your job and how you protect yourself. • Where is the safety manual? • What do you do if you are injured on the job? • When threats to worker or patient safety are identified in the area, how are they mitigated or removed? • What items are monitored during hazard surveillance rounds? • How do you respond to safety recalls of equipment? • What did the hazard analysis reveal about this area that is different from the radiology area in the other building location? How is safety planning different?	

continues

Management of the Environment of Care

Standard	Comments	Evidence	Staff Questions	Reference
EC.1.1, EC.1.1.1, EC.1.5.1, EC.2.1, EC.2.8, and EC.2.10.1 *continued*		• Policies for caring for patients with radiation implants and compliance with the policies evident at the bedside (screening before and after discharge, following movement from one area to another, badge readouts for staff members caring for implant patients) • Precautions for pregnant staff • Policies for identifying if patients could be pregnant • Procedures for radiation shielding during procedures • Fire response plan • Safety training records *Site inspection* • Area free of hazards such as exposed electrical wiring, hallway obstructions • Nearby key for locked doors (e.g., bathrooms) • Negatively vented rooms for airborne isolation • Exit signs visible and operational • Policies and procedures manual accessible to staff • Hallways unobstructed • Fire alarms/extinguishers functional • Patient and staff safety provided for in department design • Evidence in personnel files of staff receipt of training in safety program		

continues

Management of the Environment of Care

Standard	Comments	Evidence	Staff Questions	Reference
EC.1.1.2	Standard concerns enforcement of the organization's non-smoking policy in all areas of the organization, including visitor areas. Note: Please consult state regulations for specific requirements for smoking area restrictions within a stated distance from the building. Compliance is measured on an organizational basis, not related to individual departmental compliance.	• Orientation and continuing education material on efforts to communicate and enforce the nonsmoking policy • Nonsmoking policy and procedure • Patient and family education materials on smoking cessation programs, activities • "No smoking" signs posted, as appropriate • Surveyor inspection of department and surrounding areas for presence/absence of smoking materials, noticeable smell of smoke, evidence of butts outside of back exits outside of smoking areas or in hidden stairwells or unused areas	• Where can I smoke in the organization? • Describe how patients, families, visitors, and staff learn about the nonsmoking policy. • What do you do if a patient asks to smoke? • If you observe someone smoking in the building, what is the procedure to follow? • Has the organization been involved in any PI projects to promote smoking cessation?	
EC.1.2, EC.2.2, and EC.2.8	Standards relate to the organizationwide security management plan and its implementation for the security of patients, staff, and visitors. Include the requirement for educating staff on content and expectations for compliance.	• Evidence of implementation of organizationwide security plan and related policies and procedures • Staff knowledge of the following policies and procedures: – Identification badge inspection/visitor control – Security incidents, including civil disturbances, handling VIPs and the media, and staffing during disasters – Workplace violence – Patients with weapons – Kidnapping – Managing patient property	• When did you last receive security training? • How did you receive education on department security? • Who do you call if a patient or visitor threatens violence? What is the telephone number? • What do you do if you see someone without an ID or badge? • How do you file a security incident report? • What do you do if there is a bomb threat? Who is notified first? • What do you do if you locate an unidentified box or package during a bomb threat? • What do you do if a patient's belongings are missing?	

continues

Management of the Environment of Care

Standard	Comments	Evidence	Staff Questions	Reference
EC.1.2, EC.2.2, and EC.2.8 *continued*		–Safe treatment of potentially violent patients or visitors –Metal detector use, if applicable –Care of prisoner guidelines –Access and security of sensitive areas –Method for reporting missing patient/ family property • Procedures for controlling the area during internal or external disasters • Procedures for responding to infant/child abduction • Records of previous incidents, if retained at department level • Orientation manual with department-specific security information • Documentation of orientation session and other education program, attendance sheets • Safety/security meeting minutes showing evaluation of program and/or changes to the program based on identified risks • Tools for monitoring security risks, action plans in response to trends *Site inspection* • Identification badges inspected • Existence of barriers such as locked doors to prevent public access to certain areas • Panic buttons for staff	• What do you do if the media come to the radiology department? • What do you do if a patient has a weapon? • How is the radiology department staffed during a disaster? • Give me an example of a security problem that was resolved. • What are your most common security incidents? What have you done to handle the increase in the need for security? • How do you identify a staff member in the radiology department? • What do you do if you see a suspicious person? • Are there any specific procedures in place to protect infants/children or other at-risk groups during their stay in the department? • What security improvements have been made in your department?	

continues

Management of the Environment of Care

Standard	Comments	Evidence	Staff Questions	Reference
EC.1.2, EC.2.2, and EC.2.8 *continued*		• Testing of mechanical and staff response to alarm or security alert		
EC.1.3, EC.2.3, and EC.2.8	Standards relate to the organizationwide hazardous materials and waste management plan and its implementation for the protection of patients, staff, and visitors. Include the requirement for educating staff on content and expectations for compliance.	• Hazardous materials and waste management plan, including any department-specific aspects or component plans. • Policies addressing receiving, storing, and logging radioactive drugs • Training regarding the handling and use of radioactive drugs • Evidence of state licensing and other legal certifications • Sample policies for hazardous waste • Bloodborne policy for CAT scan • Material Safety Data Sheets (MSDSs) for hazardous substances accessible to staff • Reporting procedures for hazardous materials spills • Availability of hazardous waste spill kits as appropriate to materials used in the department • Inspection showing proper use and disposal of hazardous materials • Hazardous materials labeled according to federal, state, and local regulation, in a manner adequate to protect patient, visitor, and staff safety • Hazardous material containers of appropriate size and type to minimize potential	• What do you do if there is a hazardous material spill? What if a patient or staff member is exposed to such a spill? • How did you receive education on hazardous waste? • How do you dispose of contaminated sharps or gauze contaminated with body fluids? • How can staff access MSDSs? • How are hazardous materials stored in the radiology department? How do you obtain these materials? Who has access to these materials? • What do you do if you encounter an unknown chemical? • Where do you keep information regarding poisons? • What procedures do you have for treating patients with poisoning? • How do hazardous spill evacuation procedures differ from fire or disaster evacuation procedures?	4–45 4–47 4–85 4–86

continues

Management of the Environment of Care

Standard	Comments	Evidence	Staff Questions	Reference
EC.1.3, EC.2.3, and EC.2.8 *continued*		harm to patients, staff, and visitors • Hazardous waste containers appropriately located throughout the radiology department		
EC.1.4, EC.2.4, EC.2.8 through EC.2.9.1	Standards relate to the organizationwide emergency management plan and its implementation in the case of internal or external disasters. Include the requirement for educating staff on content and expectations for compliance. Of particular interest in the past year due is planning on an organizational basis and in conjunction with local authorities for communitywide disasters. Expectations include planning for four phases of emergency management activities: mitigation, preparedness, response, and recovery. Drills are required twice yearly at specified intervals.	• Emergency preparedness plan, including any department-specific aspects or component plans • Radiology personnel knowledgeable about the emergency preparedness plan and able to answer questions about it • Evidence of staff education and training on the emergency preparedness plan • Evidence of participation of radiology staff in emergency preparedness drill • Annual evaluation of emergency preparedness program, including relevant measures • Policy for communication in the department in the event of an emergency • Documentation that communication system is operational • Backup communication plan • List of duties to be performed in an emergency *Site inspection* • Emergency supplies accessible, stocked • Supplies (including electrical) in working condition	• How did you receive education on emergency preparedness? • Where is your department safety plan kept? • When was your last emergency preparedness drill? What was your role? How often do you have drills? • In an emergency, how do you manage patients in need of radioactive or chemical isolation and decontamination? • Please describe your evacuation routes, role in an evacuation, and who authorizes an evacuation. • In the event of an emergency, how do you obtain additional supplies that may be needed?	4–39 4–42

continues

Management of the Environment of Care

Standard	Comments	Evidence	Staff Questions	Reference
EC.1.4, EC.2.4, EC.2.8 through EC.2.9.1 *continued*		• Education and procedures for managing emergencies posted (utility systems failure guide, bomb threat procedures) • Evacuation route posted • Access to procedures for dealing with loss of power, water, electricity, lighting, communication, and other essential services and any evidence of implementation of backup plan during mock or actual event		
EC.1.5, EC.2.5, EC.2.8, EC.2.9.2, and EC.2.10.2	Standards relate to the organizationwide fire safety plan and its implementation for prevention, mitigation, and response. Include the requirement for educating staff on content and expectations for compliance. Particular attention is placed on life safety when construction is present. Requirements apply to procedures for fire safety in addition to fire retardant materials and environment. Consult specific standards for comprehensive requirements for organizationwide compliance. Drills are required on a quarterly basis for hospitals with less frequent drills allowed for business occupancies as outlined in the standards.	• Life safety/fire prevention plan, including any department-specific aspects or component plans • Radiology personnel knowledgeable about the life-safety plan and able to answer questions about it • Personnel given education and training on the life-safety plan • If general anesthesia is used in the department, fire safety requirements met in the area in which it is used • Fire response plan and evacuation routes posted in respective areas *Site inspection* • Up-to-date inspection tags on life-safety equipment • Department compliance (e.g., hallways unobstructed) • Portable fire extinguishers properly identified, counted, inspected	• How did you receive education on life safety? • Is access to a patient or exit from an area ever blocked? • How do you participate in fire drills? How do you evacuate the area during a fire drill? How do contract staff know what to do in case of a fire? How often do you have fire drills? • Where are fire extinguishers? • What is the process for periodic checking of fire extinguishers? • Who is responsible for turning off oxygen valves in the event of a fire? • What is your role during fire alarm activation? • Who can authorize an evacuation? What is the evacuation process and route? How do you evacuate patients? • How are medical records protected during and following an evacuation?	4–39 4–42 4–45

continues

Management of the Environment of Care

Standard	Comments	Evidence	Staff Questions	Reference
EC.1.5, EC.2.5, EC.2.8, EC.2.9.2, and EC.2.10.2 *continued*		• Interim life-safety measures in effect during relevant construction projects (e.g., access to normal exit, entrance blocked, etc.) • Reporting of fires • Data from past fire drills or alarms and any identified risk factors or resulting action plans	*Fire safety questions* • How often do you have fire drills? What is the requirement? • Do you perform these at least 50 percent of the time on all shifts with all unannounced? • Are these drills conducted without notice? • Is staff performance evaluated during drills? • Do you receive feedback? • What do you do if there is a fire? • Where is the closest fire exit? • Do exit signs lead to open exits? • Are any exits obstructed either by locks or obstructions outside? • If construction is occurring in department or adjoining area(s), are exits unobstructed? Are interim life-safety measures in place and are staff aware of their content? Where are these measures posted? • If fire exits are obstructed due to construction, have emergency signs been modified or moved/removed so as not to confuse during a fire? • Are egress routes that lead outside kept free of snow and ice? • Are portable heaters prohibited in patient treatment and sleeping areas? • Are waiting areas that open to corridors sprinklered? Is furniture arranged so not to obstruct evacuation? • What procedures do you follow to contain smoke and fire?	

continues

Management of the Environment of Care

Standard	Comments	Evidence	Staff Questions	Reference
EC.1.5, EC.2.5, EC.2.8, EC.2.9.2, and EC.2.10.2 *continued*			• How do contract or temporary staff learn about fire alarm procedures in the department? • Where are the fire extinguishers? Do you know how to use one? • Who is responsible for turning off oxygen valves in the event of a fire? Closing doors and windows? • How do you evacuate the area during a fire? • Where is the nearest fire alarm? How do you operate it? How do you know when the alarm is being tested? • How often do you receive training for fire safety, hazardous communication, and other response procedures? • What does "R.A.C.E." (or similar fire response pneumonic) stand for? • What does "P.A.S.S." (or similar fire response pneumonic) stand for?	
EC.1.6, EC.2.6, EC 2.8, and EC.2.10.3	Standards require the development, implementation, and ongoing monitoring of an equipment management program. Largely relate to medical equipment used for the diagnosis and treatment of patients rather than office or other low-risk equipment. Allow the organization to delineate the types of equipment to be monitored by the program. Do not require centralized mechanism for monitor-	• Staff and leadership interviews • Staff education and training • Equipment properly maintained, carrying inspection tags • Equipment program maintenance and service logs completed • PI studies, measurement of performance standards, action plans in response to medical equipment management (e.g., staff knowledge in response to equipment failure, preventive maintenance, etc.)	• Equipment management plan, including any department-specific aspects or checklists • How did you learn how to use this piece of equipment? • How do you know it is safe to use on a patient? • How do you find out about equipment recalls for equipment in your department? • How often is the equipment serviced? Who tracks the information to see that it is completed? • What do you do if this piece of equipment malfunctions?	4–47

continues

Management of the Environment of Care

Standard	Comments	Evidence	Staff Questions	Reference
EC.1.6, EC.2.6, EC 2.8, and EC.2.10.3 *continued*	ing equipment, only compliance with the established plan, largely based on manufacturer recommendations.	• Check of radiological technique before exposure • Quality assurance of shielding devices • Exposure badges • Equipment inspection and maintenance schedules • Reporting of equipment malfunction • Evidence of routine testing of equipment • Record of incident reports regarding equipment • Policies on personnel monitoring • Procedure for equipment failure • Training materials	• How do you operate this piece of equipment? • Who do you inform if there is an equipment failure? • How often is this equipment serviced? How do you know? • Who performs this check? How do you know? • Who is credentialed to use this equipment? • How often is the crash cart checked? How often are the contents replaced? How do the staff know what is in the crash cart? • Do you lend equipment to other organizations? What is the process? • Who is responsible for equipment maintenance when it is borrowed by other organizations?	
EC.1.7, EC.1.7.1, EC.2.7, EC.2.8, EC.2.10.4, and EC.2.10.4.1	Standards require the development, implementation, and ongoing monitoring of the utility management program. Focus on contingency planning for loss of single or multiple utilities, particularly emergency power. Include integration of response with local authorities in the case of disasters.	• Utility management plan, including any department-specific considerations or plans • Staff and leadership interviews • Organizationwide utility management plan and policies, and the radiology department's role in implementing plan • Report of utility failure events and any follow-up action plans • Log of utility monitors and *down time* testing • Emergency generator testing log and measures for monitoring effectiveness of backup power	• How did you receive education on utility systems? Please describe the orientation and continuing education you receive. • What do you do if the power goes out? • If you had to turn off medical gas, how would you? • What do you do if you learn the water is unsafe for drinking? • How do you report a utility problem, failure, or user error?	4–42

continues

Management of the Environment of Care

Standard	Comments	Evidence	Staff Questions	Reference
EC.1.7, EC.1.7.1, EC.2.7, EC.2.8, EC.2.10.4, and EC.2.10.4.1 *continued*		• Orientation, continuing education materials, attendance records for education programs on utilities • PI projects, measurement of performance standards, action plans in response to utilities (e.g., staff knowledge of actions to take in a utility system failure) • Documentation in meeting minutes of any utility management issues within the radiology department • Inspection records of preventive maintenance, testing of utilities (most likely reviewed during review of environment of care [EC] documents or building tour) *Site inspection* • Location of emergency shutoff controls for radiology department utilities • Labeling of control panels within department (performed during EC building tour)		
EC.3 through EC.3.4	Standards address the design and modification of the environment of patient care to preserve the privacy, dignity, and positive self-image of patients. Recently added the requirement for a risk assessment of sentinel events or safety issues and modification of the environment for prevention or mitigation. This risk assessment is considered	• Policy for patient confidentiality and privacy • Documentation of risk assessment related to planned construction or renovation that might compromise patient care in the radiology department *Site inspection* • Appropriate space (including light and ventilation) for services • Adequate auditory and visual privacy for patients	• Could you accommodate a patient need for making a telephone call if not contraindicated by their condition? • Is there enough space in exam rooms to run a code effectively? • How is patient confidentiality protected? • Has the organization recently remodeled the department? If so, did you participate or suggest any modifications? If so,	

continues

Management of the Environment of Care

Standard	Comments	Evidence	Staff Questions	Reference
EC.3 through EC.3.4 *continued*	during demolition, construction, or renovation work. Surveyors will also consider any known violations or noncompliance with state requirements or building code.	• Overhead paging system not violating patients' privacy • Appropriate patient clothing, considering clinical condition • Availability of a place for private conversations • Doors closed, where appropriate • Environment is safe, clean, and attractive • Ventilation allows for removal of odors • Auditory privacy (hallways) • Clearly marked exterior circulation • Paths to the radiology department	what criteria did you use? • Was there evidence that you considered in modifying the environment (e.g., patient complaints of privacy violations in a certain area)? • Does the department serve a specialty population that may require special furniture (e.g., bariatric patients)? If so, do you have equipment available for accommodating their needs?	
EC.4 through EC.4.3	Standards largely govern the evaluation of each of the seven management plans and any action planning for identified deficiencies. Require annual evaluation of each plan. Include the monitoring and response from the patient safety program. Assign an individual to monitor and respond to deficiencies. Multidisciplinary reaction to known issues is expected to resolve issues in the environment.	• Evidence of meeting minutes, reports, multidisciplinary PI teams analyzing environment of care findings, plans for improvement to resolve any identified issues • Outcomes, improvement reports, including annual reports of the scope, objectives, effectiveness for each of the environment of care plans; reports demonstrate that recommendations for the environment of care have been communicated at least annually to hospital leaders for consideration • Environment of care data, environmental safety issues, and recommendations for improvement are integrated into the hospitalwide patient safety program	• What data have you collected to measure the effectiveness of the environment of care plans in your area? • What strategies have you implemented to improve the environment of care in your unit? • How do you monitor the effectiveness of any new environment of care recommendations implemented? • Describe how you resolve environment of care issues identified in your system? Service area? • What other disciplines have you worked with to improve the environment of care?	

MANAGEMENT OF HUMAN RESOURCES

Standard	Comments	Evidence	Staff Questions	Reference
HR.1 and HR.2, HR.2.1	The radiology department must verify that there are sufficient staff within the department who have education, training, licensure, and knowledge consistent with legal requirements and organization policy. Organizational leaders analyze data on patient outcomes (clinical/services indicators) and staffing data (HR indicators) as a screen to ensure staffing effectiveness.	• Current staffing plan • Technologist qualifications policy • Policy for practicing diagnostic radiologists • Current job descriptions that reflect state law requirements for licensing and scope of practice • Competency assessment programs • Staff development plans • Records of inservice training • Department orientation program with records of attendance by staff members • Orientation handbook • Contract with provisions related to staffing if the department makes use of contracted personnel • Radiology organizational chart • Lists of procedures that may be performed by types of practitioners • Employee evaluations/competencies • Assessment tools • Staff development plans • Quality improvement (QI) studies regarding appropriate staffing levels and skills • Contracts, if the radiology department uses contracted personnel • Minutes of meetings where human resources (HR) issues are discussed • Licensure and certification records that show compliance with job descriptions and the law	• How are you competent to do your job? • What is your staffing pattern? • How were you trained to perform this procedure? • Is this department adequately staffed at all times? • How do you match staff responsibilities to education and experience? • What are your policies on staff supervision? *For the director* • Are they consistent with what requirements are needed by staff members? • What credentials do the staff members have? • Who defines qualifications for staff members? • How are job descriptions developed for newly created positions? • Can you demonstrate that there are adequate nursing staff, considering job responsibilities and qualifications, for medical imaging? • What training have you attended in the past year? • May I see your continuing education files? • How do you educate the night shift? • What was the last training session you attended? • What age-specific competencies are in place for relevant staff? • How do you monitor staff education requirements? • How do you identify staff learning needs? • How do you prioritize staff education requirements?	4–52 to 4–55 4–67 4–73 to 4–77

continues

Management of Human Resources

Standard	Comments	Evidence	Staff Questions	Reference
HR.1 and HR.2, HR.2.1 *continued*		• Completion of policy competencies by all new employees and cross-trained employees • Graphs of data comparisons between clinical/service indicators and HR screening indicators • Data on clinical/service screening indicators such as family or patient complaints, patient falls, injuries to patients • Data on HR screening indicators such as overtime, sick time, staff turnover and vacancy rates, staff satisfaction, understaffing as compared to the hospital's overall staffing plan	• How do you accomplish age-specific training and competency assessment? • Are any of your staff included in the analysis of staffing effectiveness? • What clinical service indicators were chosen? Do any of your staff influence these indicators? If yes, did the analysis show any correlation between low staffing and negative outcomes? • What HR indicators were chosen? Do any of your staff influence these indicators? If yes, did the analysis show any correlation between low staffing and negative outcomes?	
HR.3 through HR.3.1	Standards relate to ongoing evaluation and improvement of competencies of staff and measure how well an organization focuses on opportunities for self-improvement and self-learning.	• Competency lists for categories of staff members in the department (may be contained within the performance evaluation document) • Job descriptions • Performance evaluations • Self-training tests • Inservice training • Outside seminars or other continuing education programs • Credential review process • Cross-training program • Employee participation in QI projects or teams • Reward program for employee suggestions that are implemented • Age-specific competency assessment specific to the job	*For manager* • How do you ensure that staff have the skills needed for their jobs? • What ages of patients do you care for? What age-specific competencies are in place? Can someone demonstrate how he or she changes care based on the age of the patient? • Describe how you identify staff learning needs and how you prioritize and monitor staff education requirements. • What training have you planned for your department within the past year? • How do you educate the night shift? • Do staff pursue higher education and training?	4–52 to 4–55 4–68 4–73 to 4–77

continues

Management of Human Resources

Standard	Comments	Evidence	Staff Questions	Reference
HR.3 through HR.3.1 *continued*		responsibilities of a given job category • Education calendar showing educational opportunities available to staff • Agreed-upon goals as part of the employee evaluation • Employee handbook that explains evaluation methods	• What access do staff have for expanding their knowledge in areas of interest? *To staff* • What type of staff educational activities are available? How often? • Do education programs have continuing education units (CEU) credits? If yes, how many CEU education programs are provided annually? • What resources does your organization devote to continuing education (e.g., journals, books, videos, seminars, college credits, etc.)? • What was the last training session you attended? Has it helped you to improve patient care? • Can you describe your self-learning opportunities? • How many training opportunities have you had in the last year?	
HR.4	Standard outlines requirements for department orientation program and the hospitalwide orientation program.	• New employee orientation documentation and attendance records • Orientation handbook • Department policies and procedures related to orientation attendance • Policy on new employee orientation • Staff and leadership interviews	• How were you oriented to the radiology department and your job responsibilities? • Describe how you were oriented to the hospital. • Do you have volunteers working in the department? If so, what kind of orientation do they receive to the department and the hospital?	4–52
HR.4.1 through HR.4.2	Standards outline specific requirements for education of general and forensic staff on the care of forensic patients	• Schedule of inservice training • Results of self-assessment programs	• Can you give me an example of how training has improved radiology department performance? Your personal performance?	

continues

Management of Human Resources

Standard	Comments	Evidence	Staff Questions	Reference
HR.4.1 through HR.4.2 *continued*	in a multidisciplinary manner. Include need for education on patient safety that promotes the reporting of medical errors.	• Library of written, audio, video, and other resources • Staff and leadership interviews • Documentation of hospitalwide and departmental training programs concerning job-related aspects of patient safety • PI studies related to staff education • Records and staff files indicating job descriptions, orientation, verification process, performance evaluations, competencies, and continuing education contracts	• Can you describe the educational curriculum for staff (program goals and opportunities), results of self-assessment programs, and training programs specifically designed for your job classification and patient population? • Can you describe methods of team training you have participated in regarding patient safety and reporting of medical/health care errors? • When forensic patients are present in the department, how do radiology staff and forensic staff know how to care for the patient while maintaining his correctional safety?	
HR.4.3	Standard charges the organization with showing compliance with the aggregation of data concerning competency patterns to report to the board that competency is maintained and improved over time. May include compliance with existing competency programs, addition of patient safety elements, and changes reflective of patient needs or services.	• Records showing that applicable data were submitted to the hospital committee or department spearheading this effort • Aggregated competency scores from annual evaluations of staff competency • Staff and leadership interviews	*For manager* • How do you know that your staff are able to perform their roles? • What changes have been made in staff education in response to staff requests? In response to patient needs? • Who is responsible for educating staff? • Describe trends in your staff's competency and performance evaluations. • Do your data pinpoint training needs? If yes, how are you planning to improve your program? • If applicable, what changes have been made in staff education based on data collected?	
HR.5	Standard addresses the requirement for periodic evaluation of staff	• Policies and procedures related to age-specific competencies	• How often do you assess your competencies for age-specific patient groups?	4–73 to 4–77

continues

Management of Human Resources

Standard	Comments	Evidence	Staff Questions	Reference
HR.5 *continued*	member's ability to meet the performance expectations stated in his or her job description, including any age-related aspects of care.	• Examples of age-specific competencies • Current job descriptions • Staff training records • Staffing plan	• How do staff modify their job duties based on the age of the patient? How does competency assessment reflect these modifications?	
HR.6 through HR.6.2	Standards support staff members' right to request not to participate in a patient's care for ethical, religious, or cultural reasons. Require the organization to have procedures in place to accommodate these requests.	• Staff and leadership interviews • Policy and procedure (sometimes known as "staff rights" or "exclusion from patient care") concerning standard • Meeting minutes, ethics committee consultations, patient records documenting implementation of policy • Logs of staff requests, evaluations • Preemployment processes to assess whether job duties would conflict with the person's cultural values or religious beliefs	• How have managers attempted to accommodate the religious and ethical concerns of staff members? What is the policy for this accommodation? • How does the department ensure that patients receive the needed treatments? • What would you do if you did not wish to care for a patient due to religious, ethical, or cultural reasons?	

MANAGEMENT OF INFORMATION

Standard	Comments	Evidence	Staff Questions	Reference
IM.1	Standard concerns the need for information management (IM) plan created by assessing the organization's information needs. Representatives from the radiology department should participate in the creation of this plan to ensure that the department's IM needs are assessed and incorporated into the overall IM planning process. Surveyors may focus on how radiology leaders make their department's IM needs known to senior leaders.	• Staff and leadership interviews • Evidence of an IM Steering Committee that prioritizes projects, requests, and needs for the organization • IM plan for organization, including input from radiology services • Radiology department participation in IM planning documents, strategic plans, needs assessment surveys, requests to administration • Meeting minutes indicating IM planning for the radiology department • Performance improvement (PI) projects in the radiology department or organizationwide displaying plans and outcomes to improve the flow of patient information (e.g., plans for or observation of new computer system, charting, scheduling system, etc.)	• How do you participate in IM planning? Are physicians and other clinicians involved in the process? • How has the organization assessed your IM needs? Can you give an example of how you had an IM need met? • What resources are available for staff to support information needs, including any computer programs or automated data resources?	
IM.2 through IM.2.1	Radiology should ensure that IM security practices comply with organization policies and procedures while allowing access to data and information in a timely fashion. To protect confidentiality, the radiology department limits access to patient information based on the need to know. Systems must be implemented to protect	• Staff, leadership, and patient interviews • Policy for shredding confidential documentation in medical imaging • Policy for film ownership and use • Policy for destruction of archival film • Policy for who has access to medical record information • Policy and procedures for release of records	• How are medical records ordered? • Who has access to the patient's medical record? Who has access to the computer terminal where records are kept? • What do you do if a family member asks to look at a patient's record? • How do you protect the security of medical record information? • What information do you have access to on the computer?	4–78 4–79 4–81 to 4–84

continues

Management of Information

Standard	Comments	Evidence	Staff Questions	Reference
IM.2 through IM.2.1 *continued*	the integrity of the data (e.g., medical record, computer system, stored records, etc.), including protection against loss, destruction, tampering, and unauthorized access or use.	and/or films to patients or physicians • Policy on what information is released to family, media, telephone inquirers • Staff "contracts" to keep information confidential • IM plans/policies for protecting the integrity of data (e.g., operation of backup systems, contingency plans, down-time procedures, data retrieval, measures for protection against emergencies, security systems that include passwords, codes) • Outline of computerized protection for confidentiality of patient information *Site inspection* • Patient information not discussed in areas where confidential information may be overheard by individuals other than the patient • Computer terminals logged off when not being used • Security of any clinical information identifying the patient • Security of active and inactive records • Protective measures implemented to prevent distribution of sensitive information to public (e.g., procedural schedules, not having patient sign-in log where patient information could be viewed by others)	• What is your policy on releasing clinical information, copies of the record? Do you get a consent for the release of information? • How do you manage inquiries regarding patients? • How are you trained on confidentiality and security of information issues? What special procedures do you have to protect patient information (e.g., staff sign confidentiality statements on hire or when using computer system)? • What measures does the hospital take to protect information and data from being revealed to individuals not having permission? What processes protect the data or information from security breaches, harm, or being altered?	

continues

Management of Information

Standard	Comments	Evidence	Staff Questions	Reference
IM.2 through IM.2.1 *continued*		• Measures to protect records from damage (e.g., sprinklers, fireproof cabinets)		
IM.3	Expectation of the use of standard terminology, definitions, and abbreviations, as well as uniform data collection methodologies.	• Abbreviations, or a standard approved book that would include any examples from radiology • Standard data definitions for a medical record, automated data tables/dictionary on computer system • Medical record accuracy, use of approved terminology • Medical and clinical policies on abbreviations, terminology, data definitions, collection of data, etc.	• Do you have a policy on abbreviations or standard data definitions? • How do you ensure that data are collected in a uniform manner? • When definitions or abbreviations are added to the list, are safety aspects of terms considered before adoption?	
IM.4	Standard concerns IM resources available to transform data into information. Standard addresses the availability of data measurement and analysis processes in addition to statistical tools for the analysis of results toward improving care based on the data.	• Policies outlining the confidentiality, security, and access to use of computers and software. Data collection techniques, processes for ensuring accuracy of collecting data; using data, exchanging information, and interpreting data. PI tools and techniques for using data to support decision making, access to literature, and library services • Interview of manager and others about access to data management and analysis resources for improving care *Site inspection* • Staff interactions, use of data, computer system	• What education have you received in support of IM purposes, processes, and tools available for use? • What radiology indicators are collected to improve systems and processes? How do you ensure consistency when gathering the data? Have you trended your data? Do you use statistical techniques to interpret the data? • What resources does the organization have to support staff knowledge of IM principles, tools, and techniques? • *Managers:* What systems for data collection, analysis, and presentation do you have access to?	

continues

Management of Information

Standard	Comments	Evidence	Staff Questions	Reference
IM.4 *continued*		• Department resources (e.g., literature, computer software, videos) available to the staff • Examination of PI reports for presentation of data and reports of care improvements		
IM.5 through IM.5.1	Address the timely and accurate transmission of data and information in either paper or electronic format. Include appropriate communication of information between practitioners in support of patient care processes. Specific to the radiology department, address the timeliness and accuracy of reports and studies to practitioners for diagnosis and treatment.	• Radiology department adherence to hospital policy, for example – Test results from radiology transcribed in the medical record within the time frame established by organization – PI studies on the turnaround time for stat imaging examinations – Turnaround time from a request to report release • Timeliness of transmission of study results for patients transferred to other organizations for further treatment • Policies and procedures, indicators, organizationwide or specific to the radiology department specific to data transmission and use • Mechanism for ensuring that systems are compatible for accurate transmission and assimilation of data • PI data, chart reviews, practices that ensure the accuracy of data and information (e.g., use of standard abbreviations, codes, definitions, turnaround time, chart completion rates)	• Describe any mechanisms you use to ensure that data are collected in a timely and precise manner. • Give examples of how the organization standardizes data and information (e.g., approved abbreviation lists, data definitions). • What is the expected turnaround time for the following: – Radiology reports – Lab tests – Blood tests • What is the turnaround time for dictated radiology reports? • Describe your process for notifying physicians of discrepancies in radiology or lab results. • What is your procedure for notifying patients of the results of diagnostic studies?	4–35

continues

Management of Information

Standard	Comments	Evidence	Staff Questions	Reference
IM.5 through IM.5.1 *continued*		• PI studies addressing the timeliness and accuracy of components of the medical record • Standardization of the record toward improving the accuracy of the medical record		
IM.6	Governs expectations for the integration of clinical and operational information systems for the improvement of patient care. Includes the availability and use of reference databases as a mechanism for monitoring and improving care.	• IM system structure that collects, organizes, analyzes, and assists with interpreting data • IM plans, policies, and procedures on data management • Interviews with staff members who collect and use data • Agreement with reference or external databases • Reports demonstrating the integration of data from various sources, clinical with nonclinical information • Examples of reports or studies utilizing reference databases • Examples of data being used for individual care, management, research, chart documentation, education	• When you need to relate data from clinical and operational data systems, how is this accomplished? • If you have clinical systems, are they linked to your financial, billing system? • How are department clinical systems linked (e.g., food and nutrition with laboratory)? • Do you trend reports on volumes, staffing patterns, billing records?	
IM.7 through IM.7.2	Each patient must have a medical record to document treatment rendered. Only authorized individuals make entries into the medical record. The medical record must contain information that identifies the patient and describes the diagnosis and relevant	• Staff interviews • Open and closed medical records • Department policies and procedures based on the radiology department setting and patient population • Quarterly medical record review results involving radiology records, use of data,	• Who is responsible for reviewing the patient's medical records before an exam is performed? • Where is this medical record kept following discharge? • Who can document in the medical record? *Reviewing of medical record in the radiology department*	4–21 4–22 4–26

continues

Management of Information

Standard	Comments	Evidence	Staff Questions	Reference
IM.7 through IM.7.2 *continued*	testing results to manage the patient's condition, plan of care, progress of case, prognosis, and outcome depicting the continuity of care. This process displays how the organization defines, captures, analyzes, transforms, transmits, and reports patient data and information. Medical records must be retained based on state law and the organization's regulations. Patient care, research, performance improvement, legal requirements, and educational endeavors may also contribute to the length of time a record is retained. Patient-specific data and information may be used in a variety of ways: for clinical care; for financial, PI, and risk management purposes; to support research projects; and for decision making. Standards outline the elements necessary in the medical record for caring for patients.	and outcomes (involving those elements listed in the intent) • Involvement with PI studies regarding patient care documentation issues (e.g., evidence of appropriate orders, consultations, timely operative reports, discharge summaries, discharge instructions) • Assessment mechanisms • Consent forms • PI activities and their results aimed at improving the quality of the medical record • Review of open and closed medical reocrds for elements outlined in the standard	*(questions limited to those asked in the department)* • Where is the patient's identification data (e.g., name, age, and race)? • Why did this patient come to the department? What was the diagnosis and treatment plan? Chief complaint? • Where is the evidence of informed consent, as applicable? • Were any referrals made to internal or external care providers to ensure that the patient's continuing care needs are met? Where would that be documented? • Where are the discharge instructions? Where is the transfer or discharge summary? What education did the patient receive? *Other pertinent questions* • Where is this medical record kept while in the department? • Who can document in the medical record? • How long are your records maintained?	
IM.7.3 through IM.7.3.5	Standards govern the documentation required for operative and other invasive procedures, including those requiring sedation and anesthesia. As defined by the medical staff, this may include invasive procedures performed in the radiology department.	• Procedural forms or flowsheets • Dictation of procedure report • Progress notes documenting informed consent prior to procedure as required • Progress note post-procedure outlining items set forth in the standard to assist in continuity of care.	• What procedures are performed in this department? Do they include the use of sedation or anesthesia? • For those requiring sedation or anesthesia or those considered high risk by the medical staff, is there a record of a preoperative diagnosis prior to the procedure?	

continues

Management of Information

Standard	Comments	Evidence	Staff Questions	Reference
IM.7.3 through IM.7.3.5 *continued*		• Includes documentation of compliance with discharge criteria prior to discharge to lower level of care	• Are all the elements present in the chart as outlined in the standard?	
IM.7.4 and IM.7.4.1	Standards apply to the radiology department only when patients present for continuing services such as a series of treatments or tests. Require a summary list be developed for each ambulatory care patient by the patient's third visit.	• Records of patients receiving ambulatory care services containing summary lists with the required information	• Do you have a policy on summary sheets? • Who is responsible for initiating the summary sheet? • What is the process for ensuring that the patient's summary sheet is established by the third visit? How do you monitor compliance?	
IM.7.5 through IM.7.5.1	Standards largely address the special requirements for patients presenting for emergency care. Include specific requirements for documentation of patients leaving against medical advice (AMA).	• Existence of organizational policies and procedures for patients who refuse exam or do not want to continue treatment • EMTALA and AMA policies, including patient requests to leave from other departments outside of emergency department • Open and closed medical records • Staff interviews • Meeting minutes discussing AMA (any potential Emergency Medical Treatment and Active Labor Act [EMTALA] issues), risk management issues, PI activities • Trending tool of AMA patients • Medical record monitoring of compliance with standard elements	• Where in the medical record do you document time and means of arrival for patients presenting initially to the radiology department? • Describe the policy to follow when a patient leaves against medical advice. Where is this documented? What steps are being taken to reduce the number of patients leaving against medical advice?	4–26 4–36 4–37
IM.7.5.2	Outlines specific medical record content following emergent, urgent, or immediate	• Discharge handout containing instruction for self-care and	• Please describe your discharge planning process.	4–25 4–26

continues

Management of Information

Standard	Comments	Evidence	Staff Questions	Reference
IM.7.5.2 *continued*	care. Includes documentation of discharge instructions.	indicating when to return for medical care • Policies for discharge follow-up instructions for patients discharged from the emergency room • Referrals to community resources • Quality management analysis of discharge teaching • Conclusions and other required elements included in medical records • Indication in medical records that discharge instructions were given • PI studies on discharge teaching, planning, and outcomes • Evidence of care paths or teaching pathways • Medical record reviews of compliance with requirements over time	• Where in the record would I find the conclusions following treatment, final disposition, follow-up instructions for further care, referrals, etc.? • What do you do if your patient/family has barriers to understanding the instructions given (e.g., learning disabilities, financial barriers, psychosocial issues)? • Do you have a call-back program? Does it have an impact on your patients' continuum of care? How is it helpful with patient and family education? • What measures have you identified to evaluate effectiveness of teaching and follow-up care? • Have you made changes to practices based on information obtained from your call-back program?	
IM.7.5.3	Standard requires authorized release of emergency care records to internal and external practitioners to facilitate continuity of care following treatment in the emergent care setting. It requires the patient's or legal representative's consent for release of information to other providers providing follow-up care.	• Policies for transfer of information • Release of information policy • Open and closed medical records • Presence of release of information forms on discharge charts	• Describe your policy on releasing emergency records to other practitioners providing follow-up care. • If a radiology patient goes to another facility, how do you release the patient's records to that facility?	4–81
IM.7.6	Standard addresses the timeliness of medical record management. Although time requirements are specified by	• Departmental policies and procedures on medical record completion that comply with organizational policies	• Who is responsible for completing this patient's medical record? • Describe your policy for ensuring the timely entry	4–35

continues

Management of Information

Standard	Comments	Evidence	Staff Questions	Reference

IM.7.6 *continued*	the hospital, the Joint Commission and CMS requires records to be completed within 30 days of discharge.	and procedures for medical record completion
		• Radiology department adherence to hospital standards, for example:
		  – Physical review of medical records indicating that each patient's history and physical examination is documented prior to operative or invasive procedures as set forth by the medical staff
		  – Records completed in fewer than 30 days after discharge
		• Physician profiling—physical chart completion statistics
			of clinical information into the medical record.
			• How has the organization improved in timely completion of record entries? Do physicians receive data on their performance with timely completion of records? Is it used in their profiles for reappointment decisions?
			• How long do medical record components remain in radiology before being sent to the medical records department? What is the time frame for reports sent to open medical records?	

IM.7.7 (LINK new Medication Use Standards)	Standard governs the use of verbal orders by authorized individuals. Emphasis is on limiting their use and delegating their transcription to authorized individuals through well established policies. Increased emphasis expected with new medication use standards in 2004.	• Policies on verbal orders, including delineation as to who can give them, who can take them • Compliance with medical staff bylaws, rules, and regulations • Compliance with verbal order policy and procedure • Open and closed medical records demonstrating that verbal orders are accepted by appropriate staff, properly transcribed, dated, and authenticated • Record review of the verbal order authentication process • Data collection of the unit's performance with verbal orders	• Please describe your verbal order policy and procedure. • Who may transcribe a verbal order?	

continues

Management of Information

Standard	Comments	Evidence	Staff Questions	Reference
IM.7.8	Standard focuses on the dating and authentication of medical record entries. Main focus is on the authentication of histories and physicals, consultations, discharge summaries, and operative reports. Authentication may include electronic or stamped signature. However, these authorizations require safeguards for ensuring use only by the practitioner.	• Radiology representation on organizational medical record review committee or participation in medical record review function • Medical record review for properly authenticated entries • List of radiology staff authorized to document in the medical record • Open and closed medical records demonstrating compliance with policies and procedures—may ask staff to identify the date and author of entries within a selected record • Medical staff bylaws, rules, and regulations delineating requirements for medical record entry authentication • PI data on record review regarding this standard	• What medical record entries are required to be authenticated? What processes are in place to ensure that they have been authenticated? What is the designated time frame for authenticating entries? • How do you track compliance with authentication?	
IM.7.9	Requires systems and processes in place to bring portions of the medical record together when indicated to ensure access by treating practitioners. Includes the ability to retrieve radiology reports and/or films when patients arrive for emergency care.	• Mechanisms for medical record retrieval from radiology department and other areas after hours • Departmental policies and procedures • Site survey showing compliance with the standard (e.g., observation of access to fax machines, computer records) • Use of a computer patient information system • Medical staff rules and regulations • Interviews with staff, leaders	• How do you retrieve old medical records after hours? • How do you obtain old films for comparison with a new study? • If a patient was seen in the ambulatory clinic today, can you obtain his medical record when he shows up in the ED for recurring symptoms tonight? How would you go about obtaining this information? Let's try to do it now. • Describe your medical record system for assembling clinical information for patient care.	

continues

Management of Information

Standard	Comments	Evidence	Staff Questions	Reference
IM.7.9 *continued*			• How do you access this patient's record? • How quickly can you assemble a record from different settings (e.g., hard copy or screen display)? • Does the record system alert users when components are stored in other locations? • How do you order medical records for a radiology patient? • How long are records kept in the radiology department after a patient has been discharged, admitted, or transferred?	
IM.7.10 through IM.7.10.1	Standards require a quarterly review of records to ensure that the medical records are comprehensive and accurate, and that documentation is timely. The goal of the review is to improve the quality of documentation, including its timeliness. Standards outline the required elements for review. The medical record review should represent a cross section of the types of patients served in the settings in which they are served. Separate review process for the radiology department is not necessary if a representative sample is included in the organizational review. A multidisciplinary approach to the review is required—including medical staff, nursing, and other clinical caregivers.	• Quarterly reports on medical record review results • A review of a significant sample of records to draw conclusions from the data • Staff and leadership interviews • Open and closed review of records for items listed in the standard (e.g., identification data, histories, assessments, consents, consults, orders, discharge instructions, summaries, etc.) • Minutes that include the outcome from medical record reviews, including chart completion statistics • Minutes, reports that include feedback from leaders/staff on strategies to improve documentation deficiencies identified • PI studies, outcomes of reviews (e.g., appropriate treatment of patients)	• How does the radiology department participate in the organization's medical record review? How often? What clinicians participate in the review? • Describe any improvements or plans for improvement based on data collected from chart reviews. • Have you identified further needs for education, skills reviews based on the record review? • What indicators do you monitor during quarterly chart reviews?	

continues

Management of Information

Standard	Comments	Evidence	Staff Questions	Reference
IM.8	Standard references the need to collect, aggregate, and analyze data for the improvement of patient care processes.	• PI data reports, use of aggregate data in system • Minutes of meetings indicating use of data and information • Documentation illustrating that the radiology department uses data to make patient care decisions and management decisions, to reduce risks to patients, to look for trends over time, to compare with other organizations, and for any other PI	• Show me a sample of a report where you aggregate the data and use them for decision making. • What information do you collect, aggregate, and analyze to improve patient care processes? How do you select what to collect? What mechanisms are in place to assist in this process?	
IM.9 through IM.9.1	Standards concern knowledge-based ("literature") IM needs of staff. Mainly address knowledge-based information on site. A hospital is not required to have an on-site library but must demonstrate that information may be obtained in a timely manner by sharing services with another hospital or resource.	• Staff and leadership interviews • Systems, resources, literature searches, use of library services • Listing of library literature, periodicals, practice guidelines, texts, indexes, abstracts, on-line services, satellite services, research data, etc. • Needs questionnaires to determine knowledge-based needs versus resources	• Describe resources available to meet your knowledge-based ("literature") IM needs. • Do you have access to the Internet? An intranet? • Do your staff have access to the latest resources available in radiology services (e.g., latest standards of care, care planning books, reference literature, articles, etc.)? • How have you used knowledge-based information to support clinical, management decisions, PI? • What resources provide you with evidence based techniques for decreasing risks of sentinel events for patients?	
IM.10	Standard encourages the use of databases for benchmarking and comparative studies to improve care over time. The basis for the ORYX and core measure	• Staff and leadership interviews • IM Plan • Participation in comparative databases (e.g., SR Gallup, Press	• What data do you report to external databases (e.g., Department of Human Services, Board of Health, Occupational Safety and Health Administration [OSHA],	

continues

Management of Information

Standard	Comments	Evidence	Staff Questions	Reference
IM.10 *continued*	requirements. Survey inquiry based largely on the results of ORYX/ core measures and changes resulting from the data received.	Gainey, ORYX, internal system comparisons) • Core measures and comparative data	Centers for Medicare and Medicaid Services (CMS)? Do you receive reports from the external sources? How are the data used? • Do you have ORYX indicators pertinent to radiology services? Have the data been used for performance improvement? Have you achieved any improvement in outcomes? • Describe the aggregate data you use to support patient care and operation decision making. • What external databases are used by the organization for comparative data? What data does your organization contribute? • Do you use any external comparative databases to measure the effectiveness of your department? If so, which ones? What comparative data does it provide? • How have you used comparative data to improve care in your organization?	

SURVEILLANCE, PREVENTION, AND CONTROL OF INFECTION

Standard	Comments	Evidence	Staff Questions	Reference
IC.1 (LINK MMWR Vol. 51, No. RR-16; Oct. 25, 2002)	Standard outlines requirements for the monitoring, prevention, and control of infection or risks of potential infection in the hospital. Requires comprehensive program that screens for potential infection, monitors for actual infection to prevent its spread, and mitigates hospital-acquired infections through a comprehensive prevention program. This area has become increasingly important in recent months as increased media attention has focused on infectious events and revised guidelines from the CDC.	• Records of employees who have been exposed to or contracted significant infections • Data collection that complies with hospital requirements • Documentation of radiology representation on hospital infection control committee • Organizational and radiology-specific infection control policies and procedures • Infection control and prevention policy and procedure for the medical imaging department • Basic aseptic technique • Universal precautions guidelines • Staff education materials • Staff interviews • Observation of patient care and use of universal precautions/aseptic technique • Presence of supplies needed for universal precautions (hand gel, gloves, gowns, masks, as indicated) • Observation of sanitization of surfaces between patients	• How do you report a patient with a communicable disease? • How do you treat a patient who presents a risk of an epidemiologically important nosocomial infection? • What is a bloodborne pathogen? • How is the safety of staff treating a patient in tuberculosis (TB) isolation ensured? • What infection control issues have you encountered this year? • What was done to resolve those issues? • Describe infection control training programs you have attended. • Where are the infection control policies and procedures kept within the radiology department? • Where is the personal protection equipment kept? • Is a patient with an active infection treated differently while in the department? Why or why not? What if the patient needs to use the restroom during the visit?	4–85 to 4–87
IC.1.1	Requires the assignment of infection control processes to an individual for coordination with other areas.	• Report of employee infection or communicable disease	• Who do you contact in the hospital to discuss nosocomial infections? • What do you do if you have a question about infection control? • How do you find out about the activities of the infection control committee?	

continues

Surveillance, Prevention, and Control of Infection

Standard	Comments	Evidence	Staff Questions	Reference
IC.2 through IC.3	Standards address hospital data collection and surveillance of infection control and employee health issues. Require notification of infections to appropriate reporting agencies as applicable by law.	• Department-level infection control policies and procedures available to staff • Observation and interviews with staff to review infection control strategies • Implementation of organizationwide and departmental infection control policies and procedures (must be consistent) • Records of infection control and/or safety team surveillance rounds, reporting, and follow-up activities • Department data collection that complies with organization requirements • Records of employees who have contracted significant infections	• Describe your process for collecting data on nosocomial infections and employee health issues. • What is a nosocomial infection? • What is a bloodborne pathogen? • How do you monitor compliance with infection control procedures? • What infection control issues have you encountered this year? • Where are your infection control policies located in the department? • Who makes reports to the local and state health departments? • Describe the activities that make up your approach to preventing nosocomial infections in all areas of the hospital. • What education is provided to staff members regarding infection prevention and control? To patients?	
IC.4 through IC.5	Standards relate to reducing the risk of infection and responding to outbreaks appropriately. Applicable to all areas of the organization, inpatient, and outpatient.	• Department policy on reporting infections to public health authorities and hospital officials • Staff education records • Department-specific infection control policies and procedures • Records of employees who have contracted significant infections • Universal precautions guidelines • Report of employee infection or communicable disease • Basic aseptic technique	• How and when do you report a patient with a communicable disease? • What do you do if you think you have contracted an infection? • What precautions do you take when a patient may have TB or human immunodeficiency virus (HIV), etc.? • What are universal precautions? Do you follow them? • How do you monitor compliance with infection control procedures? • How were you educated about infection control?	4–85 to 4–87

continues

Surveillance, Prevention, and Control of Infection

Standard	Comments	Evidence	Staff Questions	Reference
IC.4 through IC.5 *continued*		• Observation and interviews with staff • Orientation, continuing education material, attendance records for infection control training • Radiology staff participation in any performance improvement (PI) projects to control the identified outbreaks of infections • Minutes of infection control discussions, activities *Site inspection:* • Proper disposal of waste that may transmit infection • Gloves, gowns, goggles, shields, and other protective gear worn when contacting blood or body fluid • Protective gear stored appropriately • Staff demonstrating proper handwashing techniques • Separation of soiled and clean linen • Clean room not contaminated • Open solution bottles dated and maintained according to policy • Linen hampers not overfilled, bagged linen not on floors • Food refrigerators: – Free of outdated containers – Patient food containers dated – Patient and employee food separated – Food and non-food items separated	• When were you last trained in infection control techniques? • What do you do with soiled linens? Where are clean linens stored? • How do you protect patients from discarded waste? How do you protect housekeeping staff from discarded waste? • What have you done to decrease the risk of infection for radiology patients and staff? • Are there any patients who should be immediately removed from the waiting room? Which patients? • What is the procedure to follow in the event of a sharps exposure? • Do you have special procedures when patients at increased risk of infection present to the radiology department (e.g., patients on chemotherapy)?	

continues

Surveillance, Prevention, and Control of Infection

Standard	Comments	Evidence	Staff Questions	Reference
IC.4 through IC.5 *continued*		– Thermometer in medication refrigerator, free from food, clean – Food/beverages away from possible contamination • Needle boxes not overflowing, off floor and located in position so as not to prove a risk to patients or visitors, including children		
IC.6 through IC.6.2	Standards concern hospitalwide efforts to reduce the risk of infection transmission, with an emphasis on data collection, analysis, and improvement efforts. Include the availability of human and automated resources to track data and improve processes through data analysis.	• Radiology quality improvement or other monitoring/trending tools related to infection control • Staff knowledge of the objectives of the infection control program and how it relates to PI	• What have you done to reduce the risk of infection in the radiology department? • How do you evaluate infection control procedures? Who monitors staff compliance with infection control procedures? • How are employee health programs integrated with infection control practices?	4–85 to 4–87

PART 4

Reference Materials for Radiology Department Compliance

The following materials serve as examples. Hospitals should consult with counsel or other appropriate advisors before adapting the materials in this part to suit particular purposes.

PATIENT RIGHTS AND ORGANIZATIONAL ETHICS

4–1
Code of Ethics

PURPOSE STATEMENT

To identify the ethical guidelines by which _____ Hospital functions in its dealings with the patients, staff, physicians, and community

POLICY STATEMENT

1. Health care institutions, by virtue of their roles as health care providers, employers, and community health resources, have special responsibilities for ethical conduct and practices. The many patient care, education, public health, social service, and business functions they undertake are essential to the health and well-being of their communities. In general, the public expects that health care institutions will conduct themselves in an ethical manner that emphasizes a basic community-service orientation.

2. These guidelines are intended to assist the staff of the hospital to better define the ethical aspects and implications of institutional policies and practices. They are not intended to, in themselves, create a legal duty or obligation. They are offered with the understanding that individual decisions seldom reflect an absolute ethical right or wrong and that each institution's leadership in making policy and decisions must take into account the needs and values of the institution, its medical community, its employees, individual patients, their families, and the community as a whole.

3. The board of directors of the hospital is responsible for establishing and periodically evaluating the ethical standards that guide institutional practices. The chief executive officer is responsible for ensuring that hospital medical staff, employees, and volunteers understand and adhere to these standards and for promoting an environment sensitive to differing values and conducive to ethical behavior.

4. The guidelines examine the hospital's ethical responsibilities to its community and patients as well as responsibilities derived from its organizational roles as an employer and a business entity. Although some responsibilities may also be included in legal and accreditation requirements, it should be remembered that legal, accreditation, and ethical obligations often overlap and that ethical obligations often extend beyond legal and accreditation requirements.

POLICY GUIDELINES

Community Role

1. The hospital is concerned with the overall health status of the community as well as the provision of direct patient services. This principle requires that the organization communicate and work with other health care providers, payers, educational institutions, and social agencies to improve the availability and provision of health promotion, education, and prevention services as well as patient care and to take a leadership role in enhancing public health and continuity of care in the community.

2. The hospital collaborates with area educational institutions to enhance health education for the community and for the hospital's patients and employees. Educational institutions with whom the hospital affiliates are expected to abide by the hospital's policies and procedures as well as its ethical guidelines with respect to activities at the hospital covered by the affiliation.

3. The hospital is responsible for fair and effective use of available health care delivery resources to promote access to comprehensive and affordable health care services of high quality. This responsibility extends beyond the resources of the institution to include efforts to coordinate with other health care providers and to share in community solutions for providing care for the medically indigent and others.

continues

4–1 continued

4. The hospital has community-service responsibilities, which include care for the poor and the uninsured, provision of needed services and educational programs, and various programs designed to meet the specific needs of the community. The staff are particularly sensitive to the importance of providing and designing services for the community, with a preferential option for and special concern for the needs of the poor.

5. The hospital depends on community confidence and support and is accountable to the public through its board of directors. Therefore, communications and disclosures of information and data related to the institution are to be clear, accurate, and sufficiently complete to ensure they are not misleading. Such disclosures are aimed primarily at better public understanding of health issues, the services available to prevent and treat illness, and patient rights and responsibilities related to health care decisions.

6. As health care institutions operate in an increasingly competitive environment, the hospital considers the overall welfare of the community in determining their activities, service mixes, and business ventures, and conducts its business activities in an ethical manner.

Patient Care

1. The hospital is responsible for ensuring that the care provided to each patient is appropriate and of the highest quality the hospital is able to provide. The hospital has established and follows procedures to verify the credentials of physicians and other health professionals to assess and improve quality of care and to review appropriateness of utilization.

2. The hospital adopts and promulgates policies related to the protection of patient rights that are consistent with the overall philosophy of the institution and that may be required by law, licensure, or accreditation requirements.

3. The hospital has policies and practices that support the process of informed consent for diagnostic and therapeutic procedures and that respect and promote the patient's responsibility for decision making.

4. The hospital is responsible for ensuring confidentiality of patient-specific information in both written and oral communication. This responsibility includes providing safeguards to prevent unauthorized release of information and establishing procedures for authorized release of data.

5. The hospital ensures that psychological, social, spiritual, and physical needs, and cultural beliefs and practices of patients and families are recognized, and it promotes employee and medical staff sensitivity to the full range of such needs and practices.

6. The hospital ensures respect for and reasonable accommodation of individual religious and social beliefs and customs of patients whenever possible.

7. The hospital has specific mechanisms or procedures to resolve conflicting values and ethical dilemmas among patients, their families, medical staff, employees, the institution, and the community.

8. The hospital discloses, as may be required by law, its ownership interest in any entity to which patients may be referred.

9. The hospital will engage in continuous quality improvement efforts in all areas of patient care.

10. The hospital will emphasize continuing education of patients and staff as a core value essential for the delivery of optimal patient care.

Admission of Patients

1. The hospital does not discriminate in the admission of patients or the provision of accommodations based on race, creed, color, disability, or national origin. Emergency services are available to all without regard to ability to pay.

continues

4–1 continued

Transfer and Discharge

1. The hospital has adopted policies related to the transfer and discharge of patients that are in keeping with all applicable laws and accreditation standards.

2. The hospital will inform patients of the need for and alternatives to such transfers/discharges.

3. The hospital will ensure reasonable continuity of care and inform patients of care alternatives when acute care is no longer needed.

Financial/Billing Practices

1. The hospital distributes accurate, comprehensible, and timely bills to patients and payers for the services provided by the hospital. The hospital is responsive and courteous to all inquiries and requests for assistance concerning this issue.

Marketing/Public Relations

1. The hospital reflects integrity, honesty, good taste, high professional standards, and compliance with applicable laws in all marketing and public relations activities affecting the public it serves.

2. The hospital will not intentionally damage the professional reputation of other organizations or individuals or make public judgments on the ethics of others.

3. The hospital will not make damaging remarks that would affect another institution when it writes or speaks of the institution's unique services, facilities, equipment, or philosophy.

Organizational Conduct

1. The policies and practices of the hospital respect the professional ethical codes and responsibilities of its employees and medical staff members and are sensitive to institutional decisions that employees might interpret as compromising their ability to provide high-quality health care.

2. The hospital has policies and practices that provide for equitably administered employee policies and practices.

3. To the extent possible, and consistent with ethical commitments of the institution, the hospital tries to accommodate the desires of employees and medical staff to embody religious moral values in their professional activities.

4. The hospital has written policies on conflicts of interest that apply to officers, governing board members, physicians, and others who make or influence decisions for or on behalf of the institution. These policies recognize that individuals in decision-making or administrative positions often have a duality of interest that may not ordinarily present conflicts. However, the hospital provides mechanisms for identifying and addressing conflicts when they do exist.

5. The hospital communicates its mission, vision, values, strategic plan, and priorities to its employees and volunteers whose patient care and service activities are the most visible embodiment of the institution's ethical commitments and values.

Source: Adapted from Bakersfield Memorial Hospital, Bakersfield, California.

4–2
Radiology Standards

Effective Date: _____

Original/Revision by: _____

Revised Date: _____

Reference: The Radiation Control for Health and Safety Act of 1968

Department Primarily Affected: Radiology

Cross-Reference: _____

STATEMENT OF PURPOSE

[Enter a statement of the purpose of this policy]

The X-ray technologist should know the X-ray performance standard to provide a safe environment for the patient.

PROCEDURE

A radiation safety performance standard that includes diagnostic X-ray systems and their major components has been issued under The Radiation Control for Health and Safety Act of 1968 (P: 90-602). This standard becomes effective for all medical and dental X-ray equipment manufactured after August 1, 1974. While the major responsibility of complying with the standard belongs to the manufacturers, it is recognized that X-ray technologists may operate a unit years after its initial installation. The performance standard sets forth specifications for the following components: tube housing assemblies, tables, cradles, film changers, cassette holders, and beam-limiting devices. This summary has been prepared to provide the technologist with a general knowledge of the performance standard and what it will mean to him/her on a daily basis.

Normally, a technologist will not be concerned with the tube housing: in fact, as long as the minimum amount of filtration permanently in the useful beam is known, and complete cooling curves and tube rating charts are available, the technologist really need not be concerned with additional information. Moreover, X-ray generators are not normally of major concern in daily operation. The only requirement in the standard for cassette holders, film changers, table tops, and cradles is that they shall not exceed an individual pre-determined aluminum equivalent of material. This also should not be of any concern in daily work since these particular items are used as they stand and are seldom modified. Therefore, of the above nine (9) different performance components only three (3) are of major concern to a technologist. These specifications are divided as shown below. These are X-ray controls, fluoroscopic imaging assemblies, and beam-limiting devices.

In addition to knowing the following information for these three components, the technologist should know that the manufacturer must supply certain items. These items are the necessary and sufficient instructions to cover the proper operation of the unit, maintenance schedule, various duty cycles of components, and any special radiation safety precautions for unique design features.

X-Ray Controls

1. The technique factors used during an exposure shall be indicated before the exposure begins, except when using automatic exposure controls. This indication shall be visible from the operator's position, except for spot film.

2. The control panel will conspicuously have the label "WARNING: This X-ray unit may be dangerous to patient and operator unless safe exposure factors and operating instructions are observed."

continues

4–2 continued

3. When using automatic exposure control, if an exposure has been terminated by the backup timer, an indication shall be made on the control panel. Manual resetting is required before making further automatically timed exposures, so that the operator will know something is wrong.

4. The X-ray control shall provide visual indication whenever X-rays are produced. An audible signal shall indicate the termination of exposure.

5. For multiple tubes controlled by one exposure switch, the tube or tubes selected shall be clearly indicated, both at the control panel and on or near the tube selected.

6. Except during serial radiography, it shall be possible to end the exposure at any time during an exposure greater than ½ second. In serial radiography the user can complete any single exposure of a series. End of exposure shall cause automatic resetting of timer to zero or its initial setting. You cannot make an exposure when timer is set to zero or "off."

7. The radiation output must be linear between adjacent mA settings, i.e., output increases in proportion to the increase in mA as well as being reproducible.

FLUOROSCOPIC IMAGING ASSEMBLIES

1. X-rays shall not be produced unless a primary barrier intercepts the entire useful beam. If it does not, then production of X-rays is prevented by an interlock.

2. X-ray production must be controlled by a continuous pressure device.

3. When the unit is in its high output mode, a continuous audible signal must be heard.

4. X-ray tube potential (kVp) and current (mA) shall be continuously indicated.

5. The following minimum X-ray tube to target distances shall exist:

   Stationary units 38cm

   Mobile units 30cm

   Special units 20cm

6. The maximum cumulative time for tube exposure shall not exceed five minutes without resetting. A signal must indicate the completion of the time and it will remain on until time is reset.

BEAM-LIMITING DEVICES

1. In general, there must be some means of restricting the dimension of the X-ray field. Other provisions are:

   –visually defining the perimeter of the field

   –indication when the axis of the beam is perpendicular to the plane of the image receptor

   –general purpose systems shall be capable of operation such that the field size at the image receptor can be smaller than the image receptor

   –beam limiting device shall numerically indicate the field size to which it is adjusted in inches or centimeters

2. Means shall be provided for positive beam limitation (PBL) on stationary general purpose units, which will either cause automatic adjustment of the field to the image receptor size within a certain time period or prevent production of X-rays until adjustment is completed.

continues

4–2 continued

3. PBL may be bypassed under certain conditions; however, when these conditions cease, return to PBL shall be automatic.

4. It is possible to override PBL by means of a key; however, it shall be impossible to remove key in override.

5. There are beam-limiting requirements for spot film equipment, which allows for a smaller adjustment of the field size in plane of film than the size of the film that has been selected on the spot film selector. Also, the size of the X-ray beam must be automatically limited to the size of the portion of the spot film selected *before* the beam enters the patient.

RADIOLOGY DEPARTMENT

The hospital has diagnostic X-ray facilities available. If therapeutic X-ray services are also provided, they—as well as the diagnostic services—must meet professionally approved standards for safety and personnel qualifications.

A. *Standard: Radiological services*—The hospital maintains or has available radiological services according to needs of the hospital. For example, the hospital has diagnostic X-ray facilities available in the hospital building proper or in an adjacent clinic or medical facility that is readily accessible to the hospital patients, physicians, and personnel.

B. *Standard: Hazards for patients and personnel*—The radiology department is free of hazards for patients and personnel. The factors explaining the standard are as follows:

1. Proper safety precautions are maintained against fire and explosion hazards, electrical hazards, and radiation hazards.

2. Periodic inspection is made by local or state health authorities or a radiation physicist, and hazards so identified are promptly corrected.

3. Radiation workers are checked periodically for amount of radiation exposure by the use of exposure meters or badge tests.

4. With fluoroscopes, attention is paid to modern safety design and good operating procedures; records are maintained of the output of all fluoroscopes.

5. Regulations based on medical staff recommendations are established as to the administration of the application and removal of radium element, its disintegration products, and other radioactive isotopes.

C. *Standard: Personnel*—Personnel adequate to supervise and conduct the services are provided, and the interpretation of radiology examinations is made by physicians competent in the field. The factors explaining the standard are as follows:

1. The hospital has a qualified radiologist, either full-time or part-time on a consulting basis, both to supervise the department and to interpret films that require specialized knowledge for accurate reading. If the hospital is small, and a radiologist cannot come to the hospital regularly, selected X-ray films are sent to a radiologist for interpretation.

2. If the activities of the radiology department extend to radiotherapy, the physician in charge is appropriately qualified.

3. The amount of qualified radiologist and technologist time is sufficient to meet the hospital's requirements. A technologist is on duty or on call at all times.

4. The use of all X-ray apparatus is limited to personnel designated as qualified by the radiologist or by an appropriately constituted committee of the medical staff. The same limitation applies to personnel

continues

4–2 continued

applying and removing radium element, its disintegration products, and radioactive isotopes. The use of fluoroscopes is limited to physicians.

D. *Standard: Signed reports*—Signed reports are filed with the patient's record and duplicate copies kept in the department. The factors explaining the standard are as follows:

1. Requests by the attending physician for X-ray examination contain a concise statement of reason for the examination.

2. Reports of interpretations are written or dictated and signed by the radiologist.

3. X-ray reports and roentgenographs are preserved or microfilmed in accordance with the statute of limitations.

DOCUMENTATION _____

APPROVED BY _____ _____ _____
                                           Name   Title   Date

Courtesy of Rick Sellers, Department of Radiology, Tanner Medical Center, Carrollton, Georgia.

4–3
Advance Directives Policy

PURPOSE

To define the rights of patients to establish decisions concerning their medical and psychiatric care, including the right to formulate Advance Directives.

POLICY

1. **Definition**

   Advance Directives are defined as living wills, health care power of attorney, or other instructions of a patient about medical and psychiatric care.

2. For all adult inpatients Admitting personnel assess whether patients have designated a medical decision maker. This information is documented on the admit Form (SN 1175). A patient handbook containing advance directive information is provided to the patient upon admission. Exception: Outpatient surgery staff complete this information with their patients.

3. Inquiry is made of all adult patients as to whether they possess or wish to execute an Advance Directive. This information is obtained and documented on admission by the registered nurse who completes the Patient History/Assessment and Discharge Record or other approved unit-specific admission form. This information is obtained and documented on the ambulatory care record by the nurse during the initial clinic visit. Information regarding Advance Directives will be provided to those patients desiring more information. Forms are available at no cost to the patient.

4. If the patient already possesses an Advance Directive but does not have a copy, the patient's wishes may be documented in the patient's medical record in lieu of the actual advance directive. If the patient elects to have the original directive used rather than completing a new one, the nurse attempts to briefly document the contents of the directive prior to the copy arriving.

5. If the patient has an Advance Directive, the inpatient registered nurse or ambulatory care nurse will notify the patient's primary physician that the patient has an Advance Directive.

6. If the patient desires further information on executing an Advance Directive or desires to execute a directive, the nurse may consult case management to assist with additional information and/or execution of the directive. If case manager is not available, the inpatient registered nurse or ambulatory care nurse shall assist the patient with the additional information and/or execution of the directive. (Form SN 1288)

7. Case Managers/Social Service Personnel are available to all units and clinics during regular business hours.

8. The Case Manager/Inpatient Registered Nurse/Ambulatory Care Nurse shall meet with the patient to provide additional information and answer any questions the patient may have about Advance Directives. If an Advance Directive is executed by the patient, the Case Manager/Nurse shall place it in the patient's medical record and contact the unit registered nurse or clinic nurse. The nurse shall then contact the patient's primary physician so that appropriate planning of care may be accomplished.

9. Refer to Hospital Policies 5.21 "Withholding or Withdrawal of Life Sustaining Treatment" or 5.19 "Do Not Resuscitate" for additional information.

_____

Administrator

_____

Date

Source: Louisiana State University Health Sciences Center, Shreveport, Louisiana.

4–4
Advance Health Care Directive

INSTRUCTIONS

Part 1 of this form lets you name another individual as agent to make health care decisions for you if you become incapable of making your own decisions, or if you want someone else to make those decisions for you now even though you are still capable. You may also name an alternate agent to act for you if your first choice is not willing, able, or reasonably available to make decisions for you.

Your agent may not be an operator or employee of a community care facility or a residential care facility where you are receiving care, or your supervising health care provider or an employee of the health care institution where you are receiving care, unless your agent is related to you or is a coworker.

Unless you state otherwise in this form, your agent will have the right to:

1. Consent or refuse consent to any care, treatment, service, or procedure to maintain, diagnose, or otherwise affect a physical or mental condition.

2. Select or discharge health care providers and institutions.

3. Approve or disapprove diagnostic tests, surgical procedures, and programs of medication.

4. Direct the provision, withholding, or withdrawal of artificial nutrition and hydration and all other forms of health care, including cardiopulmonary resuscitation.

5. Donate organs or tissues, authorize an autopsy, and direct disposition of remains.

However, your agent will not be able to commit you to a mental health facility, or consent to convulsive treatment, psychosurgery, sterilization, or abortion for you.

Part 2 of this form lets you give specific instructions about any aspect of your health care, whether or not you appoint an agent. Choices are provided for you to express your wishes regarding the provision, withholding, or withdrawal of treatment to keep you alive, as well as the provision of pain relief. You also can add to the choices you have made or write down any additional wishes. If you are satisfied to allow your agent to determine what is best for you in making end-of-life decisions, you need not fill out Part 2 of this form.

Give a copy of the signed and completed form to your physician, to any other health care providers you may have, to any health care institution at which you are receiving care, and to any health care agents you have named. You should talk to the person you have named as agent to make sure that he or she understands your wishes and is willing to take the responsibility.

You have the right to revoke this advance health care directive or replace this form at any time.

PART 1—POWER OF ATTORNEY FOR HEALTH CARE

DESIGNATION OF AGENT: I designate the following individual as my agent to make health care decisions for me:

Name of individual you choose as agent: _____

Address: _____

_____

Telephone: _____
       (home phone)   *(work phone)*   *(cell/pager)*

continues

4–4 continued

OPTIONAL: If I revoke my agent's authority or if my agent is not willing, able, or reasonably available to make a health care decision for me, I designate as my first alternate agent:

Name of individual you choose as first alternate agent: _____

Address: _____

_____

Telephone: _____
            (home phone)   *(work phone)*   *(cell/pager)*

OPTIONAL: If I revoke the authority of my agent and first alternate agent or if neither is willing, able, or reasonably available to make a health care decision for me, I designate as my second alternate agent:

Name of individual you choose as second alternate agent: _____

Address: _____

_____

Telephone: _____
            (home phone)   *(work phone)*   *(cell/pager)*

AGENT'S AUTHORITY: My agent is authorized to make all health care decisions for me, including decisions to provide, withhold, or withdraw artificial nutrition and hydration and all other forms of health care to keep me alive, except as I state here:

_____

_____

_____

_____

_____

_____

(Add additional sheets if needed.)

WHEN AGENT'S AUTHORITY BECOMES EFFECTIVE: My agent's authority becomes effective when my primary physician determines that I am unable to make my own health care decisions._____
                                                                                    (Initial here)

OR

My agent's authority to make health care decisions for me takes effect immediately._____
                                                                                    (Initial here)

AGENT'S OBLIGATION: My agent shall make health care decisions for me in accordance with this power of attorney for health care, any instructions I give in Part 2 of this form, and my other wishes to the extent known to my agent. To the extent my wishes are unknown, my agent shall make health care decisions for me in accordance with what my agent determines to be in my best interest. In determining my best interest, my agent shall consider my personal values to the extent known to my agent.

continues

4–4 continued

AGENT'S POSTDEATH AUTHORITY: My agent is authorized to make anatomical gifts, authorize an autopsy and direct disposition of my remains, except as I state here or in Part 3 of this form:

_____

_____

_____

_____

(Add additional sheets if needed.)

PART 2—INSTRUCTIONS FOR HEALTH CARE

If you fill out this part of the form, you may strike any wording you do not want.

> ***END-OF-LIFE DECISIONS:*** I direct that my health care providers and others involved in my care provide, withhold, or withdraw treatment in accordance with the choice I have marked below:
>
> **Choice *Not To* Prolong Life:**
>
> I do not want my life to be prolonged if (1) I have an incurable and irreversible condition that will result in my death within a relatively short time, (2) I become unconscious and, to a reasonable degree of medical certainty, I will not regain consciousness, or (3) the likely risks and burdens of treatment would outweigh the expected benefits,
>
> *(Initial here)*
>
> ***OR***
>
> **Choice *To* Prolong Life:**
>
> I want my life to be prolonged as long as possible within the limits of generally accepted health care standards.
>
> *(Initial here)*

RELIEF FROM PAIN: Except as I state in the following space, I direct that treatment for alleviation of pain or discomfort be provided at all times, even if it hastens my death:

_____

_____

_____

_____

_____

(Add additional sheets if needed.)

continues

4–4 continued

OTHER WISHES: (If you do not agree with any of the optional choices above and wish to write your own, or if you wish to add to the instructions you have given above, you may do so here.) I direct that:

_____

_____

_____

_____

_____

_____

(Add additional sheets if needed.)

PART 3—DONATION OF ORGANS AT DEATH (OPTIONAL)

Upon my death:

I give any needed organs, tissues, or parts _____
(Initial here)

OR

I give the following organs, tissues, or parts only: _____   _____
(Initial here)

My gift is for the following purposes:

Transplant_____   Research_____
(Initial here)   *(Initial here)*

Therapy _____   Education_____
(Initial here)   *(Initial here)*

PART 4—PRIMARY PHYSICIAN (OPTIONAL)

I designate the following physician as my primary physician:

Name of Physician:_____   Telephone: _____

Address: _____

_____

OPTIONAL: If the physician I have designated above is not willing, able, or reasonably available to act as my primary physician, I designate the following physician as my primary physician:

Name of Physician:_____   Telephone: _____

Address: _____

_____

continues

4–4 continued

PART 5—SIGNATURE

The form must be signed by two qualified witnesses, or acknowledged before a notary public.

SIGNATURE: Sign and date the form here:

Date:_____

Name:_____   _____
      (sign your name)   *(print your name)*

Address: _____

                  _____

STATEMENT OF WITNESSES: I declare under penalty of perjury under the laws of California (1) that the individual who signed or acknowledged this advance health care directive is personally known to me, or that the individual's identity was proven to me by convincing evidence (2) that the individual signed or acknowledged this advance directive in my presence, 3) that the individual appears to be of sound mind and under no duress, fraud, or undue influence, (4) that I am not a person appointed as agent by this advance directive, and (5) that I am not the individual's health care provider, an employee of the individual's health care provider, the operator of a community care facility, an employee of an operator of a community care facility, the operator of a residential care facility for the elderly, nor an employee of an operator of a residential care facility for the elderly.

First Witness

Name of Physician:_____   Telephone: _____

Address: _____

                  _____

Signature of Witness:_____   Date:_____

Second Witness

Name of Physician:_____   Telephone: _____

Address: _____

                  _____

Signature of Witness:_____   Date:_____

ADDITIONAL STATEMENT OF WITNESSES: At least one of the above witnesses must also sign the following declaration:

I further declare under penalty of perjury under the laws of California that I am not related to the individual executing this advance health care directive by blood, marriage, or adoption, and to the best of my knowledge, I am not entitled to any part of the individual's estate upon his or her death under a will now existing or by operation of law.

Signature of Witness:_____

Signature of Witness:_____

continues

4–4 continued

YOU MAY USE THIS CERTIFICATE OF ACKNOWLEDGMENT BEFORE A NOTARY PUBLIC INSTEAD OF THE STATEMENT OF WITNESSES.

State of California   }

                                                                       } SS.

County of _____   }

On *(date)* _____, before me, *(name and title of officer)* _____,

personally appeared *(name(s) of signer(s))* _____

☐ personally known to me   OR   ☐ proved to me on the basis of satisfactory evidence

to be the person(s) whose name(s) is/are subscribed to the within instrument and acknowledged to me that he/she/they executed the same in his/her/their authorized capacity(ies), and that by his/her/their signature(s) on the instrument the person(s), or the entity upon behalf of which the person(s) acted, executed the instrument.

WITNESS my hand and official seal. (Civil Code Section 1189)

Signature of Notary:_____

PART 6—SPECIAL WITNESS REQUIREMENT

If you are a patient in a skilled nursing facility, the patient advocate or ombudsman must sign the following statement:

STATEMENT OF PATIENT ADVOCATE OR OMBUDSMAN

I declare under penalty of perjury under the laws of California that I am a patient advocate or ombudsman as designated by the State Department of Aging and that I am serving as a witness as required by Section 4675 of the Probate Code.

Date:_____

Name:_____   _____
          (sign your name)   *(print your name)*

Address: _____

           _____

4–5
Advance Health Care Directive (Spanish)
Directiva por anticipado de la atención de la salud

SECCIÓN 4701 DEL CÓDIGO TESTAMENTARIO DE CALIFORNIA

INSTRUCCIONES

La Sección 1 de este formulario le permite nombrar a otro individuo como representante para que tome las decisiones de atención de la salud por usted en caso que llegue a ser incapaz de tomar sus propias decisiones o si usted quiere que alguien más tome esas decisiones por usted ahora aunque todavía siga siendo capaz. También puede nombrar a un representante suplente que actúe por usted si su primera elección no está dispuesta, no es capaz o no está razonablemente accesible para tomar decisiones por usted.

Su representante no puede ser un operador o empleado de un establecimiento de atención comunitaria y un establecimiento de atención residencial donde lo estén atendiendo, ni su proveedor de atención de la salud encargado de la supervisión o un empleado de la institución de atención de la salud donde usted esté recibiendo la misma, a menos que su representante esté emparentado con usted o sea compañero de trabajo.

A menos que indique lo contrario en este formulario, su representante tendrá el derecho de:

1. Prestar o negar el consentimiento a cualquier atención, tratamiento, servicio o procedimiento para mantener, diagnosticar o afectar de otro modo una enfermedad física o mental.

2. Seleccionar o rechazar proveedores e instituciones de atención de la salud.

3. Aprobar o desaprobar pruebas diagnósticas, procedimientos quirúrgicos y programas de medicamentos.

4. Dirigir el proveimiento, la negación o la retirada de nutrición e hidratación artificial y todas las demás formas de atención de la salud, incluyendo resucitación cardiopulmonar.

5. Donar órganos o tejidos, autorizar una autopsia y ordenar la disposición final de los restos.

Sin embargo, su representante no podrá internarlo en un establecimiento psiquiátrico ni dar su consentimiento para que usted sea sometido a tratamiento convulsivo, psicocirugía, esterilización o aborto.

La Sección 2 de este formulario le permite dar instrucciones específicas acerca de cualquier aspecto de su atención de la salud, ya sea que usted nombre un representante o no. Se proporcionan opciones para que usted exprese sus deseos acerca del proveimiento, la negación o la retirada del tratamiento para mantenerlo vivo, así como el proveimiento de alivio del dolor. También se proporciona espacio para que usted aumente las opciones que haya hecho o que anote cualesquier deseos adicionales. Si está conforme con dejar que su representante determine lo que sea mejor para usted al tomar decisiones relacionadas con el final de la vida, no es necesario que llene la Parte 2 de este formulario.

Entrégueles copias del formulario firmado y debidamente llenado a su médico, a cualesquier otros proveedores de atención de la salud que pueda tener, a cualquier institución de atención de la salud en la que lo estén atendiendo y a todos los representantes de atención de la salud que haya nombrado. Deberá hablar con la persona que haya nombrado como representante para asegurar que él o ella entienda sus deseos y esté dispuesta a asumir la responsabilidad.

Usted tiene derecho a revocar esta directiva por anticipado de la atención de la salud o a reemplazar este formulario en cualquier momento.

continues

4–5 continued

PARTE 1—PODER NOTARIAL PARA ATENCIÓN DE LA SALUD

DESIGNACIÓN DEL REPRESENTANTE: Designo al siguiente individuo como mi representante para que tome las decisiones de atención de la salud por mí:

Nombre del individuo que usted elija como representante _____

Dirección: _____

_____

Teléfono: _____
          (en casa)   *(teléfono en el trabajo)*   *teléfono celular / localizador*

OPCIONAL: Si revoco la autoridad de mi representante o si mi representante no está dispuesto, no es capaz o no está razonablemente accesible para tomar una decisión de atención de la salud por mí, designo como mi primer representante suplente a:

Nombre de la persona que usted elige como primera alternativa: _____

Dirección: _____

_____

Teléfono: _____
          (en casa)   *(teléfono en el trabajo)*   *teléfono celular / localizador*

OPCIONAL: Si revoco la autoridad de mi representante y mi primer representante suplente o si ninguno de los dos está dispuesto, es capaz o está razonablemente accesible para tomar una decisión de atención de la salud por mí, designo como mi segundo representante suplente a:

Nombre del individuo que usted elija como su segundo representante suplente _____

Dirección: _____

_____

Teléfono: _____
          (en casa)   *(teléfono en el trabajo)*   *teléfono celular / localizador*

AUTORIDAD DEL REPRESENTANTE: Mi representante está autorizado para tomar todas las decisiones de atención de la salud por mí, incluyendo las decisiones para proveer, negar o retirar la nutrición e hidratación artificial y todas las demás formas de atención de la salud para mantenerme vivo, excepto como lo consigno aquí:

_____

_____

_____

_____

(Si es necesario, agregue hojas adicionales.)

continues

4–5 continued

CUÁNDO ENTRA EN VIGENCIA LA AUTORIDAD DEL REPRESENTANTE: La autoridad de mi representante entra en vigencia cuando mi médico de atención primaria determine que soy incapaz de tomar mis propias decisiones de atención de la salud. _____

Escriba sus iniciales aquí. (Initial here.)

La autoridad de mi representante para tomar las decisiones de atención de la salud por mí entra en vigor inmediatamente.

Escriba sus iniciales aquí. (Initial here)

OBLIGACIÓN DEL REPRESENTANTE: Mi representante tomará decisiones de atención de la salud por mí de acuerdo con este poder notarial para atención de la salud, todas las instrucciones que yo proporcione en la Parte 2 de este formulario y mis demás deseos en la medida conocida para mi representante. En la medida que mis deseos sean desconocidos, mi representante tomará decisiones de atención de la salud por mí de acuerdo con lo que mi representante determine que es en mi mejor interés. Para determinar mi mejor interés, mi representante deberá considerar mis valores personales en la medida conocida por el mismo.

AUTORIDAD DEL REPRESENTANTE DESPUÉS DE LA MUERTE: Mi representante está autorizado para hacer donaciones anatómicas, autorizar una autopsia y ordenar la disposición final de mis restos, excepto como yo lo consigno aquí o en la Parte 3 de este formulario:

_____

_____

_____

_____

_____

(Si es necesario, agregue hojas adicionales.)

NOMBRAMIENTO DEL CONSERVADOR: Si es necesario que una corte designe para mí un conservador de mi persona, yo nombro al representante designado en este formulario. Si ese representante no está dispuesto, no es capaz o no está razonablemente accesible para actuar como conservador, nombro a los representantes suplentes que he designado, en el orden en que lo he hecho.

PARTE 2—INSTRUCCIONES PARA LA ATENCIÓN DE LA SALUD

Si usted llena esta parte del formulario, podrá tachar cualquier texto que no quiera.

DECISIONES DEL FINAL DE LA VIDA: Ordeno que mis proveedores de atención de la salud y otros que participen en mi atención provean, nieguen o retiren el tratamiento de acuerdo con la elección que yo haya marcado abajo:

☐ Elección de no prolongar la vida

No quiero que mi vida sea prolongada si (1) tengo una enfermedad incurable e irreversible que resulte en mi muerte dentro de un periodo relativamente corto, (2) pierdo el conocimiento y, con un grado razonable de certidumbre médica, no lo recuperaré o (3) los riesgos y cargas probables del tratamiento serían más mayores que los beneficios previstos, O

☐ Elección de prolongar la vida

Quiero que mi vida sea prolongada tanto como sea posible dentro de los límites de las normas de atención de la salud generalmente aceptadas.

---

continues

4–5 continued

ALIVIO DEL DOLOR: Excepto como lo consigno en el siguiente espacio, ordeno que se me proporcione en todo momento tratamiento para el alivio del dolor o las molestias, aunque acelere mi muerte:

(Si es necesario, agregue hojas adicionales).

OTROS DESEOS: (Si usted no está de acuerdo con alguna de las elecciones opcionales que aparecen arriba y desea anotar las suyas propias, o si desea aumentar las instrucciones que ha proporcionado arriba, puede hacerlo aquí). Ordeno que:

_____

_____

_____

_____

_____

(Si es necesario, agregue hojas adicionales.)

PARTE 3—DONACIÓN DE ÓRGANOS DESPUÉS DE LA MUERTE (OPCIONAL)

Después de mi muerte

Dono todos los órganos, tejidos o partes necesarios, _____

Escriba sus iniciales aquí. (Initial here)

O

Dono solamente los siguientes órganos, tejidos o partes. _____

Escriba sus iniciales aquí. (Initial here)

Mi donación es para los siguientes propósitos (tache cualquiera de los siguientes que usted no desee):

Trasplante _____   Investigación _____
  Escriba sus iniciales aquí. (Initial here)   *Escriba sus iniciales aquí. (Initial here)*

Terapia _____   Educación _____
  Escriba sus iniciales aquí. (Initial here)   *Escriba sus iniciales aquí. (Initial here)*

PARTE 4—MEDICO DE ATENCIÓN PRIMARIA (OPCIONAL)

Designo al siguiente como mi médico de atención primaria:

Nombre del Médico: _____   Teléfono: _____

Dirección: _____

_____

OPCIONAL: Si el médico que he designado no está dispuesto, no es capaz o no está razonablemente accesible para actuar como mi médico de atención primaria, designo al siguiente para que desempeñe este papel:

Nombre del Médico: _____   Teléfono: _____

Dirección: _____

_____

continues

4–5 continued

PARTE 5—FIRMA

El formulario debe ser firmado por dos testigos calificados o certificado ante un notario público.

FIRMA: Firme y ponga aquí la fecha en el formulario:

Fecha: _____

Nombre: _____   _____
              (ponga su firma)   *(escriba su nombre con letra de molde)*

Dirección: _____

_____

DECLARACIÓN DE LOS TESTIGOS: Declaro bajo pena de perjurio conforme a las leyes de California (1) que el individuo que firmó o certificó esta directiva por anticipado de la atención de la salud es conocido personalmente para mí, o que la identidad del individuo me fue demostrada con evidencia convincente, (2) que el individuo firmó o certificó esta directiva por anticipado en mi presencia, (3) que el individuo parece encontrarse en buen estado mental y bajo ninguna presión, fraude o influencia indebida, (4) que no soy la persona designada como representante en esta directiva por anticipado y (5) que no soy el proveedor de atención de la salud del individuo, un empleado del proveedor de atención de la salud del individuo, el operador de un establecimiento de atención comunitaria, un empleado de un operador de un establecimiento de atención comunitaria, el operador de un establecimiento de atención residencial para ancianos, ni un empleado de un operador de un establecimiento de atención residencial para personas de edad avanzada.

Nombre _____   Teléfono: _____

Dirección: _____

_____

Firma del testigo: _____   Fecha: _____

SEGUNDO TESTIGO

Nombre _____   Teléfono: _____

Dirección: _____

_____

Firma del testigo: _____   Fecha: _____

DECLARACIÓN ADICIONAL DE LOS TESTIGOS: Por lo menos uno de los testigos mencionados arriba también debe firmar la siguiente declaración:

Declaro además bajo pena de perjurio conforme a las leyes de California que no estoy emparentado por lazos sanguíneos, matrimonio o adopción con el individuo que formaliza esta directiva por anticipado de la atención de la salud, y que a mi leal saber y entender, no tengo derecho a parte alguna del caudal hereditario del individuo después de su muerte bajo un testamento actualmente existente o por ministerio de ley.

Firma del testigo: _____

Firma del testigo: _____

continues

4–5 continued

PARTE 6—REQUERIMIENTO DE TESTIGO ESPECIAL

Si usted es paciente en un establecimiento con servicio de enfermería especializada, el abogado o defensor cívico del paciente debe firmar la siguiente declaración:

DECLARACIÓN DEL ABOGADO O DEFENSOR CÍVICO DEL PACIENTE

Declaro bajo pena de perjurio conforme a las leyes de California que soy abogado o defensor cívico del paciente designado por el Departamento de la Senectud del Estado y que estoy sirviendo como testigo como lo estipula la Sección 4675 del Código Testamentario.

Fecha: _____

Nombre: _____   _____
         (ponga su firma)   *(escriba su nombre con letra de molde)*

Dirección: _____

_____

PATIENT ASSESSMENT

4–6
Magnetic Resonance Imaging (MRI) Screening Sheet

PATIENT ELIGIBILITY/SCREENING

M.R. exam #: _____   Patient name: _____

Date: _____   Date of birth: _____

Area to be examined: _____

Diagnosis: _____

Referring physician/phone: _____

ELIGIBILITY CRITERIA *(CIRCLE Y OR N)*

1. Possibility of pregnancy?	Y	N	15. Orbital prosthesis?	Y	N
2. Hx of claustrophobia?	Y	N	16. Braces/dentures/retainers?	Y	N
3. Pacemaker?	Y	N	17. Wig?	Y	N
4. Heart valve prosthesis?	Y	N	18. Epilepsy?	Y	N
5. Coronary bypass clips?	Y	N	19. I.U.D.?	Y	N
6. Renal transplant clips?	Y	N	20. Neurostimulator (TENS unit)?	Y	N
7. Aneurysm clips?	Y	N	21. Insulin pump/infusion pump?	Y	N
8. Intracranial clips?	Y	N	22. Shunt?	Y	N
9. Other vascular clips?	Y	N	23. Previous surgery?	Y	N
10. Joint replacement?	Y	N	If yes, what part of body? _____		
11. Shrapnel?	Y	N	24. Allergies to medications?	Y	N
12. Gunshot wound?	Y	N	If yes, to what? _____		
13. Hearing aids?	Y	N	25. Exposure to metal fragments in eyes?	Y	N
14. Middle ear prosthesis?	Y	N			

Comments: _____

_____

Technologist's Signature: _____

I have understood and accurately answered all of the above questions.

Patient's Signature: _____

Signature of parent, guardian, substitute consenter, or other legally responsible person if the patient is a minor, disabled, or otherwise unable to give consent:

_____   Signature

_____
Witness

Date   Time AM/PM

Printed Name

Relationship to Patient

continues

MAGNETIC RESONANCE IMAGING
(With Prohance)

Your Magnetic Resonance Imaging examination may include images made after an injection of gadoteridol (subsequently referred to as Prohance). The Prohance injection may allow the radiologist to identify additional details about your condition, which might not be apparent without the use of Prohance. In some areas the examination is much less useful if Prohance is not used.

Prohance will be injected into a vein, at which time there may be slight burning at the injection site. Prohance is filtered out of the bloodstream by your kidneys and eliminated from your body in your urine. Prohance will be eliminated from your body approximately 24 hours after injection.

Side effects are very rare; the most common are nausea and/or vomiting, headache, and local discomfort at the injection site. Severe reactions and death are extremely rare.

We do not currently use Prohance in patients who are pregnant or nursing or in patients with certain kinds of anemia or sickle cell disease. Please complete the checklist below regarding these situations.

Anemia   ☐ Yes ☐ No   Pregnant   ☐ Yes ☐ No

Sickle Cell ☐ Yes ☐ No   Nursing   ☐ Yes ☐ No

Have you ever experienced an adverse reaction to Prohance?   ☐ Yes ☐ No

If yes, please explain: _____

If you wish to discuss your examination further with a physician, please inform the technologist.

I understand I have the right to refuse the use of Prohance and still undergo the Magnetic Resonance Imaging scan, although it may limit the usefulness of this scan. I have read and understand the above explanation and choices, and consent to the examination.

Patient Signature: _____   Date: _____

Signature of parent, guardian, substitute
consenter, or other legally responsible
person if the patient is a minor, disabled,
or otherwise unable to consent:_____   Date: _____

Signature of Witness:_____   Date: _____

Courtesy of Monica Riccardo, Holy Cross Hospital, Silver Spring, Maryland.

4–7
MRI Patient Screening Record

Name: _____

DOB: _____   Sex: _____   Weight: _____

Doctor: _____   Insurance: _____

     Pre-Cert Required No _____ Yes _____ Number _____

Exam Date: _____   Exam Time: _____   Type of Exam: _____

Diagnosis: _____

Please answer the following questions to ensure a quality MRI examination:

Have you ever had any of the following exams for the area that is being scanned? If yes, please bring the films with you. (Example—if you are having an MRI of the knee, please bring any previous knee films with you.)

1. MRI   Y   N

2. CT scan   Y   N

3. Regular X-rays   Y   N

4. Do you have a pacemaker?   Y   N
    (If yes, no MRI can be scheduled—please notify your physician.)

5. Have you ever had any surgery in your lifetime?   Y   N
    (especially head, heart, vascular, lumbar) If yes, what surgery? _____

    Brain: If you are not sure what kind of surgery, please bring X-rays or ask your physician for the type of surgery. If you had clips, you should have a card (make, model) from the hospital.
    Heart: Bypass/Open Heart (okay to have MRI). Any valve replacements? If yes, you should have a card from the hospital.

6. Do you have any metal fragments in your eyes?   Y   N
    Have you EVER done any grinding in a foundry?   Y   N
    Have you ever worked as a machinist, mechanic, in a steel mill, or have you EVER
    done any welding (including both home and work)?   Y   N
    (If yes to any of these questions, please notify your physician. You will need to have an
    X-ray of your eyes before the MRI exam.)

7. Do you have cochlear implants?   Y   N
    (If yes, please notify your physician because you cannot have an MRI.)
    Hearing aids must be removed.

8. Are you pregnant?   Y   N
    (If yes, please notify your physician.)

9. Do you use an IUD?   Y   N

10. Medications?   Y   N
    If yes, list _____

11. Are there any surgical clips, screws, pins, or metal plates in your body?   Y   N
    (Hip/knee replacement—cannot do that joint but can do another part of the body.
    Surgery must be 3 weeks old.)

continues

4–7 continued

12. Do you have any shrapnel or bullets in your body?   Y   N
    (If yes, where? _____) (Can do MRI if not near brain, heart, or
    lungs.)

13. Do you wear any type of nitrotransdermal patch?   Y   N
    (If yes, you will be asked to remove the patch. Please bring an extra patch to the exam.)

14. Are you using a TENS (neuro pulse stimulator) unit?   Y   N
    (Need make, model, etc.) _____

15. Are you on any monitoring equipment?   Y   N
    (If yes, what type? IV, portable oxygen) _____

16. Do you have a history of a medical condition?   Y   N
    (If yes, what?) _____

17. Do you have a history of cancer?   Y   N
    (If yes, where and when?) _____

18. Have you ever had a seizure?   Y   N
    (If yes, what medication?) _____

19. Have you ever had asthma?   Y   N
    (If yes, what medication?) _____

20. Do you have any allergies?   Y   N
    Type _____ Medications _____

21. Do you have an insulin pump?   Y   N

22. Do you have any type of artificial limb?   Y   N
    (If yes, where? _____ Removable? _____)

23. Do you have dentures?   Y   N
    (If yes, must be removed for neck and brain work.)

24. Do you have a penile prosthesis?   Y   N
    (Usually are plastic, but may have a metal clamp. X-rays are needed to see what it is
    made of, unless you have had a previous MRI with no problems.)

25. Do you have any type of kidney disease, renal failure, or are you on dialysis?   Y   N
    (If yes, you cannot have contrast—please notify your physician.)

26. Are you claustrophobic?   Y   N
    (If yes, please ask your physician for sedation. If sedation is taken, please bring
    someone with you to drive you home after the exam because you will not be able to drive.)

Signature: _____   Date: _____

Courtesy of Rick Sellers, Department of Radiology, Tanner Medical Center, Carrollton, Georgia.

4–8
Department of Radiology Elective Scheduling Form

STAMP WITH ADDRESSOGRAPH OR PRINT

UNIT # _____   NAME _____   D.O.B. _____/_____/_____

This form must be filled out by all female patients between the ages of 12–50 yrs. who will be scheduled for a radiology exam.

Patient is being seen from: _____   Patient Phone # _____

☐ Emergency department   ☐ In-Patient   ☐ OPC/COPC _____

1. Beginning of Last Menstrual Period _____	

(¿Quando Empezo su Ultimo Periodo?)   Month (Mes)   Day (Dia)   Year (Año)

2. Pregnant? (¿Esta Embarazada?)   ☐ Yes (si)   ☐ No (no)   ☐ Maybe
   (Quizae)

3. Birth Control Pills (Usa Pastillias Anti-conceptivas)   ☐ Yes (si)   ☐ No (no)

4. IUD (¿Tlene Dispositivo Intrautarion?)   ☐ Yes (si)   ☐ No (no)

5. Hysterectomy (¿Ha Tenido Historectomia?)   ☐ Yes (si)   ☐ No (no)

6. Tubal Ligation (¿Tiene Los Tubos Ligados?)   ☐ Yes (si)   ☐ No (no)

7. Other _____
   _____

☐ I have read and understand the above information. (Ha Leido y compredidio la informacion antedicho.)

_____
Patient Signature (Firma del Paciente)

FOR OFFICE USE ONLY:

Date _____   Signature _____
      Month   Day   Year

Exam(s):

FLUOROSCOPY
☐ 10-Day:
  ☐ Gallbladder
  ☐ Upper G.I.
  ☐ I.V.P.
  ☐ Barium Enema
  ☐ Cystogram
  ☐ Hysterosalpingogram
  ☐ Small Bowel
☐ 10-Day
  ☐ Angiography
  ☐ Digital Angiography

CT SCAN
☐ 10-Day:
  ☐ Abdomen
  ☐ Pelvis
  ☐ Lumbar: Spine

PLAIN FILMS
☐ 28-Day:
  ☐ Mammography
  ☐ Abdomen
  ☐ Pelvis
  ☐ Hips
  ☐ Lumbar Spine
  ☐ Sacrum
  ☐ Coccyx
  ☐ Sacroilliac Joints

NUCLEAR MEDICINE:
☐ 28-Day:
  ☐ Brain Scan
  ☐ Liver Scan
  ☐ Lung Scan
  ☐ Blood Pool
  ☐ Thyroid Uptake
  ☐ Thyroid Scan
  ☐ Bone Scan
  ☐ Renal Scan
  ☐ Schillings
  ☐ Cistemogram
  ☐ Gallium Scan

☐ 10-Day:
  ☐ Radiation Therapy
  ☐ Hyperthyroidism
  ☐ Other

MAGNETIC RESONANCE IMAGING
☐ ALL EXAMS
  28 DAY

Patient referring Physician: _____

Patient Delayed? ☐ Yes ☐ No   Date of Appointment _____
                                                  Month   Day   Year

If the patient is more than   ☐ 10 days from the beginning of her last menstrual period but the examination is
                              ☐ 28 days

necessary anyway, please state reason.

_____

_____

Courtesy of Parkland Health & Hospital System, Dallas, Texas.

4–9
Patient Assessment Policy for Interventional Procedures

PURPOSE

To maintain patient stability throughout procedure and to enable the patient to tolerate the procedure with minimal difficulty. These procedures include arteriography, myelograms, nephrostomies, biliary drainage, and biopsies.

POLICY

1. Information required to perform exam:

   - physician order for procedure

   - date procedure to be performed

   - diagnostic indication for procedure to be performed

2. Procedure prioritization: Priority of test request is designated as routine, ASAP, preop, and stat.

3. Prior to test, the following assessments are performed and documented by the registered nurse:

   - history and physical obtained from primary physician

   - lab values

   - allergies

   - contraindicated medications for the procedure

   - consent obtained

4. During the procedure, the following assessments are performed and documented by the registered nurse:

   - vital signs

   - electrocardiogram (ECG)*

   - oximetry*

   - blood pressure (BP)*

   - peripheral pulses*

   - medications given

   *For arteriography

5. Postprocedure

   - Reassessment is done every 15–30 minutes postprocedure, accordingly, if the patient remains in radiology. Any significant change in the patient's condition is reported to the radiologist or to the patient's physician, with appropriate treatment initiated as indicated and then documented accordingly.

   - All materials used for procedures are documented, including contrast, guidewires, and catheters.

   - Start time and finish time of procedures are documented.

   - Copies of assessment are maintained in the patient's medical record and the radiology file.

Source: Adapted from Bloomington Hospital, Bloomington, Indiana.

4–10
History Sheet for Iodinated Contrast Studies

PATIENT NAME: _____ DATE: _____ EXAM: _____

M.R. #: _____ ROOM #: _____ DOCTOR: _____

AGE: _____ SEX: _____ TECHNOLOGIST: _____ STUDENT: _____

HISTORY OF ALLERGIES ☐ YES ☐ NO IF YES, TO WHAT? _____

PATIENT TAKING GLUCOPHAGE? ☐ YES ☐ NO

HISTORY OF HAYFEVER or ASTHMA ☐ YES ☐ NO PREVIOUS CONTRAST INJECTIONS ☐ YES ☐ NO

PREVIOUS PROBLEM or REACTION ☐ YES ☐ NO IF YES, WHAT TYPE? _____

CURRENT or OLD RENAL PROBLEMS ☐ YES ☐ NO HYPERTENSION _____ RENAL FAILURE _____

CURRENT or OLD CARDIAC PROBLEMS ☐ YES ☐ NO ARRHYTHMIA _____ INFARCT _____ CHF _____

ANGINA _____ PULMONARY HYPERTENSION _____

CURRENT HISTORY _____

CONTRAST SELECTION _____ IONIC _____ NON-IONIC _____
Radiologist signature

INJECTION INFORMATION

CREATININE LEVEL: _____ CONTRAST TYPE: _____ AMOUNT: _____ cc

INJECTION START TIME: _____ INJECTION END TIME: _____

INJECTION ROUTE: ☐ IV ☐ IA ☐ SPINAL ☐ OTHER _____

CONTRAST INJECTED BY: _____ M.D. R.T. R.N.

CONTRAST REACTION: ☐ YES ☐ NO PHYSICIAN CONTACTED: _____

TYPE OF REACTION: _____

TREATMENT GIVEN: _____

MEDICATIONS GIVEN: _____ AMOUNT GIVEN: _____

GIVEN BY: _____ TIME GIVEN: _____

ROUTE OF ADMINISTRATION: ☐ IM ☐ IV ☐ IA ☐ ORAL ☐ OTHER

REPORT TO FLOOR BY: _____ REPORTED TO: _____ TIME: _____

Source: Aspen Publishers, Inc.

4–11
Interventional Radiology Procedure Record

TIME IN DATE	MODE OF ENTRY	Smoking	Nursing Plan
	☐ Ambulatory ☐ Ambulance ☐ W/C ☐ Stretcher ☐ Inpatient ☐ Outpatient	☐ No ☐ Yes _____ pk ___ yr	Admit Nurse

PROCEDURE:

GENERAL APPEARANCE OF SKIN	LIMITATIONS IN COMMUNICATIONS	LEVEL OF RESPONSIVENESS	CHIEF COMPLAINT:		PATIENT TEACHING
☐ Warm & dry ☐ Diaphoretic ☐ Pale ☐ Other ☐ Jaundiced	☐ Hearing ☐ None ☐ Sign ☐ Other ☐ Speech	☐ Alert & oriented ☐ Confused/ disoriented	Are there spiritual/ cultural/ family needs impacting procedure? ☐ No ☐ Yes	ADMISSION VITAL SIGNS	☐ CVIR Protocol Pre-Procedure Person being taught: ☐ Patient ☐ Responsible adult Assessment of ability to learn. Deficit that interferes with learning: ☐ No ☐ Yes (explain):

ADMISSION VITAL SIGNS:
Temp.	BP	Pulse
HT	WT	Resp.

ALLERGIES/ANESTHETIC REACTIONS

DISCHARGE PLAN	NAME/RELATIONSHIP	☐ WAITING AREA	☐ PHONE CONTACT Number _____

☐ Orient patient to area.
☐ Review procedure/plan of care.
☐ Review D/C instructions.
☐ Pt/responsible adult verbalizes understanding of teaching.
☐ No   ☐ Yes

DAILY MEDICATIONS: ☐ NO ☐ YES

	YES	NO
NPO 2° PRIOR TO PROCEDURE		
ID band on patient		
Operative consent signed		
Allergy band on patient		
Safety factors observed		

REVIEW OF SYSTEMS—PAST MEDICAL HISTORY	NO	YES	ADMISSION ASSESSMENT
RESPIRATORY (i.e., COPD, asthma, bronchitis, tuberculosis)			
CARDIAC (i.e., heart sounds, MVP, HTN, CHF, MI, dysrhythmia, CABG, CAD)			
DIGESTIVE: Upper GI disorder (i.e., ulcers, gastritis, esophagitis, hiatal hernia) Lower GI disorder (i.e., colitis, Crohns, polyps, cancer, bleeding)			
URINARY (i.e., dialysis, prostate, kidney stones, renal insufficiency-failure)			
MUSCULOSKELETAL (i.e., physical disabilities, arthritis, fxs, degenerative muscular disorder)			
CIRCULATION (i.e., Raynauds, PVD, phlebitis, DVT, bleeding disorders)			
PREVIOUS SURGERY			
NEUROLOGICAL (i.e., seizure disorder, TIA, CVA) Include behavior.			
LIVER (i.e., hepatitis, jaundice, hx drug use, ETOH use, cirrhosis)			
ENDOCRINE/DIABETIC			
PERTINENT FAMILY HISTORY			

NURSING DIAGNOSIS ☐ 1. Knowledge deficit related to procedure   PLAN ☐ 1. Pre-procedure education and review OUTCOME ☐ 1. Verbalizes understanding
☐ 2. Anxiety   ☐ 2. Provide alternatives to reduce anxiety   ☐ 2. Anxiety diminished

MEDICAL-SURGICAL SEDATION ASSESSMENT

DIAGNOSIS INDICATION _____

LUNGS _____ HEART _____

NEURO _____ ABDOMEN _____

REVIEW OF SYSTEMS/PAST MEDICAL HISTORY AS NOTED ABOVE ☐

Physical Status Classification of American Society of Anesthesia (ASA)

STATUS (Circle)	DESCRIPTION
1	Healthy patient
2	Mild systemic disease
3	Severe systemic disease, not incapacitating
4	Severe systemic disease that is a constant threat of life
5	Moribund, not expected to live 24 hrs. irrespective of operation

*An E is added to status number to designate an emergency operation.

- PREVIOUS ADVERSE REACTION TO SEDATION
  ☐ NO ☐ YES EXPLAIN: _____
- PLANNED SEDATION: ☐ IV ☐ PO ☐ OTHER: _____
Patient has been re-assessed immediately prior to procedure and is an appropriate candidate for the planned sedation and procedure. Risks, benefits, alternatives to procedure, and planned sedation explained to the patient, next of kin, or guardian. ☐ Yes

Physician Signature:_____ Date:_____ Time:_____

PATIENT IDENTIFICATION   **CVIR PROCEDURE RECORD**

continues

4–11 continued

NURSING DIAGNOSIS	☐ 1. Knowledge deficit related to procedure	PLAN ☐ 1. Pre-procedure education and review	OUTCOME ☐ 1. Verbalizes understanding
	☐ 2. Anxiety	☐ 2. Provide alternatives to reduce anxiety	☐ 2. Anxiety diminished

Physician: _____

Technologist: _____

Nurse: _____

Procedure: _____

ROOM TIME

In: _____

Out: _____

☐ DENTURES ☐ UPPER ☐ LOWER ☐ PARTIAL PLATE

☐ GLASSES ☐ HEARING AID ☐ OTHER:

☐ CONTACT LENSES Pregnant ☐ No ☐ Yes Last Menses:

PUNCTURE SITE _____

CONTRAST

NAME   AMT

TIME IN   TIME OUT

Venous   _____   _____

Arterial   _____   _____

_____   _____

TOTAL _____

Pulses:	Pre		Post		IV Site _____ Cath _____
	Right	Left	Right	Left	Nurse _____
DP	___	___	___	___	Fluids _____
PT	___	___	___	___	_____
Other	___	___	___	___	_____

PROCEDURE POSITIONS

☐ Supine ☐ Ⓛ Lateral

☐ Prone ☐ Ⓡ Lateral

OUTPUT:

Urine:

Other:

Foley: ☐ No ☐ Yes

Lab Results Date _____

			OTHER		
			DATE	LAB	RESULT
NA _____	CO_2 _____	Cereal _____	_____	_____	_____
K+ _____	Glucose _____	PT _____	_____	_____	_____
CL _____	BUN _____	PTT _____	_____	_____	_____
WBC _____	HgB _____	HCT _____	_____	_____	_____
PLAT _____					

MEDICATION/IVs

MEDICATION	DOSE	ROUTE	TIME	TOTAL
VITAL SIGNS PRE-SEDATION ➔				

PROCEDURE VITAL SIGNS

TIME	NIBP	ABP	RESP	SAO_2	HR	CARDIAC RHYTHM	GENERAL APPEARANCE OF SKIN	LOC

LOC (Level of consciousness)
1. Alert and oriented
2. Sleepy/drowsy
3. Slightly drowsy/cooperative
4. Resistive
5. Uncomfortable/restless/vocal
6. Confused/disoriented

☐ PREPPED & DRAPED ☐ MONITORS IN PLACE

NURSE'S NOTES:

Report given to

_____RN

RN SIGNATURE _____ DATE _____

INTERVENTIONAL TREATMENT RECORD

TIME	LESION	BALLOON SIZE	ATM	INFLATION TIME	ACT	PATIENT REACTION

PATIENT IDENTIFICATION

CVIR PROCEDURE RECORD

Courtesy of Inova Alexandria Hospital, Alexandria, Virginia.

4–12
Pre-Visit Form

Complete this form and bring it with you to your first doctor's visit.

PATIENT INFORMATION

Patient Name: _____

Today's Date: _____

Referring Physician: _____

Family Physician: _____

Date of Birth: _____   Age: _____

Height: _____ ft _____ in   Weight: _____

Gender: ☐ female   ☐ male

Marital Status: ☐ single   ☐ married   ☐ widowed   ☐ divorced

Number of Children: _____

PERSONAL HEALTH HISTORY

What is the reason for this visit? _____

_____

Have you ever had a heart problem?   ☐ Yes   ☐ No

If yes, please explain: _____

_____

Do you have or have you ever had any of the following?

☐ Rheumatic fever   Date: _____

☐ Heart murmur   Date: _____

☐ Heart attack   Date: _____

☐ Chest pain/pressure   Date: _____

☐ Heart failure   Date: _____

☐ Rapid heart beat or irregular pulse   Date: _____

☐ Lightheadedness   Date: _____

☐ Dizziness   Date: _____

☐ Fainting   Date: _____

☐ Swelling of the ankles   Date: _____

☐ Pain in calf muscles when walking   Date: _____

☐ Congestive heart failure   Date: _____

☐ Shortness of breath   Date: _____

continues

4–12 continued

Have you ever had any of the following heart studies?

☐ EKG   ☐ Echocardiogram   ☐ 24-hour monitor

☐ Cardiac Catheterization   ☐ Treadmill   ☐ Chest X-ray

Other: _____

Have you ever had a reaction to the dye used in certain cardiac X-rays?

☐ Yes   ☐ No   ☐ I have never had this type of X-ray

Do you have any allergies to medication?   ☐ Yes   ☐ No

If yes, which medications: _____

_____

Do you currently smoke?	☐ Yes ☐ No	Pack per day:	_____
		Number of years:	_____
Have you ever smoked?	☐ Yes ☐ No	Date stopped:	_____
Do you have elevated cholesterol?	☐ Yes ☐ No	Last checked:	_____
Do you have high blood pressure?	☐ Yes ☐ No	How many years:	_____
Do you drink alcoholic beverages?	☐ Yes ☐ No	How much each day:	_____
Are you generally stressed?	☐ Yes ☐ No		
Do you drink beverages containing caffeine?	☐ Yes ☐ No	How much:	_____
Do you exercise?	☐ Yes ☐ No		

If yes, what is your exercise routine? _____

_____

Are you following a special diet?   ☐ Yes   ☐ No

If yes, please describe: _____

_____

Occupation: _____

Describe your job tasks: _____

_____

Are you retired?   ☐ Yes   ☐ No   Date _____

Are you disabled?   ☐ Yes   ☐ No   Date _____

If yes, describe your disability: _____

_____

Describe any surgeries you have had:

Surgery   Year

_____   _____

_____   _____

_____   _____

_____   _____

_____   _____

continues

4–12 continued

Please check any other health condition you have or have had in the past:

☐ Scarlet fever   ☐ Menstrual dysfunction

☐ Anxiety   ☐ Kidney disease

☐ Emphysema   ☐ Breathing problems

☐ Ulcer   ☐ Venereal disease

☐ Anemia   ☐ Sexual dysfunction

☐ Arthritis   ☐ Asthma

☐ Stomach or bowel disorder   ☐ Allergies/Hay Fever

☐ Fatigue   ☐ Gout

☐ Urinary problem   ☐ Thyroid disease

☐ Rheumatic fever   ☐ Diabetes/high blood sugar

☐ Depression   ☐ Migraine headache

☐ Constipation   ☐ Liver disease

☐ Cancer _____   ☐ Other _____

FAMILY HISTORY

Do you have a history of heart disease in your family?   ☐ Yes   ☐ No

If yes, indicate relation and age problems started? _____

_____

_____

_____

Family Member(s)	Alive	Deceased	Current Age or Age at Death	Cause of Death
Mother	☐	☐	_____	_____
Father	☐	☐	_____	_____
Sister(s)	☐	☐	_____	_____
	☐	☐	_____	_____
	☐	☐	_____	_____
Brother(s)	☐	☐	_____	_____
	☐	☐	_____	_____
	☐	☐	_____	_____

CARE OF PATIENTS

4–13
Latex Sensitivity Policy for Medical Imaging Services

Division: Clinical

Original issue date: _____

Latest revision date: _____

Authorization signature: _____ Date: _____
Director, Medical Imaging

Department/Division Affected

Medical Imaging

APPROVAL DISTRIBUTION LIST

Approved by	Title	Date
	Medical Director, Medical Imaging Services	
	AVP, Clinical Services	
	Director, Infection Control	

PURPOSE

To provide guidelines to identify and provide care for the latex sensitive patient while in the medical imaging department. To provide alternative product list for the latex sensitive patient.

POLICY

All latex sensitive or suspected latex sensitive patients will be identified, evaluated, and treated in a safe manner by all care providers while in the medical imaging department.

- Inpatients will be assessed for latex sensitivity when admitted to the hospital.

- Outpatients will be given a screening assessment when checking in.

Responsibilities

Each employee in medical imaging is responsible for being aware of and strictly adhering to the hospital and department's latex allergy policy. This should ensure that the latex sensitive patient is not inadvertently exposed to latex products.

- Refer to the hospital policy on latex sensitivity located in the administrative policy manual.

continues

4–13 continued

- Employees who suspect they have a latex allergy must report to Employee Health. Latex has a cumulative effect and a minor irritation could be a sign of future serious allergic reaction. Please refer to the administrative policy manual.

- Technologists performing an exam where latex products are being used must question the patient about possible latex allergy, check for a Medic Alert bracelet, and check the requisition for this information.

- Scheduling personnel, receptionists, and transporters must convey latex allergy information brought to their attention to the staff performing the exam on the patient.

- The radiology nurse must be notified of all known latex allergic patients who are scheduled, prior to their arrival.

Latex sensitivity will be documented in the medical record along with other allergies.

Latex Sensitive Patient Information

All patients who have been identified as latex sensitive (documented or suspected) will be managed in a latex safe environment.

- The employee should secure the latex-free tackle box and order additional products as needed.

- Latex-free products are listed in the purple/lavender three-ring reference binder located in the QC area of diagnostic radiology and the injection uptake room in nuclear medicine.

Each medical imaging employee will be responsible for knowing the location, purpose, and procedure of the latex sensitive tackle box and catalog.

- The latex sensitive tackle box is located in the QC area of diagnostics and in the injection uptake room in nuclear medicine.

- The purpose of the tackle box is for a quick admission without prior notification and/or crisis intervention on a latex sensitive patient.

- When items are used from the tackle box, the employee that used the items is responsible for ordering and restocking the tackle box.

- The three-ring binder accompanying the tackle box contains

    –an item file catalog with "L" or "LF"

    –copies of the order sheets

    –articles and bibliography to use as references

    –a brochure called "Latex Sensitivity"

    –"latex sensitive" door and chart stickers

PROCEDURES

Scheduled Procedures

- All patients scheduled for exams will be asked if they have a latex sensitivity during their pre-screening assessment. The severity of the sensitivity will be assessed during the interview when the patient comes in for the procedure.

continues

4–13 continued

- Patients with known latex sensitivity should be scheduled as the first patient of the day if at all possible.
- The medical imaging staff will document the latex sensitivity on the schedule and any information sheets that are filled out.

Prior to Admission

- The radiologist assigned to the case (for interventional procedures) will make the decision to implement the latex allergy protocol or proceed with the study.
- The latex-free product list is reviewed by all personnel who will be in contact with the patient. Products that are latex-free need to be available for the study.

Latex Protocols

Before admission or after identification of sensitivity

- notify the medical imaging manager, quality/safety coordinator, or the hospital safety officer of expected admission and sensitivity to latex
- the patient exam rooms should have all of the latex products removed or confined and terminally cleaned by environmental services the night before. No patient activity should take place in these rooms after the cleaning.
- the patient should be the first patient on the schedule
- the product list should be double-checked to verify items that contain latex. Obtain latex-free products or research alternative equipment if no latex-free product or equipment is available.
- contact the radiologist to review and revise any care plan. The radiologist assigned to the case will make the decision to implement the latex sensitive protocol or proceed with the study.
- contact the pharmacy about mixing medications for the patient

Resource people for questions relating to latex sensitivity will be the infection control staff or administrative coordinator. If the infection control office is closed, the administrative coordinator on duty will be the resource person.

General Information

Latex sensitivity is often presented to the medical imaging personnel without advance warning. Care is centered around eliminating exposure to products containing latex. Latex sensitivity can develop by repeated exposure. While some individuals have a contact sensitivity resulting in urticaria, others have immediate hypersensitivity reactions similar to hay fever or severe food allergies. Anaphylaxis can result with small amounts of latex contact. Exposure may cause a local response at the site of contact or systemically.

High-risk patients include

- patients with myelodysplasia or urological deformities
- patients who have had multiple surgeries
- health care workers
- patients with spinal cord injuries

continues

4–13 continued

- patients with a history of occupational contact with latex products

- patients with a history of atopic dermatitis, eczema, and fruit allergies

Room Preparation

- Patients with known latex sensitivity should be scheduled early in the day.

- The exam room should have all of the latex products removed or confined and terminally cleaned the night before.

- No patient activity should take place in these rooms after cleaning.

- The technologist must damp wipe the room to remove any airborne settled latex particles before the patient is brought into the room.

Signs and Symptoms in a Latex Sensitive Patient

Symptoms usually occur within 30 minutes from exposure, but the time can range from 10 to 280 minutes.

Awake Patient	Anesthetized Patient
Itchy eyes	Tachycardia
Generalized pruritus	Hypotension
Shortness of breath	Wheezing
Feeling of faintness	Bronchospasm
Feeling of impending doom	Cardiorespiratory arrest
Nausea and/or vomiting	Flushing
Abdominal cramping	Laryngeal edema
Diarrhea	Urticaria
Wheezing	

Treatment for a Latex Sensitive Patient

- Avoid all contact with latex products and limit the amount of latex air products.

- Stop the procedure or treatment immediately if reaction occurs.

- Maintain airway and administer 100% oxygen.

- Maintain hemodynamic volumes via Ringer's lactate or normal saline.

- Medication treatment may include epinephrine bolus, Benadryl, Solu-Medrol, and Zantac.

- Notify unit receiving patient of latex allergy as soon as possible so they may prepare in advance.

Many medical imaging supplies contain latex; when in doubt, check with the manufacturer. Staff should always be careful when using any items that are black. They usually contain latex. This includes positioning sponges—avoid their use if possible. If sponges must be used, they should be covered, and the patients should have a sheet barrier between their skin and the covered sponge.

Manufacturers are now required to label prepackaged items as to their latex content.

Source: Adapted from Nancy Hughes, Holy Cross Hospital, Silver Spring, Maryland.

4–14
Criteria for Determining Allergic Reaction to Contrast Media

POLICY

The following criteria have been established as a guideline for identifying allergic reactions to contrast media used for certain procedures in the radiology department.

PROCEDURE

1. If the radiologist is not in the department at the time the contrast media is to be injected, the ED physician must be alerted of the procedure to be done so as to alert him/her of potential need for his/her service. If he/she is not readily available, the procedure should not be performed until such time as there is a physician available.

2. *Flushness and a hot feeling* are frequently associated with invasive procedures requiring contrast media. While these feelings need to be alleviated, they are not considered to be an allergic reaction to the contrast media. The application of a cold, wet cloth to the patient's forehead and neck will help reduce these feelings.

3. *Nausea and vomiting* sometimes follow the flushness and hot feelings. The cold, wet cloth will help these feelings also. An emesis basin shall be easily within reach in case vomiting begins.

4. *Urticaria and sneezing* are considered to be mild reactions. A physician shall be called to check the patient and give instructions or medications that he/she feels are necessary. The physician shall be informed of the patient's condition at the time of the call. If any medications are to be given, the physician or a nurse shall be responsible for the administration.

5. *Facial swelling and respiratory distress* are considered moderate reactions. The physician shall be called to check the patient and give instructions or medications that he/she feels are necessary. The physician shall be informed of the patient's conditions at the time of the call. Respiratory therapy shall be called immediately after the physician. These changes usually occur slowly enough to allow these calls. If they occur too quickly for one person to make the two calls, they shall be made by two people at the same time or a "Code 99" should be called.

6. *Anaphylactic shock* (such as losing consciousness, severe respiratory distress, and cardiac arrest) is considered to be a severe reaction. "Code 99" shall be called, even though a full cardiac arrest is not apparent.

7. Any of these changes mentioned above shall be recorded on the Radiology Agent Data form for that procedure, and an Adverse Drug Reaction report will be completed and turned into pharmacy.

Attachments: None

_____   _____
Radiology Director   Date

_____   _____
Chief or Staff Radiologist   Date

Reviewed/Revised: _____
                                              Date

Distribution: Radiology

Courtesy of Rick Sellers, Department of Radiology, Tanner Medical Center, Carrollton, Georgia.

4–15
Injection of Contrast Material in Medical Imaging

Division: Clinical Services

Original issue date: _____

Latest revision date: _____

Authorization signature: _____   Date: _____
Director, Medical Imaging Services

Department/Division Affected

Medical Imaging Services

APPROVAL DISTRIBUTION LIST

Approved by	Title	Date
	Medical Director, Medical Imaging Services	
	Assistant Vice President, Clinical Services	

PURPOSE

To identify persons authorized to inject contrast material and the guidelines that are to be followed

POLICY

Persons Certified To Inject Contrast Material

All persons who inject contrast material must be certified in cardiopulmonary resuscitation (CPR). Qualified individuals include radiologists or other physicians and, following completion of training that demonstrates proficiency, registered nurses and registered technologists.

Guidelines for Injections

- Ensure proper identification of patient.
- Ensure that a radiologist is available in the department before injection is done.
- Obtain history from patient and medical record.

  –Determine allergies.

  –Confirm pertinent indications for the exam.

  –Determine previous injections and/or reactions to contrast material.

  –Document present medications, medical history, and lab data.

continues

4–15 continued

Contraindications for Contrast Injections

- history of previous adverse reaction to contrast material
- elevated BUN and creatine
- asthma
- multiple myeloma
- congestive heart failure
- sickle-cell disease
- diabetic patient taking metformin (Medication must be stopped two days prior to and two days following intravenous contrast administration.)

Injections through Existing IVs

- The following lines should not be used for high-pressure injections:
  - –central venous pressure lines
  - –subclavian lines
  - –Swan-Ganz lines
  - –PICC lines
- IV lines should not be closed for a period longer than needed to inject contrast material.

Resuscitative Equipment Readily Available

- emergency box
- O_2 set up
- suction set up and available

Observation of Patient for Adverse Reactions

- Inform patient of normal sensations to be expected.
- Notify radiologist and RN immediately of any adverse reaction.
- Do not leave patient alone after injection. (A reaction may occur up to 30 minutes after the injection.)
- Major reactions include bronchospasm, shock, and cardiopulmonary arrest.

Documentation of Adverse Reactions

- Technologist responsibilities
  - –enters reactions and medications given into Clinstar under Exam Data Entry
  - –stamps radiology master jacket with "Reaction to Contrast" stamp
  - –fills out Adverse Drug Reaction Form
  - –places white and canary copies in designated area in quality control
  - –places pink copy in patient's master radiology jacket
- Radiologist responsibilities
  - –dictates reaction in patient's final radiology report

Exceptions

- All pediatric patients must be injected by a radiologist, RN, or pediatric physician.

Source: Adapted from Nancy Hughes, Holy Cross Hospital, Silver Spring, Maryland.

4–16
Patient Preparation for Radiological Studies

AUDIENCE

The information in this document is applicable to all nursing, medical, and radiology personnel.

POLICY

A physician's order is required for all radiological studies.

Unless otherwise specified by the physician, the patient preparation standard approved by the Department of Radiology will be used to prepare patients for studies.

Questions and/or discussion of individual patient preparation requirements can be made by contacting the section Chief for each procedure.

Preparation requirements will be performed as outlined. Deviation from method of preparation will be made only after consultation between the Department of Radiology and the patient's physician. Contraindication to the procedure or method of preparation must be determined by the patient's physician.

GUIDELINES

Requests for intravenous pyelogram (IVP), gallbladder (GB), gastrointestinal tract (GI), and barium enema (BE) received before 2:00 PM each day will usually be scheduled for the following day. An appointment for examination will be given to the unit upon receipt of the request. The daily X-ray schedule is confirmation of this appointment (this does not apply to outpatient examinations).

If the patient is to have all four examinations, he/she should usually be scheduled in the following order:

> IVP—First Day
>
> GB—Second Day
>
> GI—Third Day
>
> BE—Fourth Day

These can also be scheduled on the same day, if necessary. The barium enema should be done before the GI series if there is a possibility of intestinal obstruction. It is preferable to schedule IVPs, cholecystograms, or ultrasound studies before contrast studies using barium are done.

Notify the Department of Radiology if there are any special requirements for patient care prior to bringing him/her to the department for studies.

continues

4–16 continued

PROCEDURE

Step	Action
1	Verify the physician's order for the radiological study.
2	If no specific patient preparation is ordered by the physician, or if "routine preparation" is ordered by the physician, consult the on-line listing of approved patient preparation protocols for radiological studies.
3	Locate and review the preparation procedure.
4	Obtain any needed supplies or equipment. Prepare the patient for the study as outlined in the radiological procedure manual.
5	Document the study ordered, patient preparation done, time, patient response, and other pertinent information as appropriate.

PATIENT/FAMILY EDUCATION

1. Explain to the patient/family the preparation for the study to be performed.

2. Explain to the patient/family his/her role in the preparation, if applicable.

Source: University of Texas Medical Branch, Galveston, Texas.

4–17
Radiology Preps—Adult and Pediatric

PURPOSE

To prepare the patient for radiological procedures that require contrast media for visualization.

POLICY

1. The radiological procedure shall be ordered by the physician and entered into the computer by a member of the nursing staff, following computer prompts.

2. The physician/nurse shall obtain the appropriate pre-printed X-ray prep order sheet, and place it in the chart. (Pre-printed prep order sheets are available from General Service store.) The following is a list of available pre-printed prep orders and their stock numbers:

   - Adult UGI   S/N 1405
   - Adult BE/IVP   S/N 1406
   - Adult Gallbladder   S/N 1411
   - Pediatric UGI   S/N 1407
   - Pediatric Gallbladder   S/N 1410
   - Pediatric IVP   S/N 1412
   - Pediatric BE with Air Contrast   S/N 1408
   - Pediatric BE without Air Contrast   S/N 1409

   (Note: The last is a two-page order sheet that will be padded p.1, then p.2 consecutively.)

3. The physician shall complete and sign the order sheet.

4. When the nurse transcribes the orders, a copy shall be sent to Pharmacy.

5. A daily schedule of the patients that need preparation shall be delivered to each nursing unit by Radiology personnel. The nursing unit staff is responsible for verifying that a scheduled exam is listed on the Radiology schedule and for clarifying any discrepancies with Radiology.

6. As a general rule, only one contrast X-ray examination on a patient should be done per day.

7. When ordering more than one radiological exam requiring contrast media, the following order sequence should be followed:

Adult:

1. IVP/Excretory Urogram
2. G.B. Series - G.I. Series
3. Barium Enema

continues

4–17 continued

Pediatric:

1. KUB

2. GB Series

3. Voiding Cystourethrogram

4. IVP

5. Barium Enema

6. Upper GI Series

7. Small Bowel Series

8. **Other fluoroscopic studies.** The following fluoroscopic studies require no preparation:

   - Chest Fluoroscopy

   - Trachea and/or Bronchi Fluoroscopy

   - Sinus Tract Injection

   - Vaginography and Hysterosalpingography

9. Special Considerations

   - Emergency IVPs require no preparation, especially for patients who have had abdominal trauma.

   - Barium enema

     - Barium enemas should be scheduled as far in advance as possible, and in no case less than 24 hours before the desired examination time. For selected cases, barium enema and excretory urograms may be done on the same day. All barium enemas are routinely done in the morning.

     - The preparation should begin one day prior to the scheduled examination. The prescription of any cathartic may be contraindicated if certain clinical problems are present (e.g., acute regional enteritis and ulcerative colitis; toxic megacolon; small or large bowel obstruction; any time perforation may be imminent). In such cases, no preparation may be required, but it is suggested that the patient's physician consult the radiologist regarding appropriate prep.

     - Barium enema examinations should not be done within 24 hours of a sigmoidoscopy or colonoscopy. If a biopsy has been performed, the radiologist should be informed and a barium enema examination should be delayed for a period of several days.

   - For patients who have had a recent barium enema study, laxative and cleansing enemas are recommended prior to obtaining additional abdominal studies. However, the patient's physician shall be contacted regarding orders for such.

10. **After care.** The patient's physician should be contacted regarding orders for after care for any radiological studies involving contrast media and/or barium.

11. **Radiological procedures ordered on an outpatient basis:**

    - The nursing unit or clinic shall schedule the examination per Invision. During business hours, an appointment card with the date/time of exam shall be given to the patient. The nursing unit/clinic shall be responsible for mailing an appointment card to the patient.

continues

4–17 continued

- The nursing unit or clinic shall give written and verbal prep instructions to the patient, with documentation noted in the nursing discharge instruction sheet or clinic record.

- For outpatients, a radiology consultation form shall be completed by the physician and routed to the Radiology Department by the outpatient clinic. Radiology procedures cannot be done without the completed consultation form.

Director, Patient Care Support Services

_____   _____
Signature   Date

Acting Assistant Hospital Administrator for Patient Care Services

_____   _____
Signature   Date

4–18
Guidelines of Care and Practice: Radiology Patients

I. OUTCOME GOAL

The provision of safe and effective care for all patients undergoing diagnostic and interventional radiologic procedures.

II. POLICY

Defines the minimum guidelines for nursing care for all patients undergoing diagnostic and interventional radiology procedures including during transport to and from the Radiology Department and during all Radiology procedures and studies.

III. EQUIPMENT/SUPPLIES

If patient has an artificial airway and requires artificial ventilation:

A. Full Oxygen (O_2) Cylinder (2000 PSI) with patient-specific supplies

B. Resuscitator bag with mask

C. Pulse Oximeter

D. $ETCO_2$ monitor as deemed necessary by MD, RN, and/or Respiratory Care personnel

E. Cardiac Monitor

F. Medications for resuscitation as defined by unit-specific standards

G. Extra endotracheal tube and/or tracheostomy tube (as deemed needed by RN)

H. Portable suction machine and suction kits (as deemed needed by RN)

I. Transport ventilator for patients who require a Positive End Expiratory Pressure >15cmH$_2$O (and/or appropriate resuscitator bag with mask & Positive End Expiratory Pressure capability)

If patient has an artificial airway, but does not require artificial ventilation:

A. Full oxygen (O_2) cylinder (2000 PSI) with supplies specific to patient's need

B. Resuscitator bag with mask or tracheostomy adapter

C. Obturator for tracheostomy tube

D. Portable suction machine and suction kit (as deemed necessary by RN)

If patient is on supplemental oxygen, but does not have an artificial airway:

A. Full oxygen (O_2) cylinder (2000 PSI) with supplies specific to patient's need

B. Supplemental O_2 equipment (i.e.,nasal cannula, face mask, etc.)

C. Pulse oximeter (MD, RN, or RCP deemed necessary)

D. Call Respiratory Care (RCP) for patients with high oxygen requirements

continues

4–18 continued

Monitoring (continuous):

A. ECG Monitor (as deemed necessary by MD, RN)

B. Pulse oximeter (as deemed necessary by MD, RN)

C. Other transport monitoring systems as deemed necessary by MD, RN (i.e., ICP monitoring, Arterial line monitoring, ETCO$_2$ monitoring for mechanically ventilated patients, etc.)

IV. PROTOCOL

A. A licensed nurse from the unit will accompany patients during transport to and from Radiology and remain in Radiology if the patient is in an ICU-monitored bed. ***Exception: Patients in an ICU with written orders to be transferred to a non-monitored bed.***

B. A licensed nurse shall accompany all monitored patients not in an ICU. The RN responsible for the patient will determine (in collaboration with the physician) the need to continue or discontinue monitoring during transport and will obtain a physician's order when discontinuation of monitoring for transport and procedure/study time is deemed appropriate.

C. A licensed nurse from the unit/floor shall accompany all hemodynamically unstable or potentially high-risk patients during transport to and from the Radiology Department and remain with the patient during the procedure/study.

   Monitoring includes: SaO$_2$ and/or apnea and/or cardiac.

D. When a monitored patient is transported to the Radiology Department without a monitor per MD order, or monitoring has been discontinued within two hours of the transport, the nurse taking care of the patient will communicate report directly to a member of the Radiology nursing staff prior to transport. The unit/floor nurse is to call the Radiology Control Desk extension 3-3310, who will page the Radiology Charge Nurse (M-F 8a-4p) or nurse on-call for report. This report will include:

   1. Patient's related history

   2. Hemodynamic status

   3. Potential high-risk considerations

   4. Whether monitoring is to be continued during the procedure/study while in Radiology

   5. Notification if multiple radiologic procedures are ordered

   6. Infection control (Isolation) status (when applicable)

E. Assessment parameters will be based on the patient's condition and the specific procedure to be performed.

F. All patients will have a brief history obtained prior to administration of any medication and/or contrast media. The history will include, but not be limited to, history of prior contrast administration and allergies.

G. Pediatric patients will be supervised at all times.

H. An RN will monitor all patients undergoing invasive arterial/venous procedures. Monitoring will minimally include the following:

   1. Cardiac monitoring

   2. Blood pressure monitoring

   3. Pulse oximetry

continues

4–18 continued

4. Vital signs at least every 15 minutes

5. Neurological assessment during neurovascular studies

I. RN will monitor all patients undergoing procedures requiring conscious sedation according to the guidelines stated in hospital policy 20-09 (Sedation & Analgesia of Patients at Vanderbilt University Medical Center).

J. Patients may receive medication to decrease their anxiety, discomfort, and/or pain during procedures as medically indicated.

1. Only a licensed nurse will administer medications. Only an RN or MD may administer IV medication.

    Exception: Radiopharmaceutical and contrast agents may be administered by Radiology Technologists.

2. Prior to the administration of medication, the following information must be obtained (per nurse-to-nurse report for inpatients or from medical record, patient, and/or family members for outpatients), when possible:

    a. Age

    b. Weight

    c. Past medical history

    d. History of sedation

    e. Allergies

    f. Length of study

    g. Specific ports to be used for administration of medications and/or contrast media

    h. Determination of other procedures that may require sedation and/or nursing support.

3. Prior to the administration of any medication for the purpose of conscious sedation, the guidelines listed in hospital policy 20-09 (Sedation & Analgesia of Patients at Vanderbilt University Medical Center) will be followed.

K. The patient's status, interventions, and any adverse reactions during and after a Radiology procedure/study with Radiology nursing involvement will be communicated verbally to the staff of the unit/floor receiving the patient after the procedure and will be documented in the patient's medical record.

L. Preprocedure preparation for scheduled procedures will be communicated to the patient care units/floors to: 1) minimize radiation time, 2) reduce the need to repeat examinations, 3) decrease the hospital stay.

M. Policies and procedures related to the nursing care of Radiology patients will be available as a resource for all Vanderbilt University Medical Center medical staff and faculty. These policies and procedures will be reviewed and/or revised at least every three years.

N. Whenever possible, multiple radiology procedures and studies will be coordinated through the Control Desk (ext.: 3-3310) and/or the Radiology Charge Nurse (hospital pager #2280) in order to minimize the number of required transports off the unit.

O. While in the Radiology Department, patients will receive safe, appropriate, efficient, coordinated care in the event of an emergency:

1. All Radiology RNs will be ACLS/PALS certified and have critical care experience.

2. All Radiology nursing staff will be required to attend all mandatory inservices applicable to their role.

3. Emergency drugs, equipment, and supplies will be inventoried daily to ensure control, availability, and proper functioning.

continues

4–18 continued

V. PROCEDURE(S)

A. Considerations:

1. Time required for transport to and from Radiology

2. Staff needed to transport (including timely notification of Respiratory Care)

3. Equipment needed to transport (i.e., O_2 cylinder/ventilator, resuscitation bag and mask, cardiac monitoring, emergency drugs, etc.)

4. Clamp any gastric or duodenal tubes for transport time with information given for care during procedure to staff/RN with patient.

5. Appropriate staff available to receive patient and assume responsibility for care *or* appropriate staff available to travel and/or stay with patient for time in Radiology

6. All chest tubes are at least to water-seal drainage with MD order or per unit standards (suction may need to be applied immediately upon transport to patient care area or procedure room).

7. Need for procedure rescheduling (i.e., conflicts with other procedure, deterioration of condition, patient's ability to tolerate transport and procedure)

8. Patient's need for sedation and/or pain control

9. Patient's airway needs (i.e., ET tube, tracheostomy, stomas, ability to maintain own secretions, history of seizure disorder, trauma or surgical intervention)

10. Patient's ability to communicate (i.e., artificial airway, language barriers, cultural differences)

11. Security needs for the patient

12. Infection Control needs for the patient

13. Communication needs for technical, transport, physician, and nursing staff

B. MD/RN need to evaluate the appropriateness of each transport (consideration should be taken to get multiple testing done in a single travel if at all possible), adjusting ventilation parameters, ensuring adequate and appropriate analgesia and sedation ordered, and need for cardiac monitoring.

VI. PATIENT/FAMILY EDUCATION

A. All Radiology procedures and studies will be explained to the patient, including the location of the procedure/study, the approximate length of time for the transport and procedure/study, along with a detailed description of the reasons for the procedure/study. Teaching will be appropriate for age and level of learning.

B. Any equipment, possible risks, and the roles of the individuals involved in the procedure/study will be explained to the patient prior to the study/procedure.

C. All patient and family questions will be addressed in a timely manner.

D. Explanations will be given regarding any required sedation/analgesia.

E. Any post study/procedure instructions and/or transport needs will be explained to patients, families, and receiving staff on inpatient unit/floor for inpatients; to patients, families, and/or responsible caregivers for outpatients prior to discharge (i.e., post arteriogram orders for body positioning requirements).

F. All instruction will be provided with appropriate age-specific focus including assessment of challenges to learning, previous knowledge/experience, and level of participation in teaching/learning experience.

continues

4–18 continued

VII. DOCUMENTATION

A. Time of transport, mode of transport, and equipment used during transport to and from Radiology will be documented.

B. Patient assessments according to level of care (RN involvement only) will be documented.

C. All invasive procedures will be documented including but not limited to IV starts and catheter placements.

D. All medication administrations including contrast agents will be documented including patient response.

E. Continuing needs of patients post-procedure/transport will be documented.

F. Patient and family education will be documented including the information from *VII Patient/Family Education* requirements section *F.*

G. Report given prior to procedure and post-procedure will be documented with individual giving and receiving report specified in the documentation.

Source: Vanderbilt University Medical Center, Nashville, Tennessee.

4–19
Radiation Safety: Permissible Exposure Levels

DOSE LIMITS

Dose limits are established by the Nuclear Regulatory Commission (NRC) and are the legal requirements that must be met for work with radioisotopes. These limits are given in Table 1 and are based on the recommendations of nationally and internationally recognized committees such as the National Council on Radiation Protection (NCRP) and the International Committee on Radiation Protection (ICRP). The present limits were adopted by the NRC in 1991, and the values given in Table 1 are taken from 10 CFR Part 20.1201. For occupational workers the basic whole body limit requires the Total Effective Dose Equivalent (TEDE) be less than 5 rems per year. The TEDE is the sum of the Deep Dose Equivalent (the dose from external radiation) and the Committed Effective Dose Equivalent (the dose from internally deposited radionuclides). In addition to the TEDE limit, there is a limit of 50 rems per year to individual organs, skin, and extremities. The eye has a special limit of 15 rem per year. There is also a special limit for declared pregnant workers of 0.5 rem to the fetus for the duration of the pregnancy and of 0.1 rem for members of the general public.

The NRC also requires that doses be kept "as low as reasonably achievable" (ALARA). The limits are set as maxima that must not be exceeded, but the goal is to keep doses as far below these limits as is practical.

TABLE 1 Dose Limits per Year

Radiation Workers	Dose
Total Effective Dose Equivalent (TEDE)	5 rem
Dose Equivalent to the Eye	15 rem
Shallow Dose Equivalent to skin, extremities	50 rem
TEDE to any other individual organ	50 rem
TEDE to embryo/fetus of declared pregnant woman	0.5 rem
Minors	Ten percent of worker limit
Members of the Public	0.1 rem

DOSE LIMITS FOR PRENATAL EXPOSURE

The fetus is more sensitive to radiation damage than the adult; therefore, the Nuclear Regulatory Commission requires that radiation exposure to the fetus be limited to less than 0.5 rem during the nine months of development for a declared pregnant woman. The Nuclear Regulatory Commission's *Regulatory Guide 8.13* discusses the possible health risks to children of women who are exposed to radiation during pregnancy. This guide should be read by all female radiation workers. The Institute is committed to keeping the dose below 0.5 rem for those who declare their pregnancy.

Female radiation workers who become pregnant or who are anticipating pregnancy are encouraged to discuss their radiation exposure situation with the Radiation Safety Officer and supervisor, especially if it is likely that an abdominal exposure of up to 0.5 rem over a nine-month period could be received.

continues

4–19 continued

DOSE DETERMINATION

The TEDE is calculated by adding the dose determined from the badge dosimeter (external deep dose equivalent) to that determined from urine and thyroid bioassay procedures (internal committed effective dose equivalent). If monitoring is required, it is very important that monitoring badges be returned promptly and that urine or thyroid assay schedules be followed. If any badges are lost or if an assay schedule cannot be met, the Radiation Safety Office must be informed and a form completed for an estimate of the dose.

Source: Adapted from "Permissible Exposure Levels," *Radiation Safety Manual,* National Institutes of Health.

4–20
Radiology Agent Protocols

PURPOSE

To provide information and guidance on all agents administered by radiology personnel

POLICY

Agents commonly used in radiology

Optiray

Agent	OPTIRAY
Strength	320
Dosage	100cc for patients over 111 lbs. (BUN = <30; creatinine = <1.3)
	50cc for patients 110 lbs. and under (BUN = <30; creatinine = 1.3 to 1.9)
	1 cc per pound for pediatrics
	None to be given if BUN = 31 and above and creatinine = 2.0 and above

Patients age 45 and older must have BUN and creatinine prior to exam. Patients must be within the normal range to inject. If not, technologist must consult with radiologist or attending ED physician.

Normal Ranges	BUN = 4 – 20 Creatinine = .5 – 1.3
Administration	Agent is injected by IV or through butterfly needle into vein. Agent is used to visualize vascular structures and organs.
A.R.R.T.	Technologists are the only personnel authorized from radiology to inject.
Onset of action	Immediately
Peak effect	Varies
Duration	Varies
Adverse reactions	Hives, rash, shortness of breath, difficulty in breathing, shock, and cardiac arrest

Gastroview

Agent	GASTROVIEW
Strength	660mg diatrizoate meglumine and 100mg diatrizoate sodium
Dosage	10cc oral for stomach and upper abdomen, mix with 480cc juice (CT)
	20cc oral for pelvis, mix with 480cc juice (CT)
	5cc mixed with 500cc water (CT) for rectum and sigmoid colon
Administration	Injected orally or into rectum.
Onset of actions	Immediately
Peak effect	N/A
Duration	N/A
Adverse reactions	Considered mild and transitory, nausea, vomiting, diarrhea, skin rashes, itching, heartburn, dizziness, and/or headache

continues

4–20 continued

Conray

Agent	CONRAY
Strength	30–60ml for adults and children age 14 and older
	Adults must have BUN and creatinine within normal limits.
	5ml under 6 months
	8ml 6–12 months
	10ml 1–2 years
	12ml 2–5 years
	15ml 5–8 years
	18ml 8–12 years
	20–30ml 12–14 years
Administration	Through IV or catheter
Onset of action	Immediately
Peak effect	Varies
Duration	Varies
Adverse reactions	Nausea, vomiting, facial flush, body warmth, S.O.B., choking, tightness in chest, syncope, convulsions, headache, trembling, chills without fever, temporary renal shutdown, coma, and/or death

Cystografin

Agent	CYSTOGRAFIN
Strength	USP 30%
Dosage	25–100ml depending on patient age and bladder irritability.
Administration	Infused by gravity through urinary catheter allowing visualization of urinary bladder and urethras.
Onset of action	Immediately
Peak effect	Immediately
Duration	N/A
Adverse reactions	Hematuria, allergic reactions as above

Technetium

Agent	TECHNETIUM
Strength	5mCi–25mCi
Dosage	.2ml–1.9ml. Children may receive lower amount of dosage compared to adults.
Administration	Agent is injected into vein by needle or IV. Agent is used to visualize the gallbladder, liver, kidneys, bones, testicles, brain, and blood pool exams.
Onset of action	Immediately
Peak effect	N/A
Duration	T½–6 hours.
Adverse reactions	Allergic reaction to binding agent

I123

Agent	I123
Strength	200uCi
Dosage	2 capsules; children to receive smaller doses.

continues

4–20 continued

Administration	Patient swallows capsules. Agent is used to visualize the thyroid.
Onset of action	Immediately
Peak effect	6 hours
Duration	6 hours and 24 hours
Adverse reactions	Reaction to iodine

CCK

Agent	CCK
Strength	.1mcg/CC
Dosage	.01mcg/KG
Administration	IV
Onset of action	Immediately
Peak effect	12 minutes
Duration	60 minutes
Adverse reactions	Pain, nausea, vomiting

Telepaque

Agent	TELEPAQUE
Strength	500mg (iopanoic acid)
Dosage	3G (6–500mg tablets)
Administration	Orally ingested with water in the evening after a fat-free dinner, about 14 hours before exam.
Onset of action	
Peak effect	14–19 hours after ingestion
Duration	
Adverse reactions	Nausea, rash, diarrhea, dysuria, and/or goiter

The above agents have been reviewed and approved for the use and administration in the department of radiology.

_____   _____
Radiology Medical Director   Date

REVISED: _____

Courtesy of Rick Sellers, Department of Radiology, Tanner Medical Center, Carrollton, Georgia.

4–21
Patient Priority Procedures

Division: Clinical Services

Original issue date: _____

Latest revision date: _____

Authorization signature: _____   Date: _____
Director, Medical Imaging Services

Departments/Divisions Affected

Medical Imaging Services

Nursing Services

Medical Staff

APPROVAL DISTRIBUTION LIST

Approved by	Title	Date
	Medical Director, Medical Imaging Services	
	Assistant Vice President, Clinical Services	
	Senior Vice President, Patient Care Services	
	Vice President, Medical Affairs	

PURPOSE

To identify the priority of patients when the technologist has the responsibility of choosing which study to do first

POLICY

The priority of patient exams is as follows:

- Operating room patients under anesthesia
- Stat requests in order of priority
  1. code blue
  2. neonatal intensive care unit (NICU)
  3. intensive care unit (ICU), critical care unit (CCU), ED, postanesthesia care unit (PACU)
  4. other—anywhere else in the hospital

continues

4–21 continued

- In and outs—stats/ASAP from emergency department or floor because of patient's condition and/or isolation purposes (e.g., patients with tuberculosis who enter the department must be treated as in-and-out patients)
- patients for postreductions
- patients for repeats
- emergency department patients non-stat requests
- examinations ordered to be returned by specific time or early AM for surgery
- examinations ordered to be returned by specific time anywhere in hospital
- physicians waiting in the department for urgent requests
- fasting patients
  - –very young or very old
  - –inpatients
  - –outpatients
- routines—determined by time of order

Source: Adapted from Nancy Hughes, Holy Cross Hospital, Silver Spring, Maryland.

4–22
Patient Handling: Care of Back

PURPOSE

To ensure that employees follow proper procedures when handling/moving patients, particularly as they relate to back care

POLICY

- Extreme caution should be used when lifting and transferring patients.

- Lift with legs. Do not bend over at the waist.

- Move feet so as not to twist.

- Place feet to allow for weight shift during transfer.

- Maintain broad base of support to allow stability by placing one foot slightly ahead of the other.

- Do not lock knees and stand rigid. Relax knees and maintain pelvic tilt.

- When moving patient, position yourself so that you can shift weight or walk in the direction that you are moving.

- Move as close as possible to the patient so as to combine center of gravity, as much as possible. Try to maintain closeness so that the patient's center of gravity does not pull you over.

- When using more than one person in a transfer, be sure to count to ensure that all people work together and combine strength.

- Place larger/stronger people in key places where maximum effort is needed; taller people where height is needed.

- Take time to analyze the situation carefully to determine the best course of action.

- A slow-steady-sustained-smooth motion is better than a quick jerk.

- Be sure to bend knees and maintain pelvic tilt when lowering, as well as lifting patient.

- When transferring patient from cart to table

  – the patient transfer board should be used for all patient transfers from cart to table, table to cart

  – attempt to have transfer surfaces at equal heights

  – lock equipment

  – whenever possible, position equipment so that the patient is moving toward his/her good side

  – in cart to bed transfers, first bring patient to the edge so as to minimize transfer distance

  – those transferring the patient should stand at patient's shoulder and hip level

  – use as many people as the situation dictates, probably five, never less than three

- At all times, think safety.

- Report all unsafe conditions to management.

Courtesy of Inova Alexandria Hospital, Alexandria, Virginia.

4–23
Timely Completion of X-ray Interpretations

Original/Revision by: _____   **Effective Date:** _____

Reference: _____   **Revised Date:** _____

Departments Primarily Affected: Radiology, Medical Records, ER

Cross-Reference: _____

STATEMENT OF PURPOSE

To provide a reasonable time for the radiology interpretations to be entered onto the patient's chart or to provide radiology interpretation to the referring physician

PROCEDURE

1. Once the radiology request is received, the paperwork is prepared and then the process to X-ray the patient begins.

   Times after the radiology request is received:
   - OR—within 10 minutes
   - Stats—within 10 minutes
   - ED—within 30 minutes
   - Outpatients—within 30 minutes of appointment time
   - Inpatients—within two (2) hours

2. If applicable, the patient is transported to radiology or the portable is taken to the patient's room.

3. The radiograph is taken and when all films are completed, they are taken to the radiologist's office for reading.

4. If the radiologist is not present, the radiographs will be placed in the radiologist's reading cart, except for ED films. They will be taken to ED for the attending physician to view. After the ED physician has viewed the films, they are placed in the radiologist's reading cart.

5. The radiologist will interpret the radiographs, and the medical transcriptionist will transcribe the dictation.

6. Once the radiology reports have been signed, they are distributed to the appropriate departments within four (4) hours.

7. Physicians can review the results on the computer after they have been transcribed.

Documentation _____

Approved by: _____   _____   _____
                                Name   Title   Date

Courtesy of Rick Sellers, Department of Radiology, Tanner Medical Center, Carrollton, Georgia.

4–24

Radiation Safety Policy: Patients Who May Be Pregnant and Need To Have Radiographs, CT Scans, or MRI

POLICY

Radiological technologists shall inquire if the patient is pregnant before any radiographic procedures can be completed. This is asked of all female patients with reproductive capacity. If there is a chance the patient is pregnant, and/or she is unsure of the pregnancy, a lab test, called serum pregnancy test, will be drawn by a laboratory technologist. This test should be ordered by the referring physician and/or the emergency department physician.

If the test is positive, all imaging procedures shall be deferred until completion of the first trimester, unless advised by the referring physician and radiologist that the radiological examination is required due to compelling medical reasons.

This policy/procedure applies to all imaging modalities, with the exception of nuclear medicine and ultrasound. No nuclear medicine studies are completed when findings are positive. Ultrasound can be completed.

If radiographs and scans are to be completed, please do as follows:

- Shield the patient's abdomen when the examination is of a different anatomical area.

- Take as few films as possible.

- The radiologists will inform technologists of specific views to be filmed.

- When the examination is of the fetus (for positioning), film AP projection only.

- If the abdomen film is technically poor due to technique, do not repeat without showing film to the radiologist.

Please indicate on the requisition that the patient was asked if she is pregnant. Also indicate the LMP, lab test results, and date when completed.

Courtesy of Douglas County Hospital, Alexandria, Minnesota.

4–25
Consent for IV Persantine Test

I, _____ , authorize Dr. _____ and such assistants as he or she may designate, to administer and conduct the IV Persantine test.

This test is designed to (1) determine the presence or absence of clinically significant heart diseases, and/or (2) evaluate the effectiveness of my current therapy.

I understand that I will be injected with IV Persantine. During the performance of the test, my electrocardiogram will be monitored and my blood pressure will be measured and recorded at periodic intervals.

I understand that, during the test, it is possible that I may notice certain symptoms. These include nausea, pain in the chest, shortness of breath, dizziness, and changes in heart rate and/or blood pressure.

I understand that there are risks involved with this test. These include rapid heart rhythms, abnormal blood pressure, and very rare instances of heart attacks. Every effort will be made to avoid these by careful observation during the test. Emergency equipment is available and ready for unusual situations that may arise.

I have read the foregoing and I understand it, and any questions that may have occurred to me have been answered to my satisfaction.

_____
Date

_____
Signed

_____
Witness

_____
Physician supervising the test

Source: Adapted from Nancy Hughes, Holy Cross Hospital, Silver Spring, Maryland.

4–26
Cardiac Stress Testing with Radioisotope

ICD9.CM Code: 92.05

CPT Codes: 784; 930

INDICATOR

1. Number of patients who experienced either of the listed conditions following cardiac stress testing with a radioisotope/Number of patients who had cardiac stress testing with a radioisotope during the relevant study period:

   A. development of a hematoma at the intravenous insertion site

   B. cardiovascular complications associated with the test

CRITICAL PATHWAY REVIEW

Assessment

The record contains a current patient assessment, with documentation of any of the following indications for a stress test with a radionuclide:

2. The presence of one or more of the following conditions, documented in the record prior to the procedure:

   A. angina not responsive to medical management, in association with coronary artery disease risk factors or history

   B. angina of unknown origin, not responsive to medical management

   C. the need to evaluate the status of valvular or congenital cardiac disease

3. History documented, including:

   A. any allergies or drug sensitivities

   B. any medications currently or recently taken

   C. patient's and significant other's level of knowledge concerning the planned procedure and anticipated results

   D. verification that food and liquids (other than small sip of water with prescribed medication) have been withheld since previous midnight

   E. verification that the patient has not taken coffee or smoked on the day of the test

4. Physical examination documented, including:

   A. vital signs

   B. peripheral circulation

   C. skin temperature and color

   D. patency of intravenous route for fluids and medications

continues

4–26 continued

5. Laboratory studies documented:

  A. prothrombin time (PT)

  B. partial prothrombin time (PTT)

  C. recent creatinine level

Documentation and Transmission of Requests and Reports

6. Written request for cardiac stress test with radionuclide received from the attending physician:

  A. provisional diagnosis and reasons for procedure reported in the written request/order

7. Radiologic report filed in medical record within 24 hours following procedure

8. Duplicates of stress test/perfusion report:

  A. filed in radiology department

  B. sent to attending physician on request

Management/Intervention

9. Patient prepared for planned procedure:

  A. patient given reassurance that his or her condition will be monitored throughout the test

  B. patient told that X-rays will be taken before and immediately following the stress test

  C. intravenous line placed

  D. patient instructed to report any chest or arm discomfort, breathing difficulty, dizziness, or fatigue to technician or physician promptly

10. Resting scan obtained with injected 101TI thallium, 3 mCi by weight:

Weight	Dose
< 185	3.0
185–224	3.5
225–250	4.0
>250	4.5

    High-resolution collimator
    30% window 68–80 keV
    20% window 167 keV
    180 degrees, 64 projections
    20 seconds per frame
    Butterworth .5
    Image 10 minutes after injection

11. Exercising scan obtained with injected Tc-99m sestamibi Cardiolite, 25 mCi by weight, during exercise at 85% of the patient's age-predicted maximum (or as tolerated):

Weight	Dose mCi
<185	2.5
185–224	3.0
225–250	3.5
>250	4.0

continues

4–26 continued

High-resolution collimator
64 projections
20 seconds per frame
Gaited ECT
Butterworth .6
P .10
Images obtained 20 minutes after injection

12. Report by physician covering the following, dictated immediately after the test:

   A. pretest diagnosis

   B. procedures performed

   C. description of patient's condition and response to procedure

13. Radiology report prepared

14. Posttest care provided:

   A. pulse and respirations recorded every 15 minutes until stable, then every hour until discharge

   B. patient monitored for evidence of side effects and complications

Management of Complications and Side Effects

15. Cardiovascular complications:

   A. cardiac emergency plan promptly implemented, with administration of oxygen, fluids, and vasopressors

Discharge Status

16. Patient discharged under the following conditions:

   A. patient meeting PADS criteria

   B. patient and family given written instructions regarding:

      i.   any applicable activity limitations

      ii. dosages, schedules, and side effects of any medications

      iii. scheduled follow-up visit to physician

Source: Jean Gayton Carroll, "Cardiac Stress Testing with Radioisotope," *Monitoring Patient Progress: Using Indicators To Evaluate Quality*, Aspen Publishers, Inc., © 2000.

EDUCATION

4–27
Scheduling of Patient Receiving Metformin (Glucophage)

POLICY

Metformin is an oral antihypoglycemic drug. The most serious, but very rare, potential adverse effect reported is lactic acidosis. Renal or hepatic dysfunction can increase the risk of Metformin accumulation and, therefore, increase the incidence of lactic acidosis.

Precautions should be taken for patients on Metformin undergoing radiologic studies involving the use of iodinated contrast materials such as an intravenous urogram, intravenous cholangiography, angiography, and CT scans with contrast materials. Studies with parenteral contrast involving iodinated materials can lead to acute renal failure and have been associated with lactic acidosis in patients receiving Metformin.

PROCEDURE

• Patients scheduled for radiologic studies involving the use of iodinated contrast materials will be advised to refrain from taking Metformin (Glucophage) 48 hours following the procedure.

• The primary physician will consult with the patient for the best alternative therapy while the patient is off Metformin.

• Patients currently receiving Metformin and undergoing an emergency procedure involving the use of iodinated contrast materials will be advised by their primary physician, as well as the technologist, of the risks of performing the procedure.

Courtesy of Inova Alexandria Hospital, Alexandria, Virginia.

4–28
Generic Consent—Radiological Procedure with Contrast Injection

U.R. No	(Please place patient label here)		
Surname			
Given Names			
D.O.B.		Sex M F	
GP			

A. INTERPRETER/ CULTURAL NEEDS

An Interpreter Service is required   yes☐ no☐
If yes, is a qualified Interpreter present? yes☐ no☐
A Cultural Support Person is required   yes☐ no☐
If yes, is a Cultural Support Person present?
                                          yes☐ no☐

B. CONDITION AND PROCEDURE

The doctor has explained that I have the following condition: *(Doctor to document in patient's own words)*

This condition requires the following procedure: *(Doctor to document)*

C. ANESTHETIC

See "About your anesthetic" information sheet for information about the anesthetic and the risks involved. If you have any concerns, talk these over with your anesthetist. If you have not been given an information sheet, please ask for one.

D. SUITABILITY FOR A CONTRAST INJECTION

By answering the following questions, you will assist us to decide if you are suitable to have a contrast injection.

- Have you ever had asthma?   Yes☐ No☐
- Are you allergic to any drug or food (especially iodine or seafood)?   Yes☐ No☐
- Have you ever had an injection of contrast medium before?   Yes☐ No☐
- Have you ever had a reaction to contrast media before?   Yes☐ No☐
- Are you pregnant or breastfeeding?
                                         Yes☐ No☐
- Are you being treated for heart or kidney disease?   Yes☐ No☐
- Are you taking any medications for diabetes mellitus?   Yes☐ No☐
- Do you have a disease such as multiple myeloma, liver failure, sickle cell, hepatitis, HIV/AIDS?   Yes☐ No☐

E. RISKS OF THIS PROCEDURE

There are some risks/**complications**, which may happen specifically with this type of procedure.

♦ They include : *(Doctor to document)*

(a)

(b)

(c)

(d)

(e)

(f)

(g)

There are some **risks/ complications, with injection of radiographic intravenous contrast media.** They include:

(a) Mild nausea, which should pass within a few minutes.

(b) Occasionally, mild reactions such as flushes, sneezing, hives, vomiting, dizziness, and vein or tissue injury.

(c) Rarely, more severe reactions such as asthma, shock, and convulsions. In very rare cases this may result in death.

(d) Death in extremely rare cases - about 1 in 250,000 to 400,000 injections.

Occasionally, due to unforeseen factors such as blood clotting, test results, or pulses being unsatisfactory, the procedure may need to be deferred or cancelled.

F. SIGNIFICANT RISKS AND RELEVANT TREATMENT OPTIONS

The doctor has explained any significant risks and problems specific to me, and the likely outcomes if complications occur.

The doctor has also explained relevant diagnostic options as well as the risks of not having the procedure.

(Doctor to document in Medical Record if necessary. Cross out if not applicable.)

PROCEDURAL CONSENT FORM

continues

4–28 continued

U.R. No		(Please place patient label here)
Surname		
Given Names		
D.O.B.		Sex M F
GP		

G. PATIENT CONSENT

I acknowledge that:

The doctor has explained my medical condition and the proposed procedure. I understand the risks of the procedure, including the risks that are specific to me, and the likely outcomes.

The doctor has explained other relevant diagnostic options and their associated risks. The doctor has explained my prognosis and the risks of <u>not</u> having the procedure.

I have been given a Patient Information Sheet on Anesthesia. The doctor has explained the risks of anesthesia and the factors that increase the risks of anesthesia.

I was able to ask questions and raise concerns with the doctor about my condition, the procedure and its risks, and my treatment options. My questions and concerns have been discussed and answered to my satisfaction.

I understand that the procedure may include a blood transfusion.

I understand that a doctor other than the Consultant may conduct the procedure. I understand this could be a doctor undergoing further training.

The doctor has explained to me that if immediate life-threatening events happen during the procedure, they will be treated accordingly.

I understand that no guarantee has been made that the procedure will diagnose the condition, and that the procedure may make my condition worse.

On the basis of the above statements, **I REQUEST TO HAVE THE PROCEDURE.**

Name of Patient/ Substitute decision maker and relationship ....

Signature

....

Date ....

Substitute Decision Maker   Under the Powers of Attorney Act 1998 and/ or the Guardianship and Administration Act 2000. If the patient is an adult and unable to give consent, an authorized decision maker must give consent on the patient's behalf.

H. INTERPRETER'S STATEMENT

I have given a translation in ....
(*state the patient's language here*) of the consent form and any verbal and written information given to the patient/parent or guardian/substitute decision maker by the doctor.

Name of Interpreter ....

Signature ....

Date ....

I. ADVANCE HEALTH DIRECTIVE

The patient has an Advance Health Directive/ Enduring Power of Attorney and will provide the doctor with a copy on admission.   yes ☐ no ☐

J. DOCTOR'S STATEMENT

I have explained

- the patient's condition

- need for treatment

- the procedure and the risks

- relevant diagnostic options and their risks

- likely consequences if those risks occur

- the significant risks and problems specific to this patient.

I have given the patient/ substitute decision maker an opportunity to

- ask questions about any of the above matters

- raise any other concerns

which I have answered as fully as possible.

I am of the opinion that the patient/substitute decision maker understood the above information.

Name of Doctor ....

Signature ....

Date ....

continues

4–28 continued

CONSENT INFORMATION - PATIENT COPY

GENERIC CONSENT -
Radiological Procedure with Contrast Injection

ANESTHETIC

See "About your anesthetic" information sheet for information about the anesthetic and the risks involved. If you have any concerns, talk these over with your anesthetist.

If you have not been given an information sheet, please ask for one.

D. SUITABILITY FOR A CONTRAST INJECTION

I have answered the following questions, to assist you in deciding if I am suitable to have a contrast injection.

- Have you ever had asthma? Yes☐ No☐
- Are you allergic to any drug or food (especially iodine or seafood)?Yes☐ No☐
- Have you ever had an injection of contrast medium before? Yes☐ No☐
- Have you ever had a reaction to contrast media before? Yes☐ No☐
- Are you pregnant or breastfeeding? Yes☐ No☐
- Are you being treated for heart or kidney disease? Yes☐ No☐
- Are you taking any medications for diabetes mellitus? Yes☐ No☐
- Do you have a disease such as multiple myeloma, liver failure, sickle cell, hepatitis, HIV/AIDS? Yes☐ No☐

SPECIFIC RISKS OF THIS PROCEDURE

There are some risks/complications, which may happen specifically with this procedure. The doctor has listed these on the consent form.

There are also some **risks/complications, with injection of radiographic intravenous contrast media.** They include:

(e) Mild nausea, which should pass within a few minutes.

(f) Occasionally, mild reactions such as flushes, sneezing, hives, vomiting, dizziness, and vein or tissue injury.

(g) Rarely, more severe reactions such as asthma, shock, and convulsions. In very rare cases this may result in death.

(h) Death in extremely rare cases - about 1 in 250,000 to 400,000 injections.

Occasionally, due to unforeseen factors such as blood clotting, test results, or pulses being unsatisfactory, the procedure may need to be deferred or cancelled.

I ACKNOWLEDGE THAT:

The doctor has explained my medical condition and the proposed procedure. I understand the risks of the procedure, including the risks that are specific to me, and the likely outcomes.

The doctor has explained other relevant diagnostic options and their associated risks. The doctor has explained my prognosis and the risks of <u>not</u> having the procedure.

I have been given a Patient Information Sheet on Anesthesia. The doctor has explained the risks of anesthesia and the factors that increase the risks of anesthesia.

I was able to ask questions and raise concerns with the doctor about my condition, the procedure and its risks, and my treatment options.

My questions and concerns have been discussed and answered to my satisfaction.

I understand that the procedure may include a blood transfusion.

I understand that a doctor other than the Consultant may conduct the procedure. I understand this could be a doctor undergoing further training.

The doctor has explained to me that if immediate life-threatening events happen during the procedure, they will be treated accordingly.

I understand that no guarantee has been made that the procedure will diagnose the condition, and that the procedure may make my condition worse.

On the basis of the above statements, **I REQUEST TO HAVE THE PROCEDURE.**

4–29
Consent for Insertion of Peripheral Central Catheter (PICC Line)

U.R. No	(Please place patient label here)	
Surname		
Given Names		
D.O.B.	Sex M F	
GP		

A. INTERPRETER/ CULTURAL NEEDS

An Interpreter Service is required   yes☐ no☐
If yes, is a qualified Interpreter present? yes☐ no☐
A Cultural Support Person is required   yes☐ no☐
If yes, is a Cultural Support Person present?
                                          yes☐ no☐

B. CONDITION AND PROCEDURE

The doctor has explained that I have the following condition: *(Doctor to document in patient's own words)*

The following procedure will be performed:

A PICC line is a narrow tube (catheter) about the size of a heart monitor lead. This goes into the arm. A small amount of local anesthetic is injected into the arm. The tip of the catheter is passed along the vein through the arm into the major blood vessel next to the heart. The catheter does not go into the heart. Drugs can then be given down the catheter rather than by repeated injections.

Ultrasound may be used to find a suitable vein. Radiographic contrast agent may be injected to show the position of the catheter. A few stitches are put through the skin to hold the catheter in place and a dressing is put over that to keep it clean.

C. SUITABILITY FOR A CONTRAST INJECTION

By answering the following questions, you will assist us to decide if you are suitable to have a contrast injection.

- Have you ever had asthma?   Yes☐ No☐
- Are you allergic to any drug or food (especially iodine or seafood)?   Yes☐ No☐
- Have you ever had an injection of contrast medium before?   Yes☐ No☐
- Have you ever had a reaction to contrast media before?   Yes☐ No☐
- Are you pregnant or breastfeeding?   Yes☐ No☐
- Are you being treated for heart or kidney disease?   Yes☐ No☐
- Are you taking any medications for diabetes mellitus?   Yes☐ No☐
- Do you have a disease such as multiple myeloma, liver failure, sickle cell, hepatitis, HIV/AIDS?   Yes☐ No☐

D. ANESTHETIC

See "About your anesthetic" information sheet for information about the anesthetic and the risks involved. If you have any concerns, talk these over with your anesthetist.

If you have not been given an information sheet, please ask for one.

E. RISKS OF THIS PROCEDURE

There are some risks/complications, which include:

(a) Infection in the wound with resultant redness, pain, and possible discharge or abscess formation.
(b) Puncture of the artery, which may not seal across, and the blood leaks from the puncture site. It may form a lump and a large bruise, which may rarely need surgical treatment.
(c) Clotting may occur in the deep veins of the arm, and rarely the clot may break off and go to the lungs. This could be fatal.
(d) Failure to access the vein in one arm. If this happens, the other arm may be used.
(e) Infrequently, the procedure may not be successful.
(f) Low risk of infection. This will be treated according to your condition. The doctor must be informed if you have any signs of redness, pain in the arm, or swelling at the site of the insertion.

There are some **risks/complications, with injection of radiographic intravenous contrast media.** They include:

(a) Mild nausea, which should pass within a few minutes.
(b) Occasionally, mild reactions such as flushes, sneezing, hives, vomiting, dizziness, and vein or tissue injury.
(c) Rarely, more severe reactions such as asthma, shock, and convulsions. In very rare cases this may result in death.
(d) Death in extremely rare cases - about 1 in 250,000 to 400,000 injections.

F. SIGNIFICANT RISKS AND RELEVANT TREATMENT OPTIONS

The doctor has explained any significant risks and problems specific to me, and the likely outcomes if complications occur. The doctor has also explained relevant treatment options as well as the risks of not having the procedure.

PROCEDURAL CONSENT FORM

continues

4–29 continued

(Doctor to document in Medical Record if necessary. Cross out i not applicable.)

U.R. No	(Please place patient label here)
Surname	
Given Names	
D.O.B.	Sex M F
GP	

G. PATIENT CONSENT

I acknowledge that:

The doctor has explained my medical condition and the proposed procedure. I understand the risks of the procedure, including the risks that are specific to me, and the likely outcomes.

The doctor has explained other relevant treatment options and their associated risks. The doctor has explained my prognosis and the risks of not having the procedure.

I have been given a Patient Information Sheet on Anesthesia. The doctor has explained the risks of anesthesia and the factors that increase the risks of anesthesia.

I have been given a Patient Information Sheet (Version 2: 09/02) about the procedure and its risks.

I was able to ask questions and raise concerns with the doctor about my condition, the procedure and its risks, and my treatment options. My questions and concerns have been discussed and answered to my satisfaction.

I understand that the procedure may include a blood transfusion.

I understand that a doctor other than the Consultant may conduct the procedure. I understand this could be a doctor undergoing further training.

The doctor has explained to me that if immediate life-threatening events happen during the procedure, they will be treated accordingly.

I understand that no guarantee has been made that the procedure will improve the condition, and that the procedure may make my condition worse.

On the basis of the above statements, **I REQUEST TO HAVE THE PROCEDURE.**

Name of Patient/ Substitute decision maker and relationship

Signature

Date

Substitute Decision Maker   Under the Powers of Attorney Act 1998 and/ or the Guardianship and Administration Act 2000. If the patient is an adult and unable to give consent, an authorized decision maker must give consent on the patient's behalf.

H. INTERPRETER'S STATEMENT

I have given a translation in ……………..……………. (*state the patient's language here*) of the consent form and any verbal and written information given to the patient/ parent or guardian/substitute decision maker by the doctor.

Name of Interpreter ------------------------------

Signature ------------------------------

Date ------------------------------

I. ADVANCE HEALTH DIRECTIVE

The patient has an Advance Health Directive/ Enduring Power of Attorney and will provide the doctor with a copy on admission.   yes ☐ no ☐

J. DOCTOR'S STATEMENT

I have explained

- the patient's condition
- need for treatment
- the procedure and the risks
- relevant treatment options and their risks
- likely consequences if those risks occur
- the significant risks and problems specific to this patient.

I have given the patient/substitute decision maker an opportunity to

- ask questions about any of the above matters
- raise any other concerns

which I have answered as fully as possible.

I am of the opinion that the patient/substitute decision maker understood the above information.

Name of Doctor ------------------------------

Signature

Date ------------------------------

continues

4–29 continued

CONSENT INFORMATION - PATIENT COPY

INSERTION OF PERIPHERAL CENTRAL CATHETER (PICC LINE)

PROCEDURE

A PICC line is a narrow tube (catheter) about the size of a heart monitor lead. This goes into the arm. A small amount of local anesthetic is injected into the arm.

The tip of the catheter is passed along the vein through the arm into the major blood vessel next to the heart. The catheter does not go into the heart. Drugs can then be given down the catheter rather than by repeated injections.

Ultrasound may be used to find a suitable vein. Radiographic contrast agent may be injected to show the position of the catheter.

A few stitches are put through the skin to hold the catheter in place and a dressing is put over that to keep it clean.

ANESTHETIC

See "About your anesthetic" information sheet for information about the anesthetic and the risks involved. If you have any concerns, talk these over with your anesthetist.

If you have not been given an information sheet, please ask for one.

RISKS OF THIS PROCEDURE

There are some risks/complications, which include:

(g) Infection in the wound with resultant redness, pain, and possible discharge or abscess formation.

(h) Puncture of the artery, which may not seal across, and the blood leaks from the puncture site. It may form a lump and a large bruise, which may rarely need surgical treatment.

(i) Clotting may occur in the deep veins of the arm, and rarely the clot may break off and go to the lungs. This could be fatal.

(j) Failure to access the vein in one arm. If this happens, the other arm may be used.

(k) Infrequently, the procedure may not be successful.

(l) Low risk of infection. This will be treated according to your condition. The doctor must be informed if you have any signs of redness, pain in the arm, or swelling at the site of the insertion.

There are some **risks/complications, with injection of radiographic intravenous contrast media.** They include:

(e) Mild nausea, which should pass within a few minutes.

(f) Occasionally, mild reactions such as flushes, sneezing, hives, vomiting, dizziness, and vein or tissue injury.

(g) Rarely, more severe reactions such as asthma, shock, and convulsions. In very rare cases this may result in death.

(h) Death in extremely rare cases - about 1 in 250,000 to 400,000 injections.

I ACKNOWLEDGE THAT:

The doctor has explained my medical condition and the proposed procedure. I understand the risks of the procedure, including the risks that are specific to me, and the likely outcomes.

The doctor has explained other relevant treatment options and their associated risks. The doctor has explained my prognosis and the risks of not having the procedure.

I have been given a Patient Information Sheet on Anesthesia. The doctor has explained the risks of anesthesia and the factors that increase the risks of anesthesia.

I have received a Patient Information Sheet (Version 2: 09/02) about the procedure and its risks.

I was able to ask questions and raise concerns with the doctor about my condition, the procedure and its risks, and my treatment options.

My questions and concerns have been discussed and answered to my satisfaction.

I understand that the procedure may include a blood transfusion.

I understand that a doctor other than the Consultant may conduct the procedure. I understand this could be a doctor undergoing further training.

The doctor has explained to me that if immediate life-threatening events happen during the procedure, they will be treated as appropriate.

I understand that no guarantee has been made that the procedure will improve the condition, and that the procedure may make my condition worse.

On the basis of the above statements, **I REQUEST TO HAVE THE PROCEDURE.**

4–30
Consent for Femoral Angiogram

U.R. No	(Please place patient label here)		
Surname			
Given Names			
D.O.B.		Sex M F	
GP			

A. INTERPRETER/ CULTURAL NEEDS

An Interpreter Service is required   yes☐ no☐
If yes, is a qualified Interpreter present? yes☐ no☐
A Cultural Support Person is required   yes☐ no☐
If yes, is a Cultural Support Person present.
                                                   yes☐ no☐

B. CONDITION AND PROCEDURE

The doctor has explained that I have the following
condition: *(Doctor to document in patient's own
words)*

The following procedure will be performed:

An X-ray of the blood vessels of the leg. A needle is
inserted into the artery. This is usually in the groin
and contrast media is injected and multiple X-rays
are taken. Local anesthetic will be used. This is
injected into the area where the needle is inserted
to numb the area.

C. ANESTHETIC

See "About your anesthetic" information sheet for
information about the anesthetic and the risks
involved. If you have any concerns, talk these over
with your anesthetist. If you have not been given
an information sheet, please ask for one.

D. SUITABILITY FOR A CONTRAST INJECTION

**By answering the following questions, you will
assist us to decide if you are suitable to have a
femoral angiogram.**

- Have you ever had asthma?   Yes☐ No☐
- Are you allergic to any drug or food (especially
  iodine or seafood)?   Yes☐ No☐
- Have you ever had an injection of contrast
  medium before?   Yes☐ No☐
- Have you ever had a reaction to contrast media
  before?   Yes☐ No☐
- Are you pregnant or breastfeeding?
          Yes☐ No☐
- Are you being treated for heart or kidney
  disease?   Yes☐ No☐
- Are you taking any medications for diabetes
  mellitus?   Yes☐ No☐
- Do you have a disease such as multiple
  myeloma, liver failure, sickle cell, hepatitis,
  HIV/AIDS?   Yes☐ No☐

E. RISKS OF THIS PROCEDURE

There are some risks/complications, which include:

(a) Infection in the wound with resultant redness,
    pain, and possible discharge or abscess
    formation.

(b) The puncture in the artery may not seal across,
    and the blood leaks from the puncture site. It
    may form a lump and a large bruise, which may
    need surgical treatment.

(c) The circulation to the leg may be interfered with
    due to complications of the needle insertion,
    and urgent treatment including surgery may be
    necessary.

(d) Clotting may occur in the deep veins of the leg
    or pelvis, and rarely the clot may break off and
    go to the lungs. This could be fatal.

(e) Infrequently, the procedure may not be
    successful.

(f) Death is possible during or after the angiogram
    due to severe complications.

There are some **risks/complications, with
injection of radiographic intravenous contrast
media.** They include:

(a) Mild nausea, which should pass within a few
    minutes.

(b) Occasionally, mild reactions such as flushes,
    sneezing, hives, vomiting, dizziness, and vein or
    tissue injury.

(c) Rarely, more severe reactions such as asthma,
    shock, and convulsions. In very rare cases this
    may result in death.

(d) Death in extremely rare cases - about 1 in
    250,000 to 400,000 injections.

Occasionally, due to unforeseen factors such as
blood clotting, test results, or pulses being
unsatisfactory, the procedure may need to be
deferred or cancelled.

F. SIGNIFICANT RISKS AND RELEVANT TREATMENT OPTIONS

The doctor has explained any significant risks
and problems specific to me, and the likely
outcomes if complications occur.

The doctor has also explained relevant
diagnostic options as well as the risks of <u>not</u>
having the procedure.

*(Doctor to document in Medical Record if
necessary. Cross out if not applicable.)*

PROCEDURAL CONSENT FORM

continues

4–30 continued

	U.R. No	(Please place patient label here)	
	Surname		
	Given Names		
	D.O.B.	Sex M F	
	GP		

G. PATIENT CONSENT

I acknowledge that:

The doctor has explained my medical condition and the proposed procedure. I understand the risks of the procedure, including the risks that are specific to me, and the likely outcomes.

The doctor has explained other relevant diagnostic options and their associated risks. The doctor has explained my prognosis and the risks of <u>not</u> having the procedure.

I have been given a Patient Information Sheet on Anesthesia. The doctor has explained the risks of anesthesia and the factors that increase the risks of anesthesia.

I have been given a Patient Information Sheet (Version 2: 09/02) about the procedure and its risks.

I was able to ask questions and raise concerns with the doctor about my condition, the procedure and its risks, and my treatment options. My questions and concerns have been discussed and answered to my satisfaction.

I understand that the procedure may include a blood transfusion.

I understand that a doctor other than the Consultant may conduct the procedure. I understand this could be a doctor undergoing further training.

The doctor has explained to me that if immediate life-threatening events happen during the procedure, they will be treated accordingly.

I understand that no guarantee has been made that the procedure will diagnose my condition, and that the procedure may make my condition worse.

On the basis of the above statements, **I REQUEST TO HAVE THE PROCEDURE.**

Name of Patient/ Substitute decision maker and relationship   ....

Signature

....

Date   ....

Substitute Decision Maker   Under the Powers of Attorney Act 1998 and/ or the Guardianship and Administration Act 2000. If the patient is an adult and unable to give consent, an authorized decision maker must give consent on the patient's behalf.

H. INTERPRETER'S STATEMENT

I have given a translation in .... (*state the patient's language here*) of the consent form and any verbal and written information given to the patient/ parent or guardian/substitute decision maker by the doctor.

Name of Interpreter   ....

Signature   ....

Date   ....

I. ADVANCE HEALTH DIRECTIVE

The patient has an Advance Health Directive/ Enduring Power of Attorney and will provide the doctor with a copy on admission.   yes ☐ no ☐

J. DOCTOR'S STATEMENT

I have explained

- the patient's condition

- need for treatment

- the procedure and the risks

- relevant diagnostic options and their risks

- likely consequences if those risks occur

- the significant risks and problems specific to this patient.

I have given the patient/substitute decision maker an opportunity to

- ask questions about any of the above matters

- raise any other concerns

which I have answered as fully as possible.

I am of the opinion that the patient/substitute decision maker understood the above information.

Name of Doctor   ....

Signature   ....

Date   ....

continues

4–30 continued

CONSENT INFORMATION - <u>PATIENT COPY</u>

FEMORAL ANGIOGRAM

PROCEDURE

An X-ray of the blood vessels of the leg. A needle is inserted into the artery. This is usually in the groin and contrast media is injected and multiple X-rays are taken. Local anesthetic will be used. This is injected into the area where the needle is inserted to numb the area.

ANESTHETIC

See "About your anesthetic" information sheet for information about the anesthetic and the risks involved. If you have any concerns, talk these over with your anesthetist.

If you have not been given an information sheet, please ask for one.

RISKS OF THIS PROCEDURE

There are some risks/complications, which include:
(a) Infection in the wound with resultant redness, pain, and possible discharge or abscess formation.

(b) The puncture in the artery may not seal across, and the blood leaks from the puncture site. It may form a lump and a large bruise, which may need surgical treatment.

(c) The circulation to the leg may be interfered with due to complications of the needle insertion, and urgent treatment including surgery may be necessary.

(d) Clotting may occur in the deep veins of the leg or pelvis, and rarely the clot may break off and go to the lungs. This could be fatal.

(e) Infrequently, the procedure may not be successful.

(f) Death is possible during or after the angiogram due to severe complications.

There are some **risks/complications, with injection of radiographic intravenous contrast media.** They include:
(e) Mild nausea, which should pass within a few minutes.

(f) Occasionally, mild reactions such as flushes, sneezing, hives, vomiting, dizziness, and vein or tissue injury.

(g) Rarely, more severe reactions such as asthma, shock, and convulsions. In very rare cases this may result in death.

(h) Death in extremely rare cases - about 1 in 250,000 to 400,000 injections.

I ACKNOWLEDGE THAT:

The doctor has explained my medical condition and the proposed procedure. I understand the risks of the procedure, including the risks that are specific to me, and the likely outcomes.

The doctor has explained other relevant diagnostic options and their associated risks. The doctor has explained my prognosis and the risks of <u>not</u> having the procedure.

I have been given a Patient Information Sheet on Anesthesia. The doctor has explained the risks of anesthesia and the factors that increase the risks of anesthesia.

I have received a Patient Information Sheet (Version 2: 09/02) about the procedure and its risks.

I was able to ask questions and raise concerns with the doctor about my condition, the procedure and its risks, and my treatment options.

My questions and concerns have been discussed and answered to my satisfaction.

I understand that the procedure may include a blood transfusion.

I understand that a doctor other than the Consultant may conduct the procedure. I understand this could be a doctor undergoing further training.

The doctor has explained to me that if immediate life-threatening events happen during the procedure, they will be treated as appropriate.

I understand that no guarantee has been made that the procedure will diagnose my condition, and that the procedure may make my condition worse.

On the basis of the above statements, **I REQUEST TO HAVE THE PROCEDURE.**

4–31
Policy for Pregnant or Potentially Pregnant Patients

PURPOSE

Guidelines for providing diagnostic exams to pregnant and potentially pregnant patients.

BACKGROUND INFORMATION

In accordance with the guidelines found in the University of Utah's Radiation Safety Manual and Procedures relative to Radiation Safety in Diagnostic Radiology (RPR 23), users of ionizing radiation for diagnostic purposes are responsible for the protection of employees and patients. While the NCRP places a limit of 500-mrem/gestational period to the developing fetus, it is generally recognized that since the embryo or fetus is more sensitive to ionizing radiation than the adult, precautions should be taken to ensure that pregnant female patients are not accidentally exposed.

GUIDELINES

Therefore, the following general guidelines shall be observed:

All female patients of childbearing age shall be asked the question during the registration process whether they are pregnant. In the event the patient indicates she is pregnant, the technologist performing the exam will be notified. The technologist will in turn confer with the attending Radiologist before proceeding. All patient reception and waiting areas shall have signs posted informing female patients to notify the receptionist if they are pregnant. In the event a patient indicates she is pregnant, the same procedure will be followed as indicated above. Precautions shall be taken to shield the abdomen/pelvis area of all female patients of child-bearing age (12–50 years) for all general X-ray exams of the extremities, chest, and skull, and head CT scans. Listed below is the procedure that will be followed for all female patients of child-bearing age who are to receive a body CT, Nuclear Medicine, or X-ray exam of the abdomen/pelvis region:

1. When a request of a Radiological exam is initiated from the nursing floors, clinics, or a referring physician, a form will be filled out and witnessed *(see attachment)* indicating that to the best knowledge of the patient she believes that she is not pregnant. In the event the patient indicates that she is pregnant, the technologist performing the exam will confer with the Radiologist assigned to the case before proceeding. The Radiologist's recommendations will be included at the bottom of the form.

2. If the patient believes that she is not pregnant, but the time period since her last menstrual period is more than 30 days, the Radiologist assigned to the case may elect to order a pregnancy test be performed (depending on the type of exam and circumstances surrounding the case) prior to the diagnostic procedure.

3. In the event that the patient is a minor (i.e., over 12 and under 18 years of age), a parent or guardian is not required to sign the above-mentioned form. (Note: Utah's informed consent statute indicates that any female regardless of age or marital status is empowered to consent to any health care not prohibited by law, when given in connection with her pregnancy or childbirth.)

4. The Patient Pregnancy Questionnaire will be filed with the patient's Diagnostic films.

5. This policy would not apply to trauma patients sent to the Radiology Department from the Emergency Department, patients from the Critical Care Units, or Operating Rooms.

continues

4–31 continued

The following should be observed for all female patients of childbearing age who are to receive a 2-view (PA,LAT) chest X-ray exam:

1. The technologist will ask the patient whether she is pregnant or if there is any chance she might be pregnant. If the answer is affirmative, the technologist will take a PA view only.

2. The technologist will then consult with the assigned radiologist. A LAT view will then be taken, if necessary, following review of the PA film by the radiologist.*

PROCEDURE FOR PREGNANT OR POTENTIALLY PREGNANT PATIENTS

1. Precautions shall be taken to shield the abdomen/pelvis area of all female patients of childbearing age (12–50 years) for all general x-ray exams of the extremities, chest, and skull, and head CT scans.

2. The Technologist should question female patients of childbearing age scheduled for a 2-view (AP and LAT) chest whether she is or may be pregnant. If the answer is affirmative, a PA view will only be taken. The Technologist will then consult with the assigned Radiologist whether a LAT view is needed.

3. Whenever a body CT, MRI, Nuclear Medicine, or an X-ray of the abdomen/pelvis region is ordered, a flag will flash on the order screen indicating that if the patient is female and between the ages of 12–50 years, that a Pregnancy Questionnaire must be filled out by the patient. A Pregnancy Questionnaire will then be attached to the patient's registration forms, and routed through the system. Note: Trauma patients from the ED, patients from the OR, or any of the Critical Care Units do not need to fill out the questionnaire.

4. Questionnaires for outpatients meeting the criteria should be signed and witnessed in Reception. Inpatient or non-trauma ED patient signature will be obtained and the questionnaire witnessed by either the Department Public Relations Representative in the department or the technologist assigned to the patient, depending on the surrounding circumstances.

5. The questionnaire will be checked and the question will again be asked "are you pregnant?" by the technologist prior to proceeding with the ordered exam. If the patient is pregnant or is uncertain whether she is pregnant (i.e., more than 30 days have elapsed since the onset of her last menstrual period), the technologist will confer with the attending Radiologist. The Radiologist will then determine whether a pregnancy test is needed before proceeding, to cancel the exam, or to proceed. This decision will be noted by the Radiologist at the bottom of the questionnaire.

6. Following the exam, the Pregnancy Questionnaire will be filed with the patient's report in her film jacket.

PREGNANCY QUESTIONNAIRE FORM

Patient Name _____ Medical Record No. _____

Age _____ Patient Date of Birth _____

In accordance with the Radiation Protection guidelines** adopted by the University of Utah Hospital, steps must be taken to ensure that pregnant female patients are not accidentally exposed to ionizing radiation in the pelvic or abdominal areas of the body. Therefore, it is necessary to answer the following questions to aid the Radiology Medical Staff prior to diagnostic exams. We appreciate your cooperation.

*Source: NCRP Report No. 33.
**These guidelines are available to you upon request. We will be pleased to answer your questions or concerns.

continues

4–31 continued

1. Do you believe that you are pregnant? (yes or no)

2. If no, please answer the following:

   a. Please indicate the approximate date of the first day of your last menstrual period.

   b. Are you currently using any form of contraception? (yes or no)
      Please specify _____

3. Are you currently breastfeeding? (yes or no)

Patient Signed_____   Date_____

Witnessed by_____   Date_____

To be filled out by Radiologist:

Radiologist's recommendations in the event the patient is pregnant: _____

_____

_____

_____

Signed_____

Date _____

Source: University of Utah Radiological Health Department, Salt Lake City, Utah.

4–32
Resolution of Concerns Regarding Medical Management Issues in Patient Care

PURPOSE

To provide direction and delineate guidelines for nurses to follow when questioning medical management of a patient's care

POLICY

1. The unit nurse shall first clarify the issue/order with the involved physician. If the issue cannot be resolved with the involved physician, the decision algorithm shall be followed until the issue is resolved.

2. When a variance report is completed, as noted in the algorithm, it is submitted to Quality Management, who will then forward a copy to the involved attending staff MD.

DECISION ALGORITHM

Staff Nurse Notifies

(Working Hours)	(After Hours, weekends, and holidays)	
Unit Manager if not resolved, notifies	**Charge Nurse** if not resolved, notifies	
Nursing Director if not resolved, **Nursing Director** notifies	**House Manager** ⟶ If not resolved, House Manager notifies	**Manager Administrative Support**
Upper Level resident if not resolved, **Nursing Director** completes Variance Report per policy and notifies	**Upper Level resident** if not resolved, **House Manager** completes Variance Report per policy and notifies	↓
Chief Resident of Involved Service if not resolved, **Nursing Director** notifies	**Chief Resident of Involved Service** if not resolved, **House Manager** notifies	**Nursing Director**
Attending Staff M.D. if not resolved, **Nursing Director** notifies	**Attending Staff M.D.** if not resolved, **House Manager** notifies	↓
Clinical Chief of Services if not resolved, **Nursing Director** notifies	**Clinical Chief of Services** if not resolved, **House Manager** notifies	**Administrator on call**
Associate Dean for Clinical Affairs/Medical Director	**Associate Dean for Clinical Affairs/Medical Director**	

continues

4–32 continued

Director, Patient Care Support

_____   _____
Signature   Date

Assistant Hospital Administrator for Patient Care Services

_____   _____
Signature   Date

CONTINUUM OF CARE

4–33
Policy for Transfer of Isolation Patients to X-ray

PURPOSE

To establish guidelines for the proper precautions and steps to be taken when transporting isolation patients

POLICY

1. The mode of transportation will be determined by the patient's condition and isolation procedure.
2. The wheelchair or stretcher is draped with a clean sheet or bath blanket, which is wrapped around the patient.
3. Contact the nurse giving care to isolation patient for special instructions prior to transporting to Radiology.
4. All X-ray personnel having contact with the isolation patient wear attire required by isolation type, and follow all isolation precautions specified on the patient's door.
5. All linen is considered contaminated and processed appropriately.
6. The patient is covered with a clean sheet or blanket and returned to the room.
7. Stretcher linens are stripped and left in the linen hamper in the patient's room.
8. Equipment, including wheelchair, stretcher, and portable X-ray equipment in contact with vancomycin resistant enterococci (VRE) isolations patient, must be cleaned using germicide before reuse.
9. X-ray room is cleaned according to procedures for terminal cleaning following procedures performed on patients in VRE isolation.
10. Toilet facilities used by VRE patients in X-ray department are to be washed down, with close attention being paid to commode seat and faucet handles.
11. All personnel wash hands thoroughly following patient contact and cleaning procedures.
12. The patient's chart accompanies the patient but does not touch patient or linens.

4–34
Patient Follow-Up for Continuum of Care in the Radiology Department

PURPOSE

To identify studies where continuum of care may be necessary and to describe the documentation method

STUDIES REQUIRING CONTINUUM OF CARE

- Venous access port placement
- Biliary drainage procedure
- Urological drainage procedures
- Angioplasty
- IV infiltration
- Allergic reactions

DOCUMENTATION METHODS

- Patient medical record
- Logbook—maintained by RN in radiology
- Infiltrations and allergies—maintained in a file kept in radiology

Source: Adapted from Bloomington Hospital, Bloomington, Indiana.

4–35
Teleradiology

Original/Revision by: _____   **Effective Date:** _____

Reference: _____   **Revised Date:** _____

Department Primarily Affected: Radiology

Cross-Reference: _____

STATEMENT OF PURPOSE

To provide a means for the radiologist to review radiology images away from the facility via laptop or home computer for the attending physician's diagnosis

PROCEDURE

Once the attending physician declares a procedure an emergency, the radiology technologist will perform the procedure, load procedure onto the teleradiography system, and notify the radiologist via phone or pager when scan is completed.

Radiologist will review scan and contact the emergency department via phone or fax with patient's diagnosis.

Final interpretation will be dictated the next working day.

Documentation: Teleradiology Log

May be performed by: Radiology Technologist

Approved by: _____   _____   _____
                          Name   Title   Date

Courtesy of Rick Sellers, Department of Radiology, Tanner Medical Center, Carrollton, Georgia.

4–36
Patient's Refusal of Medical Treatment

POLICY

The competent adult patient or the parent/legal guardian of a minor or incompetent adult has the right to refuse part or all of the recommended care prescribed by the physician.

PROCEDURE

- All episodes of patient refusals will be documented appropriately in the patient's medical record.

- The Patient's Refusal Form (see 4–37) can be completed when the refusal may result in the deterioration of an existing condition.

- The attending physician is responsible for informing the patient/guardian of the risks of refusal and the proposed benefits of the recommended treatment, which may include transfer to another facility. The physician must document his/her discussion with the patient of the benefits and possible risks in the medical record.

- The Patient Refusal Form must be completed when the refusal relates to transfer of the patient (per Section 1867 of the Medicare Act COBRA).

- When completed, the form becomes part of the patient's permanent medical record.

Courtesy of Inova Alexandria Hospital, Alexandria, Virginia.

4–37
Patient Refusal Form
for/against Medical Advice Use—Discharge against Medical Advice

I, _____, refuse to allow anyone to

__perform a medical screening examination

__transfer me to another health care facility

__other_____

_____

_____

I understand that my refusal for such examination/transfer/treatment could seriously imperil my life or cause adverse health consequences. Nevertheless, it is my wish, desire, and direction to refuse regardless of attendant risks and peril to my life or health. I understand that I am doing so against medical advice.

I hereby release and hold harmless _____ Hospital, its nurses and employees, together with all physicians in any way connected with me as a patient from liability for respecting and following my wish and direction.

_____   _____
(Patient/Guardian signature)   *(Date)*

_____
(Print name, relationship)

_____   _____
(Witness)   *(Date)*

IMPROVING ORGANIZATION PERFORMANCE

4–38
Performance Improvement Plan—Imaging Services

PURPOSE/OBJECTIVE

The Imaging Services Department participates in Hospitalwide Performance Improvement (PI) Program designed to monitor, evaluate, and improve the quality and appropriateness of clinical services.

> Identify opportunities through continuous assessment of systems and processes of care through a collaborative, interdisciplinary focus and,

> Implementing solutions and actions which will bring about desired change to

> Facilitate a positive outcome while maintaining a safe environment for personnel, patients, and visitors.

RESPONSIBILITY

The Director of Imaging Services is responsible for establishing and implementing an Imaging Service PI Program. The program shall integrate imaging services performance, improvement, and QC activities into a system that will foster improvement in patient care. The Director shall also delegate responsibilities for monitoring action, evaluation, and reporting.

The Director and Assistant Director will report all imaging service performance improvement activities to the hospitalwide quality council for their review and recommendations.

SCOPE OF CARE

Patient services are provided to the inpatient, outpatient, and emergency department population 24 hours a day. Patients of all ages, race, sex, and financial status are serviced, which may include:

- diagnostic radiographic testing
- ultrasound
- computer tomography
- magnetic resonance imaging
- nuclear medicine studies
- mammography
- bone densitometry

Range of treatment for procedures, invasive/non-invasive and with or without the use of contrast.

DESCRIPTION OF P.I. PROCESS

Projects are initiated by determining aspects of care: high risk, problem prone, high volume, safety and infection control measures. A specific form is filled out to determine important aspects of care. Radiology personnel fill out form and forms are returned to Radiology assistant director. Projects are initiated according to priority, high risk, and problem prone areas. Process for PI: Plan, Do, Check, Act.

continues

4–38 continued

Project leaders are clinical directors who meet quarterly to discuss needs and concerns of each department: mammography, US, CT, NM and radiology. The minutes are available if requested. QA, QC personnel chart on following page shows tasks that individuals perform and methodology for each task. All radiology personnel are involved in documentation on patient care services. Performance improvement is everyone's business.

The approach used to complete a project deals with determining indicator/problems, gathering data, daily logs, reports, meeting minutes, stats, etc. Evaluate conclusion, recommend solutions for the process, system, and education. Action follow: what was done to improve the system/process/problem. A follow-up is completed by looking back at previous years to compare percentages. If no improvement, continue monitoring. If improvement is made, monitor is discontinued and/or reviewed again if deemed necessary, documented in P.I. radiology manual.

Persons responsible for evaluating results are: QA Council, Radiologists, Department Director, Clinical Director, and Assistant Director. Improvement results are shared at monthly department meetings and/or quarterly reports.

Courtesy of Douglas County Hospital, Alexandria, Minnesota.

4–39
Quality Assessment and Improvement Plan—Imaging Department

This plan serves as a supplement to the hospitalwide quality improvement plan and is intended to meet the specific needs of the in-house imaging department and the outpatient imaging facilities.

The plan provides a process by which the quality of care and patient outcomes are monitored and assessed and opportunities for improvement are identified.

THE IMPORTANT FUNCTIONS FOR ASSESSING QUALITY

- Infection control
- Management of information
- Management of human resources
- Management of the environment
- Leadership
- Improving organizational performance
- Continuum of care
- Education
- Care of patients
- Assessment of patients
- Patient rights/organizational ethics

THE DIMENSIONS OF PERFORMANCE IN ASSESSING QUALITY

- Efficacy
- Appropriateness
- Availability
- Timeliness
- Effectiveness
- Continuity
- Safety
- Efficiency
- Respect/Caring

SELECTION OF PERFORMANCE MEASURES CRITERIA

- The topic/condition makes a significant impact on the quality and cost of health care.
- It is a condition in which improvement in quality would affect a large population or significantly benefit a narrower target group.
- There is sufficient, clinical consensus or treatment approaches to evaluate quality of care using practice guidelines.

continues

4–39 continued

- The topic/condition is amenable to design and implementation of a quality screen analysis.
- Comparison to efficacy of available treatments is possible.
- The current type and amount of care being provided supports evaluation.

THE FOLLOWING STEPS ARE NECESSARY FOR EFFECTIVE MONITORING AND EVALUATION OF THE QUALITY OF OUR SERVICES

1. Assign responsibility.
2. Delineate scope of care.
3. Identify important aspects of care.
4. Identify indicators related to these aspects of care.
5. Establish thresholds for evaluation related to the indicators.
6. Collect and organize data.
7. Evaluate care when thresholds are reached.
8. Take action to improve care.
9. Assess the effectiveness of the action and document improvement.
10. Communicate relevant information to quality resource management.

Responsibility

Ultimate responsibility for quality improvement lies with the governing board. The medical director of the imaging department maintains provisional responsibility for the quality improvement program. He or she, in turn, has delegated ACCOUNTABILITIES to department staff in performing the monitoring and evaluation activities including the following:

A. The planning of a systematic and ongoing process for monitoring, evaluating, and improving the quality of care provided to patients.
B. When patient care problems and opportunities to improve care are identified, actions are taken and the effectiveness of the actions is evaluated.
C. Identifying major aspects of care.
D. Identifying clinical indicators.
E. Collecting data.
F. Evaluating data.
G. Taking action and monitoring for follow-up.

Scope of Care

The imaging department provides a full spectrum of imaging services for inpatients, outpatients, and emergency department patients of all ages. Our imaging services include consultative, diagnostic, and therapeutic procedures.

continues

4–39 continued

Modalities and Services

   A. X-ray

   B. Ultrasound

   C. Fluoroscopy

   D. Angiography

   E. Mammography

   F. Magnetic resonance imaging

   G. Tomography

   H. Interventional procedures

   I. Nuclear medicine

   J. Computerized axial tomography

Diagnostic imaging services are available at our outpatient imaging facilities Monday through Friday, 8:00 AM–5:00 PM. Diagnostic imaging services are available 24 hours a day in the hospital. During those hours when an in-house radiologist is not provided, the radiologists are available and are able to respond in 30 minutes or less. Staff technologists are available 24 hours a day, seven days a week. The medical staff radiologists are board certified by the American Board of Radiology. The radiologists are consultants, responsible for performing procedures, interpreting images, and advising referring physicians on which imaging procedures to do and in what sequence.

The radiographic technical staff are certified by the state of Florida and are registered or registry eligible with the American Registry of Radiologic Technologists. The ultrasound personnel are registered or registry eligible with the American Registry of Diagnostic Medical Sonography.

The radiology nurses are registered and further certified in critical care services.

Aspects of Care

The important aspects of care are identified as those aspects that have the greatest impact on patient care, that is, those aspects that are high-risk, high-volume, or problem-prone aspects of care. The imaging department has identified the following:

	High Risk	High Volume	Problem Prone
Contrast usage/evaluation	x	x	
Accurate and timely interpretation and reporting	x	x	
Infection control	x	x	x
Patient safety	x	x	x
Employee protection/safety	x	x	x
Appropriateness of ordered exams based on documented clinical indications of the patient	x	x	
Patient/staff education	x	x	x
Technical proficiency		x	x

continues

4–39 continued

Identify Indicators Related to These Aspects of Care

An INDICATOR is a measurable variable relating to the structure, process, or outcome of care.

Contrast Usage and Evaluation

  A. Allergic reactions to contrast media

  B. Total contrast injections

  C. Any patient who receives greater than 45 mg of injected contrast media within 24 hours

Accurate and Timely Interpretation and Reporting

  A. CT-guided biopsies/pathology report correlation

  B. Pathology reports/imaging report correlations

  C. Breast needle localization/pathology correlations

  D. Radiologist cross-check readings

  E. Trauma c-spines (complete exam before discharge)

  F. TST and cardiac catheterization correlation

  G. Hepatobiliary imaging/pathology report correlation

  H. 24-hour turnaround time (echoes)—exam completion within 24 hours of order and dictated within 72 hours after exam completion

Infection Control/Safety

  A. Follow OSHA universal precautions guidelines.

  B. Follow up complications of invasive procedures.

  C. Check survival of contrast hypersensitivity reactions.

  D. Check integrity of lead aprons and gloves.

  E. Query for pregnancy.

  F. Document time of fluoroscopy.

  G. Ensure imaging equipment is safe and performs properly.

  H. Complete dosimetry badge reports.

  I. Follow up special procedures/invasive procedure.

Appropriateness of Ordered Exams

A pertinent reason for examination is provided—exams are performed only when indicated.

Technical Performance

  A. Quality of study

  B. Film reject analysis

  C. Film critique

continues

4-39 continued

Establish Thresholds for Evaluation

The threshold for evaluation is the predetermined level or points at which evaluation of care is triggered. Setting a threshold at 0% or 100% means that even one occurrence would initiate evaluation and quality assessment. The thresholds are set from national norms, departmental historical experience, and to set up high-quality standards derived from the American College of Radiology.

Collect and Organize Data

Data are collected for each aspect of care. The data are collected on an ongoing basis. The data sources include the following:

A. Patients' medical record

B. Occurrence/incident reports

C. Imaging reports

D. Pathology reports

E. MARS computer data collection

F. Statistical data

G. OC computer-generated orders

H. Meeting minutes

I. Direct observation

Evaluate Care When Thresholds Are Reached

Data will be reviewed monthly in the department meetings and quarterly by the Quality Resource Management department. The quarterly report will also be forwarded to the Medical Executive Committee.

The findings will be reviewed to determine whether a problem or an opportunity for improvement in care exists. This evaluation includes analysis of patterns or trends in patient care that relate to specific shifts, staff, skills, and/or structure. If the evaluation identifies an opportunity to improve care or solve a problem, a plan of action is formulated. Action plans identify who and what are expected to change and where the responsibility lies for action implementation. If interdepartmental action exceeding the authority of the department is needed, recommendations are forwarded to the authorizing body. If unresolved, the issue is then referred to the Hospital Quality Improvement Committee.

Take Action To Improve Care

If evaluation identifies a problem or an opportunity for improvement, the committee forms an action plan and forwards that recommendation to the individual or group with the authority to act. Other recommendations may be forwarded to the Medical Director of imaging services. Some possible actions include the following:

A. **Systems Problems**—Changes in communication channels, changes in organizational structure, adjustments in staffing, changes in equipment or chart forms

B. **Knowledge Problems**—Inservice education, continuing education, and circulating informational material

C. **Behavior Problems**—Informal or formal counseling, changes in assignments, and disciplinary action

continues

4–39 continued

Assess the Effectiveness of the Action/Document Improvement

The imaging department staff and Quality Improvement Committee are responsible for assessing the effectiveness of actions taken to improve care. If the level of performance improves notably, the action was probably successful. Even if the care appears to be improved, periodic monitoring and evaluation of the indications will be continued to ensure that the improvement is sustained and to identify opportunities for even further improvement.

Communicate Relevant Information to Quality Resource Management

To "close the loop" of the monitoring and evaluation process, the following information is reported to the hospitalwide Quality Improvement Committee, the Medical Executive Committee, and the Governing Board.

A. Conclusions/findings

B. Recommendations

C. Actions

D. Results of actions taken

Source: Adapted from Delray Medical Center, Delray Beach, Florida.

4–40
Risk Management Process

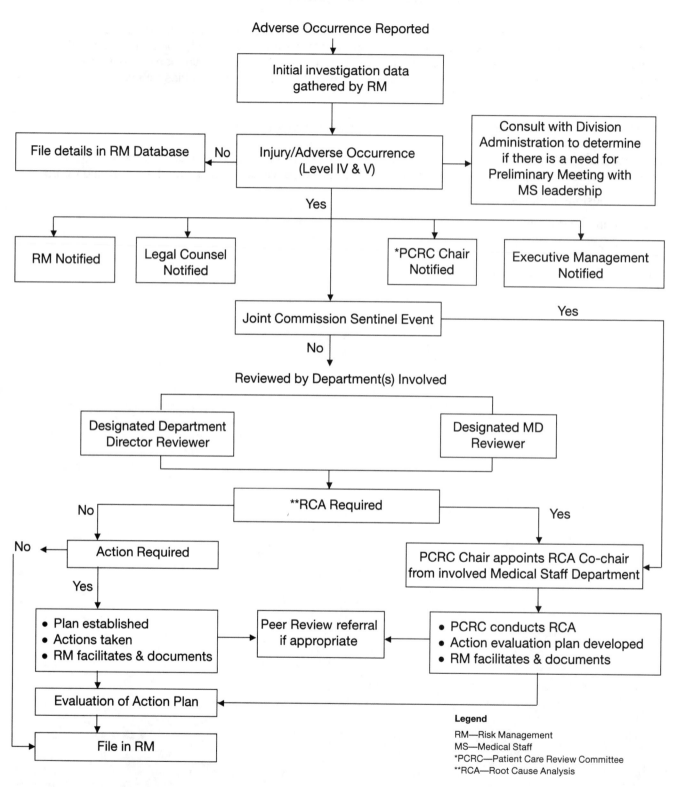

Source: Rusty McNew, JCAHO Quality Manager, Tenet Health System.

4-41
Response after a Significant Adverse Occurrence

To swiftly and effectively manage the personal and organizational impacts of a significant adverse occurrence (patient, visitor, or employee injury or death related to health care delivery), an interdepartmental, multidisciplinary meeting will be held within a day or two of the occurrence. The purpose of this meeting is to:

- Provide support to those involved in the occurrence.
- Obtain information about what happened (chronology of events).
- Determine what processes and/or procedures may have impacted the course of events.
- Direct communication.
- Determine what additional information, discussion, and/or investigation is needed and summarize next steps.

When an adverse occurrence is reported to Risk Management, the Risk Management staff will validate the type and severity of the occurrence. The Risk Manager will contact hospital and Medical Staff leadership to discuss the occurrence and determine what type of response should occur. The following outlines the role and responsibilities of leadership and Risk Management (before, during, and after the initial response).

HOSPITAL AND MEDICAL STAFF LEADERSHIP SHALL

- Identify persons directly involved with the occurrence and determine who should attend the initial response meeting.
- Provide support for the process of system & process review for improvement purposes and eliminate finger pointing or blame identification/shifting.
- Designate person(s) to manage communications with the patient and family.
- Encourage limiting/reducing unit/department discussions regarding the occurrence (rumor control).
- Arrange for staff and leadership to meet within a day or two of the occurrence.
- Participate actively in the initial review, follow-up discussions and, when applicable, a root cause analysis for the development and implementation of action plans.
- Educate and/or update staff on process improvements.

RISK MANAGER WILL

- Facilitate initial response meeting and promote the completion of follow-up activities.
- Document process and system changes and educational efforts.
- Report to Hospital Senior Management and UTSWMC Legal Department as needed.
- Ensure that Root Cause Analysis is conducted according to Joint Commission Standards.

Source: Rusty McNew, JCAHO Quality Manager, Tenet Health System.

4-42
Radiology Report Turnaround Time for Inpatients—QI Process

The length of time it takes for radiology reports to reach patients' charts is a constant source of concern for patients, referring physicians, radiologists, the radiology director, and staff.

The radiology and medical records departments at _____ Medical Center thought the turnaround time for radiology reports was adequate. It was assumed that the reports were reaching the floor within six hours. Continual complaints from referring physicians prompted the radiology department to take a closer look at the current process.

In December of 1994, the radiology director met with the quality assurance director and the director of medical records to develop a strategy for evaluating and improving turnaround time for reports in radiology. This process would be radiology's quality improvement (QI) process for 1995.

In January of 1995, the radiology director met with the diagnostic services clerks and the X-ray technologists in radiology to discuss collection of data to study the process. What needed to be collected, when to start the collection, and how long to collect data were also discussed. With the help of the staff of radiology and medical records, it was decided to collect the following data:

1. the time the exams were performed

2. the time the reports were dictated

3. the time the reports were transcribed

4. the time the reports were signed or approved

5. the time the reports were printed

6. the time the reports were delivered to the floor

The data collection would occur the last two weeks of January.

Next, the director and the clerical staff developed a flowchart of the current process. This first flowchart indicated various situations where the report process could be detained, so the group decided to narrow the focus and start the process at "X-ray taken" and end the process at "delivered."

The new flowchart had the following monitoring times:

1. X-ray taken

2. radiologist dictated

3. transcription typed

4. physician signed

5. reports printed

6. reports delivered to the floor

The areas on the flowchart from computer update through reports brought over were insignificant for this study because they did not take much time. The areas of echocardiography, cardiac cath, NIIC, and C-arms were eliminated from the study because echoes and cardiac cath are not reported through Radcom, NIIC is outpatient procedures, and C-arms require no dictation.

continues

4–42 continued

From the data collected, the team discovered the following:

- Films leave the department unread on more occasions than presumed.

- X-rays taken after 3:00 PM often result in a report being delivered to the floor after 10:00 AM the next day.

- Reports were not being printed and delivered often enough.

- Reports were waiting too long for approval.

- Reports were delivered to physician mailboxes before being delivered to the floors.

- The average turnaround time from the time the films are placed in the physician's reading room to final report delivery was approximately 8.5 hours.

The team also discovered that the average time from point of dictation to transcription completed was under two hours 92.3 percent of the time. This time does not need to be improved. So, believing that the transcription department was doing the best that it could, the team focused on processes to change in the radiology area. They are as follows:

- A policy was established that all films will be read before they leave the department, unless after 6:00 PM and before 7:00 AM.

- The radiologists agreed to check their cue for reports awaiting approval more often.

- The radiologists requested instructions on how to correct their own reports, which should decrease delays.

- The process was changed so that reports are delivered to the floors before the physicians' mailboxes.

- Clerks now print and deliver inpatient reports every two hours.

- For the X-rays taken after 3:00 PM that are dictated and transcribed but not approved, the 6:00 AM clerk prints unapproved copies of the reports and delivers all inpatient reports before 7:00 AM. The clerk stamps the report "unofficial" in red ink and replaces it with the "official" report when the reports are available.

Radiology tested the changes and collected new data in February of 1995. The average turnaround time from the time the films were placed in the reading room until the report was delivered was now 3.7 hours, a significant improvement. Because the improvements were all in the radiology area, radiology will look at this process again every March unless the need arises to monitor the process sooner.

Source: Adapted from Kootenai Medical Center, Coeur d'Alene, Idaho.

4–43
Radiologists Peer Review Program

The peer review of the Consulting Radiologists is performed by agreement with Renaissance Radiology Group. The Radiological Technologist will select and forward, on a quarterly basis, four (4) X-rays and X-ray reports along with the approved Peer Review Form to the radiology group to perform the peer review.

The Radiological Technologist will select films, in consultation with the Lead Physician, using a variety of methods including random selection, by diagnosis or by specific request for review.

One of the firm's other radiologists will review the films and the reports and complete the peer review form. The form and any comments provided will be reviewed and signed by the radiologist who read the films and wrote the X-ray report. The reports will be returned to Student Health Services and reviewed and signed by the Lead Physician and the Director.

Significant problems discovered during the process will be reviewed by the Lead Physician or the Director with the administrator of the radiology group.

The completed Radiology Peer Review form will be filed in the appropriate credentialing folder and stored for a minimum of three years.

The completed Radiology Peer Review forms will be reviewed annually and will be used as a part of the basis for renewing or discontinuing the contract with the consulting radiology group.

Source: Cal Poly Pomona Student Health Services, Pomona, California.

4–44
Radiologist Peer Review Evaluation Form

MR#: _____   Exam date: _____

Type of exam: _____

Reading radiologist: _____

Review evaluation:

_____ 1. Interpretation expected and acceptable. Reviewer comfortable with interpretation.

_____ 2. Interpretation varies slightly, but not totally unexpected. Reviewer still comfortable with interpretation.

_____ 3. Interpretation varies moderately. Reviewer uncomfortable with interpretation.

_____ 4. Interpretation varies significantly. Reviewer very uncomfortable with interpretation.

EXAM Clinically indicated: YES   NO

Recommendations:

_____

_____

_____

_____

_____

_____

_____

Comments:

_____

_____

_____

_____

_____

_____

_____

Reviewer: _____   Date: _____

MANAGEMENT OF THE ENVIRONMENT OF CARE

4–45
Emergency Management Plan for Medical Imaging and Cardiology

Division: Acute Care Services

Original issue date: _____

Latest revision date: _____

Authorization signature: _____ Date: _____
Director, Medical Imaging

Departments/Divisions Affected

Medical Imaging and Cardiology Services

APPROVAL DISTRIBUTION LIST

Approved by	Title	Date
	Medical Director, Medical Imaging	
	SR VP Patient Care Operations	
	Director, Security	
	VP Support Services	
	Ex. Director, Outpatient Services	

TITLE

Emergency Management Plan for Medical Imaging and Cardiology

PURPOSE

To ensure staff can react appropriately in an event of an emergency.

REFERENCE

HCH Safety Manual: Emergency Management Plan (ER4)

POLICY

When a Disaster alarm is sounded (Signal D over the Hospital intercom system), the Manager or Lead Technologist (if no Manager is on duty) will assess the situation. The Manager will immediately initiate the recall of personnel using the Medical Imaging Disaster recall list if needed.

continues

4–45 continued

Available Staff Should Begin Preparing the Department for the Emergency

- All stretchers should be moved to the inpatient holding area.
- All patient waiting room chairs should be pushed aside to allow for stretcher holding area.
- Disaster kit located under the cabinet next to dressing area in front hallway shall be removed from cabinet and assembled on the side of the front desk (across from inpatient waiting area), ready for use.

All Medical Imaging Staff Shall be Under the Direction of the Manager

- The Manager will assess the situation continually and call in additional staff if needed.
- The Lead Technologist and the Medical Imaging nurse shall be stationed at Control Desk.
- An ECG and Echo technician will report to the Emergency Department, and one remains in ECG department for emergency calls.
- Available technologists will be assigned to Rooms 6 and 7, and will remain with these rooms to aid disaster patients.
- Rooms 2, 6, and 7 are available for patients requiring negative pressure rooms. A negative pressure machine is available to prepare another room for those patients.
- Additional rooms shall be taken over for the emergency as the need arises.
- Angio, Ultrasound, CT, MRI, and Nuclear Medicine technologists shall stand by their areas for use as needed.
- Available staff will be called as needed to transport.
- All other personnel will report to the Manager for assignment. These employees may be assigned to the hospital Personnel Pool, which is located in the cafeteria.

All patients shall be processed using the procedure for the Emergency Plan located in Holy Cross Hospital Safety Manual (ER4). Nurse will assess disaster patients and orders for treatment.

Radiologists will write the interpretation on the patient's request form in longhand, which will go with the patient back to the Emergency Department. Images will be viewed on the workstation.

Mobile X-ray units not needed on the patient floors will be brought to the department for use as needed.

Radiologist and technologists may be assigned by the Manager to monitor patients for radioactivity using the radiation meters available.

(During drills, normal patient care will not be disrupted except for use of Room 7 for the mock disaster.)

continues

4–45 continued

MEDICAL IMAGING DEPARTMENT PROCEDURE FOR EMERGENCY MANAGEMENT

Location

Control Desk will be located at the side of the front desk.

Supplies

- non-computer (downtime) X-ray requests
- pens (ball point and flair)
- check-in documents
- metal file box
- paper clips
- clipboard
- yellow legal pad
- radiology jackets

Set-up: *On-duty personnel shall set up the disaster desk.*

Set up counter as follows: (Left to right)

    Station #1—X-ray requests, clipboard, paper, pens

    Station #2—Check-in documents, paper clips, X-ray folders, marking pens

Procedure: Station #1—Receptionist Responsibilities

- Logs in the patient using triage disaster number found on patient
- Writes the disaster number and exam on X-ray request
- Removes billing copy and places in metal box

Station #2—Film Librarian Responsibilities

- Makes up a folder, attaches request, and hands folder to Radiologist.

Station #3—Manager and/or Designee

- Radiologist writes interpretation on patient requisition, removes one copy, and gives the original request and report to the Manager and/or designee.
- The Manager will then put the report with the patient and send the patient back to the appropriate location.
- **No patient will leave Medical Imaging without his or her report.**

Procedure for Portables:

- Technologist taking films will put patient's name/disaster number on cassette.

Source: Monica Riccardo, Holy Cross Hospital, Silver Spring, Maryland.

4–46
Disaster Plan

Division: Clinical Services

Original issue date: _____

Latest revision date: _____

Authorization signature: _____ Date: _____
Director, Medical Imaging Services

Department/Division Affected

Medical Imaging Services

APPROVAL DISTRIBUTION LIST

Approved by	Title	Date
	Medical Director, Medical Imaging Services	
	Assistant Vice President, Clinical Services	

PURPOSE

To ensure that employees can react appropriately in the event of a disaster policy

- When a disaster is called, the supervisor on duty will immediately initiate the recall of personnel using the medical imaging disaster recall list.

- Available staff should begin preparing the department for the disaster.

  - All stretchers should be moved to the inpatient holding area.

  - All patient waiting room chairs should be pushed aside to allow for stretcher holding area.

  - Disaster kit shall be removed from storage location and prepared for use.

- All staff shall be under the direction of the manager.

  - A manager, team leader, and a radiology nurse shall be stationed at the control desk next to the dressing area in the front hallway.

  - The team leader technologist should be assigned to match films and jackets and be responsible for the flow of films to the radiologists for stat readings.

  - Available technologists shall be assigned to treatment rooms to aid disaster patients.

  - Additional rooms shall be taken over for the disaster as the need arises.

  - In the event the disaster affects the main radiology treatment area, alternate locations should be determined for patient relocation

continues

4–46 continued

- Angiography, ultrasound, CT, MRI, and nuclear medicine technologists shall stand by their areas ready for service, as needed.

- Radiology assistants will be made available to transport patients.

- All other personnel will report to the manager for assignment.

- All disaster patients shall be processed using the facility's disaster procedure.

- After patients have been treated in the radiology department, they will be assigned to available beds, in collaboration with the admitting office.

- A radiologist will be stationed in the department and be responsible for film interpretation as the films become available. Radiologists will immediately enter the film interpretation into the patient's record. The record will accompany the patient to his/her destination in the hospital. X-ray films will not leave the department.

- Mobile X-ray units not needed on the patient floors will be brought to the department for use as needed.

- The Radiology supervisor will check with the Emergency Department to determine if additional X-ray Units are needed in that location.

- In the event that it is believed that patients have been contaminated by ionizing radiation, the Radiation Safety Officer will be contacted to measure contamination levels and to assist in decontamination of exposed individuals.

Practice Drills

- During drills, normal patient care will not be disrupted, except for one area for use in the mock disaster.

PROCEDURE FOR DISASTER

Location

Control Desk (located at receiving area of the Radiology Department).

Supplies

- view box
- metal box for storage of billing copies
- X-ray request forms
- pens (ballpoint and flair)
- check-in documents
- paper clips
- clipboard
- yellow legal paper

continues

4–46 continued

Set-up

On-duty personnel shall set up the disaster desk. Set up counter includes:

- Station #1—X-ray requests, clipboard, paper, pens
- Station #2—Check-in documents, paper clips, X-ray jackets, marking pens
- Station #3—Viewbox and pens

Station #1

- Log in the patient using triage disaster number found with patient.
- Write the disaster number and exam on X-ray request.
- Remove billing copy and place in metal box.
- Write up the check-in document.
- The triage disaster number will also be the X-ray number.

Station #2

- Make up a folder, write triage number on jacket in Flair Pen, attach request and flashcard to the folder, and hand to the supervisor or designee.

Station #3 (Radiologist)

- Write interpretation on patient requisition, remove one copy, and place the original request, and report back with the patient. Send patient to appropriate location.

Portables

- Technologist taking films will put patient's name/disaster number on cassette.
- Runner will bring cassette to disaster desk and leave with supervisor.

Source: Rusty McNew, JCAHO Quality Manager, Tenet Health System.

4–47
Safety Management Performance Improvement Plan

I. INTENT OF THE SAFETY MANAGEMENT PLAN

This Safety Management (SM) Plan outlines the methodology that _____ utilizes to improve processes, practice(s), outcomes, satisfaction regarding safety management, cost, and efficiency related to the seven (7) Environment of Care programs:

- Safety Management Program
- Life Safety Management Program
- Hazardous Materials & Waste Management Program
- Utility Systems Management Program
- Security Management Program
- Emergency Preparedness Program
- Equipment Management Program

II. PURPOSE OF SAFETY MANAGEMENT

To establish and monitor performance standards based on safety management criteria. To identify processes that can improve the safety management of the hospital district.

III. OBJECTIVES OF THE SAFETY MANAGEMENT PLAN

A. Describe the structure of the SM Program.

B. Define hospital district's Patient Care Division responsibilities for SM.

C. Identify a consistent and systematic methodology for SM.

D. Identify systemwide SM priorities.

E. Identify SM internal continuous indicators and external benchmarking comparisons.

F. Establish mechanisms for reporting SM activities.

IV. ROLE & RESPONSIBILITY OF SAFETY MANAGEMENT

A. Board of Managers

1. Oversee the services provided by the Dallas County Hospital District by reviewing SM activities.

2. May make recommendations for actions.

3. Receive SM status reports at least quarterly from the Safety Management Committee.

4. May establish systemwide priorities.

continues

4–47 continued

B. Safety Management Committee (SMC)

1. Chaired by the **(to be determined).**

2. Scope of the SMC is a high-level monitoring of the safety management performance of the hospital district.

3. Take an active role in working with Divisional PICs and hospital departments to improve safety management performance of the hospital district.

4. Use influence to improve processes and change behavior to conform to the values and mission of _____ related to safety management.

5. Annually establish systemwide SM priorities (October).

6. Annually evaluate SM priorities to determine impact on system (October).

7. Meet no less than quarterly.

8. Committee attendance = 70%

9. Membership:

Safety Management Chairperson	Director of Quality Management	Director of Facilities Management	Designee from Risk Management	Director of DPS
Manager of Infection Control	Director of Training & Development	Director of Emergency Services	Director of Engineering	Director of Trauma Services

10. Communicate to the Division PICs, Departments, Medical Advisory Council (MAC), Regulatory Advisory Group (RAG).

11. Report to the Clinical Improvement Committee.

12. Annually approve the five (5) Safety Plan components including Emergency Preparedness, Medical Equipment Safety, Utility Management, Life Safety, and Security.

13. Analyze performance standard reports from each of the components.

14. Approve proposed acquisitions from bedding, drapes, furnishings, decorations, wastebaskets, and other equipment requiring review for fire safety prior to purchase.

15. Plan actions as required and educational/training programs to meet safety requirements.

C. Executive Management

Requires that all Divisions and Departments:

1. Maintain an SM program.

2. Maintain SM employee competency program and outcome measurements.

3. Submit SM reports at least quarterly to their respective Vice President.

D. Medical Advisory Council (MAC)

Requires that each Medical Staff department be involved within their respective division's SM Program.

continues

4–47 continued

E. Clinical Division Performance Improvement Committees (PIC)

Requires that each Clinical Division PIC integrate safety management into their Divisional/Departmental PIC.

F. Non-Clinical Departments

1. Participate in their respective division's SM program.

2. Maintain quality control, regulatory requirements, and quality initiatives, which are unique within the department or function related to SM.

V. METHODOLOGY FOR IMPROVING PERFORMANCE

Annually SM will assess and assign priorities for improving care, safety management processes, practice(s), and outcomes. The methods utilized will depend on the type of initiative and desire of the team. Teams may include sub-groups, task forces, or utilize existing quality or service teams.

Performance Improvement teams use the Plan, Do, Check, Act (PDCA) model. Continuous Quality Improvement (CQI) principles are also used to plan, design, implement, and evaluate process or systems.

There are three (3) fundamental components within the PHHS SM Program. Each division/department includes these structures in their measurement and improvement prioritization:

1. *Effectiveness* relates to outcomes. The outcome of clinical interventions, service, or processes as measured against internal pre-established goals or external benchmarks

2. *Efficiency* relates to systems. The organizational processes as measured against pre-established targets or benchmarked operations

3. *Satisfaction* relates to patient/customer satisfaction. Measurement of services delivered, behaviors observed, and/or perceptions conveyed to internal and external customers.

VI. PERFORMANCE MONITORING

Reporting

Specific indicators/functions including the five (5) safety plans are continuously monitored to evaluate practice. Findings of the following committees are reported as appropriate to the:

- Clinical Improvement Committee (CIC); quarterly

- Division/Department Performance Improvement Committees; quarterly

- Non-clinical Departments; quarterly (via CIC)

- Medical Advisory Committee (MAC); quarterly (via CIC)

- Board of Managers (BOM); quarterly (via CIC)

VII. ANALYSIS OF INDICATOR & PRIORITY MONITORING

Data are presented in a format that allows for analysis. Internal and external comparisons should be utilized.

continues

4–47 continued

VIII. COMPETENCE OF PERSONNEL

Competency of staff is evaluated, measured, and exerted at four (4) levels:

1. Job Descriptions—Preemployment analysis of education, skills, & background history.

2. Orientation—General and Department Specific.

3. Annual performance appraisals for all employees.

4. Annual mandatory SM training.

IX. CONFIDENTIALITY

Safety management activities are conducted for the purpose of evaluating current practice(s), process(s), outcomes, satisfaction, are and service. Data is collected in order to make improvements in patient outcomes and perceptions, to manage costs, and to be utilized for the medical staff recredentialing process. The Performance Improvement Committee members acting in good faith shall keep all reports and information gained through these committees in strict confidence.

X. PROTECTION FROM DISCLOSURE

The performance improvement activities of the hospital system and medical staff are identified in the bylaws of the Board of Managers and the Medical Staff. Performance improvement is directed by Senior Management. Performance improvement findings shall be confidential and shall be used only for the functions of the Performance Improvement Committee members. Records may be made available to persons who have regulatory oversight authority. These accrediting or licensing agency surveyors are required to keep the information confidential.

The activities, records, and minutes of performance improvement committees are maintained under HB 4495b guidelines, which afford protection from disclosure or discovery. Records of these committees are not public records and are not subject to court subpoena.

Source: Rusty McNew.

4–48
Smoke-Free Environment

POLICY

The hospital recognizes its responsibility as the major health care provider in the community to set a positive example in health promotion and disease prevention. In view of the overwhelming body of evidence on the harmful effects of smoking or using tobacco products, and in compliance with the smoking ordinance, _____ Hospital will maintain a restricted smoking environment.

PROCEDURE

The sale, distribution, and/or use of tobacco products anywhere in the hospital is prohibited. Smoking is permissible outside the hospital in designated smoking areas, located at :_____. Receptacles are provided for safe and proper disposal of cigarettes and butts.

Smoking is prohibited within 25 feet of all doors and entrances to the hospital and all of its associated structures and facilities.

Patients are allowed to smoke inside of the hospital in specially designated smoking rooms, but only when such smoking has been authorized in writing by their attending physician or primary care nurse. Such smoking facilities are located at _____.

Enforcement Responsibility

Managers—Ensure compliance with the hospital's smoke-free environment policy; investigate reports of noncompliance; initiate appropriate actions.

Employees with patient care responsibilities must ensure that the following criteria are met before allowing a patient to smoke in specially designated areas inside of the hospital. Before a patient may sign a release the following criteria must be met:

- A physician's order to permit smoking is in the patient's chart.

- The primary care nurse has provided written approval for the patient to smoke.

All hospital employees—Comply with the smoke-free environment policy; monitor compliance of visitors, physicians, volunteers, employees, and patients; report observed noncompliance, in confidence, to their own supervisors; provide information to patients and visitors regarding the policy as requested or required.

Enforcement Procedures

Visitors—In the event of noncompliance, the visitor should be informed of the smoke-free environment policy. Continued noncompliance should be reported to security. Security should request such visitors to cease smoking or to leave the premises. In case of refusal, security should consult with the department director or designee to determine whether officials should be contacted and requested to enforce smoking prohibitions in accordance with local code requirements.

- Medical staff—Noncompliance will be reported to the administrator for action as required by the medical staff bylaws.

- Employees—Noncompliance shall be grounds for disciplinary action in accordance with personnel policy as stated in _____.

- Patients—Noncompliance should be reported to the unit director/shift supervisor and/or the admitting physician.

- Volunteers—Noncompliance should be reported to the director of volunteers and refusal or repeated noncompliance should result in dismissal.

Source: Radiology Department, University of California—Davis Medical Center.

4–49
Diagnostic Radiology

PURPOSE

This procedure defines the responsibilities for protective equipment, radiation and safety surveys, operating procedures, and quality assurance programs for X-ray machines used on humans for diagnostic purposes in the Diagnostic Radiology Division of the Radiology Department.

POLICY

The **Radiation Safety Committee** is responsible for ensuring that each individual who prescribes or uses any form of ionizing radiation in or on humans is properly qualified through training and experience that meets all regulatory requirements. Routine clinical uses of X-rays for diagnosis are controlled by qualified radiologists and radiologic technologists and are not subject to review or approval by the Radiation Safety Committee. Research or experimental applications of radiation to humans must be reviewed and approved by the Human Uses Subcommittee of the Radiation Safety Committee (RPR 40).

Radiation safety and quality assurance procedures for the diagnostic use of X-rays are prepared, implemented, and supervised by the **Diagnostic Radiological Physicist (DRP)** in the Diagnostic Radiology Division of the Radiology Department. The **DRP** submits a copy of all new or revised diagnostic X-ray procedures involving any aspect of radiation protection and quality assurance to the **Radiation Safety Officer (RSO)** for review and documentation. The **RSO** submits comments, suggestions, or proposed changes to the **DRP** for action. The **RSO** reports on the status and acceptability of the procedures to the **Radiation Safety Committee** at least annually.

Users of X-ray machines for diagnostic purposes are responsible for radiation protection of employees and patients. Quality assurance for equipment and procedures is an integral part of the responsibility for patient welfare and is, therefore, the responsibility of the medical and administrative staffs of the Radiology Department at University Hospital and Wasatch Clinic.

The **RSO** is responsible for ensuring that all equipment, facilities, procedures, and practices involving ionizing radiation comply with applicable federal and state laws and regulations, and that complete and accurate records of actions pertaining to radiation protection are maintained.

REGISTRATION

The **RSO** shall maintain complete records of the X-ray machines possessed by the Radiology Department, based on information submitted by the **DRP** for each machine. All X-ray machines must be registered annually with the Utah Division of Radiation Control (URC). To avoid duplication or omission of records, **registration forms are to be submitted to the URC only by the RSO**. The Radiology Department shall reimburse the Radiological Health Department for the cost of registration.

INSPECTIONS

Each X-ray machine must be inspected at regular intervals by a qualified expert (URC, R313-16). The inspection shall include machine function, film processing, facility design including shielding, operator procedures, documentation of operator qualifications, and evaluation of patient exposures. The **RSO** is responsible for ensuring that appropriate inspections are performed and documented for all University X-ray facilities.

continues

4–49 continued

The Radiology Department employs the **DRP** (a qualified expert) who performs the regular inspections of X-ray machines belonging to the Radiology Department and maintains the records of such surveys. Any defect or malfunction identified during such surveys is to be reported in writing to the **RSO,** who is responsible for assuring that corrections are made and for the necessary documentation.

QUALITY ASSURANCE PROGRAMS

The Radiology Department shall develop and maintain a quality assurance (QA) program in accordance with guidelines published by the U.S. Food and Drug Administration (FDA), the American Association of Physicists in Medicine (AAPM), and/or the National Council on Radiation Protection and Measurement (NCRP).

DIAGNOSTIC X-RAY PROCEDURES

All diagnostic X-ray procedures shall be performed according to radiation protection procedures in the University of Utah Radiation Safety Manual and Procedures and in compliance with URC Rules in chapter R313-28.

TRAINING

The **DRP** shall ensure that all Diagnostic Radiology personnel, Surgery personnel, and Ward personnel involved in care of patients being X-rayed have received appropriate radiation safety training. Documentation of radiation safety training for these personnel shall be provided to the Radiological Health Department.

All staff radiologists **must** be certified by the American Board of Radiology or meet the training requirements stated in chapter R313-28 of the URC Rules. Radiologic technologists **must** be certified or meet the URC training requirements.

REFERENCES

National Council on Radiation Protection and Measurements, Bethesda, MD: *Quality Assurance for Diagnostic Imaging Equipment,* NCRP Report No. 99, 1988.

Medical X-ray, Electron Beam and Gamma-ray Protection for Energies up to 50 MeV, NCRP Report No. 102, 1989.

Radiation Protection for Medical and Allied Health Personnel, NCRP Report No. 105, 1989.

Implementation of the Principle of As Low As Reasonably Achievable (ALARA) for Medical and Dental Personnel, NCRP Report No. 107, 1990.

University of Utah, *Radiation Safety Policy Manual and Radiation Safety Procedures and Records.*

Utah Department of Environmental Quality, Division of Radiation *Control, Utah Radiation Control Rules.*

Standards for protection against radiation, R313-15.

General requirements applicable to the installation, registration, inspection, and use of radiation machines, R313-16.

Use of X-rays in the healing arts, R313-28.

4–50
Tangible Research Material Transfer Request

1. Principal Investigator: _____

2. Academic Title: _____

3. SSN: _____

4. Department/Unit: _____

5. Telephone: _____

6. Fax: _____

7. E-mail: _____

8. Department Mail Account #: _____

9. Department Contact: _____

10. Telephone: _____

11. Fax: _____

12. E-mail: _____

13. Indicate whether hospital is the Provider or Recipient of the Material: ☐ Provider
                                                                                ☐ Recipient

14. Date Material Needed: _____

15. If Sooner Than 45 Days from Submittal, State Reason: _____

16. Project Title: _____

17. Project Sponsor or Funding Source: _____

18. Project Period: From: _____   To: _____

19. Optional Material Preparation and Transmittal Fee: _____

20. Material Description: _____

    _____

    _____

    _____

    _____

    _____

21. Description of Research Use: _____

    _____

    _____

    _____

    _____

    _____

continues

4–50 continued

22. Research Location(s): _____

23. **Environmental Health and Safety, Regulatory Compliance:** Indicate the safety and regulatory considerations that apply to the material being transferred or to the research being conducted by checking the appropriate box and providing additional information where requested below:

☐ Injury prevention program?

☐ Carcinogens?   If Yes, CUA #:

☐ Ionizing Radiation?   If Yes, RUA #:

☐ Pathogenic Agents?   If Yes, BUA #:

☐ Recombinant DNA?   If Yes, GUA #:

☐ Federally Regulated Drugs or Controlled Substances?

☐ Medical waste?

☐ Vertebrate Animals?   If Yes, Protocol #:

☐ Human Subjects?   If Yes, Protocol/Exemption #
Yes

24. Non-Hospital Organization Name and Address:_____

_____

25. How and why did you make contact with this organization? _____

_____

_____

_____

_____

26. Non-Hospital Scientist:	27. Telephone:	28. Fax:	29. E-mail:
30. Non-Hospital Administrative Contact:	31. Telephone:	32. Fax:	33. E-mail:
34. Non-Hospital Legal Contact:	35. Telephone:	36. Fax:	37. E-mail:

continues

4–50 continued

FOR TECHNOLOGY TRANSFER CENTER USE ONLY:

UCD MTR #: _____
UCD Master Agreement #: _____
UCD Implementing Letter #: _____

Action	**Date**
☐ Request Received at OVCR:	_____
☐ Request Received at TTC:	_____
☐ Proposed Agreement Reviewed:	_____
☐ PI Interview/Input:	_____
☐ Hospital Response #1:	_____
☐ Non-Hospital Response #1:	_____
☐ Hospital Exceptions Requested:	_____
☐ Hospital Exceptions Approved/Rejected:	_____
☐ Non-Hospital Final Response:	_____
☐ Non-Hospital Rejection:	_____
☐ Negotiations Terminated:	_____
☐ Hospital Approval:	_____
☐ Non-Hospital Approval:	_____
☐ Agreement Effective Date:	_____

Final Agreement Type:
☐ Non-Hospital (describe):
_____
☐ Hospital Single Transaction
☐ Hospital Master
  ☐ Implementing Letter
UBMTA:
  ☐ Implementing Letter
  ☐ Simple Letter Agreement
☐ Other (describe):
_____

Non-Hospital Entity Information:
☐ Non-Profit
☐ For-Profit
☐ UBMTA Signatory
☐ Government
☐ Private University
☐ Public University

Pre-existing Intel. Prop. Rights?
☐ YES
☐ NO

Entity Type Holding Those Rights:
☐ Com. Board
☐ Priv. Sponsor
☐ Other Transfer
☐ Government
☐ Pub. University
☐ Priv. University

Scope of Rights Held (briefly describe):

Publication Terms:
☐ Advance Submittal: _____ days
☐ Review Period: _____ days

Agreement Expiration Date(s):
☐ Max:
☐ Min:

By signing this form, the Principal Investigator and other required signatories agree to comply with current university and sponsor policies and regulations addressed in both the UCD Sponsored Research Manual Section 230, Exhibit A, and the UCD Technology Transfer Manual, Section 100, Material Transfer Guidelines.

	SIGNATURE	**DATE**
Principal Investigator		
Department Chair or Division Director		
Dean (if applicable):		
Other (if required):		

Source: Radiology Department, University of California—Davis Medical Center.

4–51
Recall of Drugs, Medical/Surgical Supplies, Devices, Equipment, and Other Related Hazards

I. PURPOSE

This policy establishes a program for prompt reaction to notices of product recall or product modification issued by the Federal Food and Drug Administration (FDA), any manufacturer, vendor, or other source. This program will allow this facility to respond to such notification, whether it applies to supplies, equipment, or any other material.

II. POLICY

A. Precautions should be taken to prevent the use of any item that could be considered injurious to the user.

B. The office of material management shall be responsible for the implementation, coordination, notification, follow-up, and documentation of the program.

C. The director, hospital, and clinics shall publish separate internal operating policies for the hospital, which should be used in conjunction with this PPM.

III. PROCEDURES

A. Notification of Recalls

The FDA, the manufacturer, distributor, or user via mail, telegram, telephone, or in person may notify individuals of product recall, warnings, etc. If an individual receives or reads a notice of product recall or product modification directly from the manufacturer, or personally detects a product defect or problem, that individual should telephone the recall coordinator immediately, and forward the information to Q-026.

B. Supplies and Equipment Recall (including vehicles)

1. The recall coordinator will review each recall notice to determine if it is applicable to the campus.

2. If applicable, the recall coordinator shall in conjunction with the purchasing manager, equipment manager, and storehouse manager identify departments/units that might need to be notified of the product recall.

3. The recall coordinator shall initiate a product recall warning notice with the pertinent information, then disseminate the notice to the campus department(s) deemed appropriate for action as well as to the associate director of pharmacy and office of environmental health and safety within eight working hours after receiving notification of recall notice.

4. In the case of recalls and warnings where reasonable probability of serious injury or death may result, appropriate department/unit contacts will be telephoned with written follow-ups provided.

5. Departments shall complete the product recall warning notice, take the appropriate action indicated on the form, and return the original to the recall coordinator.

6. The recall coordinator will identify collection points where applicable, supervise the disposition of all equipment and supplies affected by the recall/warning, and initiate steps to obtain the appropriate credit or replacements from the manufacturer or vendor.

7. The recall coordinator will follow up with all notified areas who have not complied with the recall, and act as liaison between vendor and/or manufacturer.

8. The recall coordinator will provide a monthly status report of recall activity to the materiel manager.

continues

4–51 continued

C. Drug Recalls

1. For drug-related recalls, the action taken depends upon FDA recall classifications. Definitions are listed below:

   a. Class One—Recalls involving a situation in which there is a reasonable probability that the use of, or exposure to, a violative product will cause serious, adverse health consequences, or death.

      Action—All products are to be immediately impounded and destroyed or returned to the manufacturer by the recall coordinator, according to instruction from the FDA or the manufacturer. FDA inspectors usually check to determine compliance with the regulations.

   b. Class Two—Recalls involving a situation in which the use of, or exposure to, a violative product may cause temporary or medically reversible adverse health consequences or where the probability of serious health consequences is remote.

      Action—All products are to be impounded from all areas but are not to be necessarily destroyed until final instructions are received by the recall coordinator from the FDA or the manufacturer.

   c. Class Three—Recalls involving a situation in which the use of or exposure to a violative product is not likely to cause adverse health consequences.

      Action: The department chair shall exercise administrative judgment in the removal of these products from all areas, and coordinate with the recall coordinator the destruction or return of products to the manufacturer.

2. Upon official notification of a drug recall, the recall coordinator shall immediately transmit a copy of the notice to the associate director, pharmacy services, as well as initiate the recall/warning process. (See III.B.3)

3. In conjunction with the purchasing manager and drug commodity buyer, the recall coordinator identifies department and staff that might be affected.

IV. RESPONSIBILITIES

A. Recall Coordinator

1. Implement the recall program.

B. Department Chairs/Unit Managers

1. Take note of recall/warning and institute action if necessary.

2. Identify departmental principal and alternate contact person to be notified of product recalls, and advise recall coordinator at Q-026.

3. Check all areas of responsibility for the recalled item.

4. Isolate recalled products.

5. Complete and return the product recall/warning notice along with any recalled stock to the collection point identified by the recall coordinator. Retain department file copy.

4–52
Product Recall Warning Notice

TO: _____   DATE: _____

IMPORTANT! READ IMMEDIATELY!

(SECTION A—To be completed by recall coordinator)

1. The Food and Drug Administration and/or the manufacturer has

   ☐ recalled   ☐ sent a warning notice

   regarding the following:

   ☐ drug   ☐ med/surgical supply   ☐ device   ☐ equipment.

   Description _____

   Brand _____   Manufacturer _____

   Unit of issue/dose _____   Product Number _____

   Lot Number _____   UCID and/or Serial Number _____

   Reason for recall/warning _____

2. It is necessary that you check your area of responsibility for the item(s) and

   ☐ clearly mark and quarantine the item(s) under recall to ensure that the items will not be used

   ☐ immediately notify the Recall Coord, Ext. _____, that you have located the item(s) described above

   ☐ return the item(s) with a copy of this form and shipping memo to _____

   _____

   If you have any questions, please call the recall coordinator on Extension _____.

(SECTION B—To be completed by department) Fill Out Immediately!

1. ☐ this item is in our stock in the following quantities _____

2. ☐ this item has been quarantined for further disposition

   Please call _____   at extension _____

3. ☐ this item is not in our area

Name of person completing form (print or type)

Name	Department	Mail Code
Signature	Date	Extension

Original—Return to recall coordinator
Copy 1—Post for one week
Copy 2—Retain for File
Retention Period: 5 years

Source: Reprinted by permission of the University of California Regents, San Diego, California.

4–53
Safety in the Medical Imaging Department

Division: Clinical Services

Original issue date: _____

Latest revision date: _____

Authorization signature: _____ Date: _____
Director, Medical Imaging Services

Department/Division Affected

Medical Imaging Services

APPROVAL DISTRIBUTION LIST

Approved by	Title	Date
	Medical Director, Medical Imaging Services	
	Assistant Vice President, Clinical Services	

PURPOSE

To maintain a safe and healthy environment for patients, visitors, and employees

POLICY

- The medical imaging department is committed to maintaining a safe and healthy environment for all patients, visitors, and employees.
- All medical imaging employees are required to participate in safety training sessions annually. These sessions will include

  –hazardous materials and hazard communication

  –fire safety and the proper use of fire extinguishers

  –infection control

  –disaster response for department disaster policy, including evacuation plans and telephone tree list

  –electrical safety

  –radiation safety
- All new employees will receive required safety training sessions during their orientation period and before they perform duties independently.
- All safety training must be documented. Attendance records and post-test documentation will be maintained by the department for three years.
- The director of medical imaging is responsible for coordinating the unit's safety program.

continues

4–53 continued

General Rules

- A visual inspection to check all external wiring to and from all components for X-ray units shall be made daily by the technologist assigned to that room. The technologist will also do a manual check of all movable parts.

- A visual check will also be made of all other equipment in the room, such as suction, blood pressure cuff, etc.

- Any *unsafe* items or conditions shall be reported immediately to the manager. Steps to correct the condition must be instituted as soon as possible.

- Special attention should be paid to the hazards associated with wet floors and blocked egress, slipping and tripping hazards, and other unsafe conditions.

- Every employee of the medical imaging department should be thoroughly familiar with the evacuation plans for his or her area.

- It is the responsibility of all employees to know and adhere to the safety policies of the hospital. The safety manuals and their locations are as follows:

  –The hospital safety manual is located in the quality control (QC) area.

  –MSDS manuals and exposure control manuals are located in the following areas: QC area, QA/safety coordinator's office, nuclear medicine QC area, and MRI.

Accident Procedure

All incidents and accidents must be recorded as soon as feasible on the incident report form. All incident reports are then given to the manager.

HAZARDOUS MATERIALS AND HAZARD COMMUNICATIONS

Hazardous chemicals are those that may present a physical, chemical, or health hazard under normal use.

- **Acids** cause severe burns on tissue. Acids must not be stored in the same area as caustics. Safe handling of acids requires proper gloves and eye goggles. The emergency spill procedure is as follows:

  –**small spills**—Mix with water to dilute, then mop up.

  –**large spills**—Acid neutralizer kits are located in the receiving department. The kit has a powder that is sprinkled on the acid spill. The powder absorbs the acid and then is swept up.

- **Caustics** cause severe burns on tissue. Caustics must not be stored in the same area as acids. Examples of caustics found in hospitals are sodium hydroxide and ammonium hydroxide. Safe handling of caustics requires proper gloves and eye goggles. A spill kit for caustics is located in the receiving department.

- Inhalation or absorption of **solvents** through the skin may cause irritation or more severe exposure symptoms. Safe handling of solvents requires proper gloves and mask. A spill kit for solvents is located in the receiving department.

- Examples of **carcinogens and suspected carcinogens** are antineoplastic drugs and formaldehyde. Only authorized and trained individuals are permitted to handle these chemicals.

In-House Emergency Response

If a hazardous chemical and/or radioactive spill occurs in the department, the manager or supervisor on duty will take the following steps:

continues

4–53 continued

1. Contain spill as safely as possible.

2. Evacuate all unneeded personnel.

3. Notify the telecommunications operator who will in turn notify security, the administrative coordinator, and maintenance. The operator will also notify the emergency department if there are injuries.

4. Assign trained personnel within the department to contain and clean up the spill.

5. Call security for support with large spills.

Emergency Procedures for Chemical Exposure

- **Skin contact**—Promptly flush the affected area with water and remove any contaminated clothing. Use a safety shower when contact is extensive. If symptoms persist after washing, seek medical attention.

- **Ingestion**—Encourage the victim to drink large amounts of water.

- **Eye contact**—Promptly flush eyes with water for a prolonged period (15 minutes) and seek medical attention.

Chemical spills are contained using the Think CLEAN Plan.

Contain the spill.

Leave the area.

Emergency: eye wash, shower, medical care.

Access MSDS.

Notify a supervisor.

Material Safety Data Sheets

- There must be an MSDS for each hazardous chemical in the medical imaging department. They are in alphabetical order along with a chemical inventory of the department.

- All hazardous chemicals should have the following labeling:

  –name of chemical

  –routes of exposure

  –PPE to use

Radioactive Isotopes

- All radioactive isotopes are stored in nuclear medicine's hot lab, which is locked unless a nuclear medicine technologist is present in the department.

- Safe handling of radionuclides requires gloves.

Disposal of Radioactive Material

- Short-lived radioactive waste is stored behind lead in the hot lab in red bags.

- Long-term radioactive waste is locked in the storage room in the basement.

continues

4–53 continued

Radioactive Spills

- Minor spills

    1. Notify people in area of spill.

    2. Prevent spread with absorbent pads.

    3. Clean up using gloves, remote handling tongs, and soap.

    4. Store all trash in the basement storage room or the hot lab.

    5. Survey and isolate any remaining contamination by blocking off or covering and labeling.

- Major spills

    1. Notify radiation safety officer, security, and anyone in the area of the spill. Anyone not involved should leave the room.

    2. Prevent spread with absorbent pads.

    3. Confine movement of contaminated personnel to prevent spread.

    4. Shield the source, if possible.

    5. Close the room and lock the door.

    6. Decontaminate personnel.

- Personnel decontamination

    1. Remove and store contaminated clothing.

    2. Flush skin thoroughly, and wash with mild soap and lukewarm water.

Source: Adapted from Nancy Hughes, Holy Cross Hospital, Silver Spring, Maryland.

4–54
Radiation Safety for Mobile Radiographic Examinations

Division: Clinical Services

Original issue date: _____

Latest revision date: _____

Authorization signature: _____ Date: _____
Director, Medical Imaging Services

Departments/Divisions Affected

Medical Imaging Services

Nursing Services

APPROVAL DISTRIBUTION LIST

Approved by	Title	Date
	Medical Director, Medical Imaging Services	
	Assistant Vice President, Clinical Services	
	Senior Vice President, Patient Care Services	
	Radiation Physicist	

PURPOSE

To ensure patient and staff safety for mobile radiation examinations

POLICY

Mobile examinations are provided at the patient bedside for those patients too ill to be transported to medical imaging. Portable exams should never be ordered as a convenience to staff and/or patient because the diagnostic quality of mobile examinations is generally not of the quality of those taken in the department.

Technologists performing mobile examinations shall use proper radiation safety procedures by following the procedures listed below:

- Provide a lead apron and gloves for personnel or family members requested to hold or immobilize the patient. Leave beam-defining light on during exposure and record name of holder on Human Holding Log.

- Wear a lead apron for all exposures.

- Use the full length of the exposure switch cord or stand at least six feet from the tubehead and patient.

- Use gonadal shielding for *all* patients except where interference with area of interest will result.

- Use collimation to restrict exposure to the site of diagnostic interest and consistent with film size.

continues

4–54 continued

• Warn all personnel in the immediate area of the patient being examined *prior* to making each exposure.

Staff Safety

The technologist shall announce "X-ray" in a loud and clear voice before making the exposure. Following the announcement, the technologist shall ensure that people have vacated the immediate area before making the exposure. Should anyone be still in the immediate area, a second announcement shall be made before the exposure is made. Provide lead aprons to individuals in close vicinity (six to eight feet) who cannot leave the area.

Patient Safety

The technologist performing mobile examinations shall drape the patient's abdomen for all chest examinations with a lead apron and shall provide gonadal shielding where appropriate as well. Radiologists are encouraged to look for evidence of shielding as well as for collimation on all portable examinations.

Shielding is essential on all pediatric, nursery, and neonatal patients. Every effort must be taken to shield the abdomen during chest examination and male gonads during abdominal examinations. Small lead shields are provided on the mobile units for this purpose. Radiologists are encouraged to report any of the above radiographs that do not show evidence of shielding.

Source: Adapted from Nancy Hughes, Holy Cross Hospital, Silver Spring, Maryland.

4–55
MRI Safety and Screening Guidelines

Original/Revision by: _____   **Effective Date:** _____

Reference: _____   **Revised Date:** _____

Departments Primarily Affected: Radiology/MRI

Cross-Reference: _____

STATEMENT OF PURPOSE

To provide guidelines for safety and prescreening of MRI patients

PROCEDURES

Qualifying personnel with knowledge of safety guidelines and potential contraindications shall conduct prescreening and MRI scans.

1. It is highly recommended that patients come to the radiology department for prescreening and to ask questions prior to their appointment times.

    A. Patients will fill out a prescreening questionnaire.

    B. Patients will receive an information pamphlet explaining magnetic resonance imaging.

    C. Patients will be prescreened for:

        a. Prior surgeries

        b. Pacemakers and implants

        c. Metal splinters in the body (may require X-ray exam of the orbits)

        d. Tattoos

        e. Claustrophobia (recommend patient speak with his/her doctor about sedation)

        f. If the patient is female, check for pregnancy/possible pregnancy (see 2 D)

    D. Recommend patient arrive for his or her exam wearing plain T-shirt/sweatshirt and elastic waist shorts/sweatpants, no make-up, and no jewelry.

    E. The radiology department will provide a locker where the patient can secure wallets, purses, or loose objects.

    F. The radiology department will also provide hearing protection for the patient.

2. The following are indications where patients **cannot** be scanned:

    A. Aneurysm clips—neurosurgical only

    B. Permanent pacemakers

    C. Intraoccular metal

    D. Pregnancy (review with radiologist prior to scheduling)

    E. STARR-Edwards pre6000 (1960–1964) heart valves

continues

4–55 continued

   F. Cochlear implants (3M/house and 3M/Vienet)

3. All patients shall remove:

   A. Bobby pins

   B. Dentures/bridge work (if performing head or neck exams)

   C. Hearing aids

   D. Makeup

   E. Hair pieces

   F. All metal to include but not limited to: watches, coins, jewelry, keys, pocket knives, fingernail clippers, bra, necklaces, pens, etc.

4. Patients that can be scanned but may have degraded images are those with:

   A. Hip pins and replacements

   B. Bone rods and pins

   C. Herrington rods (must usually be away from the area being scanned)

   D. Most implants, but not all (see 2, above)

   E. Some large metal within the body—if questionable, call the physician

   F. Abdominal and thoracic surgical clips

   G. Dural clips and wire mesh secondary to brain surgery

   H. Braces

5. Inpatient items that **cannot** enter magnet area:

   A. Oxygen tanks

   B. IV pumps—IMED, McGaw etc.

   C. ECG monitor

   D. Temporary pacemakers

   E. Ventilators/respirators

   F. Crash carts

   G. Holster monitors

   H. Gowns with snaps

   I. Metallic restraints

   J. Sandbags (check carefully in magnet before scanning)

6. All personnel to include nurses and ambulance personnel shall remove any loose metallic objects to include scissors, paper clips, needles, safety pins, ID badges, analog watches, keys, hemostats, etc.

7. The MRI technologist will remove any patient that codes from the magnet area immediately and bring him or her into the control room. The code response team will not enter the magnet area, but will wait in the control room for the patient.

continues

4–55 continued

8. In case of fire, patients will be immediately removed from the area by the MRI technologist and the fire code called.

9. All patients requiring constant monitoring will be monitored by the radiology/MRI monitor system by a trained nurse. The patient will be attached to the monitor prior to entering the scan room. The monitoring system will be replaced with a regular monitor as soon as possible after the scan is completed and the monitor returned to the radiology department.

10. Any patient requiring conscious sedation will be accompanied by another individual for escorting/driving home. No conscious sedation patient will be released to his or her own efforts to drive home.

Documentation: MRI Patient Screening Record

May be performed by: Trained MRI technologist or (monitoring) trained nurse.

Approved by: _____   _____   _____
                                      Name   Radiology Manager   Date

Courtesy of Rick Sellers, Department of Radiology, Tanner Medical Center, Carrollton, Georgia.

4–56
Protocols To Minimize Radiation Hazards Associated with High-Dose Fluoroscopic Procedures

Division: Clinical Services

Original issue date: _____

Latest revision date: _____

Authorization signature: _____ Date: _____
Director, Medical Imaging Services

Departments/Divisions Affected

Medical Imaging Services
Cardiology
Medical Staff

APPROVAL DISTRIBUTION LIST

Approved by	Title	Date
	Medical Director, Medical Imaging Services	
	Assistant Vice President, Clinical Services	
	Radiation Safety Officer	
	Vice President, Medical Affairs	
	Director, Cardiopulmonary Services	
	Radiation Physicist	

PURPOSE

To reduce the risk of serious X–ray-induced skin injuries to patients during fluoroscopic guided procedures

POLICY

- Exposure times should be kept as short as possible, consistent with the requirement of the study.

- The kilovoltage should be kept as high as possible, consistent with imaging needs. This minimizes the radiation to both patient and staff.

- The field size shall be collimated to the smallest area required for the study.

- All fluoroscopic equipment must be properly maintained and tested for proper radiation output annually.

- The patient should be located as close to the image intensifier as practical (except for magnification studies).

- All users of fluoroscopic equipment must be properly trained and credentialed as required.

continues

4–56 continued

- A licensed radiology technologist or physician must operate portable fluoroscopic equipment.

- Use of portable fluoroscopic equipment should be limited to patients who, for health reasons, may not be safely transported to stationary, shielded fluoroscopic facilities.

- Use of high-dose mode of operation should be limited to procedures where the standard imaging mode does not provide sufficient diagnostic image quality.

- Because radiation exposure is directly proportional to cine frame rates and run times, the lowest frame rates and shortest run times should be used consistent with patient care needs.

- Because radiation exposure is directly proportional to fluoroscopic dose rates, the lowest dose rate should be used consistent with patient care needs.

- Units with last image hold capability should be used for fluoroscopic studies when available.

Source: Adapted from Nancy Hughes, Holy Cross Hospital, Silver Spring, Maryland.

4–57
Personnel Monitoring, Personnel Dosimeters, Film Badges/Ring Badges

Division: Clinical

Original issue date: _____

Latest revision date: _____

Authorization signature: _____   Date: _____
Director, Medical Imaging Services

Departments/Divisions Affected

Medical Imaging
Cardiology
Surgical Services
Speech Therapy

APPROVAL DISTRIBUTION LIST

Approved by	Title	Date
_____	Medical Director, Medical Imaging Services	_____
_____	Assistant VP, Clinical Services	_____
_____	Radiation Safety Officer	_____
_____	Radiation Physicist	_____
_____	Sr. V.P., Patient Care Services	_____
_____		_____
_____		_____

PURPOSE

To effectively measure the amount of radiation an employee is receiving during working hours

POLICY

Personnel dosimeters will be provided to all radiation workers (e.g., radiologists, radiology technologists) and various personnel involved with frequent fluoroscopy procedures and/or therapeutic doses of radioactive material (e.g., speech pathologist, minor surgery nurses, cysto nurse, etc.). The dosimeters shall be worn at all times while doing procedures.

The body badges should be worn at the waist or on the collar except when lead aprons are being worn. When wearing a lead apron, the body badge shall be worn on the collar outside of the apron. Ring badges shall be worn whenever there is a possibility of radiation exposure to hands (e.g., fluoroscopy, special procedures,

continues

4–57 continued

nuclear medicine, etc.). When two badges are worn, one badge should be worn on the inside under the apron at the waist and one badge worn on the collar outside the apron.

Personnel dosimeters will be distributed by the assistant radiation safety officer on the 1st of the month. The previous month's badges should be returned to the assistant radiation safety officer no later than the 8th of the month following distribution. This will allow the weekend staff to change badges.

Maximum annual total effective dose equivalent (TEDE) is 5rem, as set by state and federal regulatory agencies. An investigation will be made of all the film badge exposures exceeding 400 millirem in a monthly period. The investigation will be initiated by the radiation safety officer and will require a statement from the individual involved and his or her manager. Any actions taken will be dependent upon the circumstances and severity of the exposure.

A copy of the monthly dosimeter exposure report will be posted on the bulletin board in the employees' lounge.

Personnel dosimeters shall not be worn when medical radiation procedures (e.g., X-rays, isotope procedures, etc.) are being performed on the wearer.

Source: Adapted from Nancy Hughes, Holy Cross Hospital, Silver Spring, Maryland.

4–58
Workplace Violence Checklist

TRUE NOTATIONS INDICATE A POTENTIAL RISK FOR SERIOUS SECURITY HAZARDS:

_____ T _____ F This industry frequently confronts violent behavior and assaults of staff.

_____ T _____ F Violence occurs regularly where this facility is located.

_____ T _____ F Violence has occurred on the premises or in conducting business.

_____ T _____ F Customers, clients, or coworkers assault, threaten, yell, push, or verbally abuse employees or use racial or sexual remarks.

_____ T _____ F Employees are **NOT** required to report incidents or threats of violence, regardless of injury or severity, to employer.

_____ T _____ F Employees have **NOT** been trained by the employer to recognize and handle threatening, aggressive, or violent behavior.

_____ T _____ F Violence is accepted as "part of the job" by some managers, supervisors, and/or employees.

_____ T _____ F Access and freedom of movement within the workplace are **NOT** restricted to those persons who have a legitimate reason for being there.

_____ T _____ F The workplace security system is inadequate—i.e., door locks malfunction, windows are not secure, and there are no physical barriers or containment systems.

_____ T _____ F Employees or staff members have been assaulted, threatened, or verbally abused by clients and patients.

_____ T _____ F Medical and counseling services have **NOT** been offered to employees who have been assaulted.

_____ T _____ F Alarm systems such as panic alarm buttons, silent alarms, or personal electronic alarm systems are **NOT** being used for prompt security assistance.

_____ T _____ F There is no regular training provided on correct response to alarm sounding.

_____ T _____ F Alarm systems are **NOT** tested on a monthly basis to ensure correct function.

_____ T _____ F Security guards are **NOT** employed at the workplace.

_____ T _____ F Closed circuit cameras and mirrors are **NOT** used to monitor dangerous areas.

_____ T _____ F Metal detectors are **NOT** available or **NOT** used in the facility.

_____ T _____ F Employees have **NOT** been trained to recognize and control hostile and escalating aggressive behaviors, and to manage assaultive behavior.

_____ T _____ F Employees cannot adjust work schedules to use the "Buddy system" for visits to clients in areas where they feel threatened.

_____ T _____ F Cellular phones or other communication devices are **NOT** made available to field staff to enable them to request aid.

_____ T _____ F Vehicles are **NOT** maintained on a regular basis to ensure reliability and safety.

_____ T _____ F Employees work where assistance is **NOT** quickly available.

Source: Creighton University, Omaha, Nebraska.

4–59
Radiation Oncology—Brachytherapy Policy

PURPOSE

This procedure provides general instructions for developing, maintaining, and documenting radiation protection procedures for the use, storage, inventory, and quality control of sources used for brachytherapy; for training of personnel responsible for such use; and for the management of patients treated by brachytherapy.

POLICY

The **Radiation Safety Committee** is responsible for ensuring that each individual who prescribes or uses any form of ionizing radiation in or on humans is properly qualified through training and experience that meets all regulatory requirements. Routine clinical uses of radiation sources for brachytherapy are controlled by qualified radiation oncologists and are not subject to review or approval by the Radiation Safety Committee. Research or experimental applications of radiation to humans must be reviewed and approved by the Human Uses Subcommittee of the Radiation Safety Committee (RPR 40).

Radiation safety procedures for the therapeutic use of sealed radiation sources are prepared, implemented, and supervised by the **Clinical Medical Physicist (CMP)** in the Radiation Oncology Division of the Radiology Department. The **CMP** submits a copy of all new or revised brachytherapy procedures involving any aspect of radiation protection to the **Radiation Safety Officer (RSO)** for review and documentation. The **RSO** submits comments, suggestions, or proposed changes to the **CMP** for action. The **RSO** reports on the status and acceptability of the procedures to the **Radiation Safety Committee** at least annually.

MISADMINISTRATIONS

Procedures for the Quality Management Program (QMP) and misadministrations shall be in accordance with URC Rules in chapter R313-32 and based on recommendations in NRC Regulatory Guide 8.33. MISADMINISTRATIONS (RPR 22) contains a general description of the required procedures.

CONTROL AND STORAGE OF SEALED SOURCES

All radioactive sealed sources used for clinical therapeutic purposes shall be under the control of and stored within the confines of Radiation Oncology, University Health Sciences Center. The acquisition or storage of such sources by other departments or persons must be approved by the Radiation Safety Committee.

BRACHYTHERAPY SOURCE HANDLING

All procedures for brachytherapy source handling (emergency procedures, source inventory, package receipt, waste disposal, etc.) shall be performed according to procedures in the *Radiation Safety Manual and Procedures*, in compliance with URC Rules, and based on recommendations in the applicable appendixes of Guide DRC-MED, July 1996 and in applicable NCRP Reports.

BRACHYTHERAPY SOURCE IMPLANTATION

Most temporary implants will be inserted into the patient in the patient's room. Some temporary implants and all permanent implants will be inserted into the patient in the operating room. Implantation procedures shall utilize all necessary precautions in accordance with established radiation safety procedures. These procedures shall be based on URC Rules from chapter R313-32, recommendations in Appendix Q of Guide DRC-MED, July 1996, and recommendations in applicable NCRP Reports.

continues

4–59 continued

TRAINING

The CMP shall ensure that all Radiation Oncology personnel and nurses involved in care of patients undergoing brachytherapy have received appropriate radiation safety training. Documentation of radiation safety training for these personnel shall be provided to the Radiological Health Department.

All staff radiation oncologists involved in brachytherapy must be certified by the American Board of Radiology or meet the training requirements stated in chapter R313-32 of the URC Rules.

Medical physicists, dosimetrists, and radiation therapy technologists who independently handle brachytherapy sources must be certified or have equivalent training and experience.

SUPPORT SERVICES

The RSO shall be responsible for radiological evaluations, leak testing of sealed sources, and calibration of portable survey instruments in accordance with RADIOLOGICAL LABORATORY EVALUATIONS (RPR 50), LEAK TESTING OF SEALED SOURCES (RPR 51), and CALIBRATION AND USE OF PORTABLE SURVEY INSTRUMENTS (RPR 52).

REFERENCES

National Council on Radiation Protection and Measurements (NCRP), Bethesda, MD: *Precautions in the Management of Patients Who Have Received Therapeutic Amounts of Radionuclides,* 1970.

Protection Against Radiation from Brachytherapy Sources, 1972.

US Nuclear Regulatory Commission (NRC): *Guide for the Preparation of Applications for Medical Use Programs,* Reg. Guide 10.8, Rev. 2, 1987.

Quality Management Program, Reg. Guide 8.33, 1991.

University of Utah, *Radiation Safety Manual and Procedures,* Radiation Procedures and Records.

Utah Department of Environmental Quality, Division of Radiation Control: Radioactive Material License No. UT 1800001 issued to the University of Utah.

Guide DRC-MED, July 1996.

Standards for Protection against Radiation, *Utah Radiation Control Rules,* R313-15.

Medical Use of Radioactive Material, *Utah Radiation Control Rules,* R313-32.

Source: The University of Utah Radiological Health Department, Salt Lake City, Utah.

MANAGEMENT OF HUMAN RESOURCES

4–60
Manager Primer: Imaging Visit[1]

During the imaging services visit, the surveyor assesses the settings where diagnostic radiology, radiation oncology, and nuclear medicine procedures are performed. This activity lasts approximately 45 minutes. It is important to note areas may be surveyed prior to the scheduled visit. Surveyors may jump ahead of the schedule or even return to your area if they have free time.

WHO WILL PARTICIPATE?

- Medical director of radiology services
- Administrative director of radiology services
- Chief diagnostic radiology technologist
- Medical directors of appropriate settings (such as nuclear medicine services, oncology services), as appropriate
- Other staff you may designate

WHAT WILL OCCUR?

Visits to Imaging Services Include the Following Elements

- An orientation to the setting(s) with the director(s)
- A meeting with staff members and a review of medical records
- A tour of the area

The surveyor begins the visit by briefly discussing the site and the purpose of the visit with all directors of sections, services, or departments providing imaging services. He or she will select standards to address during this activity based on issues raised in the document review and other survey activities.

WHAT DOCUMENTS NEED TO BE AVAILABLE?

Information accompanying any patients who are in the area at the time of the visit. Quality control data may also be reviewed.

Sample Questions the Surveyor May Ask during the Visit

1. Describe how patients are involved in giving informed consent. (RI.1.2.1)

2. How does your hospital demonstrate respect for the following patient needs:

    - Confidentiality (RI.1.3.1)
    - Privacy (RI.1.3.2)
    - Security (RI.1.3.3)
    - Resolution of complaints (RI.1.3.4)

3. Does the environment provide for patients' privacy? (RI.1.3.2)

---

[1]These questions serve as an adjunct to the Joint Commission Continual Readiness Process. Please see the Hospital Joint Commission Intranet site for additional survey preparatory tools.

continues

4–60 continued

4. When the report of diagnostic testing should include clinical interpretation, is adequate clinical information provided with the request? (PE.1.5.1)

5. Describe how radiographic contrast media are stored, controlled, distributed, administered, and monitored. (TX.3.3)

6. Is there appropriate equipment available should patients require resuscitation services? (TX.8)

7. What assessment procedures do you use to determine the individual's acceptance for entry to this service? (CC.2)

8. What essential information do you need to determine the appropriateness of the individual's entry to this setting? (CC.2.1)

9. How do you provide for coordination among the health professional(s) and service(s) or setting(s) involved in patient care? (CC.5)

10. What aspects of care provided in this setting do you measure, analyze, and improve? (PI.3–PI.5)

11. How does performance in this service relate to your hospital's mission and strategic planning processes? (LD.1.1–LD.1.1.1)

12. Are the services appropriate to the scope and level of care? (LD.1.3.2)

13. What information is available relative to patient satisfaction with the services provided? (LD.1.3.3.1)

14. Are services available in a timely manner to meet patient needs? (LD.1.3.4–LD.1.3.4.1)

15. Do the leaders collaborate with departmental staff for the development of departmental budgets? (LD.1.5.2)

16. Are there any issues relating to uniform performance of patient care processes? (LD.1.6)

17. Are the goals and scope of the setting's services defined? (LD.1.7.1)

18. What programs do you have to promote recruitment, retention, development, and recognition of staff members, especially job-related educational programs? (LD.1.9–LD.1.9.1)

19. Is there evidence on bulletin boards of educational opportunities for staff? (LD.1.9)

20. Has the hospital considered clinical practice guidelines in the design or improvement of clinical processes? (LD.1.10)

21. If clinical practice guidelines are used, how do hospital leaders identify or set criteria to guide the selection and implementation of the guidelines? (LD.1.10.1)

22. Who is involved in the review and approval of clinical practice guidelines selected prior to implementation? (LD.1.10.2)

23. Describe the process for how clinical practice guidelines are monitored for their effectiveness. (LD.1.10.3)

24. Do department directors determine the qualifications and competence of department personnel who are not licensed independent practitioners, but are involved in the provision of health care? (LD.2.5)

25. Is there evidence of communication across the hospital? If so, what? (LD.3–LD.3.4; LD.4.3.1–LD.4.3.3)

26. Within this patient care setting, is there evidence of plans and performance standards for the following programs:

   - Safety (EC.2.1)

   - Security (EC.2.2)

   - Hazardous materials and waste (EC.2.3)

continues

4–60 continued

- Emergency preparedness (EC.2.4)
- Life safety (EC.2.5)
- Medical equipment (EC.2.6)
- Utilities (EC.2.7)

27. Have staff members been oriented to the environment of care and educated about environment of care issues? Do they perform their responsibilities under the environment of care management plans? (EC.2.8)

28. Do you have regular emergency drills? (EC.2.9.1)

29. Do you have fire drills on a quarterly basis? (EC.2.9.2)

30. Have you performed hazard surveillance surveys in this setting at least every six months? (EC.2.10.1)

31. Has your setting maintained, tested, and inspected life safety elements of the environment of care? Has your hospital documented the required testing of fire alarm, detection, and extinguishing systems? (EC.2.10.2)

32. Have you maintained, tested, and inspected medical equipment in this setting? (EC.2.10.3)

33. Has your department maintained, tested, and inspected utility systems, including the emergency power system? (EC.2.10.4–EC.2.10.4.1)

34. Is there adequate privacy to reflect sensitivity to and respect for the patient? (EC.3.3)

35. How do your leaders define the following:

- The qualifications and responsibilities of staff working in this setting
- A system to evaluate how well staff responsibilities are met
- The number of staff needed to fulfill the setting's mission (HR.1–HR.2)

36. How do you monitor and adjust staffing levels based on patient needs? (HR.2)

37. How do you encourage and support staff self-development and learning? (HR.3.1)

38. Do staff members receive an orientation to the department and initial job training and information? (HR.4)

39. Does each staff member participate in ongoing inservice education sessions and other related training to increase his or her knowledge of specific work-related issues? (HR.4.2)

40. How does the department manager determine whether staff are competent to perform assigned duties and, when appropriate, provide care for the special needs and behaviors of specific age groups? (HR.5)

41. Are the information and data you require for patient care provided in an accurate and timely fashion? (IM.5)

42. What types of aggregate data do you have available to staff to support patient care and operations decisions? (IM.8)

43. Do you have adequate resources and services available to meet the knowledge-based information needs of the medical staff? (IM.9)

44. Describe the following:

- The process for reporting information about infections (IC.3)
- Actions you have taken to reduce the risk of or prevent nosocomial infections (IC.4)
- Actions you have taken to control outbreaks of identified nosocomial infections (IC.5)

Source: Rusty McNew.

4–61
Reporting Noncompliant Conduct in Research or Sponsored Programs

I. PURPOSE

The primary purpose of the research compliance reporting process is to provide nonthreatening ways for employees and agents of _____ to report any activity or conduct that they suspect is not in compliance with the *Research and Sponsored Programs Compliance Plan* (Plan) or with applicable federal or state laws and regulations. Information received through the research compliance reporting process will be used to investigate, verify, and correct any identified noncompliant conduct in research or sponsored program activity.

II. POLICY

Employees, students, and agents of _____ who know or suspect that noncompliant conduct is occurring or has occurred in any research or sponsored program activities conducted and/or approved through _____ should report such conduct. No person shall be retaliated against by _____ or any of its employees, students, or agents for making a good-faith report of suspected noncompliant conduct in research or sponsored program activities.

III. SCOPE

This policy applies to all full-time and part-time faculty, administrators, staff, volunteers, students, and agents of _____.

IV. PROCEDURE

A. Reporting Noncompliant Conduct

1. **University research oversight committees, boards, and offices:** Individuals who know or suspect that noncompliant conduct is occurring or has occurred should first discuss their concerns with their immediate supervisor, if appropriate. As necessary, concerned individuals should then contact the appropriate University research oversight committee, board, or office responsible for the element of research compliance in question, as described in the Plan. Concerned individuals who do not know which committee, board, or office to contact or who have a general research compliance concern should contact the Research Compliance Officer.

2. **Research Compliance Hotline:** The Research Compliance Officer shall establish and maintain a Research Compliance Hotline to allow individuals to anonymously report noncompliance in research or sponsored program activities. Any person may call the confidential Research Compliance Hotline to report any known or suspected noncompliant conduct in research or sponsored program activities. Anyone who intentionally makes a false report or misuses the Research Compliance Hotline shall be subject to discipline.

B. Confidentiality of Individuals Reporting Noncompliant Conduct

All reports regarding suspected noncompliant conduct shall be maintained in a confidential manner to the extent allowed by law. Persons who wish to remain anonymous may report concerns using the Research Compliance Hotline.

Individuals receiving reports of noncompliant conduct shall maintain the confidentiality of the person making the report, shall utilize the procedures in this policy to obtain information, and shall confidentially submit the

continues

4–61 continued

information to the Research Compliance Officer for further action. Except as required by law, no one shall disclose the name of anyone making a report of noncompliant conduct without the express consent of the person making the report.

A caller who uses the Research Compliance Hotline and wishes to remain anonymous will be assigned a tracking number. Callers who do not want to provide contact information will then be able to follow up by calling the Research Compliance Hotline and referencing their assigned tracking number.

C. Notice of the Research Compliance Hotline Number

The Research Compliance Officer shall provide a current notice of the Research Compliance Hotline number to all University vice presidents, deans, and department heads to be posted in noticeable locations for employees, students, and agents working in those locations.

D. Procedures for Receiving Reports of Noncompliant Conduct

All reports of noncompliant conduct shall be handled in a confidential manner, according to the following guidelines:

1. **Recording Information:** Persons receiving reports of noncompliant conduct shall use the Report of Noncompliant Conduct Information Sheet (Attachment A) to obtain the information necessary for investigating the complaint. The completed Report of Noncompliant Conduct Information Sheet shall be forwarded to the Research Compliance Officer, who shall maintain the confidential information in a secure location.

2. **Handling Calls to the Research Compliance Hotline:** Calls to the Research Compliance Hotline shall be handled by the Research Compliance Office. The following procedures are to be followed in answering a call to the Hotline:

   a. **Identification:** Callers shall be asked if they want to give their name, department, and contact telephone number. If a caller wishes to remain anonymous, a tracking number shall be assigned to the caller. Anonymous callers can follow up by calling the Research Compliance Hotline and referencing their assigned tracking number.

   b. **Calls During University Business Hours (Monday–Friday, 8:00 AM–4:30 PM):** In most cases, calls to the Research Compliance Hotline during University business hours will be handled by the Research Compliance Officer. If the Research Compliance Officer is unavailable, the caller will have the option of either leaving a message on voice mail or contacting Associate General Counsel to report any suspected noncompliant activity or conduct. A caller who chooses to contact Associate General Counsel will have the option of remaining anonymous.

   c. **Calls Outside Regular Business Hours (including weekends and holidays):** During non-business hours, calls to the Research Compliance Hotline will be handled through the voicemail system for the Research Compliance Hotline. Hotline callers will be given three options:

   - To call back during business hours if they do not want to leave information on the voicemail system.

   - To leave their name and phone number or other contact information on the voicemail system. Callers who leave contact information will be contacted within a reasonable time, preferably the next business day.

   - To leave a voicemail message regarding the suspected noncompliant conduct or activity. Callers who leave a message regarding noncompliant conduct or activity should also leave contact information or should call back on the next business day to follow up on the report.

continues

4–61 continued

E. Investigating Reports of Noncompliant Conduct

Before initiating investigation of any report of noncompliant conduct, the Research Compliance Officer shall contact the General Counsel's Office. The General Counsel's Office shall decide whether or not to oversee any investigation. If the General Counsel's Office decides not to oversee the investigation, then the Research Compliance Officer shall be primarily responsible for conducting or supervising the investigation. In most cases, the Research Compliance Officer will forward anonymous Research Compliance Hotline reports (using only the tracking number for identification) to the appropriate University research oversight committee, board, or office for further investigation and action according to its policies and procedures for addressing noncompliance. The written results of such investigations, including any corrective action taken or recommended, shall be given to the Research Compliance Officer.

After receiving the written investigation results, the Research Compliance Officer shall ensure that appropriate corrective action, if any is required, has been taken or is implemented. The Research Compliance Officer, in consultation with the General Counsel's Office, shall determine if any government or private funding agency must be notified prior to, during, or after any investigation.

V. ADMINISTRATION AND INTERPRETATIONS

Questions regarding this policy may be addressed to the Research Compliance Officer or General Counsel.

VI. AMENDMENTS OR TERMINATION

This policy may be amended or terminated at any time.

continues

4–61 continued

REPORT OF NONCOMPLIANT CONDUCT
INFORMATION SHEET

Date: _____   Time (if applicable): _____

Reporter's name (optional and confidential): _____

If anonymous, tracking number: _____

Reporter's department (optional and confidential): _____

Reporter's phone number (optional and confidential): _____

Report received and recorded by: _____

Method of contact:

☐ Telephone, Research Compliance Hotline   ☐ E-mail
☐ Telephone, other   ☐ Other _____
☐ In person

Information to obtain from reporter:

a. Name(s) and department of individuals involved in alleged noncompliance: _____

_____

_____

_____

b. Description of suspected noncompliance, including date(s) and location(s), as applicable: _____

_____

_____

_____

c. Name(s) of any other persons who may have knowledge regarding this matter (to remain confidential for
    purposes of investigating the alleged misconduct): _____

_____

_____

_____

d. Has the suspected noncompliant conduct been reported to anyone else?   ☐ Yes   ☐ No

e. If Yes, obtain the following information:

   1. Name of person(s) reported to: _____

   2. Date the report was made: _____

   3. Was the report written or oral? _____

f. Can the reporter provide any documentation to assist in an investigation?   ☐ Yes   ☐ No

g. Is the reporter willing to meet with the Research Compliance Officer and/or the chair
    of the associated regulatory committee?   ☐ Yes   ☐ No

continues

4-61 continued

The following is to be completed by the Research Compliance Officer.

This report has been received by and/or forwarded to the following (check all that apply) for investigation and follow-up:

☐ Research Compliance Officer

☐ Research Compliance Committee

☐ Institutional Review Board

☐ Institutional Animal Care and Use Committee

☐ Institutional Biosafety Committee

☐ Radiation Safety Committee

☐ Campus Safety Committee

☐ Grants Administration

☐ Controller's Office

☐ General Counsel's Office

☐ Internal Audit Department

The Research Compliance Officer shall attach information related to investigation, follow-up, and any disciplinary action taken.

Date investigation and file closed: _____

Source: Creighton University, Omaha, Nebraska.

4–62
Adverse/Unanticipated Events Report: Internal

IRB #: _____

AE ID: _____

1. PI: [Name of Principal investigator or Student Investigator]

   Phone(s):   Fax: E-Mail:

   Address:

2. Contact: [Name of person you designate to be the primary contact for all IRB communication]

   Phone(s):   Fax: E-Mail:

   _____

3. Study Title: [Must match exactly the titles for protocol and funding proposal]

   _____

4. Type of Report: ☐ Initial   ☐ Follow-up for report dated:

5. A. Date of event (onset):

   B. Date report of event received:

   C. Date this test article (i.e., drug, biologic, device, or procedure) was initiated with this participant:

   D. Is this event continuing: ☐ Yes.   ☐ No. Date event ended:

   E. Is the use of this test article continuing with this participant?

      ☐ Yes.   ☐ No. Date use ended:

6. Was this event serious?

   ☐ No.
   ☐ Yes. Please answer A <u>and</u> B:

   A. Severity of AE: (check one)   B. Outcomes of AE: (check all that apply)

      ☐ Mild   ☐ Hospitalization of subject
      ☐ Moderate   ☐ Prolonged hospitalization of subject
      ☐ Severe   ☐ Permanent disability of subject
      ☐ Life-threatening   ☐ Death of subject—Was an autopsy performed?
      ☐ Fatal   ☐ Yes ☐ No

7. A. In your opinion, was this event related to the use of a test article (i.e., drug, biologic, device, or procedure)?

      ☐ Yes   ☐ Maybe   ☐ Unknown   ☐ No. If no, please indicate cause:
                                                ☐ Underlying disease (including progression)
                                                ☐ Concomitant medication
                                                ☐ Other: [Please specify]

   B. Please discuss how you reached this conclusion:

continues

4–62 continued

8. Was this event unanticipated? ☐ Yes ☐ No

9. Subject ID# (if applicable): _____ Age: _____ Gender: _____

10. At which site did the event occur:

11. Please describe the AE, including relevant history and clinical observations; also discuss any pre-existing conditions (specify whether active or inactive at time of AE) that could have precipitated this event:

12. Please discuss all relevant actions taken and/or treatments provided to resolve this AE:

13. Has the same reaction occurred previously in this study?
    ☐ No.
    ☐ Yes.
       A. How many times locally:
       B. If applicable, what is the total number of times this same reaction has occurred at all sites and what is the total number enrolled at all sites:

14. Does this study involve recombinant DNA or gene transfer?
    ☐ No.
    ☐ Yes. Is this AE related to the recombinant DNA or gene transfer test substance?
       ☐ No.
       ☐ Yes. Please attach a copy of your NIH/OBA Serious Adverse Event Report
          (www.4.od.nih.gov/oba/rac/documents1.htm) <u>and</u> submit a copy NIH/OBA SAER to
          the Institutional Biosafety Committee.

15. In your opinion, do any of these events require a change in the currently approved informed consent document?
    ☐ Yes. Please attach one copy with the changes highlighted <u>and</u> one clean copy.
    ☐ No. Please explain why these events should not be included in the consent form:

16. Should the protocol be modified to protect subjects?
    ☐ Yes. Please attach one copy with the changes highlighted <u>and</u> one clean copy.
    ☐ No. Please explain why the study should be continued without modification of the protocol:

17. Do other agencies need to be notified (e.g., funding agency, FDA, NIH)?
    ☐ No.
    ☐ Yes. Has this AE been reported to these agencies?
       ☐ Yes.
       ☐ No. Please explain why not:

continues

4–62 continued

18. Was this AE Report submitted late?
    ☐ No.
    ☐ Yes. Please explain:

19. Principal Investigator's Statement of Assurance

    I confirm the accuracy of this report.

    I certify that this research study is being conducted in accordance with the terms of the *Assurance* and the policies of _____ and its affiliates for the protection of human subjects participating in research.

    _____   _____
    Signature of Principal Investigator   Date

    (or Student Investigator)

Instructions for submitting this AE Report

1. Use this AE Report for adverse events/safety reports that have occurred in studies in which the study personnel are employed by _____ or its affiliates.

2. Please designate an **AE ID** to identify this AE for use in all correspondence with the IRB. Place this identification code at the top of the first page of this form.

3. Please submit two copies of this completed AE Report with all supporting documentation to:

Division of Research Compliance
(Address)
Fax number: (xxx) xxx-xxxx

Source: University of South Florida Office of Research, Tampa, Florida.

4–63
Training and Experience Form:
Medical Authorized User or Radiation Safety Officer

1. Name of proposed authorized user or radiation safety officer

2. Certification—Please attach a copy of certificate

SPECIALTY BOARD	CATEGORY	MONTH AND YEAR CERTIFIED

3. Training received in basic radioisotope handling techniques

		Type and Length of Training	
FIELD OF TRAINING A	LOCATION AND DATES OF TRAINING B	LECTURE/ LABORATORY COURSES (HOURS) C	SUPERVISED LABORATORY EXPERIENCE (HOURS) D
a. Radiation physics and instrumentation			
b. Radiation protection			
c. Mathematics pertaining to use and measurement of radioactivity			
d. Radiation biology			
e. Radiopharmaceutical chemistry			

4. Experience with radiation (actual use of radioisotopes or equivalent experience) (Use back if more space is needed.)

Isotope	Maximum amount per procedure	Duration of experience From To	Type of use ❏ Diagnostic ❏ Therapeutic
Institution			Phone number ( )
Address (number, street)		City State	ZIP code
Duties and responsibilities if Radiation Safety Officer (RSO)			

Isotope	Maximum amount per procedure	Duration of experience From To	Type of use ❏ Diagnostic ❏ Therapeutic
Institution			Phone number ( )
Address (number, street)		City State	ZIP code
Duties and responsibilities if Radiation Safety Officer (RSO)			

Isotope	Maximum amount per procedure	Duration of experience From To	Type of use ❏ Diagnostic ❏ Therapeutic
Institution			Phone number ( )
Address (number, street)		City State	ZIP code
Duties and responsibilities if Radiation Safety Officer (RSO)			

I hereby certify that all information contained in this statement is true and correct.	
Signature of proposed user	Date

continues

4–63 continued

This part must be completed by the applicant's physician's preceptor. If more than one preceptor, obtain a separate statement from each. (**NOTE**: Physicians who have obtained their Diagnostic Radiology, Nuclear Medicine, or Oncology board certification within the last five years need not submit the preceptor statement.)

1. Clinical training and experience
    KEY TO COLUMN C—Personal participation consists of:

    a. Supervised examination of patients to determine the suitability for radionuclide diagnosis and/or treatment and recommendation for prescribed dosage.

    b. Dose calibration and actual administration of dose to the patient including calculation of the radiation dose and related measurements.

    c. Supervised interpretation of results of diagnostic studies.

    d. Adequate period of training to enable physician to manage radioactive patients and follow patients through diagnosis and therapy.

ISOTOPE A	CONDITIONS DIAGNOSED OR TREATED B	NUMBER OF CASES INVOLVING PERSONAL PARTICIPATION C	COMMENTS (Additional information or comments may be submitted in duplicate on separate sheets) D
	Thyroid scan		
	Thyroid uptake		
	Lung perfusion scan		
	Xenon ventilation study		
	Aerosol ventilation scan		
	Renal flow scan		
	Brain scan		
	Liver/spleen scan		
	Bone scan		
	Gastroesophageal study		
	LeVeen shunt study		
	Cystogram		
	Dacryocystogram		
	Cardiac perfusion scan		
	Cardiac stress ventriculogram		
	Cardiac rest ventriculogram		
	Gallium scan		
P-32 (soluble)	Treatment of polycythemia vera, leukemia and bone metastases		
P-32 (coltoidal)	Intracavitary treatment		
I-131	Treatment of thryoid carcinoma		
	Treatment of hyperthyroidism		
Au-196	Intracavitary treatment		
Co-60 or Ca-137	Interstitial treatment		
	Intracavitary treatment		
I-125 or Ir-192	Interstitial treatment		
Co-60 or Ca-137	Teletherapy treatment		
Sr-90	Treatment of eye disease		
	Radiopharmaceutical preparation		
Mo-99/Tc-99m	Generator		
Sn-113/In-113m	Generator		
Tc-99m	Reagent kits		
Ir-192	HDR		
	LDR		
Co-60	Gamma knife		

continues

4–63 continued

ISOTOPE A	CONDITIONS DIAGNOSED OR TREATED B	NUMBER OF CASES INVOLVING PERSONAL PARTICIPATION C	COMMENTS (Additional information or comments may be submitted in duplicate on separate sheets D
Other			

2. Dates and total number of hours received in clinical radioisotope training

LOCATION	DATES		CLOCK HOURS OF TRAINING
	FROM	TO	

The training and experience indicated above was obtained under the supervision of:

Name of preceptor	Name of institution		
Mailing address (number, street)	City	State	Zip Code
Materials license number(s)			
Preceptor's signature	Print preceptor's name		Date

Source: California Department of Health Services, Sacramento, California.

4–64
Request for Radiation Exposure History and/or Training Verification
(Please type or print legibly)

Organization _____

Address _____

_____

_____

_____

Attention   Radiation Safety Officer, if known, or Supervisor *(indicate which)*

To whom it may concern:

Please send the following to the address indicated below:

☐ My radiation exposure history

☐ Verification that I received radiation safety training appropriate for independent work with radioactive materials or radiation-generating machines.

Surname: _____   Given names: _____

Previous (maiden) or other surnames known by: _____

Soc. Sec. No.: _____

Inclusive dates of work with radiation—From: _____   To: _____

Please send the requested information to:

Radiation Safety Officer
Radiological Health Department
123 Street
City, State 00000

Signature: _____   Date: _____

Source: The University of Utah Radiological Health Department, Salt Lake City, Utah.

4–65
Radiation User Training and Personal Data
(Please type or print legibly)

Surname (family or last name): _____

Given names (first and middle or initial): _____

Previous (maiden) or other surnames known by: _____

Soc. Sec. No. (not University ID No.): _____ Sex: Male ☐ Female ☐

Institution affiliation, if other than the University: _____

Birth date: Month _____ Day _____ Year _____ Degrees: _____

Job Title or Duties: _____

Department: _____ Division/Section: _____

Work Location: _____ Phone: _____

Responsible User: _____ RU #: _____ or Supervisor: _____

Date of first radiation use at University: _____ Date(s) of University Training: _____

Required radiation safety training includes the following topics:

1. nature of radiation sources
2. biological effects and risk estimates
3. risks to the unborn and control of prenatal exposure
4. ALARA principle and minimizing exposure
5. correct use of protective devices
6. provisions of regulations and licenses
7. response to radiation emergencies
8. responsibilities and rights of radiation users
9. availability of monitoring and inspection reports, and, for radioisotope users only
10. safe handling and storage of radioactive materials

Have you had previous work experience involving occupational radiation exposure?   Yes ☐   No ☐

Have you received training on ALL of the topics listed above at another institution?   Yes ☐   No ☐

If you checked "Yes" for either of the above statements, complete a "Request for Radiation Exposure History and/or Training Verification" for each institution or employer. Note: Substitution of prior training needs approval from the RSO and may require passing a written exam.

All radiation users with board certification who will be responsible for prescribing, computing, preparing, or delivering any kind of radiation doses to *humans* must have a copy of their specialty board certificate on file in your department.

The information above is accurate and complete. I understand that I may communicate directly, in confidence and without prejudice, with the Radiation Safety Officer, the State Division of Radiation Control, or the U.S. Nuclear Regulatory Commission on any matter concerning radiation protection.

Signature: _____ Date: _____

Source: The University of Utah Radiological Health Department, Salt Lake City, Utah.

4–66

Recommendations Regarding Pregnant Employees in the Radiology Department

PURPOSE

To provide guidelines for pregnant employees

BACKGROUND INFORMATION

Exposure limits during pregnancy are based on NCRP requirements, which state that exposure shall not exceed 0.5 rem (to the fetus) during the entire gestational period (limited to 50 mrem per month)

The embryo or fetus is subject to greater risk of injury than an adult per unit radiation dose. However, the University cannot be aware of or control the dose without the full cooperation of the pregnant employee. Any employee who believes she may be pregnant should notify her supervisor. With the cooperation of the employee, the University will take all reasonable actions to evaluate and limit the embryonic-fetal dose as required.

A report titled "A Concept and Proposal Concerning the Radiation Exposure of Women" prepared under contract with the Bureau of Radiological Health, by Brown, Shaver, and Lamel of the University of California Medical Center, San Francisco, makes the following recommendations regarding pregnant radiological technologists:

GUIDELINES*

Therefore, the following general guidelines shall be observed:

1. Review the previous six months' exposure records.

2. If these records indicate exposure rates of less than 0.5 rem per year, the same work assignments can continue with periodic monitoring for guidance. This provision will cover nearly all-diagnostic and therapeutic technologists except those concerned with implant therapy, and certain radioisotope technologists.

3. If the guidelines of above paragraph are not practical, then the work assignment should be changed before the exposure estimates reach 0.5 rem for the fetus.

    A review of radiation exposure data for Radiology Department personnel indicates that by far the majority of readings fall within the required limit of 50 mrem per month. This is in accord with the comments of experts who have stated that pregnancy does not automatically require that a female technologist or radiologist be removed from the clinic (see Bushong, S.C., "The Development of Radiation Protection in Diagnostic Radiology, CRC Press, P. 41, and J. Nucl Med. Technol, 14, Dec. 1986, p. 218-224). The same texts also recommend that pregnant employees not be assigned to "high risk" areas, such as Fluoroscopy, Special Procedures, radionuclide therapy, etc.

    MRI involves three types of electromagnetic fields: a static magnetic field, a radio frequency field, and magnetic gradient fields that are pulsed on and off. Each of these forms of electromagnetic radiation can produce significant biological effects in humans if applied at sufficiently high exposure levels. While numerous studies have been performed to identify potential biological effects of MRI and none of these has determined significant hazards, the data are insufficient to assume absolute safety. Therefore, the FDA has issued guidelines for exposure to the above-mentioned electromagnetic radiation.

    Because of the shielding design of an MRI facility, only a very low-level static magnetic field (5 gauss) is present in the areas outside the room housing the magnet. In addition, RF and gradient electromagnetic fields are also virtually self-contained.

*FDA Guidelines for MRI.

continues

4–66 continued

The FDA guideline for static magnetic fields recommends maximum exposures of 2T for the head and trunk, and 5T for extremities. In addition, the FDA suggests that pregnancy may be contraindication for patient scanning.

While no definitive guidelines have been published for employees, many institutions around the United States have adopted the policy that pregnant technologists working at MRI facilities should not be exposed long term to static fields greater than 10 gauss (0.001 T). In addition, such technologists should not be exposed to the high levels of RF and gradient electromagnetic fields. Thus pregnant technologists should not be in the magnet room during a patient scan, and should limit their time in the magnet room before and after patient scans.

RECOMMENDATIONS

1. Pregnant personnel should not be assigned to work in "high risk" areas. These would include Special Procedures and Fluoroscopy in Diagnostic Radiology; the simulator and radioactive storage room in Radiation Therapy; and the hot lab in Radiopharmacy.

2. They should not work with uncontained radioactive materials. This would apply to Nuclear Medicine and would include work in the Radiopharmacy and any "clean-up" responsibilities for spills and accidents.

3. They should not be assigned responsibilities requiring them to work in close proximity to radiation sources. For example, they should not hold patients during radiographic procedures in Diagnostic Radiology. They should not work with patients containing therapeutic radionuclides in Radiation Therapy or Nuclear Medicine (I-131, P-32, etc). These restrictions should apply regardless of whether or not protective shielding is used.

4. They should work in protected areas or wear protective clothing whenever radiation sources are present or active. Adaptable work areas would include control booths or control stations in Diagnostic Radiology or Radiation Therapy. May operate cameras or scanners in Nuclear Medicine. Nuclear Medicine technologist is counseled to apply time-distance and shielding whenever possible during patient scans. Lead-lined aprons afford little protection at most gamma ray energies.

5. Pregnant personnel should wear two dosimeters. One badge on the collar and one at waist level (belly). When lead aprons are worn, the belly badge should be under the apron. All radiation exposure data should be carefully monitored.

6. Pregnant technologists, with the exception of Nuclear Medicine technologists, should not be assigned weekend or night call responsibilities, because this may require violation of one or more of the above restrictions.

7. These recommendations and any supplementary materials should be read by and fully explained to the pregnant employee by either the medical physicist (or the Onsite Radiation Safety Officer in the case of Nuclear Medicine), to make sure she understands the restrictions and the reason for them. Her radiation exposure history and past performance as an employee should be evaluated to determine if there are any questions as to reliability in following the guidelines. If she agrees to continue to work, she will be required to fill out a work release and counseling form indicating that she understands the risks involved and will strictly follow all radiation safety practices together with recommended work restrictions. Her supervisors, to ensure that the guidelines are being followed, will carefully monitor her activities.

8. These recommendations do not apply to secretarial, clerical, or other employees in the department who do not work with radioactive materials or in radiation areas.

9. Pregnant employees working in the MRI Department are allowed to work in the patient scanning area. However, the employee should not be present in the magnet room during a patient scan to avoid exposure to height level RF and gradient electromagnetic fields. In addition, the employee should limit her time in the magnet room before and after patient scans to avoid lengthy exposure to high-level static magnetic fields.

continues

4–66 continued

PROCEDURES

1. When an employee who works in the Department with radioactive materials, and in the diagnostic X-ray areas, or in the MRI Department learns of her pregnancy, she is required to sign a statement indicating her responsibility, and to inform her supervisor immediately that she is pregnant, so that precautionary measures can be taken in her work assignment.

2. The supervisor will request the pregnant employee fill out a Work Release and Counseling Form.

3. The employee will sign the above form indicating her desire to continue employment in the Department. The work supervisor will determine if any changes in work assignment are needed based on the recommendations found in Section 4-25 of the Policy and Procedures Manual governing pregnant employees. The supervisor will indicate what work assignment exceptions are necessary and then sign the form.

4. The employee will then report to the Department Medical Physicist or On-Site Radiation Safety Officer for further counseling in radiation protection and the effect of electromagnetic radiation—both ionizing and non-ionizing—and static magnetic fields on fetal development. The Physicist or On-Site Radiation Safety Officer will review the work assignment, recommend any changes to the employee's supervisor, and order an additional belly badge. All declared pregnant employees will be issued a belly badge. He/she will then sign the request indicating that he/she concurs with the recommendations.

5. The employee will then sign the Counseling portion of the form indicating that she has received instruction in electromagnetic radiation—both ionizing and non-ionizing—and static magnetic fields and their effects on the fetus, and will follow all required safety practices.

6. The completed form will then be placed in the employee's personnel file.

Employee Responsibility for Reporting Pregnancy Form

(To be completed by all newly hired female employees in Diagnostic, Special Procedures, and Nuclear Medicine)

I understand that should I become pregnant, I have the option of declaring or not declaring my pregnancy to my supervisor. Should I decide to declare my pregnancy, it is my responsibility to inform my supervisor of my condition immediately, so additional protective measures can be taken in my work assignment.

Supervisor_____   Employee_____

Date _____

continues

4–66 continued

Work Release and Counseling Form

TO WHOM IT MAY CONCERN:

I, _____, wish to declare that I am pregnant, and request to continue my current work assignment in the _____ Department at the University Health Sciences Center.

Signed: _____

Date:_____

1. I have reviewed the work assignment of _____and recommend the following changes in accordance with the Department of Radiology Policy and Procedure Manual:

    Signed: _____

    Supervisor:_____

    Date _____

2. I have reviewed the above changes in work assignment and the radiation history of the employee, and do not expect that continued employment will result in a fetal dose exceeding the UDRC maximum permissible limit of 500 mRem per gestational period. I concur with the above recommendations.

    Signed: _____

    Title: Medical Physicist:_____

    Date _____

3. I have received counseling on the effects of ionizing radiation on my unborn child from the Department Medical Physicist, and will follow the above recommendations and continue to practice good radiation safety.

    Signed: _____

    Date _____

Source: University of Utah Radiological Health Department, Salt Lake City, Utah.

4–67
Radiologist On-Call Policy

RADIOLOGIST ON-CALL ("O.D.") (OR OFFICER OF THE DAY)

POLICY

The night O.D. is required to be present in the hospital, accessible to the paging system, from 5:00 PM until 8:00 AM on weekdays, from 8:00 AM Saturday until 8:00 AM on Sunday, and from 8:00 AM Sunday to 8:00 AM on Monday.

During the hours of duty, the O.D. functions as a radiology consultant/administrator, responsible for consultations with clinicians throughout the hospital complex as they are requested. Additionally, it is the O.D.'s responsibility to perform whatever emergency procedures are requested by the staff on the clinical specialties if the procedures requested are clinically indicated and providing the O.D. is competent to perform the examination. If the O.D. has not had sufficient training to perform the examination, it is his responsibility to call on the appropriate senior radiologist for assistance.

For special examinations, such as emergency arteriography, it is the responsibility of the Service requesting the procedure to contact the radiology resident to discuss the matter with him or her. The radiology resident will then contact the appropriate staff radiologist by phone or pager.

For an "after hours" neuroradiologic and peripheral angiographic procedure:

a. If the O.D. has had a rotation through neuroradiology or peripheral angiography, he and the neuroradiology staff person, neuroradiology fellow, or peripheral angiographer on call will perform the examination together.

b. If he has *not* had a rotation through neuroradiology or peripheral angiography, he will contact the senior resident on call who will come in to assist the neuroradiologist or peripheral angiographer.

The O.D. functions as a mediator between clinical staff and radiology technicians whenever this might be necessary.

All emergency procedures must be approved by the radiology O.D., specifically emergency CT scans, nuclear medicine scans, angiograms, or myelograms. The clinical staff may not contact the radiology technologist directly. It is the O.D.'s responsibility to assess the clinical indication and emergent nature of the procedure. If the procedure is warranted, the O.D. will then contact the on-call technologist by pager or phone.

All barium studies and ultrasound studies are performed by the O.D. There are no on-call ultrasound or GI technologists. Emergency excretory urograms are performed in the emergency radiology rooms with the aid of the evening technologists.

Most pediatric emergency cases should be performed in the pediatric radiology department. The pediatric staff radiologist should be consulted for all emergency studies.

All adult emergency room films should be interpreted by the O.D., and a preliminary report should be written on the requisition sheet. The ED films will be reviewed in the AM with the appropriate chest or bone staff radiologist, then dictated by the resident.

The thoracic and ICU boards should be reviewed by the O.D. several times during the night. No preliminary reading report is necessary, but the O.D. should check for possible life-threatening abnormalities such as pneumothorax, free intraperitoneal air, position of lines and tubes, etc. If any possible life-threatening abnormalities are present that require immediate attention, the O.D. will contact the appropriate service and document the contact on the requisition.

Any clinical problems that arise during the night that cannot be resolved by the O.D. should be referred to the staff radiologist of that particular track.

Source: University of Chicago Department of Radiology, Chicago, Illinois.

4–68
Radiology Nursing On-Call Guidelines

I. OUTCOME GOAL

Safe, efficient care in a timely manner maintaining continuity of care during transfers to and from Radiology as well as during the procedure.

II. POLICY

Radiology nursing staff will be on-call from 4:00 PM to 8:00 AM weekdays and on weekends to cover emergent special procedures for patients who come from general care floors and step-down units. Special procedures consist of invasive/interventional angiography procedures such as arteriograms and percutaneous transhepatic cholangiograms (PTC) and biopsy/drainage procedures.

III. SPECIFIC INFORMATION

A. Nursing staff from critical care areas (SICU, Neuro ICU, NICU, L&D, PICU, MICU, CCU, Burn ICU, CRR, PACU, and GI lab) will accompany and provide nursing care for patients during all radiological procedures.

B. Nursing staff from the ED will accompany and provide nursing care and monitoring for all patients on ventilators (not to include patients on home vent), vasoactive drips, multi-system trauma, and rapid infuser needs, and hemodynamically unstable patients that do not fall into categories listed above.

Radiology nurses will provide nursing care and monitoring for the following categories of patients:

Interventional Patients

- Pulmonary arteriogram
- Nephrostomy tube and J tube changes
- Extremities, such as gunshot wounds to legs or arms, or cold legs or extremities
- Subarachnoid bleeds that are not on vent or on vasoactive drips
- Mesenteric studies

CT Patients

- Biopsies
- Drainages
- Abscesses

MRI

- Patients with R/O subarachnoid bleeds, not on vents or vasoactive drips
- Heads
- Spines—If patient has an unstable spine (on backboard), an ED resident must be present for the removal of the backboard. In most cases, the MRI cannot be performed with the patient on a backboard.
- Patients that need moderate sedation

continues

4–68 continued

MRI nurse will need to know if the patient is NPO for 6 hours for food and milk, and NPO for 4 hours for clear liquids. Patients who require pain medicine do not necessarily have to adhere to the NPO guidelines.

C. Under the following conditions, general care or step down patients requiring an emergent procedure other than invasive/interventional procedures will require licensed staff in attendance:

1. hemodynamically unstable

2. require cardiac monitoring, and/or continuous pulse oximetry

3. require sedation during the procedure

There must be communication between the radiology resident, the patient's resident/attending, the nurse caring for the patient/charge nurse, and the technologist to determine the status of the patient. The radiology resident will determine if the radiology nurse on call is needed based on the areas identified above.

D. In some circumstances, patients may not require the care of a licensed nurse, but may require supervision for *safety* measures (e.g., confused/disoriented patients). Unlicensed staff may be appropriate to accompany and supervise the patient during these procedures. The charge nurse will determine when this is the case.

E. The primary responsibility of the radiology on-call nurse or the ICU nurse is to the patient. These responsibilities include the provision and maintenance of nursing care and do not include assisting and/or scrubbing in the technical aspects of the radiological procedure.

IV. EQUIPMENT/SUPPLIES

The following equipment will be available in the Radiology Department for use as needed for patients having a special procedure or biopsy/drainage procedure performed:

A. O_2 with tubing

B. Suction and supplies (catheters)

C. Cardiac monitor

D. Non-invasive blood pressure

E. Pulse oximeter

F. Emergency cart

G. Narcotics and sedatives

V. PROCEDURE (NURSE RESPONSIBILITIES DURING PROCEDURE)

A. Identify the patient.

B. Receive verbal report from nurse caring for patient on unit.

C. Assessment per Radiology adult or pediatric database.

D. Assist technologist as necessary in positioning of patient.

E. Ensure patient has patent IV access and restart as needed.

F. Obtain baseline VS.

continues

4–68 continued

G. Place patient on cardiac monitor, including SaO$_2$, non-invasive blood pressure, observe every 15 minutes, place alarms on.

H. Place patient on supplemental O$_2$ as ordered by radiologist.

I. Vascular cases: VS recorded VS q 5 min after IV sedation analgesia until stable then every 15 minutes with patient's condition documented every 30 minutes.

J. Neuro cases: VS recorded every 15 minutes with patient's condition documented every 15 minutes.

K. Administer medication as prescribed by the radiologist. Ensure consent obtained prior to sedation or narcotic analgesia.

L. Assess, intervene, and notify radiologist of significant change in patient condition (e.g., vagal episodes, hypotensive episodes, etc.).

M. Radiology nurse will communicate verbal report on RN caring for patient on floor/unit, including procedure, medications, changes in condition, and interventions.

N. Document patient condition and to whom report was given at the time of transfer.

O. Accompany patient back to unit if condition warrants to ensure continuity of care (e.g., sedation, unstable, cardiac or other monitoring, *puncture wound, new drain/tube placed*).

VI. CROSS-REFERENCES

Clinical Policy Manual

CL 30-02.03, "Guidelines of Care and Practice: Radiology Patients"

Operations Policy Manual

OP 20-09, "Sedation and Analgesia"

VII. ENDORSEMENT

Patient Care Services Board
Radiology
Practice Committee

APPROVED:
Director, Patient Care Services
Chair, Radiology and Radiological Sciences
Administrator, Radiology Clinical Services

4–69
Non-Hospital Employee Checklist

Instructions: Please complete this form and submit to QM prior to your clinical rotation. A form that is incomplete will not be processed. It is the responsibility of the individual student/faculty to confirm the completeness of this tool and its receipt to QM. By initialing each box, you attest to completing that element of the checklist. This checklist does not constitute a contractual agreement between the individual, student, or faculty and the Health & Hospital System.

Student: _____ School: _____
Social Security Number: _____ Semester: _____ Year: _____
Assigned Unit(s): _____ Rotation Dates/Shifts:_____

Student Category:

☐ Graduate   ☐ Nurse
☐ Undergraduate   ☐ Paramedic
☐ Out of County   ☐ OR Tech
☐ Out of State   ☐ Radiology Tech
☐ Out of Country   ☐ Other _____

School Contact:

Name: _____
Telephone: _____
Pager: _____
Fax: _____
E-mail Address: _____

I. ALL NON-PARKLAND EMPLOYEES COMPLETE THIS SECTION

Immunizations Current:

☐ TB (in the last 6 months)
☐ Hepatitis B
☐ Varicella
☐ Measles
☐ Mumps
☐ Rubella
☐ Tetanus
☐ Diphtheria

Required Safety Education:

☐ Fire & Safety
☐ Hazardous Materials
☐ Electrical Safety
☐ Disaster
☐ Infection Control

☐ Criminal background check completed in the last 6 months (Group One DFW Hospital Council-Beginning Spring 2001)
☐ Drug Screen Negative in the last 6 months (Beginning Spring 2001)
☐ Safety Test Completed
☐ Orientation manual read and will abide by rules and regulations outlined
☐ ID Badge request submitted

II. THIS SECTION FOR GRADUATE NURSING STUDENTS ONLY

☐ Course description on file
☐ Preceptor's letter of agreement (submit to Nursing School Liaison)

III. SIGNATURES

I have read and understand the above and attest to its accuracy to the best of my knowledge.

(Student) Non-Hospital Employee Signature: _____ Initials: _____ Date: _____
(Faculty) Non-Hospital Employee Signature: _____ Initials: _____ Date: _____
(Faculty) Non-Hospital Employee Signature: _____ Initials: _____ Date: _____

Attention: This form must be typewritten and received by Quality Management 1 week prior to the student's clinical rotation. Fax to Nursing School Liaison at _____.

Source: Rusty McNew.

4–70
Compliance Policy Guidelines

The Department of Radiology has a policy on resident interpretation of diagnostic images and procedures.

A teaching physician is a staff radiologist (other than a resident) who involves residents in the care of his or her patients. The teaching physician is responsible for the supervision of the activities of the resident and must review every diagnostic radiologic image.

All interventional radiology procedures require the staff radiologist to be present during the key portion(s) of the procedure. The resident or fellow initially evaluates the patient and then reports to the staff radiologist. The staff radiologist will then decide on the appropriate exam or procedure. All procedures are performed or personally supervised by the staff radiologist. Upon completion, the staff radiologist will discuss the case with the resident/ fellow and a note is written on the patient's chart. The report, including a complete procedure paragraph, is dictated by the resident/fellow or the staff radiologist. All dictated reports are reviewed, edited, and signed by the staff radiologist.

All plain-film emergency radiology examinations are contemporaneously interpreted by the on-call resident until 2300 hours. The examination is then returned to the Emergency Department with the preliminary interpretation on the Diagnostic Imaging Check-in Form (DICF). The Emergency Department Physician or Physician Assistant either agrees, disagrees, or consults with the resident. This is documented on the DICF. After 2300 hours, the Emergency Physician may consult the on-call resident about any examination. All computed tomography, magnetic resonance, ultrasound, and nuclear medicine studies must be preliminarily interpreted by the resident after the exam is performed and documented on the DICF. All other non-emergency examinations will be evaluated by the resident after the films are placed on the viewing alternator. If there are any major findings noted on the exam, the resident contacts the consulting physician and documents this on the DICF. In addition, the on-call faculty radiologist is available to review any examination performed after hours, as requested.

The above examinations are always reviewed by the on-call staff radiologist, the following morning. If there are any discrepant findings, the consulting physician is immediately notified and the findings are documented on the DICF and timed. The resident then dictates the report. All dictated reports are reviewed, edited, and signed by the staff radiologist. The finalized reports are available for the resident to review. The resident will not review any preliminary reports or electronically sign the staff radiologist's reports. All reports that are not signed-off are identified as preliminary. All faculty are encouraged to complete reports prior to a leave. If there are unsigned reports, the Chairman or his or her designee may choose to sign reports. This should affect less than one percent of the exams. Reviewing the exam may be necessary.

Occasionally, the Department of Radiology will hire a substitute radiologist to cover a service when one of the faculty is away or on vacation. The substitute radiologist will function as a faculty radiologist; however, billing will be assigned to the faculty radiologist for whom the substitute radiologist is covering for continuous cover- age periods of 60 days or less. The billing department is notified that services were provided by the substitute radiologist.

The issue of medical necessity is an important one demanded by third-party payers. The department was made aware of proper ICD-9 codes. It is important for referring physicians to provide reasons and proper indications for the examination being requested. The department also implemented a policy that exams will be performed only when a proper indication is present.

Each radiology department head has established a standard exam protocol for the technologist to perform. All exam protocols are subject to change.

The Department of Radiology follows the list of commonly used abbreviations that _____ has established.

continues

4–70 continued

All coding and billing procedures are initially handled by any of the radiology billing personnel. _____, radiology's billing supervisor, may be notified, if needed. The interpreting physician has ultimate coding authority and, occasionally, is asked for assistance. The helpline will be used when there is a discrepancy between the coding personnel and the interpreting physician. All claims are submitted in a timely fashion, currently within one week. If over/under-billing is identified, it is the University and the Department of Radiology's policy to correct the error as quickly as possible and this matter is addressed by the billing supervisor. The Department is aware that failure to correct a claim constitutes civil and/or criminal fraud and punishable by fine/imprisonment and possibly exclusion from federal and/or state health care programs.

Department compliance policies will be updated when necessary and reviewed annually. All department compliance policies and procedures must be approved by the Compliance Committee.

DEPARTMENT EDUCATION AND TRAINING

Training sessions for physicians, staff, and residents will be provided annually and as otherwise necessary. Mandatory attendance is required and a sign-in sheet must be initialed by all department personnel. Ongoing training sessions will be provided as changes occur, and these sessions are also mandatory. The Compliance Officer and Coordinator are responsible for the training/updating sessions, and the Compliance Officer shall ensure that the information is correct and current. Generally, the training sessions will be during a departmental meeting or at a Grand Rounds Conference.

DEPARTMENT MONITORING

There are monthly random coding audits of exams numbering from 3 to 5 exams per physician. This is carried out by _____, the Billing Supervisor for Radiology. If there are questions concerning billing or coding, the interpreting physician is notified and correction, if needed, is made. All department physicians will be randomly audited. Results of the audit will be made available and distributed to department personnel. Relevant findings of the audit will be incorporated into training/improvement sessions. Audit results will be reported quarterly to the department and Compliance Officer. The University Compliance Officer has also instituted regular departmental audits. A monthly billing audit is performed utilizing the HBO system at _____. All exams where a bill has not been generated are reviewed, and a bill issued.

REPORTING AND INVESTIGATION OF NONCOMPLIANT CONDUCT

When noncompliant behavior is observed, it is the Department's policy to handle the problem internally. Initially, the person is educated and trained on appropriate procedure and all pertinent regulations are discussed. If noncompliant behavior continues, a meeting with appropriate department personnel is held and a 6-month probation period is initiated. At this time, the Compliance Officer is notified of the situation and a specific plan is addressed and implemented. The compliance liaison will assist the Compliance Officer with the situation.

A Hotline is available to allow employees and agents to provide information concerning suspected violations. This can be performed in an anonymous fashion.

All radiology employees and agents must review and sign the University compliance plan annually.

Source: Creighton University Medical Center, Omaha, Nebraska.

4–71
Radiology Technologist Competency Evaluation

NAME: _____

DATE: _____

AREA: _____

1. Checks quality of radiographs before returning patients to proper areas of hospital. ___yes   ___no   ___N/A

2. Assists radiologist in the performance of all contrast exams. ___yes   ___no   ___N/A

3. Uses proper techniques to avoid retaking any films. ___yes   ___no   ___N/A

4. Sets up room with proper equipment and supplies. ___yes   ___no   ___N/A

5. Uses proper safety precautions when transporting and operating X-ray equipment. ___yes   ___no   ___N/A

6. Enters patient information and properly makes out charge slips as needed. ___yes   ___no   ___N/A

7. Assists in educating students (new techs) regarding radiology techniques. ___yes   ___no   ___N/A

8. Accepts supervision and maintains good working relationships. ___yes   ___no   ___N/A

9. Accepts and assumes responsibility for job functions performed and is accountable for the results. ___yes   ___no   ___N/A

10. Demonstrates skill in problem solving and follows through on assigned functions. ___yes   ___no   ___N/A

11. Sets priorities needed to perform job functions effectively. ___yes   ___no   ___N/A

12. Responds to patient request for assistance, information, and needs in a timely and empathetic manner. ___yes   ___no   ___N/A

13. Demonstrates knowledge of proper infection control techniques. ___yes   ___no   ___N/A

Comments:

_____

_____

_____

_____

_____

Technologist: _____   Manager: _____
                        Signature   Signature

4–72
How To Develop Competency in Your Department

1. List critical elements that have the potential for a) serious injury to patients or staff; b) catastrophic outcome if improperly conducted/given and c) serious financial or resource loss to the institution.

2. List the job positions that conduct or perform the elements in number 1.

3. List how you, as a manager, know that the staff referenced in number 2 can conduct or perform the activities in number 1. Note that this may be by demonstration, written test, verbal test, or performance of the activity. The type of competency test needs to fit the specific activity.

4. How often will testing of competency be conducted? Are there exceptions . . . for example if someone does the activity every day and you know he/she maintains good results, then retesting may not be necessary. This is your decision . . . are you comfortable with the daughter test*?

5. Who (title) is responsible for conducting the competency test? He will set up a schedule and documentation to ensure all staff are competent now and decide when retesting will occur.

    Documentation should go in the staff person's file.

Remember to limit the number of competencies . . . Nursing has about 10–12 . . . Radiology has 6 and Business office has 3. Not all employees have specific competency testing . . . only those who perform the critical elements. (All have annual mandatory education for safety etc. however.)

*Daughter test . . . would you feel comfortable with the person taking care of your daughter?

Courtesy of Parkland Health & Hospital System, Dallas, Texas.

4–73
The Joint Commission on Accreditation of Healthcare Organizations Human Resources Standard

DEPARTMENTAL REQUIREMENTS

DEPARTMENT COMPETENCY EVALUATION

Each Department shall:

1. Identify critical processes, procedures, and or services that present a high risk to patients, employees, or to the operation of the Hospital.

☐ 2. Identify who is performing these activities.

☐ 3. Determine how competency for these critical processes, procedures, and or services will be tested; define how competency testing occurs and who is responsible for conducting the testing and who will document the results.

☐ 4. Maintain documentation of competency testing in the employee's file.

AGE-SPECIFIC COMPETENCIES

Each department that provides care for children, adolescents, or geriatrics shall:

☐ 5. Identify staff who deal with children, adolescents, or geriatrics.

☐ 6. Develop specific competency criteria for each job description. These must be objective and utilized on the Performance Evaluation.

EDUCATION

Each department shall:

☐ 7. Provide each new employee and/or transferred employee a complete department orientation including specific department guidelines for safety (fire, electrical, and hazardous materials), infection control and age-related/handicap information (if appropriate).

☐ 8. Document orientation in the individual employee's file.

☐ 9. Update employee's Education Plan (which is part of the Department Organization Plan) including the department's competencies and *mandatory programs.

☐ 10. Document department education programs on an *Education Program Information* sheet. This documentation should be kept for 3 years.

☐ 11. Evaluate department education programs and utilize data to analyze and improve future programs.

☐ 12. Provide department competency education programs and utilize some type of validation testing. (This may be written questions or by demonstration, but documentation must state how competencies were tested.)

ORGANIZATIONAL PLAN

Each Department shall:

☐ 13. Revise its Departmental Organization Plan

☐ 14. Contact Quality Management if assistance is needed

Reference Person: _____ Quality Coordinator, Ext. _____

*Mandatory education programs include Fire, Safety, Emergency Preparedness, Infection Control, and Age-Specific (where information appropriate)

Courtesy of Parkland Health & Hospital System, Dallas, Texas.

4–74

Department Competency Evaluation

List High-Risk Procedures (serious injury to patient or staff, could cause catastrophic outcome if improperly conducted/given and serious financial or resource loss to the institution)	List job positions that conduct or perform	How will testing be conducted (demonstration, written test, verbal test, or performance of activity)	How often will testing be conducted? Example: (daily, monthly, semi-annually, annually)	Who (title) is responsible for conducting the competency test?

4–75
Human Resource Competencies Checklist

Employee Name:	Date:
Division:	Job Code:
Director:	Reviewer:

Competencies	Competencies Met (Yes, No, or N/A)	Comments
Current Licensure		
CPR		
Departmental Orientation Checklist Completed		
Credentialing Procedures/High Risk		
Waived Testing Competency		
Age-Specific Training		
Handicapped Inservices		
Abuse Recognition		
Unit-Specific Hazardous Material Training		
Fire/Safety Training		
Medical Equipment Training		
Required CEU		
Infection Control		
Information Management For Managers		
Current Job Description		

Courtesy of Parkland Health & Hospital System, Dallas, Texas.

4–76
Age-Specific Competencies

Division: Clinical Services

Original issue date: _____

Latest revision date: _____

Authorization signature: _____   Date: _____
Director, Medical Imaging Services

Department/Division Affected

Medical Imaging Services

APPROVAL DISTRIBUTION LIST

Approved by	Title	Date
	Medical Director, Medical Imaging Services	
	Assistant Vice President, Clinical Services	

PURPOSE

To ensure competency of the technologist in providing quality service for patients of all age groups

POLICY

The medical imaging department wants to ensure that it employs qualified and competent technologists who can and will provide quality service for patients of all age groups.

Each technologist must successfully complete competency requirements for the following age groups:

- neonatal
- pediatric
- adolescent
- adult
- geriatric

These competency requirements must be completed before the 90-day probationary period ends and then annually thereafter.

Source: Adapted from Nancy Hughes, Holy Cross Hospital, Silver Spring, Maryland.

4–77
Age-Specific Criteria for Technologists—Neonates, Infants, and Toddlers

SAFETY

- Infants and toddlers are not immobile and will not necessarily stay where they are placed.
- Keep crib/stretcher siderails up.
- Do not leave a child on an imaging table without supervision.
- Maintain a firm grasp of child while carrying or positioning. Support head, as necessary.
- Protect from suffocation and falls.
- Remove any small objects from the area that could be inhaled or ingested.

COMMUNICATION

- Communication with infants is usually non-verbal.
- Talk with the parents about the management of the child during the procedure. Establish a rapport with the parents by acting like a helpful friend. Do not lecture or scold parents about their child's behavior.
- You can promote family-centered care by explanations to the parents and the child, and by allowing them to help. Parents or caretakers should be present during the explanations.
- Be as nurturing as you can to the child while parents are out of the procedure room. The staff should be like the ideal parent—loving, honest, respectful, and consistent. Cajoling and threatening cannot help the child cope.
- Sit down, if possible, when talking to a child. You are more approachable when at their physical level. Seek to have a warm, friendly relationship without thrusting yourself on the child. How you feel about the child is more important than what you do or say.
- Talk casually. Do not bombard the child with verbal information. Convey authority without anger or threats. Do not initiate a battle of wills: give direction about a situation. "Now it is time to . . . ."
- Do not tell a child not to cry. Do not tell a child that a procedure will not hurt when it will.
- Toddlers' concept of time is now, so distraction is very effective. Say "put your hands under your back or head" rather than "don't move your hands."

SPECIFIC PARAMETERS IN DIAGNOSTIC RADIOLOGY

In performing pediatric studies, the technologist will make setting adjustments to enhance film quality in the pediatric patients. Such adjustments may include, but not be limited to

- KVP and MAS adjustment
- speed settings (exposure time)
- positioning and positioning support requirements for the child
- use of the equipment for immobilization
  - parental assistance
  - papoose board
  - use of the pig-o-stat

Courtesy of Inova Alexandria Hospital, Alexandria, Virginia.

4–78
Age-Specific Criteria for Technologists—School-Aged to Adolescents

SAFETY

- Children are not immobile and will not necessarily stay where they are placed.
- Keep crib/stretcher siderails up.
- **DO NOT** leave a child on an imaging table without supervision.
- Keep a firm grasp of child while carrying or positioning.

COMMUNICATION

- Talk with the parents about the management of the child during the procedure. Establish a rapport with the parents by acting like a helpful friend. Do not lecture or scold parents about their child's behavior.
- You can promote family-centered care by explanations to the parents and the child, and by allowing them to help. Parents or caretakers should be present during the explanations, and can be asked to explain in terms commonly used by the child when discussing body parts, processes, and problems.
- Be as nurturing as you can to the child while parents are out of the procedure room. The staff should be like the ideal parent—loving, honest, respectful, and consistent. Cajoling and threatening cannot help the child cope.
- Sit down, if possible, when talking to a child. You are more approachable when at their physical level. Seek to have a warm, friendly relationship without thrusting yourself on the child. How you feel about the child is more important than what you do or say.
- Talk casually. Do not bombard the child with verbal information. Convey authority without anger or threats. Do not initiate a battle of wills: give direction about a situation, "Now it is time to . . . ."
- Do not tell a child not to cry. Do not tell a child that a procedure will not hurt when it will.
- Tell a child what he or she will see, hear, and feel; who will be with him or her; how he or she can help with the procedure and how long it will take.
- Acknowledge their need to be in control. When possible, allow them to make some decisions about the procedure (i.e., "Which arm can we use for the shot?").
- Don't offer a choice if there is none.

SPECIFIC PARAMETERS IN DIAGNOSTIC RADIOLOGY

In performing school age to adolescent studies, the technologist will make setting adjustments to enhance film quality. In adolescent patients, such adjustments may include, but not be limited to

- KVP and MAS adjustments
- speed settings (exposure time)
- positioning and positioning support requirements for the child
- use of the equipment for immobilization
  - parental assistance
  - papoose board
  - use of the pig-o-stat

Courtesy of Inova Alexandria Hospital, Alexandria, Virginia.

4–79
Age-Specific Criteria for Technologists—Adolescents

SAFETY

Question female patients beginning at age 10 about the possibility of being pregnant.

COMMUNICATION

- If appropriate, discuss with the parents their wishes for participation during the procedure.
- Ensure that the adolescent knows the reason for the procedure, and that he or she has an opportunity to express concerns. Ask questions.
- Let the adolescent know who will be with him or her, how he or she can help, and how long the procedure will take.
- Recognize that adolescents feel very vulnerable when their bodies are exposed. Provide privacy during the procedure.
- Acknowledge the adolescent's need to be in control. Give him or her the opportunity to make some decisions concerning the procedure, if a choice is possible.
- Don't assume that because of apparent sophistication, he or she understands the basis of the procedure.
- Watch for hidden fears that may be expressed in unconventional language.
- Promote warm, accepting, supportive, and nonjudgmental feedback to the adolescent.

SPECIFIC PARAMETERS IN DIAGNOSTIC RADIOLOGY

In performing adolescent studies, the technologist will make setting adjustments to enhance film quality in adolescent patients. Such adjustments may include, but not be limited to

- KVP and MAS adjustments
- speed settings (exposure time)
- positioning and positioning support
- use of equipment immobilization
  - parental assistance
  - positioning aids

4–80
Age-Specific Criteria for Technologists—Geriatric Patients

SAFETY

This age group should be protected from falls. Possible reasons for falls are poor lighting, loose carpet pins, paper clips, etc., on the floor, or unsteady gait.

COMMUNICATION

- Acceptance, understanding, and respect must be shown to each person.
- Establish and maintain private and comfortable environment.
- Providing information about the procedure will help individuals feel less anxious.
- Avoid the indiscriminate use of first names.
- If your patients are senior citizens or adults with physical or behavioral limitations, you may find that they are not totally reliable historians. Due to the aging process, the older adult may be confused or forgetful at times especially about relating dates, remote events, or occasions accurately.
- Trust is frequently the basis of open and effective communication. The patient may trust an individual because of the role he or she occupies as health care provider. In the past patients had little control over selecting care givers. Today's patients are rejecting relationships that are superficial and are selecting health care providers with whom they can establish a more trusting relationship.
- You must be willing to listen.
- Seniors seem to accept tests or treatment more readily when they understand the rationale and the expected effects.

SPECIFIC PARAMETERS IN DIAGNOSTIC RADIOLOGY

In performing geriatric studies, the technologist will make setting adjustments to enhance film quality in geriatric patients. Such adjustments may include, but not be limited to

- KVP and MAS adjustments
- speed settings (exposure time)
- positioning and positioning support
- use of the equipment immobilization
  - posesies
  - arm and leg restraints
  - compression bands
- assist patient from wheelchair
- request assistance for lifting patient from stretchers

Courtesy of Inova Alexandria Hospital, Alexandria, Virginia.

4–81
Self-Assessment for Technologists

Division: Clinical Services

Original issue date: _____

Latest revision date: _____

Authorization signature: _____   Date: _____
Director, Medical Imaging Services

Department/Division Affected

Medical Imaging Services

APPROVAL DISTRIBUTION LIST

Approved by	Title	Date
	Medical Director, Medical Imaging Services	
	Assistant Vice President, Clinical Services	
	Director, Infection Control	

PURPOSE

To maintain a program of continuous quality improvement for each individual technologist

POLICY

A self-assessment checklist for the specific areas in medical imaging will be given to the following technologists:

• newly hired technologists upon completion of their probationary period

• technologists who have completed cross-training in a specific area

• all technologists annually

Each technologist will mark his or her comfort level for performing each individual exam/procedure.

During the year, it will be the responsibility of each technologist to improve on one or more exams/procedures that he or she marked "no experience" or "needs improvement."

The self-assessment and improvement on one or more exams in a year will be a standard for the next evaluation period.

Improving on one or more exams will result in a rating of "meets expectation" or above on the performance evaluation, depending on how many exams are improved upon.

Source: Adapted from Nancy Hughes, Holy Cross Hospital, Silver Spring, Maryland.

MANAGEMENT OF INFORMATION

4–82
Confidentiality of Patient Information

AUDIENCE

The information in this document is for use by all physicians, other health care providers, and staff who have access to patient information.

POLICY

At _____, all patient information is confidential and shall not be disclosed without the consent of the patient, the patient's representative, or unless required by law.

The Medical Practice Act states that the following patient information is confidential and cannot be disclosed except as permitted by the Act:

1. Physician-patient communications in connection with professional services.

2. Information contained in patient records.

Confidential patient information shall not be communicated to, or accessed by, any person (including health care givers) unless that person has a clear need to know (e.g., other physicians and personnel under the direction of the physician who are participating in the diagnosis, evaluation, or treatment of the patient).

Communicating confidential patient information inappropriately, carelessly, or negligently (e.g., casual discussion regarding a patient, discussion in public areas, and/or unauthorized release of information while on or off campus) is a breach of confidentiality.

ADDRESSING LEGAL OR ETHICAL ISSUES

When disclosure of patient information is required by law, consultation with the Department of Legal Affairs is recommended. When a conflict between the law and the health care provider's ethical duty to protect the patient's right of confidentiality occurs, consultation with the Ethics Consultation Service is recommended.

VIOLATIONS

Breach of confidentiality is a serious violation covered by the hospital Standards of Employee Conduct.

- Violation of this policy will result in appropriate disciplinary review and action, which may include termination.

- Documents containing a patient's name or UH number should be disposed of in a manner that conforms with assurance of confidentiality.

Source: University of Texas Medical Branch, Galveston, Texas.

4–83
Preliminary HIPAA Checklist

Review with your organization to determine if you are a covered entity or business associate and who your business associates are.

COVERED ENTITY

____ Health plan

  ____ Group health plan (50 or more participants, or administered by entity other than employer, for two or more employers)

  ____ Health insurance issuer (insurance company, service, or organization)

  ____ Health maintenance organization

  ____ Government program (Medicare Part A or B, Medicare+Choice, Medicaid, military personnel, veterans, Civilian Health and Medical Program of the Armed Services, Indian Health Service, federal employees, state child health plans, state high-risk pools)

    ____ Private insurance (Medicare supplemental, long-term care)

____ Health care clearinghouse

____ Health care provider (conducts at least one of following electronic transactions: claims, payment, coordination of benefits, claims status, enrollment, eligibility, premium payments, referral certification/authorization, first report of injury, claims attachments)

BUSINESS ASSOCIATE

1. Performs a function for or on behalf of the covered entity; and
2. Uses or discloses protected health information* as part of performing that function.

Business Associate Functions:	Name(s) of Business Associate(s)
____ Claims processing or administration	_____
____ Data analysis, processing, or administration	_____
____ Utilization review	_____
____ Quality assurance	_____
____ Billing	_____
____ Benefit management	_____
____ Practice management	_____
____ Repricing	_____
____ Legal services	_____
____ Actuarial services	_____
____ Accounting services	_____
____ Consulting services	_____
____ Data aggregation services	_____
____ Management services	_____
____ Administrative services	_____
____ Accreditation services	_____
____ Financial services	_____

*Protected health information is individually identifiable health information that is transmitted or maintained by electronic media or any other form or medium, excluding information in educational records or inmate records.

Source: Cummings & Lockwood. *HIPAA: A Guide to Health Care Privacy and Security Law.* New York: Aspen Publishers, Inc., © 2002.

4–84
Faxing of Medical Records

PURPOSE

To outline the process for appropriate release of confidential medical record information via fax in emergency situations for continued patient care purposes

AUDIENCE

All Health Information Management (HIM) employees

POLICY

Medical record information will be faxed only in emergency situations for continued patient care purposes.

PROCEDURE

Limited and specific medical record information may be faxed to other Health Care Providers in emergency/urgent situations when the following conditions have been met:

- The requesting Health Care Provider has a fax machine.
- The requester must first fax to a legible and valid authorization (on their letterhead) for release of specific medical record information that states the information may be faxed to the Health Care Provider and includes their fax number and their office number.
- The patient or his/her legal representative or the physician must sign the authorization if the patient/legal representative is unable to sign.
- If only the physician signs the authorization, it must also include a statement specifying that the requested information is needed immediately to assist with providing emergency medical care to the patient.
- If an authorization signed by the patient or his/her legal representative is not provided, the requester is asked to mail such an authorization to HIM as soon as possible.
- If the requester, on a non-urgent basis, requires additional medical record information, this is so noted and the information will be copied and mailed on the next business day.
- A cover sheet specifying the number of pages being faxed and a confidentiality statement must accompany the faxed medical record information. (A copy can be obtained from ROI.)
- Request to fax medical records of substantial length should not be honored. No more than ten (10) pages of a medical record should be released via fax transmission.
- Verify that the faxed information was received by requesting that the recipient fax a confirmation statement to us once they have received the information, verifying the number of pages received. This statement is filed in the medical record.
- If a confirmation statement is not received, the requesting party's office is called to obtain a verbal confirmation. A record of the verbal confirmation is documented on the authorization for the release of the information form.
- If the faxed information is not received by the intended recipient due to misdialing, the internal log of the fax machine is checked to obtain the misdialed fax number. Another fax is then sent requesting that we be called so that arrangements can be made for the return of the misdirected information.

continues

4–84 continued

- Misdirected fax incidents must be reported to the HIM Director or designee. They will then inform the Risk Management Department of the incident.

Requests for faxed medical information will be processed according to the following schedule:

- Between 8:00 AM and 5:00 PM, Monday–Friday (excluding holidays), the ROI team of HIM, room 1.108 McCullough Building, extension 21965 or 29257 is contacted for assistance.

- All other hours, the Main file staff at extension 22400 should be contacted for assistance.

Source: University of Texas Medical Branch, Galveston, Texas.

4–85
Shredding Confidential Documents in Medical Imaging

Division: Clinical Services

Original issue date: _____

Latest revision date: _____

Authorization signature: _____   Date: _____
Director, Medical Imaging Services

Department/Division Affected

Medical Imaging Services

APPROVAL DISTRIBUTION LIST

Approved by	Title	Date
	Medical Director, Medical Imaging Services	
	Assistant Vice President, Clinical Services	

PURPOSE

To ensure confidentiality of all patient-related information

POLICY

The medical imaging department wants to ensure that all documents containing confidential patient information are shredded.

Shredders will be placed strategically throughout the department in the following locations:

- nuclear medicine/MRI reception area
- front desk area
- file room
- quality control

Examples of the kinds of documents that will be shredded include, but are not limited to

- check-in documents
- requisitions
- medical imaging reports
- patient information sheets
- all other discarded documents related to the individual patient and his or her condition

Source: Adapted from Nancy Hughes, Holy Cross Hospital, Silver Spring, Maryland.

4–86
Film Storage and Silver Recovery

Original/Revision by: _____   **Effective Date:** _____

Reference: _____   **Revised Date:** _____

Department Primarily Affected: Radiology

Cross-Reference: _____

STATEMENT OF PURPOSE

To provide adequate film par levels and receipt of any silver and scrap film turned in

PROCEDURE

New Film Storage

1. New film will be routed to the purchasing department upon delivery from the dealer. The new film will be stored in the purchasing department until issued to the radiology department.
2. The radiology department will store a week's supply of film. The darkroom will be locked when the department is unattended. Radiology staff and nursing supervisor will have the only keys.

Silver Recovery (Silver Flake)

1. A separate company that purchases the silver flake owns the silver recovery unit in use. One lock and key is owned by the company, which retains the key to the lock.
2. The hospital has placed a second lock on the silver recovery unit. The secretary to the administration has the only key to this lock.
3. The recovery unit is cleaned periodically by the company representative and observed by the director of radiology and administrator's secretary.
4. The silver is weighed, documented, and the receipt is signed by at least two parties. A copy of this receipt is kept in the radiology director's office file.
5. The silver is purchased at the price of silver marker at the time of pick up. A check reflecting the percent of return agreed upon follows within forty-five (45) days.
6. The check is mailed to the director of radiology, who then gives the check to accounting and keeps a copy for administration and radiology. The money is recorded in the general operation fund.

Sale of Used Scrap Film

Scrap film is sold to the same company who purchases the silver flake. The film is weighed on scales, documented, and receipt is signed by the purchasing company and the director of radiology. The payment procedure is the same as for silver flake.

Documentation: Receipt from silver flake and scrap film.

Approved by: _____   _____   _____
                              Name   Title   Date

Courtesy of Rick Sellers, Department of Radiology, Tanner Medical Center, Carrollton, Georgia.

4–87
Destruction of Archival Film

Division: Clinical Services

Original issue date: _____

Latest revision date: _____

Authorization signature: _____   Date: _____
Director, Medical Imaging Services

Department/Division Affected

Medical Imaging Services

APPROVAL DISTRIBUTION LIST

Approved by	Title	Date
	Medical Director, Medical Imaging Services	
	Assistant Vice President, Clinical Services	

PURPOSE

To clarify the film retention policy and the process by which films are destroyed

POLICY

Retention of Radiographs

It is the expressed desire of the hospital to retain radiographs in their original form as long as is practical.

In all cases, however

- all films and reports on adult patients shall be retained at least five years from the date of last examination
- mammography films are kept indefinitely
- pediatric films shall be retained until the patient reaches 21 years of age
- expired patients' films and reports shall be retained for five years from the date of the last examination

Destruction

When purging is necessary, it shall be done on an annual basis and through written authorization by the director of medical imaging.

Payment

Payment for archival films shall be made upon their removal from the hospital.

Source: Adapted from Nancy Hughes, Holy Cross Hospital, Silver Spring, Maryland.

SURVEILLANCE, PREVENTION, AND CONTROL OF INFECTION

4–88
Infection Prevention and Control Policies and Procedures for the Medical Imaging Department

BLOODBORNE PATHOGEN SURVEY: JOB CLASSIFICATION AND TASKS AT RISK

Name of Institution _____   Date _____

Department _____

Location (several locations may exist, one form per location) _____

Name of Person conducting Survey _____

A. List of tasks/jobs where exposure to sharps may occur:

_____   _____   _____
_____   _____   _____
_____   _____   _____

B. List of tasks/jobs where exposure to blood or other contaminated material may occur:

_____   _____   _____
_____   _____   _____
_____   _____   _____

C. List of job classifications where employees may potentially be exposed to sharps or contaminated materials may occur:

_____   _____   _____
_____   _____   _____
_____   _____   _____

D. List of hazards that can cause exposure to sharps or contaminated material:

_____   _____   _____
_____   _____   _____
_____   _____   _____

E. Classification of hazards by severity of risk (from high to low):

_____   _____   _____
_____   _____   _____
_____   _____   _____

F. Evaluation and Comments: _____

_____

G. Recommendations: _____

_____

4–89
Sample Form To Demonstrate Compliance with
Employee Participation in Selection of Safer Needle Devices

Name of Institution _____

Department _____

Coordinator _____

Meeting Dates (maintain a separate sheet for each meeting): _____

A. Names of participants and job titles:

_____   _____   _____

_____   _____   _____

_____   _____   _____

_____   _____   _____

B. Describe all devices considered:

_____

_____

_____

_____

_____

C. List all methods and criteria used to evaluate each device:

_____

_____

_____

_____

_____

D. List justification for selection of devices to be used:

_____

_____

_____

_____

_____

4–90
Exposure Control Plan Compliance Form

Hazard evaluation has been conducted   Y_____   N_____

All job classifications listed in hazard evaluation   Y_____   N_____

All jobs and tasks listed in hazard evaluation   Y_____   N_____

Methods and time schedule for implementation of

• Compliance with universal precautions   Y_____   N_____

• Compliance with engineering controls   Y_____   N_____

• Provision of Hepatitis B Vaccination   Y_____   N_____

• Postexposure evaluation and follow-up   Y_____   N_____

• Communication of hazards to employees   Y_____   N_____

• Recordkeeping requirements   Y_____   N_____

Plan reflects changes in technology that will eliminate or reduce exposure to
bloodborne pathogens   Y_____   N_____

Documents annual consideration and evaluation of safer medical devices
designed to reduce or eliminate exposure   Y_____   N_____

Reflects solicitation of input on safer medical devices from nonmanagerial staff   Y_____   N_____

Includes use of personal protective equipment   Y_____   N_____

Includes methods for proper waste containment and disposal   Y_____   N_____

Includes methods for proper cleaning and disinfection, including laundering of
contaminated clothing and bedding   Y_____   N_____

Includes provisions for training of employees about hazards and methods used
to reduce exposures   Y_____   N_____

Is reviewed annually   Y_____   N_____

Is readily available to employees   Y_____   N_____

Is readily available to inspectors, as from OSHA   Y_____   N_____

4–91
Preconstruction Checklist

Is there a preconstruction review team that interacts with project coordinators, engineers, and safety personnel to review any construction and renovation activities that will occur in the Radiology Department?   Y_____   N_____

List the names of review team members and their job titles (do not forget to include Infection Control, Safety, Construction Project Manager, and Radiation Management Staff personnel):_____

_____

_____

_____

Describe the planned renovation/construction activity:_____

_____

What is the length of the project and the expected time of disruption of operational activities?

_____

Will transplant or respiratory impaired patients be exposed?   Y_____   N_____

Can the procedures affecting these patients be conducted elsewhere?   Y_____   N_____

Will essential services or power supplies be compromised or affected?   Y_____   N_____

Will hazardous materials be used during the project?   Y_____   N_____

If yes, list them: _____

_____

Are Material Safety Data Sheets available for all hazardous materials?   Y_____   N_____

What precautions will be used to prevent spread of dust, fumes, microorganisms?

   Barriers   Y_____   N_____

   Containment areas   Y_____   N_____

   Negative ventilation   Y_____   N_____

   Protection of air vents   Y_____   N_____

   Limited access to work area   Y_____   N_____

4–92
Isolation Procedures

Original/Revision by: _____   **Effective Date:** _____

Reference: _____   **Revised Date:** _____

Department Primarily Affected: Radiology

Cross-Reference: _____

STATEMENT OF PURPOSE

To prevent cross-contamination of infectious diseases

PROCEDURE

1. All personnel going into a patient's room marked "ISOLATION" shall be dressed properly according to the posted requirements.

2. The required precautions are posted on the patient's door.

3. All dressing garments shall be disposed of in the proper receptacle inside the patient's room.

4. All patients who are to be transported to radiology will be dressed and a mask will be worn if needed. Also, the technologist will be assigned to that patient so others will not come in contact with the patient. The technologist will wear a mask and gown according to the type of isolation.

5. If the technologist has any questions, he or she will check with the nurse prior to entering the patient's room and transporting patient.

6. Hands shall be washed inside the room before any patient care is attempted and before leaving the room.

7. The area in radiology where the patient came in contact with equipment will be wiped down with Virex TB before any other patient is to be X-rayed in that room.

Documentation: _____

May be performed by: Radiology technologist

Approved by: _____   _____   _____
                              Name   Title   Date

4–93
Sharps-Safety and Needlestick-Prevention Device Assessment Form

Device: _____

Supplier/trade name: _____

Applications: _____

Reviewer: _____

Date: _____

For each question, circle the appropriate response for the protective device being evaluated.

Health care worker safety

1. A. Does the protective device prevent needlesticks or other sharps injuries during use (i.e., before disposal)?   Yes   No

   B. Does it do so after use (i.e., does the safety mechanism remain activated through disposal of the protective device)?   Yes   No

2. A. Does the protective device provide protection in one of the following ways: either intrinsically or automatically? (Answer "No" if a specific action by the user is required to activate the safety mechanism, or if the user can somehow fail to activate the safety mechanism.)   Yes   No

   B. If "No," is the mechanism activated in one of the following ways: either by a one-handed technique or by a two-handed technique accomplished as part of the usual procedure?   Yes   No

3. During use of the protective device, do the user's hands remain behind the needle or sharp until activation of the safety mechanism is complete?   Yes   No

4. Is the safety mechanism reliable when activated properly?   Yes   No

5. Does the protective device minimize the risk of user exposure to the patient's blood?   Yes   No

Patient safety and comfort

6. Does the protective device minimize the risk of infection to the patient (e.g., through cross-contamination)?   Yes   No

7. Can the protective device be used without causing more patient discomfort than a conventional device?   Yes   No

8. For intravenous (IV) protective devices: Does the protective device attach comfortably (i.e., without causing patient discomfort) at the catheter port or IV tubing?   Yes   No

Ease of use and training

9. Is device operation obvious? That is, can the device be used properly without extensive training?   Yes   No

10. Can the protective device be used by a left-handed person as easily as by a right-handed person?   Yes   No

continues

4–93 continued

11. Is the technique required for using the protective device the same as that for using a conventional device?   Yes   No

12. Is it easy to identify the type and size of the product from the packaging?   Yes   No

13. For IV catheters and blood collection needle sets: Does the protective device provide a visible blood flashback during initial insertion?   Yes   No

14. Please rate the ease of using this protective device

   A. Under normal conditions   Excellent   Good   Fair   Poor

   B. When using the device with wet gloves   Excellent   Good   Fair   Poor

15. Please rate the quality of the inservice training   Excellent   Good   Fair   Poor

Compatibility

16. Is the protective device compatible with devices (e.g., blood collection tubes) from a variety of suppliers?   Yes   No

17. For IV protective devices:

   A. Is the protective device compatible with intralipid solutions?   Yes   No

   B. Does the protective device attach securely at the catheter port?   Yes   No

   C. Does the protective device attach securely or lock at a Y-site (e.g., for piggybacking)?   Yes   No

18. Is the protective device easy to dispose of in sharps containers of all sizes (if required)?   Yes   No

19. Does using the protective device instead of a conventional device result in only a modest (if any) increase in sharps container waste volume? (Answer "No" if the protective device will increase waste volume significantly.)   Yes   No

Overall

20. Would you recommend using this device?   Yes   No

Comments (e.g., describe problems, list incompatibilities)

_____

_____

_____

_____

_____

_____

_____

_____

Source: Reprinted with permission from ECRI, Plymouth Meeting, Pennsylvania, 2001.

4–94
Sample Sharps Injury Log

⬚⬚⬚⬚⬚⬚   ⬚⬚⬚⬚⬚

Injury ID (Please leave blank) Facility ID (Please leave blank)

Please complete a Log for each employee exposure incident involving a sharp.
Fill in the one circle corresponding to the most appropriate answer. Use block print and avoid touching lines.

Institution: _____ Department: _____

Address: _____ Page # _____ of _____

City: _____ State: _____ ZIP code: _____

Date filled out: _____ by: _____ Phone number: (____) _____

Facility injury ID#	Date of injury	Time of injury	optional	Age
⬚⬚⬚⬚⬚⬚⬚⬚⬚⬚	⬚⬚ / ⬚⬚ / ⬚⬚	⬚⬚ : ⬚⬚	Sex ○ Male	⬚⬚
	Month day year	○ AM ○ PM	○ Female	

Description of the exposure incident:	**Job classification:**	**Department/Location:**
_____	○ MD ○ Nurse	○ Patient room ○ Emergency dept
_____	○ Medical assistant	○ Operation room ○ procedure room
_____	○ Phlebotomist/lab tech	○ CCU/ICU ○ Home
_____	○ Housekeeper/Laundry	○ Clinical laboratory
_____	○ CAN/HHA	○ Medical/outpatient clinic
_____	○ Student, type _____	○ Service/utility area (disp rm./laundry)
_____	○ Other _____	○ Other _____

Procedure:	**Did the exposure incident occur:**
○ Draw venous blood ○ Heparin/saline flush	○ During use of sharp ○ Disassembling
○ Draw arterial blood ○ Cutting	○ Between steps of a multistep procedure
○ Injection, through skin ○ Suturing	○ After use and before disposal of sharp
○ Start IV/set up heparin lock	○ While putting sharp into disposal container
○ Unknown/not applicable	○ Sharp left, inappropriate place (table, bed, etc.)
○ Other _____	○ Other _____

Body part: (check all that apply)	**Identify sharp involved:** (if known)	**Did the device being used have engineered sharps injury protection?**
○ Finger ○ Face/head	Type: _____	○ yes ○ no ○ don't know
○ Hand ○ Torso	Brand: _____	Was the protective mechanism activated?
○ Arm ○ Leg	Model _____	○ yes—fully ○ yes—partially ○ no
○ Other _____	e.g., 18g needle/ABC	Did the exposure incident occur:
_____	Medical/"no stick" syringe	○ Before ○ During ○ After activation

Exposed employee: If sharp had no engineered sharps injury protection, do you have an opinion that such a mechanism could have prevented the injury? ○ yes ○ no Explain: _____	**Exposed employee:** Do you have an opinion that any other engineering, administrative, or work practice control could have prevented the injury? ○ yes ○ no Explain: _____
_____	_____
_____	_____
_____	_____
_____	_____
_____	_____
_____	_____
_____	_____

Source: Sharps Injury Control Program (Sharps), Department of Health Services, Occupational Health Branch/University of California.

PART 5

CMS and Joint Commission Standards Checklist

The following materials serve as examples. Hospitals should consult with counsel or other appropriate advisors before adapting the materials in this part to suit particular purposes.

INTRODUCTION

"CMS and Joint Commission Standards Checklist" is a tool designed to reference similarities and differences between CMS regulations and Joint Commission accreditation standards for hospital compliance. It is an invaluable tool for quality assurance nurses, directors of nursing, infection control nurses, medical records personnel, risk managers, and hospital administrators.

CMS regulations are cited in the Code of Federal Regulations (CFR). The Hospital Conditions of Participation (COPs) at 42 CFR Subpart E is cited as 42 CFR 482. CMS expects the hospital, as part of its participation agreement, to implement a demonstrable process and system to produce the desired outcome for compliance with the regulations. Citations or Statements of Deficiency (SODs) are written when the hospital fails to maintain a system to produce the desired outcome or when the hospital fails to monitor and correct undesirable outcomes. CMS can take termination actions if the intent of the regulation is not objectively met by the hospital.

"CMS and Joint Commission Standards Checklist" compares CMS regulations to Joint Commission accreditation standards in a table format. The table contains a section for the user to enter applicable state laws for a complete reference guide. **Remember,** the hospital's policies, procedures, and protocols (PPPs) must reflect the requirements of CMS, the Joint Commission, and the state to be in compliance, so it makes sense to include all of the requirements in one easy-to-use checklist.

This checklist **is intended** for use as a reference guide to aid the user in determining the most stringent requirements for compliance, so the user can formulate PPPs that meet or exceed the most restrictive requirement. It **is not intended** to be utilized as a complete set of regulations, conditions, standards, or laws governing hospitals or compliance.

Denise Casaubon, RN, Paralegal   Rose Sparks, RN, BA
a teeny tiny corporation
dba DNR Medical-Legal Consultants

AREAS OF RISK

Requirement	CMS	Joint Commission	State
Compliance with Federal, State, Local Laws	**482.11(a)** **482.11(c)**	**MA.2**—Compliance with law/regulation **MA.2.1**—CEO responds to agencies' reports and recommendations. **GO.2.4**—Compliance with law/regulation	
Governing Body [GB] Administration	**482.12** Legally responsible for the conduct of the hospital **(a)** Appoint medical staff [MS]. **(a)(4)** Approve MS bylaws and rules/regulations. **(a)(5)** Ensure MS is accountable to the GB for quality of care provided. **(b)** Appoint a CEO. **(c)** Patients under the care of a physician **(c)(2)** Patient admissions **(c)(5)** Written protocols for organ donation **(d)** Plan and budget **(d)(6)** Revised/updated annually **(d)(7)** Plan prepared under the direction of the GB **(e)** Responsible for contracted services **(f)** Emergency services	**MA.1**—CEO responsible for operating the hospital according to GB **GO.2.1**—Adopt bylaws addressing legal responsibilities **GO.2.2**—MS participation in governance **MS.1**—MS responsibility for quality of professional services provided and accountability to the GB **GO.2.3**—Select qualified CEO **MA.1.1**—CEO education/experience **MS.6.1**—Privileges granted to admit patients to inpatient services **RI.2**—Policies for procurement and donation of organs/other tissues **LD.1.5**—Approves annual budget **LD.1.5.3**—Annual audit by an accountant **LD.1.5.2**—Budget review process **LD.2.10**—Selecting outside resources for needed services **GO.2.5**—Developing, reviewing, and revising policies and procedures **GO.2.6**—GB provides for conflict resolution. **LD.1.7**—Each department's scope of services is defined in writing.	

continues

continues

Areas of Risk continued

Requirement	CMS	Joint Commission	State
Patients' Rights [PR]	**482.13**	**RI.1**—Hospital addresses ethical issues in patient care.	
		RI.1.4—Each patient receives written patient's rights.	
	Hospital must promote and protect each PR.		
	(a)(1) Inform patient or representative of PR before furnishing or discontinuing care.		
	(a)(2) Establish a patient grievance process that includes referral to utilization review (UR) and quality assurance (QA).	**RI.1.2.4**—Patients involved in resolving care decision dilemmas	
	(b) Patients have the right to participate in plan of care.	**RI.1.3.4**—Resolution of complaints	
		RI.1.2—Patients are involved in care.	
	(b)(2) Patient or representative has the right to make informed decisions for care.	**RI.1.2.1**—Informed consent obtained	
		RI.4.3—Address right to perform or refuse to perform tasks with longer length of stay	
	(b)(3) Patient has the right to formulate advance directives.	**RI.1.2.5**—Hospital addresses advanced directives.	
		RI.1.2.6–1.2.8—Resuscitation, life sustaining treatment, end of life	
	(c)(1) Right to personal privacy	**RI.1.3.2**—Privacy	
	(c)(2) Right to receive safe care	**RI.1.3.3**—Security	
	(c)(3) Right to be free from abuse or harassment		
	(d)(1) Right to confidentiality of medical records (MR)	**RI.1.3.1**—*Confidentiality*	
	(d)(2) Right to access information contained in MR in reasonable amount of time		
	(e)(1) Right to be free from restraints (physical or chemical) not medically necessary	**TX.7.1**—Restraint or seclusion use	
		TX.7.1.4.1—Restraint and seclusion limited to emergencies where patient is at risk to hurt self or others	
	(e)(2) Restraint used only to improve the patient's well-being		
	(e)(3) Use of a restraint must be		
	(e)(3)(i) used when less restrictive measures ineffective	**TX.7.1.4**—Nonphysical techniques are preferred	
	(e)(3)(ii) in accordance with a physician's order. The order must	**TX.7.1.5**—Restraint or seclusion use ordered by licensed practitioner	
	(e)(3)(ii)(A) never be written as a standing or as needed order	**TX.7.1.6**—A licensed practitioner evaluates the patient in person.	

Areas of Risk continued

Requirement	CMS	Joint Commission	State
Patients' Rights [PR] *(continued)*	(e)(3)(iii) according to written changes to patient's plan of care (e)(3)(iv) implemented in the least restrictive manner (e)(3)(v) in accordance with safe restraint techniques (e)(3)(vi) ended at earliest time. (e)(4) Patient must be continually assessed, monitored, reevaluated. (e)(5) Direct patient care staff must have ongoing education and training in safe use of restraints. (f)(1) Patient has the right to be free from seclusion and restraint imposed as coercion or discipline. (f)(2) Only used in emergency situations to protect patient/others (f)(3)(ii)(C) Practitioner must see and evaluate restraint/seclusion within 1 hour of intervention (f)(3)(ii)(D) Restraint or seclusion orders max: 4 hours adults, 2 hours age 9–17, 1 hour if under 9—for a total of 24 hours (f)(4)(i) Restraint *and* seclusion require continual face-to-face monitoring *OR* (f)(4)(ii) continuous video and audio monitoring. (f)(7) Hospital must report to CMS any death that occurs while a patient is restrained or secluded.	**TX.7.4**—Use of behavior management conforms to patient's treatment plan **TX.7.1.2**—Used correctly by trained staff **TX.7.1.11**—Restrained patients are monitored. **TX.7.1.7**—Written or verbal orders for use of restraint and seclusion are time limited. **TX.7.1.8**—Restrained or secluded patients are regularly reevaluated. **TX.7.1.15**—Collect data on use of restraints and seclusion to monitor and improve performance.	

continues

Areas of Risk continued

Requirement	CMS	Joint Commission	State
Quality Assurance [QA] Continuous Quality Improvement [CQI] Performance Improvement [PI]	**482.21**	**PI.1**—Organizationwide approach to performance measurement, analysis, and improvement (not scored at this standard)	
		GB ensures there is an effective hospitalwide program. **(a)** Written plan, ongoing activities **(a)(1)** Evaluation of contracted services **(a)(2)** Evaluation of infections and medication therapy **(a)(3)** Evaluation of medical and surgical services **(b)** Services meet medically related needs of patients. **(c)** Implementation of program and documentation of remedial actions and outcomes	**PI.4–PI.4.4**—Aggregation and analysis of data and sentinel events **PI.3–PI.3.1.3**—Collection of data to monitor performance **PI.5**—Improved performance is achieved and sustained. **NR.4**—Nursing and PI activities (not scored at this standard). **HR.4.3**—Collect data on competence patterns and trends of staff. **TX.7.5.1**—PI identifies opportunities to reduce risks of restraint use. **LD.1.4**—PI organization priorities in response to unusual events. **LD.2.7**—Directors maintain quality control programs. **LD.4–LD.4.5**—Leadership's role in PI **MS.3.1.6.1.5**—MS's participation in PI **MS.8–MS.8.4**—MS's role in PI **IM.8**—Hospital collects and aggregates data/information to support care and service delivery/operations. **ORYX specific requirements are not included in the scope of this manual.**	

continues

Areas of Risk continued

Requirement	CMS	Joint Commission	State
Medical Staff [MS]	**482.22** Organized MS responsible for the care of patients	**MS.6–MS.6.8**—Care of the patient	
	(a) Composition of MS	**MS.1.1.1**—MS includes licensed physicians and licensed independent practitioners.	
	(a)(1) Periodic peer review	**MS.5–MS.5.15.7**—Credentialing	
	(a)(2) Credentialing	**GO.2.2.1**—MS at GB meetings	
	(b) Accountable to the GB	**MS.3.1**—There is an executive committee of MS.	
	(b)(2) If MS has executive committee, majority of members are MDs or DOs.	**MS.3.1.4**—The majority of voting members are licensed physicians.	
	(b)(3) Responsibility for the organization and conduct of MS assigned to an MD or DO	**MS.4–MS.4.2.1.15**—Department leadership	
	(c) Medical staff bylaws adopted and enforced	**MS.2.2**—MS bylaws/rules/regulations	
	(c)(1) Approved by the GB	**MS.2.1**—Approved by the GB	
	(c)(2) Statement of privileges of each category of MS	**MS.1.1.3**—Delineated clinical privileges	
	(c)(3) Describe MS organization	**MS.2.3.4**—Description MS organization	
	(c)(4) Describe qualifications for MS appointment	**MS.5.4.3**—Professional criteria	
	(c)(5) History and physical [H&P] are completed 7 days before or 48 hours after admission by an MD, DO, or oromaxillofacial surgeon.	**PE.1.7.1**—H&P completed in 24 hours **PE.1.7.1.1**—H&P within last 30 days in MR with recorded changes **MS.6.2.1**—Oral and maxillofacial surgeons	
	(c)(6) Criteria for determining privileges	**MS.3.1.6.1.2 and MS.3.1.6.1.4**—Clinical privileges **MS.5.11**—Appointment for no more than 2 years	
	(d) Autopsies: securing and notification	**MS.8.5–MS.8.5.3**—Autopsies: securing, defining, and performing **PE.2–PE.2.4**—Patient reassessments **PE.4.2**—Practitioner with clinical privileges determines scope of assessment and care of patients in need of emergency care. **MS.2.3.2, MS.3.1.6.1.7, MS.5.2, MS.5.4.4.1**—Fair hearing processes **MS.2.3.3**—Mechanism for corrective action	

continues

Areas of Risk continued

Requirement	CMS	Joint Commission	State
Nursing Services [NS]	482.23	**LD.2.11**—Department directed by qualified professional	
		NR.1—Nursing services directed by RN executive	
		NR.2—Nurse executive establishes standards of nursing practices.	
	Organized, 24-hour NS under the supervision of an RN **(a)** Plan of administrative authority and delineation of responsibilities for patient care. The Director of Nursing (DON) must be an RN.	**LD.2.4**—Sufficient number qualified/competent persons to provide care	
	(b) Staffing and delivery of care ensure immediate availability of an RN for patient care.	**HR.2**—Adequate number of qualified staff	
	(b)(2) Nurses must have valid, current licenses.		
	(b)(3) RN supervises/evaluates care for each patient.	**PE.4.3**—RN assesses the patient's need for nursing care.	
	(b)(4) Current Nursing Care Plans for each patient	**PE.3–PE.3.1**—Patient care needs and care decisions	
	(b)(5) RN makes patient care assignments.		
	(b)(6) Responsibility for nonemployee nurses (registry)		
	(c) Preparation and administration of drugs and biologicals		
	(c)(2) Orders for drugs and biologicals must be in writing and signed by the practitioner responsible for the patient's care.	**TX.3.6**—Orders are verified and patients identified before medication given.	
		TX.3.3—Policies for medication orders	
	(c)(2)(i) Telephone orders PPP	**IM.7.7**—Protocols for verbal orders	
	(c)(3) Blood transfusions are administered per approved MS policies and procedures.	**MS.8.1.3**—Use of blood/blood components	
	(c)(4) Reporting transfusion and adverse drug reactions and errors in administration of drugs	**TX.3.9**—Medication effects on patients are monitored.	
		PE.1.7.1—Nursing assessment in 24 hours	
		PE.2–PE.2.4—Patient reassessments	
		NR.3—Policies, standards of patient care, and nursing practice are approved by nurse executive.	

continues

Areas of Risk continued

Requirement	CMS	Joint Commission	State
Medical Records Services [MR]/ Information Management	**482.24** MR must be maintained for every person evaluated or treated. **(a)** Must employ personnel to ensure prompt completion, filing, and retrieval of records **(b)** Form and retention of MR: accurate, promptly filed, retained, and accessible and system of author identification that protects security of entries **(b)(1)** Retained at least 5 years **(b)(2)** Coding and indexing system **(b)(3)** Procedures for ensuring confidentiality and release **(c)** Content of MR: reason for admission, patient's progress, and response to treatment **(c)(1)** Legible, complete, and authenticated (name and discipline) and dated promptly **(c)(1)(ii)** Authentication: signatures, written initials, or computer entry **(c)(2)** MR must document the following: **(c)(2)(i)** H&P 7 days before or 48 hours after admission **(c)(2)(ii)** Admitting diagnosis **(c)(2)(iii)** Results of evaluations and findings **(c)(2)(v)** Properly executed informed consent forms **(c)(2)(vi)** Information necessary to monitor the patient's condition **(c)(2)(vii)** Discharge summary, outcome, and follow-up care **(c)(2)(viii)** MR completed in 30 days after discharge.	**IM.7.1**—Hospital maintains MR for every individual assessed or treated. **IM.2**—Confidentiality, security, and integrity of data/ information are maintained. **IM.7.1.1**—Entries made in MR by authorized individuals **IM.7.6**—MR data are managed in a timely manner. **IM.7.1.2**—MR retention based on law and regulation **IM.2.1**—Protect MR against destruction, loss, tampering, and unauthorized use. **IM.7.2**—Information to identify patient, support diagnosis, justify treatment, course, and results **IM.7.8**—Entries are dated, author identified, and authenticated (when necessary). **PE.1.7.1**—H&P completed in 24 hours **IM.7.2**—As noted above **PE.1.5.1**—Test reports require clinical interpretation. **RI.3.1**—Consent forms address information in **RI.1.2.1.1–RI.1.2.1.5.** **IM.7.2**—As noted above **IM.5**—Transmission of data is timely and accurate.	

continues

Areas of Risk continued

Requirement	CMS	Joint Commission	State
Pharmaceutical Services [PS]	**482.25** PS to meet the needs of patients. MS is responsible for developing PPP that minimize drug errors. **(a)** Pharmacy or drug storage is administered in accordance with professional principles/state law. **(a)(1)** Full-time, part-time, or consulting pharmacist is responsible for developing, supervising, and coordinating activities of PS. **(a)(2)** Adequate number of personnel to ensure quality of PS **(a)(3)** Current, accurate records on receipt and disposition of all scheduled drugs **(b)(1)** Compounding, packaging, and dispensing under the supervision of a pharmacist **(b)(2)** Drugs and biologicals must be kept in a locked storage area. **(b)(3)** Outdated, mislabeled, or unusable drugs and biologicals must not be available for patient use. **(b)(4)** PPP for removing drugs when pharmacist is not available **(b)(5)** Protocol for automatic stop orders determined by the MS **(b)(6)** Drug administration errors, drug reactions, and incompatibilities reported immediately to physician **(b)(7)** Reporting of abuse and loss of controlled substances **(b)(8)** Drug information available to professional staff **(b)(9)** Established formulary	**TX.3.5.2**—Pharmacists review all prescriptions or orders. **TX.3.4**—Medications prepared/administered per law, regulation, licensure, and standard of practice **LD.2.11**—Department directed by qualified professional **TX.3.5**—Preparation/dispensing medications appropriately controlled **TX.3.5.5**—Emergency medications are available/secure in pharmacy and patient care areas. **TX.3.5.6**—System for retrieval and safe disposition for discontinued and recalled medications **TX.3.5.4**—Services are available when department is closed. **TX.3.1**—Identified selection of medications **TX.3.5.1**—A patient medication dose system is implemented	

continues

Areas of Risk continued

Requirement	CMS	Joint Commission	State
Radiologic Services [RS]	**482.26** **(a)** Hospitals must maintain, or have available, diagnostic RS. **(b)** Must be free from hazards for patients and personnel **(b)(2)** Periodic equipment inspections must be done. **(b)(3)** Use of exposure meters or badge tests **(b)(4)** Provided only on the order of practitioners with privileges **(c)(1)** Personnel: full-time, part-time, or consulting radiologist **(d)** Record of RS must be maintained. **(d)(1)** Signed reports of interpretations **(d)(2)** Retained at least 5 years	**LD.2.11**—Department directed by qualified professional **PE.1.5**—Diagnostic testing to determine patient's health care needs	

continues

Areas of Risk continued

continues

Requirement	CMS	Joint Commission	State
Laboratory Services [LS]	**482.27** **(a)** Hospitals must maintain, or have available, adequate LS. **(b)(1)** Emergency LS must be available 24 hours a day. **(b)(2)** Written description of LS must be available to the MS. **(b)(4)** MS and a pathologist must determine tissue specimens that require macroscopic or macroscopic and microscopic examinations. **(c)(1)** Potentially HIV infectious blood and blood products **(c)(2)** Services furnished by an outside blood bank **(c)(3)** Quarantine of blood and blood products pending completion of testing **(c)(4)** Patient notification of administration of potentially HIV infectious blood or blood products **(c)(5)** Time frame for notification **(c)(6)** Content of notification **(c)(7)** Policies and procedures for notification ⬤ **CLIA (waived testing) specific requirements are not included in the scope of this manual. They can be found at 42 C.F.R. 493, Subpart P.**	**PE.1.10**—LS and consultation readily available to meet patient needs **PE.1.10.1**—Hospital provides for prompt performance of examinations in pathology/clinical LS. **PE.1.5**—Diagnostic testing to determine patient's health care needs **PE.1.10.2–PE.1.10.2.2**—Laboratory testing by hospital or approved reference or contract laboratories **PE.1.11–PE.1.15.2**—Waived testing under federal law and regulation	

Areas of Risk continued

continues

Requirement	CMS	Joint Commission	State
Food and Dietetic Services [FDS] and Nutrition Care	**482.28**	**LD.2.11**—Department directed by qualified professional	

CMS (482.28):

Must have an organized FDS that is directed and staffed by adequate personnel

(a)(1) Must have a full-time employee who

(a)(1)(i) serves as the director

(a)(1)(ii) is responsible for the daily management of FDS

(a)(2) There must be qualified dietitian, full-time, part-time, or consulting.

(b)(1) Therapeutic diets must be prescribed by the practitioner(s) responsible for the care of the patient.

(b)(2) Nutritional needs must be met in accordance with recognized dietary practices.

(b)(3) Therapeutic diet manual approved by the MS and dietitian and available to staff

Joint Commission:

TX.4.3—Responsibilities for all activities are assigned.

TX.4.2—Authorized individuals prescribe food/nutrition products in a timely manner.

TX.4.5—Each patient's response to nutrition care is monitored.

PF.3.2—Patient is educated about nutrition interventions and modified diets.

PE.1.2—Nutritional status is assessed when appropriate to patient needs.

TX.4—Each patient's nutrition care is planned.

TX.4.1—Interdisciplinary nutrition therapy plan is developed and updated.

TX.4.1.1—Meals/snacks support program goals.

TX.4.4—Food/nutrition distribution and administration

TX.4.6—Nutrition meets patients' needs for special diets and altered diet schedules.

TX.4.7—Nutrition care standardized throughout the hospital

continues

Areas of Risk continued

Requirement	CMS	Joint Commission	State
Utilization Review [UR] or Continuum of Care	**482.30** **(a)** This section applies except in the following circumstances: **(a)(1)** A PRO has assumed binding review for the hospital. **(a)(2)** CMS has determined the UR procedures by the state under Title XIX of the Act are superior to the procedures required in this section. **(b)** UR committee composition **(c)** Scope/frequency of review **(d)** Determination regarding admissions or continued stays **(e)** Extended stay review **(f)** Review of professional services	**CC.1**—Patients have access to appropriate level of care and services. **CC.2.1**—Criteria define patient information necessary for appropriate care. **CC.3**—Continuity of care and services provided to patient. **CC.4**—Hospital provides for referral, transfer, or discharge of the patient based on patient needs and hospital capacity to provide care. **CC.5**—Hospital ensures clinical information is exchanged when patients are admitted, referred, transferred, or discharged. **CC.6**—Established procedures used to resolve denial-of-care conflicts.	
	These sections are compared for total content only. DO NOT compare line by line.	**These sections are compared for total content only. DO NOT compare line by line.**	

continues

Areas of Risk continued

Requirement	CMS	Joint Commission	State
Physical Environment [PE]	**"Life Safety Code"** **482.41** **(a)** PE must be developed and maintained to ensure safety of patients. **(a)(1)** There must be emergency power and lighting. **(a)(2)** There must be facilities for emergency gas and water. **(b)** Life safety from fire **(b)(2)** Must have procedures for the storage and disposal of trash **(b)(3)** Must have a written fire control plan **(b)(4)** Must maintain written evidence of inspection and approval of fire control agencies **(c)(2)** Facilities, supplies, and equipment must be maintained to ensure safety and quality. **(c)(4)** Must be proper ventilation, light, and temperature controls in PS and FDS	**EC.1.5.1**—Compliance with Life Safety Code **EC.1**—*Hospital plans for environment of care consistent with mission, services, law, and regulation (not scored at this standard).* **EC.1.7.1**—Provides reliable emergency power source **EC.1.7**—Plans for managing utilities **EC.1.3**—Hazardous materials and waste management plan **EC.1.5**—Plans for fire prevention **EC.1.2**—Plans for secure environment **EC.1.6**—Plans for managing medical equipment **EC.1.1.1**—Plans for worker safety **EC.1.1.2**—Develop policy re: smoking **EC.2**—*Hospital provides for environment of care consistent with mission, services, law, and regulation (not scored at this standard).* **EC.2.1–EC.2.10.4.1**—Implementation **EC.3–EC.3.4**—Plans and provides for other environmental concerns **EC.4–EC.4.3**—Measures outcomes of implementation	

Areas of Risk continued

Requirement	CMS	Joint Commission	State
Infection Control [IC]	**482.42**	**IC.1**—The organization uses a coordinated process to reduce risks of nosocomial infections in patients and health care workers.	
		IC.1.1—IC process is managed by one or more qualified individuals.	
	The hospital must have an active program for the prevention, control, and investigation of infections and communicable diseases. **(a)** Have designated infection control officer(s) develop and implement policies. **(a)(1)** Infection control officer(s) must develop a system for identifying, reporting, investigating, and controlling infections and communicable diseases.	**IC.2**—Provide surveillance data. **IC.3**—Report IC information internally and to public health agencies. **IC.5**—Take action to control outbreaks. **IC.6.2**—IC process includes at least one activity to prevent spread of infection.	
	(a)(2) Must maintain a log of incidents related to infections and communicable diseases **(b)** The CEO, MS, and DON must	**IC.6.1**—Management systems support the IC process.	
	(b)(1) ensure hospitalwide quality assurance and training programs address problems identified by infection control officer(s)	**IC.4**—Take action to prevent or reduce the risk of nosocomial infections.	
	(b)(2) be responsible for implementation of successful corrective action plans	**IC.6**—IC process is designed to lower the risks and improve the rates or trends of epidemiologically significant infections.	

continues

Areas of Risk continued

Requirement	CMS	Joint Commission	State
Discharge Planning [DP]	**482.43** Must have DP policies and procedures that apply to all patients **(a)** Must identify all patients who are likely to suffer adverse health consequences on discharge if there is no DP **(b)(2)** An RN, social worker, or other qualified personnel must develop or supervise the DP evaluation. **(b)(3)** Evaluation must include patient's need for post-hospital services and availability of services. **(b)(4)** Evaluation must include patient's capacity for self-care or care in the environment from which they entered the hospital. **(b)(5)** Evaluation must be completed in a timely manner, to avoid delays in discharge. **(b)(6)** Evaluation must include discussion of the plan with the patient or the individual acting on the patient's behalf and must be in the MR. **(c)(3)** Hospital must arrange for the initial implementation of the DP. **(c)(4)** Hospital must reassess DP if needs change.	**PE.1.6**—Need for DP assessment is determined. **PF.3.6**—Patient is educated about resources, care, services, or treatment to meet needs. **PF.3.8**—Education includes self-care activities. **PE.1.7.1**—Patient's screening assessment completed within 24 hours of inpatient admission. **IM.7.3.4.1**—Compliance with discharge criteria is documented in the patient's MR. **PF.3.3**—Hospital ensures patient is educated to safely use medical equipment or supplies. **TX.6.1.1**—DP from rehabilitation services is integrated into the functional assessment. **PF.3.9**—Discharge instructions are given to patient and those responsible for providing continuing care.	

continues

Areas of Risk continued

Requirement	CMS	Joint Commission	State
Organ, Tissue, and Eye Procurement [OTEP]	**482.45** **(a)** Must have and implement written protocols **(a)(1)** Agreement with a designated organ procurement organization [OPO], which the hospital must notify in a timely manner of all deaths **(a)(2)** Agreement with at least one tissue bank and one eye bank **(a)(3)** Ensures families of potential donors are informed of donation options **(a)(4)** Use discretion and sensitivity with respect to potential donors **(a)(5)** Ensure that staff is educated on donation issues, death records are reviewed to improve identification of potential donors, and potential donors are maintained while testing and placement of organs is done **(b)(1)** A hospital where transplants are performed must be a member of the Organ Procurement and Transplantation Network [OPTN], the United Network for Organ Sharing [UNOS], and abide by its rules. **(b)(2)** "Organ" means human kidney, liver, heart, lung, or pancreas. **(b)(3)** A transplanting hospital must provide data to OPTN [UNOS], the Scientific Registry, and the OPOs. These sections are compared for total content only. **DO NOT compare line by line.**	**RI.2**—Implement policies and procedures, developed with MS participation, for procuring and donation of organs and tissues **Intent of RI.2**—The OPO is identified and hospital has procedures for notifying OPO in a timely manner. The OPO determines medical suitability for organ donation. Hospital has procedures for family notification of each potential donor. Notification is made by the hospital's designated requestor or organ procurement representative. Written documentation by designated requestor for acceptance or denial of organ donation Hospital staff exercises discretion and sensitivity to the beliefs and desires of the families of potential donors. Hospital maintains records of potential donors. Hospital works with OPO, tissue and eye banks in reviewing death records to improve potential donor identification. Hospital works with OPO, tissue and eye banks in educating staff on donation issues. These sections are compared for total content only. **DO NOT compare line by line.**	

continues

Areas of Risk continued

Requirement	CMS	Joint Commission	State
	Optional CMS Services		
Surgical Services [SS]	**482.51** SS must be well organized and provided in accordance with acceptable standards of practice.	**TX.5**—MS defines the scope of assessment for operative and other procedures.	
		LD.2.11—Department directed by qualified professional	
	(a)(1) OR must be supervised by RN, MD, or DO. **(a)(2)** LPNs and scrub techs work under the supervision of an RN. **(a)(3)** RNs perform circulating duties.		
	(a)(4) SS must maintain a roster specifying surgical privileges. **(b)** Must develop policies governing surgical care	**MS.6.4**—Individuals perform surgical procedures in the scope of their delineated privileges.	
	(b)(1) Must be an H&P in every patient's chart before surgery (except in emergencies)	**PE.1.8**—Before surgery H&P, diagnostic tests and preoperative diagnosis must be completed/recorded in MR.	
	(b)(2) Properly executed informed consent form for the operation must be in every patient's chart before surgery (except in emergencies).	**TX.5.2**—*Before obtaining informed consent, risks, benefits, potential complications discussed with patient/family (not scored in this standard).*	
	(b)(3) Must have the following equipment: call system, cardiac monitor, resuscitator, defibrillator, aspirator, and tracheotomy set **(b)(4)** Must have provisions for postoperative care	**TX.5.4**—Patient is monitored postprocedure.	
	(b)(5) OR register complete and must be up-to-date **(b)(6)** Operative report written or dictated immediately following surgery and signed by surgeon	**IM.7.3.2**—Operative report is dictated or written immediately after surgery. **IM.7.3.2.1**—Operative report is authenticated by the surgeon. **IM.7.3.2.2**—If operative report is not placed immediately in MR after surgery, progress note entered. **IM.7.3.3**—Postop documentation **IM.7.3.5**—Postop documentation for DC	

continues

Areas of Risk continued

Requirement	CMS	Joint Commission	State
Anesthesia Services [AS]	**482.52** Must be provided in a well-organized manner under the supervision of a physician. (a) Organization of AS must be appropriate to scope of services anesthesia administered by (a)(1) A qualified anesthesiologist (a)(2) Doctor of medicine or osteopathy (a)(4) Certified RN anesthetist under the supervision of the operating practitioner or anesthesiologist who is immediately available (a)(5) Anesthesiology assistant who completed a 6-year program (b) Policies on anesthesia procedures must include delineation of pre-anesthesia responsibilities. The policies must ensure the following are provided: (b)(1) Pre-anesthesia evaluation performed within 48 hours prior to surgery by an individual qualified to administer anesthesiology (b)(2) Intraoperative record (b)(3) Post-anesthesia follow-up report written within 48 hours after surgery for inpatients (b)(4) Post-anesthesia follow-up evaluation for anesthesia recovery in accordance with PPP approved by MS for outpatient	**LD.2.11**—Department directed by qualified professional **TX.2**—Moderate or deep sedation and anesthesia provided by qualified individuals **TX.2.1.1**—Moderate or deep sedation and anesthesia care is planned. **TX.2.4.1**—Patients are discharged by a qualified practitioner according to criteria approved by the MS. **PE.1.8.1**—Pre-sedation or pre-anesthesia assessment **PE.1.8.3**—Patient re-evaluated immediately before induction **TX.2.3**—Patient's physiological status is monitored during sedation or anesthesia. **PE.1.8.4**—Postoperative status is assessed on admit to/discharge from recovery area. **TX.2.2**—Sedation and anesthesia options/risks are discussed with patient/family.	

continues

Areas of Risk continued

Requirement	CMS	Joint Commission	State
Nuclear Medicine Services [NMS]	**482.53** **(a)** Organization of NMS must be appropriate to scope of services. **(a)(1)** Director must be a doctor of medicine or osteopathy qualified in nuclear medicine. **(a)(2)** Qualifications, training, and responsibilities of NMS personnel must be approved by NMS director and MS. **(b)** Radioactive materials are handled in accordance with acceptable standards of practice. **(b)(1)** In-house preparation **(b)(2)** Storage and disposal **(b)(3)** Laboratory tests and quality control **(c)** The equipment must be **(c)(1)** maintained in safe operating condition **(c)(2)** inspected, tested, and calibrated at least annually by qualified personnel **(d)(1)** NMS reports must be maintained for at least 5 years. **(d)(2)** The practitioner approved by the MS to interpret diagnostic procedures must sign and date test interpretations. **(d)(3)** Must maintain records of receipt and disposition of radiopharmaceuticals **(d)(4)** NMS is ordered only by a practitioner whose scope of licensure and defined privileges allow such referrals.	**PE.1.10.1**—Hospital provides prompt performance of examinations in nuclear medicine. **LD.2.11**—Department is directed by qualified professional.	

continues

Areas of Risk continued

Requirement	CMS	Joint Commission	State
Outpatient Services [OS]	**482.54** **(a)** Must be organized and integrated with inpatient services **(b)(1)** Assign an individual to be responsible for the OS. **(b)(2)** Have appropriate professional and nonprofessional personnel available.	**LD.1.3.4.2**—MS approves sources of patient care provided outside the hospital. **LD.2.11**—Department is directed by qualified professional. **MS.6.3**—MS determines non-inpatient services for which a patient must have an H&P.	
Emergency Services [ES]	**482.55** **(a)(1)** Must be organized and under the direction of a qualified member of the MS and **(a)(2)** Services must be integrated with other hospital departments **(a)(3)** PPP governing medical care are established by and a continuing responsibility of the MS **(b)(2)** Must be adequate medical and nursing personnel qualified in emergency care to meet the needs of the facility **NOTE: THESE ARE NOT THE REQUIREMENTS FOR EMTALA. EMTALA is found at 42 C.F.R. 489.20 and 489.24.**	**LD.2.11**—Department is directed by qualified professional. **PE.4.2**—Practitioner with clinical privileges determines scope of assessment and care of patients in need of ES. **IM.7.5**—When ES are provided, time and means of arrival documented in MR. **IM.7.5.1**—MR notes if patients receiving ES left against medical advice. **IM.7.5.2**—MR of patient receiving ES notes termination of treatment, final disposition, condition at discharge, and instructions for follow-up.	

continues

Areas of Risk continued

continues

Requirement	CMS	Joint Commission	State
Rehabilitation Services [RS]	**482.56** **(a)** Organization of the RS must be appropriate to the scope of services offered. **(a)(1)** The director of RS must have knowledge, experience, and capabilities to properly supervise and administer RS. **(a)(2)** RS must be provided by staff who meet the qualifications specified by the MS consistent with state law. **(b)** Services must be furnished in accordance with a written plan of treatment. RS must be given in accordance with medical staff orders, and the orders must be incorporated in the patient's record.		
Respiratory Care Services [RCS]	**482.57** **(a)** Organization of RCS must be appropriate to the scope and complexity of services offered. **(a)(1)** Director of RCS must be a doctor of medicine or osteopathy. The director may be full- or part-time. **(b)** Services are delivered in accordance with MS directives. **(b)(1)** Written procedures for personnel and supervision **(b)(2)** Blood gases or other clinical laboratory tests **(b)(3)** Services must be provided in accordance with doctor's orders.		

Areas of Risk continued

Requirement	CMS	Joint Commission	State
Personnel Records [PR]/Human Resources	No COP titled "Personnel"	**HR.1**—Defined qualifications and performance expectations for all staff positions **HR.4**—Orientation process **HR.4.2**—Ongoing inservice and education training **HR.5**—Assess each staff member's performance expectations stated in their job description. **LD.2.8**—Directors provide orientation, inservices, and continuing education for all persons in department.	
Disaster Preparedness [DP]	No COP titled "Disaster Preparedness"	**EC.1.4**—A plan addresses emergency management.	

DEEMED STATUS

Background

The Social Security Act § 1861(e) and § 1865(a) permit for deemed status of hospitals. Deemed status means that institutions accredited as hospitals by the Joint Commission or the American Osteopathic Association (AOA) are deemed to meet all of the Medicare Conditions of Participation, except

- the requirement for utilization review as specified in section 1861(e)(6) of the Act and in 42 CFR 482.30
- the additional special requirements necessary for the provision of active treatment in psychiatric hospitals section 1861 (f) of the Act and 42 CFR 482.60
- any requirements under section 1861(e) of the Act and implementing regulations that CMS, after consulting with the Joint Commission or AOA, identifies as being higher or more precise than the requirements for accreditation in section 1865(a)(4) of the Act

Procedure

A hospital deemed to meet program requirements must authorize the accreditation organization to release to CMS, or the state agency responsible for licensing, a copy of the most current accreditation survey. The hospital must furnish the accreditation survey report to the government agency that processes the deemed status requests (CMS or the state agency).

Determination

CMS or the state agency will review the survey, and related survey information, and make a determination to grant or deny deemed status to the hospital.

If deemed status is granted, the hospital is considered in compliance with the Medicare Conditions of Participation for the period of time the accreditation is valid (usually a period of 3 years).

CMS may use a validation survey (42 CFR 488.7) or an accreditation survey or any other survey information (such as Life Safety Code requirements) to determine that a hospital does not meet the Medicare Conditions of Participation. In this case, the hospital is not granted deemed status, and may be required to submit a Plan of Correction to CMS to maintain Medicare certification.

PROVIDER-BASED DESIGNATION

Background

Provider-based, or integral-component, designation is granted by CMS for a hospital's services that receive Medicare reimbursement under the hospital's Medicare number. These services may not be provided in the actual hospital, but may be provided by the same organization that governs the hospital, such as a hospital-based outpatient diagnostic center that is located on the hospital's campus. The hospital should request provider-based designation to accommodate the correct allocation of costs and reimbursement where there is more than one type of service being given within the same organization. If the request for a provider-based designation is approved by CMS, there is an increase in the portion of the facility's general and administration costs.

Medicare is under statutory and regulatory mandates to operate as a prudent purchaser of services that will enhance the services and care to its beneficiaries. Medicare must comply with the intent of section 1861 (v)(1)(A) of the Social Security Act that requires reimbursement for services that are both cost effective and advantageous to its beneficiaries.

Policy

Changes to the provider-based status or designation have been proposed. The final regulations for determining provider-based status were published in August 2002. If a hospital or facility would like to obtain a provider-based status, it is recommended to contact your regional CMS office for assistance at this time.

Determination

CMS will determine if the entity will be granted a provider-based status or designation with the assistance of the state agency and the fiscal intermediary. The hospital will receive written approval or denial of the provider-based designation status.

ADDITIONAL RESOURCES

www.jcaho.org
www.cms.hhs.gov
www.acreditinfo.com
http://access.gpo.gov
www.cdc.gov

Index

Fire, 1:23
First aid, 1:32
Food and dietetic services, 5:11
Fraud, definition of, 1:2
Fraud and abuse, 1:1–1:2
    contract provisions, 1:3–1:4
    radiology issues, 1:2–1:3

G

Gases, 1:19
Gas storage, 1:18
Geriatric patient competency, 4:169
Glucophage scheduling, 4:64
Governing body administration, 5:1
Grooming, 1:60–1:61

H

Handwashing, 1:36
Haverfield, Addie, 2:3, 2:11
Hazard communication, 1:39
    standard, 1:44–1:45
Hazard Communication Act, 1:44
Hazardous drug exposure, 1:45–1:47
Hazardous substances, 1:44–1:47
Hazards reduction protocol,
    4:126–4:127
Health Care Financing
    Administration checklist, x–xi
Health Insurance Portability and
    Accountability Act, 1:74
    compliance, 1:78–1:79
    preliminary checklist, 4:172
Hepatitis B, 1:39
Hepatitis B vaccine, 1:38
High-dose fluoroscopic procedures,
    4:126–4:127
High-risk procedures, 1:7
Hospital-physician arrangements, 1:3
Hottinger v. Pope County, 1:61
Human immunodeficiency virus,
    1:39
Human resources, 5:22
    competency, 4:164
    management, 3:66–3:70
    standard, 4:162

I

Identification, of parties, 1:3
Imaging services
    performance improvement plan,
        4:84–4:85
    quality assessment, improvement,
        4:86–4:91

Incident notification, 1:23
Indoor air quality, 1:43
Infection control, 5:14
    prevention, 3:84–3:87; 4:178
    surveillance, 3:84–3:87
Infectious waste, 1:36–1:37
Information management, 3:71–3:83;
    5:7
Informed consent
    evidence, 1:69
    information disclosure for, 1:67,
        1:68–1:69
    radiology procedures, 1:66–1:67
    requirement, 1:66
    state laws, 1:67–1:68
Injection of contrast media, 4:38–4:39
Injury and illness recordkeeping,
    1:30–1:33
Inspections, 1:25, 1:29
Instrument calibration, 1:17
*International Union, United
    Automobile, Aerospace & Agricultural
    Implement Workers of Am v. Johnson
    Controls, Inc.*, 1:58
Interventional procedures, 4:26
    record, 4:28–4:29
Investigations, 1:4
Iodinated contrast studies, 4:27
Isolation
    patient transfer, 4:79
    procedures, 4:182

J

Joint Commission on Accreditation
    of Healthcare Organizations
    accreditation standards, x
    compliance risk areas, 5:1–5:22
    disaster response, 1:49
    environment of care standards,
        1:43
    human resources standard, 4:162
    new survey process, 2:13–2:14
    occupational safety, 1:30
    on-call schedule and, 1:57
    standards checklist, x–xi
    survey focus, 2:1–2:10
    survey Q & A, ix
    visit primer, 4:133–4:135

K–L

Kemp v. Claiborne County Hospital,
    1:62
Labeling, 1:14–1:15
Laboratory services, 5:10

Latex sensitivity, 1:43
    policy, 4:33–4:36
Lauer, Bruce, 2:4–2:5, 2:11–2:12
Leadership, 3:43–3:52
Liability
    information disclosure, 1:68–1:69
    on-call failure, 1:56–1:57
    radiology equipment
        malfunctions, 1:19–1:20
    reducing, 1:20
    staffing issues and, 1:57–1:58
    unauthorized disclosure of medical
        records, 1:74
Licensure, 1:41–1:53
    telemedicine, 1:77
    training requirements, 1:16–1:17
Life Safety Code, 5:13

M

Magnetic resonance imaging
    safety screening, 4:123–4:125
    screening, 4:21–4:22
    screening record, 4:23–4:24
Mammography, 1:5, 1:8
Management
    environment of care, 3:53–3:65
    human resources, 3:66–3:70
    information, 3:71–3:83
Material safety data sheets, 1:44.
    1:45, 1:46
Medicaid
    certification, licensure, 1:51
    nurse practitioners, 1:8
Medical event reporting, 1:22
Medical imaging, emergency
    management plan, 4:98–4:100
Medically unnecessary services, 1:9
Medical management issues, 4:77–4:78
Medical records, 1:73–1:76
    faxing, 4:173–4:174
    information management, 5:7
Medical removal, 1:31
Medical staff, 5:5
Medical treatment, 1:23, 1:31–1:32
Medicare
    certification, licensure, 1:51
    clinical nurse specialists, 1:7–1:8
    deemed status, 5:23
    equipment requirements, 1:17
    fee schedule, 1:9
    nurse practitioners, 1:7–1:8
    outpatient prospective payment
        system, 1:9
    physician's orders, 1:8
    radiation safety, 1:11–1:12